Mergers and Acquisitions

Routledge Advances in Management and Business Studies

For a full list of titles in this series, please visit www.routledge.com.

18 **Power and Influence in the Boardroom**
James Kelly and John Gennard

19 **Public Private Partnerships**
Theory and Practice in International Perspective
Stephen Osborne

20 **Work and Unseen Chronic Illness**
Silent Voices
Margaret Vickers

21 **Measuring Business Excellence**
Gopal K Kanji

22 **Innovation as Strategic Reflexivity**
Edited by Jon Sundbo and Lars Fuglsang

23 **The Foundations of Management Knowledge**
Edited by Paul Jeffcutt

24 **Gender and the Public Sector**
Professionals and Managerial Change
Edited by Jim Barry, Mike Dent and Maggie O'Neill

25 **Managing Technological Development**
Hakan Hakansson and Alexandra Waluszewski

26 **Human Resource Management and Occupational Health and Safety**
Carol Boyd

27 **Business, Government and Sustainable Development**
Gerard Keijzers

28 **Strategic Management and Online Selling**
Creating Competitive Advantage with Intangible Web Goods
Susanne Royer

29 **Female Entrepreneurship**
Implications for education, training and policy
Edited by Nancy M. Carter, Colette Henry, Barra Ó Cinnéide and Kate Johnston

30 **Managerial Competence within the Hospitality and Tourism Service Industries**
Global CulturalContextual Analysis
John Saee

31 **Innovation Diffusion in the New Economy**
The Tacit Component
Barbara Jones and Bob Miller

32 **Technological Communities and Networks**
International, National and Regional Perspectives
Dimitris G. Assimakopoulos

33 **Narrating the Management Guru**
In search of Tom Peters
David Collins

34 **Development on the Ground**
Clusters, Networks and Regions in Emerging Economies
Edited by Allen J. Scott and Gioacchino Garofoli

35 **Reconfiguring Public Relations**
Ecology, Equity, and Enterprise
David McKie and Debashish Munshi

36 The Pricing and Revenue Management of Services
A Strategic Approach
Irene C. L. Ng

37 Critical Representations of Work and Organization in Popular Culture
Carl Rhodes and Robert Westwood

38 Intellectual Capital and Knowledge Management
Strategic Management of Knowledge Resources
Federica Ricceri

39 Flagship Marketing
Concepts and Places
Edited by Tony Kent and Reva Brown

40 Managing Project Ending
Virpi Havila and Asta Salmi

41 AIDS and Business
Saskia Faulk and Jean-Claude Usunier

42 The Evaluation of Transportation Investment Projects
Joseph Berechman

43 Urban Regeneration Management
International Perspectives
Edited by John Diamond, Joyce Liddle, Alan Southern and Philip Osei

44 Global Advertising, Attitudes, and Audiences
Tony Wilson

45 Challenges and Controversies in Management Research
Edited by Catherine Cassell and Bill Lee

46 Economy, Work, and Education
Critical Connections
Catherine Casey

47 Regulatory Governance and Risk Management
Occupational Health and Safety in the Coal Mining Industry
Binglin Yang

48 Risk Management and Corporate Governance
Edited by Abolhassan Jalilvand and A. G. Malliaris

49 Careers in Creative Industries
Chris Mathieu

50 Marketing without Advertising
Brand Preference and Consumer Choice in Cuba
Joseph Scarpaci and Emilio Morales

51 Pioneers in Marketing
A Collection of Biographical Essays
D.G. Brian Jones

52 Mergers and Acquisitions
The Critical Role of Stakeholders
Edited by Helén Anderson, Virpi Havila, and Fredrik Nilsson

Mergers and Acquisitions

The Critical Role of Stakeholders

Edited by Helén Anderson, Virpi Havila, and Fredrik Nilsson

Routledge
Taylor & Francis Group
NEW YORK AND LONDON

First published in paperback 2024

First published 2013
by Routledge
605 Third Avenue, New York, NY 10158

and by Routledge
4 Park Square, Milton Park, Abingdon, Oxon OX14 4RN

Routledge is an imprint of the Taylor & Francis Group, an informa business

Publisher's Note
The publisher has gone to great lengths to ensure the quality of this reprint but points out that some imperfections in the original copies may be apparent.

Library of Congress Cataloging-in-Publication Data

Mergers and acquisitions : the critical role of stakeholders / edited by Helen Anderson, Virpi Havila, and Fredrik Nilsson
p. cm. — (Routledge advances in management and business studies ; 52
Includes bibliographical references and index.
1. Consolidation and merger of corporations. 2. Social responsibility of business. I. Anderson, Helen. II. Havila, Virpi. III. Nilsson, Fredrik.
HD2746.5.M433 2012
338.8'3—dc23
2012013085

ISBN 13: 978-0-41-553652-3 (hbk)
ISBN 13: 978-1-03-292283-6 (pbk)
ISBN 13: 978-0-20-311137-6 (ebk)

DOI: 10.4324/9780203111376

Typeset in Sabon
by IBT Global.

Contents

Figures

Tables

Acknowledgments

We would like to express our heartfelt thanks to all participants in the two workshops on mergers and acquisitions which took place in June 2009 and in August 2010. The workshops gathered researchers who had written a PhD thesis with the principal focus on mergers and acquisitions within the field of business studies in Sweden. During the workshops, we discussed and scrutinized our knowledge on mergers and acquisitions. You inspired us to initiate a process that has developed into this book. It has been a pleasure to work with you all, and we are pleased to present several of you as authors of different chapters in this book.

We are also very grateful to Bo Rydén, who encouraged us at an early stage, as well as to Lars Engwall, Rolf Lundin, and Johan Wiklund, for their constructive comments. The supportive and useful comments of the anonymous reviewers of the book proposal were also very much appreciated. Furthermore, our sincere thanks go to the SCANCOR community at Stanford University, where parts of this manuscript were carefully examined in a positive and scholarly manner. In addition, we would like to express our gratitude to the Jan Wallander and Tom Hedelius Foundations, as well as the Tore Browaldh Foundation in Sweden, for their financial support, without which this project could not have been realised. Finally, we would like to thank Peter Dahlin for his contribution in arranging the workshop on mergers and acquisitions in 2009 and Dick Wathen for his help with the language editing.

1 A Stakeholder Approach to Mergers and Acquisitions

Helén Anderson, Virpi Havila, and Fredrik Nilsson

EXTENDING THE CONTEXT FOR MERGERS AND ACQUISITIONS

Research has shown that a business relationship between two companies is connected to other business relationships (e.g., Håkansson and Snehota 1989, 1995; Johanson and Mattsson 1988). In this way, for example, customers' customers and suppliers' suppliers may have an impact on a business relationship (e.g., Gadde and Mattsson 1987). This, in turn, means that companies are connected, both directly and indirectly, to each other and form networks of business relationships (Anderson, Håkansson, and Johanson 1994). These networks are constantly changing as a result of the continuous interaction between the business parties. Sometimes they may even change in a more radical way, for example, through mergers and acquisitions (Halinen, Salmi, and Havila 1999). Mergers and acquisitions may influence not only the merging/acquiring companies themselves, such as their employees, but also directly and indirectly other connected companies, such as the companies' suppliers and customers (e.g., Anderson, Havila, and Salmi 2001). Thus, many parties may affect, or become affected, by a merger or acquisition, that is, have a *stake* in it. In stake we include both claims of interest and influence of different kinds (Mitchell, Agle, and Wood 1997).

Even though each relationship and the stakes in each are unique, there are similarities due to the type of category the relationships represent. For example, Friedman and Miles (2002: 8) differentiate between stakeholder groups with either explicit or implicit contracts (e.g., top management and suppliers), and those with no contractual relationships (e.g., environmental activists and companies connected through common trade associations). In a merger or an acquisition, the two (or more) companies involved have shareholders, top managements, employees, suppliers, and customers. If they are located in different countries, at least two governments and their agencies and municipalities may have a stake in the merger or acquisition. Also, competitors may feel that they need to act, for example, by seeking a partner with which to merge. Thus, there are different categories of stakeholders that exert influence and are influenced in different ways, depending for example on the type of contracts between them and the merging/acquiring companies.

In their article, Friedman and Miles (2002) point out that despite the vast amount of books and articles focusing on the stakeholder concept, we still know little about how and why stakeholder relations change over time. Some years later, Lamberg et al. (2008) also note that the concept of stakeholder has most often been used in the study of stable stakeholder relationships, ignoring situations of turbulence. In this book, our focus is on situations where dynamics are at work, as at least two companies will be involved: the two merging companies, or the acquiring company and the target company (see Figure 1.1).

This type of situation may influence the acquiring and the target companies' relationships in a radical way. For example, relationships with suppliers and customers of the merging/acquiring companies may be terminated because of the merger/acquisition (Havila and Salmi 2000; Salmi, Havila, and Anderson 2001). On the other hand the companies' relationships may stay unchanged. The reason may be management skills in handling the situation or the view of stakeholders that they need not react if business continues as usual. All in all, this means that a merger or an acquisition is always challenging for management (Bower 2001).

As we focus on a context with at least two companies, it will always be necessary to consider stakeholders of the same stakeholder category in both the acquiring and target company. To illustrate the multiplicity and diversity of stakeholder relationships during a merger or an acquisition, we apply a *multi-stakeholder approach*. We argue that a merger or an acquisition involves several stakeholder groups of both the acquirer and the target company. These stakeholder groups perceive the pro's and con's from their own perspective and thus act and react accordingly. Their stakes are unlikely to be the same. Further, they will probably evaluate the benefits and drawbacks of the merger process, and thus the changing stakes, in different ways.

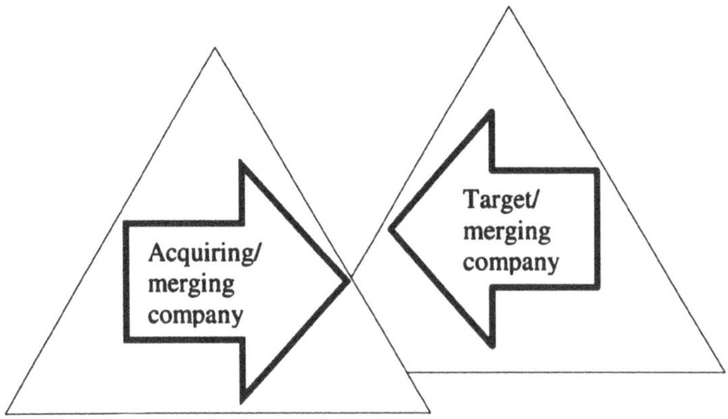

Figure 1.1 A merger or an acquisition involves at least two companies.

MERGERS AND ACQUISITIONS: FREQUENT STRATEGIC ACTIVITIES

Although the number of mergers and acquisitions seems to increase and decrease in waves (Martynova and Renneboog 2008; Shleifer and Vishny 1991), they have always been common and frequently studied. For example, according to Cartwright and Schoenberg (2006), an acquisition was made every 18 minutes all year around in 2004. Normally no business day ends without news of a merger or an acquisition in the media. It may be rumours of well-known global companies acquiring shares in each other, or it may emanate from a press conference where the CEO and the chairperson announce a merger. Whether the information is based on facts or just rumours, it still makes the headlines. The reason is simple: few other decisions and actions by shareholders, boards of directors and top management have such an impact on the company's future, on market structure and on shareholder value. Researchers who focus on mergers between two (or more) companies, or on acquisitions where the acquiring company acquires a substantial part of the shares in the target company, often see the merger/acquisition as a strategic step. In this introductory chapter, we present a brief overview of this broad field of research.

The decision to merge or acquire a company is always preceded by some sort of planning, followed by a decision of the shareholders and the board of directors. The time period from the first thoughts of the need to acquire or merge until integration can be considered complete may be short, or it may take many years. Researchers have often studied the phenomenon as if it passed through different phases or stages, such as a pre-merger phase and a post-merger phase. In their review of the literature, Calipha, Tarba, and Brock (2010) found several different ways to split the process into phases. It is not clear, however, what activities belong to which phase. Moreover, speed in integrating the companies involved has been found to be beneficial in some situations, but not in all (Homburg and Bucerius 2006).

There has been considerable research on the motives for a merger or an acquisition; that is, researchers have tried to answer the question why companies merge with/acquire other companies (e.g., Chatterjee 1992; Seth, Song, and Pettit 2000; Trautwein 1990). Examples of typical motives are: to lower costs through economies of scale, acquire new technology or increase market share. Depending on the goal, mergers can be categorised according to different types (Ansoff and Weston 1962: 50–52): vertical mergers, where a company merges with its suppliers and/or its customers; horizontal mergers, where the company's competitors are acquired; and conglomerate mergers, where unrelated product lines are combined. However, as Bower (2001: 93) states: 'The thousands of deals that academics, consultants and business people lump together as mergers and acquisitions actually represent very different strategic activities'. For example, if a company integrates upstream, that is, makes a former supplier company part of its own company, it changes at the same time the former indirect relationships with the supplier's suppliers into direct relationships. In the same way, a downstream vertical integration means that the former customer's customers become direct customers. In horizontal mergers, where former competitors integrate, the customers may not remain as loyal as expected (Lusch, Brown, and O'Brien 2011). This represents a totally different type of situation for the merging companies' managements than with a vertical downstream merger. The variety of perspectives and explanations is increased even further if we include the many forms of strategic alliances and partnerships (e.g., Ulijn, Duysters, and Meijer 2010).

The overwhelming majority of research in the field of mergers and acquisitions, however, has focused on the merging/acquiring companies. Consequently, researchers have primarily studied stakeholder groups within the merging companies, such as employees and managers (Birkinshaw, Bresman, and Håkanson 2000; Napier 1989; Raukko 2009). Stakeholder groups that are indirectly involved, such as the merging or acquiring company's suppliers and customers (if not in the role of target or acquirer), have received less attention from researchers; some recent exceptions are Holtström (2008) and Öberg (2008). Another, and still more recent, study of indirectly involved stakeholders is that of Clougherty and Duso (2011), who studied effects of horizontal mergers on non-merging rivals. More macro-level effects of mergers and acquisitions are treated in a study by Finkelstein (1997), who focused on inter-industry merger patterns, and in Dahlin (2007), who examined business networks. Even local communities and nations may have an interest in a deal involving a company that is important for their economic development (Kim 2006).

Over the years, researchers have identified many different challenges that the merging/acquiring companies' managers need to address. One challenge is how and when to communicate the decision so as to reduce uncertainty among employees (Appelbaum et al. 2000). For instance, Schweiger and Denisi (1991) found that realistic communication to employees was important. When the official announcement of the merger or acquisition is made, the chairperson of the board may explain the benefits of the merger to present and future customers, for example. Thus, one challenge is how to deal with media (Hellgren et al. 2002). Additional challenges identified during the integration phase are how to cope with cultural differences (Buono, Bowditch, and Lewis 1985; Larsson and Lubatkin 2001; Teerikangas and Very 2006) and how to manage knowledge transfer in cross-border acquisitions (Nummela 2011). The cultural dimension has gained extensive attention, as merger and acquisition activities often cross national borders (e.g., Söderberg and Vaara 2003).

Finally, the performance of the merged entity has received considerable attention from researchers. For example, Datta (1991) studied the impact of organisational differences between acquiring and target firms on post-acquisition performance. Chatterjee (1992) examined cultural differences and shareholder value in related mergers, and Capron (1999) reviewed long-term performance in horizontal acquisitions. Most researchers seem to agree that the (financial) value of a merger or an acquisition is difficult to measure (Very 2011; Zollo and Meier 2008). Often value creation, or destruction, is discussed from the perspective of the owners (i.e., shareholders). It is much less common to discuss how value is created or destroyed for other stakeholders, such as employees, customers or suppliers. One reason is probably the difficulties of defining and measuring value creation for these types of stakeholders. The emphasis on multiple stakeholders in this book aims to open the way for such an extended evaluation.

A MORE COMPREHENSIVE VIEW OF MERGERS AND ACQUISITIONS

The aim of this book is to give the reader a broader view of mergers and acquisitions by considering the different stakeholder groups that may have a stake before, during, and after a merger or an acquisition. We argue that the use of a multi-stakeholder approach has many advantages in the study of mergers and acquisitions. By acknowledging, for example, customers and suppliers as actors who have stakes in the merger or the acquisition, we open the way to studying a much more complex integration process, where the dynamics of the business network are included. Moreover, the multi-stakeholder approach, we argue, has the potential to make conflicting and interfering stakes visible; in line with this reasoning, it can also contribute to a discussion on measuring the performance of mergers and acquisitions. In the following sections we will further elaborate on our discussion of how a multi-stakeholder approach may enhance our knowledge and understanding of mergers and acquisitions.

Origins of the Stakeholder Concept

Often the book *Strategic Management: A Stakeholder Approach* by Edward R. Freeman (1984) is seen as the origin of the stakeholder concept. However, Freeman himself (2009: 97) credits numerous other scholars: 'The real pioneers were people like Eric Rhenman and Bengt Stimne [editors' note: correct spelling Stymne] from Sweden, Marion Doscher and Robert Stewart from Stanford Research Institute, Russell Ackoff, James Emshoff, Eric Trist, Ian Mitroff and Richard Mason, from Wharton and other schools, and in an earlier time frame Mary Parker Follett, Chester Barnard, and many others'.

It was in the 1960s that interest in the organizational environment really took off, influenced by advances in organisation theory (Argyris 1960; Cyert and March 1963; Presthus 1958; Thompson and Bates 1957) and vitalised by the discussion on organisational borders (see Scott and Davis 2007 for the development of the field). At the same time, interaction between the company and its environment became a focus of research (Boulding 1956; Clegg and Dunkerley 1977; Dahl and Lindblom 1953; Lawrence and Lorsch 1967). Rhenman (1964) was one of the researchers acknowledging the mutual dependence between the company and stakeholders such as suppliers, customers, employees and the local community. Rhenman introduced a stakeholder model,[1] in which he illustrated the two-way view on stakeholders: a company is dependent on the stakeholder and the stakeholder is dependent on the company in order to fulfil its goals and ambitions.

In the 1970s, Pfeffer and Salancik (1978) continued on the path of viewing organisations as open systems and argued that 'what happens in an organization [. . .] is also a consequence of the environment' (p. 3). They examined different forms of organisational interdependence, stating that a merger 'typically involves a restructuring of organizational dependence' (p. 114). They even went so far as to say that organisational effectiveness is '. . . an external *standard* of how well an organization is meeting the demands of the various groups and organizations that are concerned with its activities' (p. 11). Pfeffer and Salancik (1978) did not explicitly use the term stakeholder but helped to clarify its meaning and content by adding that interdependencies may include several conflicting interests.

In the 1980s, Freeman (1984) contributed to the consolidation of the field with his book where one important contribution was the finding that the handling of a company's many stakeholders, both within and outside the organization, may have a significant impact on the success of the firm: 'Each of these groups plays a vital role in the success of the business enterprise in today's environment' (p. 25). In 2010, Freeman et al. stated, '[a] stakeholder approach to business is about creating as much value as possible for stakeholders, without resorting to trade-offs' (p. 28). Involved in this value-creating process are the so-called primary and secondary stakeholders. The former include employees, suppliers, customers, financiers, and communities. Examples of the latter are competitors, consumer advocate groups, special interest groups, media, and the government.

We claim that it is interesting to confront the stakeholder approach with the typical view of a merger or an acquisition because this challenging strategic endeavour, with few exceptions, has a single official and ultimate aim: to create value for the owner(s). However, a stakeholder approach shows how such a narrow and one-sided focus may be detrimental in general—not only to other stakeholders within and outside the company—but also to the owner(s). Especially in a merger or an acquisition, it is quite evident that there are many different companies and other types of organisations, as well as individuals, that depend on the success or failure of the merger/acquisition. Besides monetary interest, there may be individuals and groups who have interests relating to technological or business development, to how the business best is managed, and to how the value-creation process should be organised.

A Multi-Stakeholder Approach to Mergers and Acquisitions

In this book, we study stakeholders in a context of two or more merging companies. Firstly, the fact that some of the stakeholder groups are at least doubled (sometimes more) means that there may be tensions and conflicts within each stakeholder group. For instance, some employees may be made redundant by a merger, or suppliers may suddenly realise that their product is not needed any more (Salmi, Havila, and Anderson 2001). Secondly, the dynamics depend on the character of the phenomenon as a process. For example, the situation of stakeholders may be very different during a pre-merger phase compared to a post-merger phase.

As Figure 1.2 illustrates, a merger or an acquisition creates complexity for the companies involved as several of the stakeholder categories are doubled up for the simple reason that two companies are concerned. This type of 'doubling' has a different significance for the various stakeholder categories. For example, during the pre-merger or pre-acquisition phase, the companies' owners and top management interact, often not involving other stakeholder groups until after the official announcement of the merger/acquisition. The two companies' middle management and employees are another stakeholder

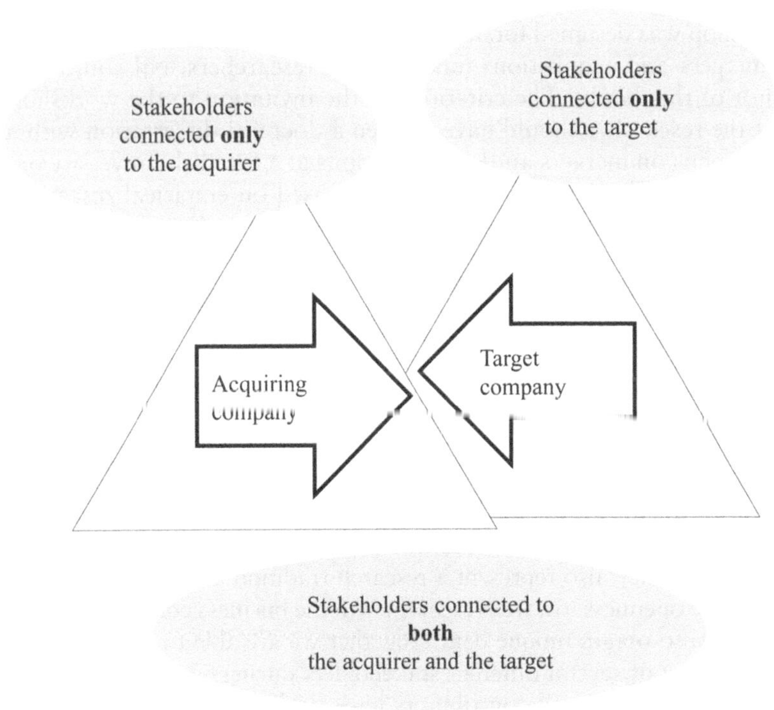

Figure 1.2 A multi-stakeholder approach to mergers and acquisitions.

category that is multiplied by two (or more if several companies merge). Finally, there are categories of stakeholders that are not doubled in case of national mergers and acquisitions, such as public bodies and other parties of public interest. However, in case of a cross-border merger or acquisition, some of these stakeholder groups may also be multiplied.

As the different stakeholders do not necessarily share the same goals and ambitions, they may play very different roles during a merger or an acquisition process. There are shifting goals and ambitions between the stakeholder groups and among stakeholders belonging to a particular category. Some suppliers to the acquiring company may, for example, perceive the acquisition as a business advantage, whereas the suppliers of the acquired company may see it as a threat. It is of course not possible or even meaningful to identify all possible stakeholders in a merger or an acquisition. Our ambition in this book is to show that acknowledging stakeholders connected to merging or acquiring companies may help not only to understand the complexities, but also to identify both opportunities and obstacles during a merger or an acquisition.

ABOUT THIS BOOK

The book project was initiated at a workshop held in June 2009 as part of a research project led by two editors of this book (Anderson and Havila). The workshop was designed for, and attracted, Swedish researchers specializing in mergers and acquisitions (one of these researchers, Nilsson, is also an editor of this book). The criterion for the invitation to the workshop was that the researcher should have written a doctoral dissertation with a primary focus on mergers and/or acquisitions at a Swedish university or business school. The resulting book is thus based on empirical research from many doctoral dissertations, as well as research conducted within different national and international research projects led by the editors.

The Empirical Base

The book builds on unique and extensive empirical material covering a great variety of industries and companies located in many different countries throughout the world. Most of the chapters are accounts from case studies based on rich empirical data. These types of accounts—'from the inside'—are rather uncommon in the literature because of the sensitive nature of most mergers and acquisitions, in addition to the difficulties of gaining access. In that respect they also represent a research tradition among Nordic researchers, where openness towards researchers in the business community has made it possible to obtain unique data. Together we are able to present a comprehensive view of several different stakeholders during a merger or an acquisition process because all contributors have studied mergers and acquisitions; some of us also have many years of practical experience in the field.

Although the majority of contributors are based in Sweden, the book covers acquiring and target companies around the world as several of the companies studied are multinationals with global business operations. For example, the acquirers come from countries that include Finland, Germany, Sweden, Switzerland, the UK, the US, and South Africa. The cases cover such highly diverse industries as bakeries, car manufacturing, chemicals, consultancy, construction, defence, electronics, insurance, information technology, materials handling, market research, metal cutting, paper and pulp, pharmaceuticals, and wine and spirits, for example.

There are many different kinds of mergers and acquisitions. Both horizontal and vertical mergers and acquisitions can be found in the cases studied. The majority of the transactions studied are so-called friendly deals, but one so-called hostile take-over is included. The companies studied are of all sizes. In total more than 50 companies are involved, either directly or indirectly, in the mergers and acquisitions studied in the cases in the book.

When one company acquires or merges with another, the process and the situation are likely to be perceived differently depending on the company with which the stakeholder is connected. Figure 1.3 illustrates this variety of perspectives. For example, stakeholders belonging to the same category, like managers, appear and act in both the acquiring and the target company. Because this is an edited book based on the work of many scholars, the stakeholder palette we present is the result of choices by the respective researchers. We have, however, asked the authors to focus primarily on a single type of stakeholder that is clearly identified in the beginning of each chapter. Some stakeholders, like managers, appear in several chapters, albeit in different positions.

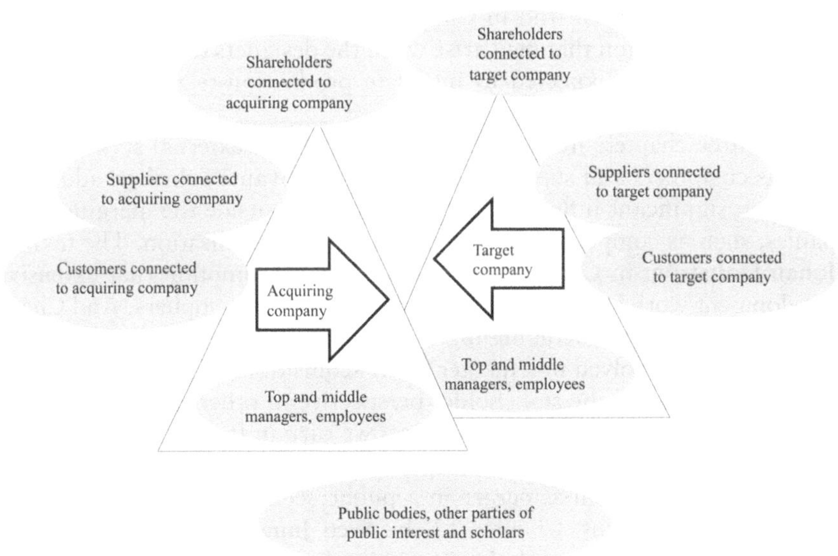

Figure 1.3 Stakeholders in focus in this book.

The Stakeholders in the Different Chapters

This book consists of 14 chapters: this first introductory chapter, 12 chapters representing different stakeholders, and a final chapter where we further discuss the critical roles of the different stakeholders during a merger or an acquisition process. We present the chapters in the following four parts:

Part I: Shareholders and top managers (Chapters 2 and 3)
Part II: Middle managers and employees (Chapters 4, 5, 6, and 7)
Part III: Suppliers and customers (Chapters 8, 9, and 10)
Part IV: Public bodies, other parties of public interest, and scholars (Chapters 11 and 12)

The chapters in Part I provide two different perspectives on shareholders and top management. In Chapter 2, **Tommy Borglund** discusses the importance of corporate social responsibility during an acquisition process and the role of shareholders in relation to other stakeholders. Chapter 3, by **Mona Ericson,** focuses on top managers and their motives and sensemaking during a hostile take-over attempt.

In Part II there are four chapters with focus on company-internal stakeholders. In Chapter 4, **Roger Schweizer** discusses the challenges faced by local subsidiary managers when they try to implement decisions made by their parent companies after the merger. Chapter 5, by **Magnus Frostenson,** addresses the issue of internal employee acceptance of changes following a merger and acquisition. In Chapter 6, **Fredrik Nilsson, Nils-Göran Olve, and Olof Arwinge** study the role that internal auditors may fulfil in an acquisition process. And in Chapter 7, **Peter Beusch** elaborates on the problematic situation that may arise when the designers of the management control system are expected to integrate production-related information systems as part of a merger.

The three chapters in Part III focus on company-external stakeholders, such as customers and suppliers. Chapter 8, by **Svante Schriber,** addresses the often significant influence that stakeholders outside the merging companies, such as competitors, may have on synergy realisation. The text by **Johan Holtström** in Chapter 9 is based on the assumption that extensive development work is conducted in collaboration with suppliers. And Chapter 10, by **Christina Öberg,** highlights customer business relationships with the companies involved in a merger or an acquisition.

Having extended the stakeholder perspective to other actors than those directly involved in the transition phase, we turn in Part IV to public bodies, other parties of public interest, and scholars. Chapter 11, by **Louise Bringselius,** focuses on a merger in a public sector context, and the role of central government. Chapter 12, by **Sven Jungerhem** and **Mats Larsson,** provides an account of changes in the Swedish banking sector from 1910–2009 and shows that bank owners, bank management, and the state played important roles in promoting and restricting bank mergers. Finally, scholars are seen as stakeholders in Chapter 13, by **Annette Risberg,** where she examines the claim of high failure rates.

In the epilogue (Chapter 14) by **Helén Anderson,** the complexity of understanding an acquisition and merger process is acknowledged and challenged by the many stakes involved. With reference to the findings in Chapters 2–13, this final chapter illustrates how different stakeholders may play critical and changing roles throughout the process, thus, ultimately affecting the outcome of the merger or acquisition.

NOTES

1. In his book, which was written in Swedish, he used the heading 'Intressebalans i företaget—en grundläggande model' (1964: 17 ff), and which usually is referred to as 'intressentmodellen' in Swedish.

REFERENCES

Anderson, H., Havila, V., and Salmi, A. (2001) 'Can you buy a business relationship? On the importance of customer and supplier relationships in acquisitions', *Industrial Marketing Management*, 30: 575–86.

Anderson, J.C., Håkansson, H., and Johanson, J. (1994) 'Dyadic business relationships within a business network context', *Journal of Marketing*, 58(October): 1–15.

Ansoff, H.I. and Weston, J.F. (1962) 'Merger objectives and organization structure', *Quarterly Review of Economics and Business*, 2(3): 49–58.

Appelbaum, S.H., Gandell, J., Yortis, H., Proper, S., and Jobin, F. (2000) 'Anatomy of a merger: behavior of organizational factors and processes throughout the pre- during- post-stages (part 1)', *Management Decision*, 38(9): 649–61.

Argyris, C. (1960) *Understanding organizational behaviour*, Oxford, England: Dorsey.

Birkinshaw, J., Bresman, H., and Håkanson, L. (2000) 'Managing the post-acquisition integration process: How the human integration and task integration processes interact to foster value creation', *Journal of Management Studies*, 37(3): 395–425.

Boulding, K. (1956) 'General systems theory—The skeleton of science', *Management Science*, 2(3): 197–208.

Bower, J.L. (2001) 'Not all M&As are alike—and that matters', *Harvard Business Review*, 79(3): 92–101.

Buono, A.F., Bowditch, J.L., and Lewis III, J.W. (1985) 'When cultures collide: The anatomy of a merger', *Human Relations*, 38(5): 477–500.

Calipha, R., Tarba, S., and Brock, D. (2010) 'Mergers and acquisitions: A review of phases, motives and success factors', *Advances in Mergers and Acquisitions*, Vol. 9: 1–24.

Capron, L. (1999) 'The long-term performance of horizontal acquisitions', *Strategic Management Journal*, 20: 987–1018.

Cartwright, S. and Schoenberg, R. (2006) 'Thirty years of mergers and acquisitions research: Recent advances and future opportunities', *British Journal of Management*, 17: S1–S5.

Chatterjee, S. (1992) 'Sources of value in takeovers: Synergy or restructuring—implications for target and bidder firms', *Strategic Management Journal*, 13(4): 267–87.

Clegg, S.R. and Dunkerley, D. (1977) *Critical issues in organizations*, London: Routledge & Keegan Paul.

Clougherty, J.A. and Duso, T. (2011) 'Using rival effects to identify synergies and improve merger typologies', *Strategic Organization*, 9(4): 310–35.

Cyert, R.M. and March, J.G. (1963) *A behavioural theory of the firm*, Upper Saddle River, NJ: Prentice Hall.

Dahl, R.A. and Lindblom, C.E. (1953) (Revised edition in 1992) *Politics, economics, and welfare*, New Brunswick, NJ: Transaction Publishers.

Dahlin, P. (2007) *Turbulence in business networks—A longitudinal study of mergers, acquisitions and bankruptcies involving Swedish IT-companies*, Doctoral Thesis No. 53, Mälardalen University.

Datta, D.K. (1991) 'Organizational fit and acquisition performance: Effects of post-acquisition integration', *Strategic Management Journal*, 12(4): 281–98.

Finkelstein, S. (1997) 'Interindustry merger patterns and resource dependence: A replication and extension of Pfeffer (1972)', *Strategic Management Journal*, 18: 787–810.

Freeman, R.E. (1984) *Strategic management: A stakeholder approach*, Boston: Pitman.

Freeman, R.E. (2009) 'Stakeholder theory: 25 years later', *Philosophy of Management*, 8(3): 97–107.

Freeman, R.E., Harrison, J.S., Wicks, A.C., Parmar, B.L., and de Colle, S. (2010) *Stakeholder theory—The state of the art*, Cambridge: Cambridge University Press.

Friedman, A.L. and Miles, S. (2002) 'Developing stakeholder theory', *Journal of Management Studies*, 39(1): 1–21.

Gadde, L.-E. and Mattsson, L.-G. (1987) 'Stability and change in network relationships', *International Journal of Research in Marketing*, 4: 29–41.

Håkansson, H. and Snehota, I. (1989) 'No business is an island: the network concept of business strategy', *Scandinavian Journal of Management*, 5(3): 187–200.

Håkansson, H. and Snehota, I. (eds.) (1995) *Developing relationships in business networks*, London: Routledge.

Halinen, A., Salmi, A., and Havila, V. (1999) 'From dyadic change to changing business networks: An analytical framework', *Journal of Management Studies*, 36(6): 779–94.

Havila, V. and Salmi, A. (2000) 'Spread of change in business networks: An empirical study of mergers and acquisitions in the graphic industry', *Journal of Strategic Marketing*, 8(2): 105–19.

Hellgren, B., Löwstedt, J., Puttonen, L., Tienari, J., Vaara, E., and Werr A. (2002) 'How issues become (re)constructed in the media: Discursive practices in the AstraZeneca merger', *British Journal of Management*, 13: 123–40.

Holtström, J. (2008) *Synergi—En studie av några industriföretag*, Doctoral Thesis No. 1231, Linköping studies in Science and Technology, Linköping University.

Homburg, C. and Bucerius, M. (2006) 'Is speed of integration really a success factor of mergers and acquisitions? An analysis of the role of internal and external relatedness', *Strategic Management Journal*, 27: 347–67.

Johanson, J. and Mattsson, L.-G. (1988) 'Internationalisation in industrial systems—A network approach', in N. Hood and J.-E. Vahlne (eds.), *Strategies in global competition*, New York: Croom Helm, pp. 287–314.

Kim, S.-K. (2006) 'Networks, scale, and transnational corporations: The case of the South Korean seed industry', *Economic Geography*, 82(3): 317–38.

Lamberg, J.-A., Pajunen, K., Parvinen, P., and Savage, G.T. (2008) 'Stakeholder management and path dependence in organizational transitions', *Management Decision*, 46(6): 846–63.
Larsson, R. and Lubatkin, M. (2001) 'Achieving acculturation in mergers and acquisitions: An international case survey', *Human Relations*, 54(12): 1573–607.
Lawrence, P.R. and Lorsch, J.W. (1967) *Organization and environment: Managing differentiation and integration*, Boston: Graduate School of Business Administration, Harvard University.
Lusch, R.F., Brown, J.R., and O'Brien, M. (2011) 'Protecting relational assets: a pre and post field study of a horizontal business combination', *Journal of the Academic Marketing Science*, 39: 175–97.
Martynova, M. and Renneboog, L. (2008) 'A century of corporate takeovers: What have we learned and where do we stand?', *Journal of Banking & Finance*, 32: 2148–77.
Mitchell, R.K., Agle, B.R., and Wood, D.J. (1997) 'Toward a theory of stakeholder identification and salience: defining the principle of who and what really counts', *Academy of Management Review*, 22(4): 853–86.
Napier, N.K. (1989) 'Mergers and acquisitions, human resource issues and outcomes: A review and suggested typology', *Journal of Management Studies*, 26(3): 271–89.
Nummela, N. (2011) 'Knowledge management in cross-border acquisitions', in M. Hassett, M. Räikkönen, and T. Rantala (eds.), *M&A as a strategic option. From opportunities to new business creation*, Helsinki: The Federation of Finnish Technology Industries, pp. 130–38.
Öberg, C. (2008) *The importance of customers in mergers and acquisitions*, Doctoral Thesis No. 115, Linköping Studies in Science and Technology, Linköping University.
Pfeffer, J. and Salancik, G.R. (1978) *The external control of organizations. A resource dependence perspective*, New York, NY: Harper and Row Publishers.
Presthus, R.V. (1958) 'Towards a theory of organizational behavior', *Administrative Science Quarterly*, 3(1): 48–72.
Raukko, M. (2009) *Key persons' organizational commitment in cross-border acquisitions*, Doctoral Thesis, Turku School of Economics.
Rhenman, E. (1964) *Företagsdemokrati och företagsorganisation: om organisationsteorins tillämpbarhet i debatten om arbetslivets demokratisering*. Stockholm: Svenska arbetsgivareföreningen (SAF).
Salmi, A., Havila, V., and Anderson, H. (2001) 'Acquisitions and Network Horizons: A Case Study in the Nordic Graphics Industry', *Nordiske Organisasjonsstudier*, 3(4): 61–83.
Schweiger, D.M. and Denisi, A.S. (1991) 'Communication with employees following a merger: A longitudinal field experiment', *Academy of Management Journal*, 34(1): 110–35.
Scott, W.R. and Davis, G.F. (2007) *Organizations and organizing. Rational, natural and open systems perspectives*, Upper Saddle River, NJ: Prentice Hall.
Seth, A., Song, K.P., and Pettit, R. (2000) 'Synergy, managerialism or hubris? An empirical examination of motives for foreign acquisitions of U.S. firms', *Journal of International Business Studies*, 31(3): 387–405.
Shleifer, A. and Vishny, R.W. (1991) 'Takeovers in the '60s and the '80s: Evidence and implications', *Strategic Management Journal*, 12: 51–59.
Söderberg, A.-M. and Vaara, E. (eds.) (2003) *Merging across borders: people, cultures and politics*, Copenhagen: Copenhagen Business School Press.
Teerikangas, S. and Very, P. (2006) 'The culture-performance relationship in M&A: From yes/no to how', *British Journal of Management*, 17: S31–S38.

Thompson, J.D. and Bates, F.L. (1957) 'Technology, organization, and administration', *Administrative Science Quarterly*, 2: 325–42.

Trautwein, F. (1990) 'Merger motives and merger prescriptions', *Strategic Management Journal*, 11(4): 283–95.

Ulijn, J., Duysters, G., and Meijer, E. (eds.) (2010) *Strategic alliances, mergers and acquisitions*, Cheltenham, UK: Edward Elgar Publishing Limited.

Very, P. (2011) 'Acquisition performance and the "Quest for the Holy Grail"', *Scandinavian Journal of Management*, 27: 434–37.

Zollo, M. and Meier, D. (2008) 'What is M&A performance?', *Academy of Management Perspectives*, August: 55–76.

Part I

Shareholders and Top Managers

2 The Growing Importance of Corporate Social Responsibility in Mergers and Acquisitions

Tommy Borglund

INTRODUCTION

Mergers and acquisitions are often described as an area where the interests of shareholders have been given priority over those of other stakeholders (Borglund 2006; Tainio et al. 2003; Tainio and Lilja 2003). In these situations companies often rhetorically express the importance of shareholder value and argue that the transaction will bring greater financial value later on. The interests of other stakeholders, such as employees, customers, and local communities, thus tend to be played down, to the advantage of shareholders.

However, with the advent of the discourse on Corporate Social Responsibility, CSR, priorities may be shifting, with other stakeholders gaining ground over shareholders as prioritized stakeholders. The interests of such stakeholders as employees, suppliers, and local communities become more important when a broader view of business responsibility is taken. This shift is likely to affect mergers and acquisitions. Today it is increasingly common to consider issues of social and environmental responsibility in connection with acquiring other companies (Knecht and Calenbuhr 2007; Konstantopoulos, Sakas, and Triantafyllopoulos 2009; Waddock and Graves 2006). This tendency is evident, for example, in more frequent taking of stakeholder perspectives in public relations by the parties involved in the transaction, as well as the increased importance of social and environmental responsibility in the due diligence process and in dialogues where companies listen to the concerns of affected stakeholders.

In more abstract terms, 'shareholder value' and 'corporate social responsibility' can be seen as two conflicting discourses on a macro level (Borglund 2006), where a discourse can be defined as a certain way of talking about and understanding the surrounding world (Jörgensen and Phillips 2000). A macro-level discourse is a shared approach to certain phenomena in society and a system for formulating ideas in a certain time frame (Alvesson and Kärreman 2000). The outcome of this struggle between discourses has implications for corporate strategy, stakeholder relations, and consequently mergers and acquisitions.

The overall purpose of this chapter is to highlight the possible role of corporate social responsibility during an acquisition process and to discuss the changing role of shareholders in relation to other stakeholders. I argue that the interests of other stakeholders are becoming increasingly important compared to the interests of shareholders, especially when the parties to the acquisition have strong links to societal interests, as in the case presented here Pernod Ricard Vin & Sprit, where the Swedish state was the seller.

This chapter is structured as follows: the first and second sections describe the development of the macro-level discourses on 'shareholder value' and 'corporate social responsibility', and their relevance for mergers and acquisitions. In the third section the new role of corporate social responsibility is exemplified in a case study of a recent acquisition in Sweden: the purchase of Vin & Sprit by Pernod Ricard. Interpretations are offered in light of the theoretical background used in the macro discourses. Comparisons are made to earlier case studies from a time when the notion of CSR was less well established in Sweden (Borglund 2006). Conclusions are drawn, and the changing role of shareholders in mergers and acquisitions is discussed.

Method

My background is in qualitative research, based on the hermeneutical tradition used in my dissertation. A hermeneutical process is one of interpretation and reinterpretation over time to obtain a holistic understanding of a problem and of reaching results in terms of credible interpretations of the phenomena involved (Alvesson and Sköldberg 1994; Kristensson Uggla 2002). To improve the credibility of the case studies, data are triangulated with a combination of interviews, observations and studies of documents (Denzin and Lincoln 2000). The approach is an explorative one focusing on finding possible explanations and suggestive interpretations in line with the case study method used (Yin 1984). It is a qualitative study with an emphasis on particular facts, and with a descriptive and inductive approach (Merriam 1988). Hence, to generalize the results and make them applicable to a larger group of companies, a quantitative method is needed, based on a positivist tradition. The qualitative approach in the case studies implies that the results are indicative and to some extent relativistic according to my interpretations, according to a postmodern tradition of social construction (Lyotard 1979).

One could say that the case studies show discourse analysis at the micro level, as distinguished from macro-level analysis of the discourses of shareholder value and corporate social responsibility (Alvesson and Kärreman 2000). The micro discourse analysis is used for the study of Pernod Ricard's acquisition of Vin & Sprit. The sources here are on a discursive level and include official sources such as press releases, web communication, and media coverage which have been compiled from data bases and websites. In addition and as a complement, some interviews and discussions were conducted with a smaller number of key parties close to the transaction and representing the seller, the purchaser, and the target. This case study focuses more on the communication of the transaction and the related messages than on a large number of formal in-depth interviews. Pernod Ricard's acquisition of Vin & Sprit was chosen as a case because it was current, access was possible through contacts, and the transaction concerned two companies advanced in CSR and operating in a sensitive industry from the standpoint of corporate reputation. My previous experience proved helpful in the research process. For 10 years I was a business journalist covering corporations and markets, including their major transactions. This experience helped me significantly in interpreting the observations in this case. In addition, I have five years of more recent experience as a consultant in corporate social responsibility, advising companies on communication and strategy. My work included several assignments involving corporate social responsibility in connection with mergers and acquisitions.

DEVELOPMENT OF THE DISCOURSE ON SHAREHOLDER VALUE

The development of the 'shareholder value' discourse is strongly related to mergers and acquisitions. The idea of shareholder value was developed in the US in the 1980s (Fligstein 2001; Holmström and Kaplan 2001; Jensen 2000; Kennedy 2000; Lazonick and O'Sullivan 2000). New models were used in the American capital market, where companies were acquired and restructured to make them create more value for shareholders. Thus, in the spread of the concept of 'shareholder value' in American business life, mergers and acquisitions played a key role. Managers started to seek 'shareholder value' because it was perceived as a successful management idea, but also in fear of otherwise being acquired (Fligstein 2001).

The concept of 'shareholder value' gave legitimacy to the notion that shareholders should be dominant in relation to other stakeholders (Aglietta 2000). To a growing extent, companies started competing to provide the best return to shareholders, representing a shift from an earlier emphasis on competing in products and production processes (Froud et al. 2000). Thus, the financial focus became stronger. A manager's pay was based on the creation of shareholder value in line with new theories of principal and agent, where the CEO was regarded as the agent of the owner, who was the principal (Jensen and Meckling 1976). To a growing extent, profits were distributed to shareholders, and programs to improve efficiency led to a substantial decrease in the number of employees at large American companies (Lazonick and O'Sullivan 2000). Overall, one could say that major American businesses stepped up the pressure on other stakeholders to focus more on the shareholders.

The notion of 'shareholder value' became prevalent among American companies during this period, and it emerged as a new business ideology that spread throughout the globe (Fligstein 2001). As a macro-level discourse it was powerful, winning over any competing discourses. During the 1990s it spread from the US to Europe and around the world. Mergers and acquisitions were a central driving force in this development. The pace of globalization was rapid, and world-wide investment soared. Much of the investment was related to mergers and acquisitions, where there were annual increases of 20 percent in the first half of the 1990s and 50 percent in the second half (UNCTAD 2001). Other driving forces were the expansion of financial markets, the development of professions like institutional investors, financial analysts, business journalists, and academics touting the importance of shareholder value, and consultants helping companies to become more shareholder-value oriented (Brodin et al. 2000; Lazonick and O´Sullivan 2000; Reberioux 2002).

In Europe this development entered different cultural territory. One may distinguish between a Continental European stakeholder model and an Anglo Saxon shareholder model of corporate governance. In the former, the influence of stakeholders plays a larger role in the management of the company (Gedajlovic and Shapiro 1998). In Europe there is tradition of broader goals for companies than maximizing financial return (Cioffi 2000; Reberioux 2002). Expectations are that companies have responsibilities and obligations to stakeholders, and there is a tradition of stakeholder value rather than shareholder value (Reberioux 2002).

During the 1990s the use of the term of 'shareholder value' was observable in countries like Germany, France, Finland, and Sweden (Lazonick and O´Sullivan 2000; Tainio, Huolman, and Pulkkinen 2001). Mergers and acquisitions thus became an arena for declaring a commitment to shareholder value for investors, analysts, and business journalists (Hellgren et al. 2003; Tainio et al. 2003; Tainio and Lilja 2003). In communication of the reasons for the M&A transaction, arguments taken from the discourse on 'shareholder value' were used. A company was expected to declare its commitment to shareholder value in order to attract investors and find support for the proposed transaction (Hellgren et al. 2003). The discourse on 'shareholder value' became well established in Europe and started to assume a major role in mergers and acquisitions.

By the mid-1990s the notion of shareholder value had become influential in Sweden. It received increasing media attention, and major companies started to declare their shareholder-value orientation, following the international trend (Brodin et al. 2000; Landelius and Treffner 1998). This commitment was new, because in Sweden it was common to view a company from a stakeholder perspective. Eric Rhenman (1964) formulated some of the early thinking about corporate democracy and stakeholder balance, influencing current stakeholder theories (Freeman 1984). Henrekson and Jakobsson (2001) described the development as the advent of a new system for Anglo-Saxon corporate governance, which represented a shift from earlier Swedish corporatism, where shareholders and capital markets had played a subordinate role for companies.

In the case studies presented in Borglund (2006), there were several examples of how the influence of the 'shareholder value' discourse affected companies.

Case Studies in the Era of Shareholder Value

In my dissertation I studied changes in stakeholder relations in Swedish companies that were becoming more international through mergers and acquisitions (Borglund 2006). The studies of mergers and acquisitions were conducted over a period from 2001 to 2005, when the shareholder value discourse was prevalent in Sweden, and the case narratives are clearly influenced by the discourse. Four cases were studied. The first was a large-scale merger in the pulp and paper industry, where Skogsföretaget merged with a Finnish competitor to form a very large concern listed on international stock markets. The second was Elektronikföretaget, a smaller enterprise acquired by a listed American company with global operations. The third was Konsultföretaget, a smaller consultancy firm acquired by a large listed British-American company. The fourth firm, Internet AB, was acquired by a recently listed German Internet company. In all cases, shareholders were becoming increasingly important from a management perspective relative to other stakeholders. There were some clear indications of the influence of the 'shareholder value' discourse, as could be observed in two ways: first through adaptation to stock market demands, and second through more financial reporting and increased control by the new owners.

The direct influence of stock market demands could be studied in the two companies that were listed on the stock market: Internet AB and Skogsföretaget. As for the case of Internet AB, it unfolded during the Internet bubble, and Internet AB played the game of the financial markets at that time. A number of measures taken were consistent with a shareholder value discourse, such as share-buyback programs, enhanced investor relations and executive incentive programs that linked managers' goals to financial value. After the M&A transaction, the stock market and investors became more dominant stakeholders. Eventually, however, the company went out of business in the stock market crash of Internet businesses. The direct expectations of the stock market for Skogsföretaget were also clear. Here shareholder value was an influential factor in the merger, the rhetoric used and the changes that came over time. For example, the company started to employ the EVA valuation model, which is used in the shareholder value discourse, as well as investor relations programs, share buyback programs and executive compensation programs based on share price. The changes in stakeholder relations were substantial; investors and the stock market became more important, whereas the Swedish nation, local communities, and local employees became less important.

The indirect stock market requirements of increased financial reporting and control were apparent in the two cases where small firms—Elektronikföretaget and Konsultföretaget—were acquired by a large listed company. New reporting systems emphasized financial considerations, and new kind of financial rationality was introduced. Thus, after a previous focus on industrial aspects, the interests of shareholders were now given priority. The requirements for listing on the stock exchange pushed these changes indirectly and led to greater financial control of the subsidiaries of listed corporations. This was the case with Elektronikföretaget, where more financial performance indicators were used and the frequency of financial reports was increasing. The owners took a much firmer grip on the company through a new system of reporting and control. Pressure was put on some of the other stakeholders, mainly the employees, who had to accept more hierarchy, less influence on decisions and increased stress. In addition, hard-fought negotiations were held with suppliers about lowering costs, exposing them to international competition. At Konsultföretaget similar developments were noted. New systems of financial reporting were introduced, putting additional pressure on the organisation. Several employees in the accounting department left in protest of the workload. A heavy emphasis on sales created frustration and alienation. New selling processes were introduced, where smaller clients were to be ignored. Furthermore, contracts with major suppliers were renegotiated in favour of cheaper alternatives. When the economy entered a downturn, there were severe consequences for employees. Salaries were frozen, and fringe benefits were eliminated. Eventually Konsultföretaget was downsized and moved to cheaper offices.

To sum up, the discourse on shareholder value affected the companies´ stakeholder relations and view of stakeholders in two ways: first, through new procedures for financial reporting and control related to the company's pursuit of its explicit goal of creating shareholder value, and second, through the expectation that companies listed on the stock market would declare their commitment to a shareholder value orientation. The companies took several steps consistent with the discourse, such as increasing communication of a shareholder-value orientation, investor relations activities, share buybacks, and introduction of incentive systems tying the compensation of managers to the creation of shareholder value.

In none of the cases did corporate social responsibility play any significant part in connection with the M&A transaction. Very rarely was the topic of CSR or related issues brought up in interviews. At that time the concept of corporate social responsibility was virtually unknown in Sweden, especially among rank-and-file employees of Swedish companies. In regard to taking responsibility for stakeholder relations, creating 'shared value' was not discussed as such in the cases. Probably the reason was that it had not yet matured as a strategic concept at this time. This notion emerged later, with the development of the CSR discourse.

DEVELOPMENT OF THE DISCOURSE ON CORPORATE SOCIAL RESPONSIBILITY

In recent years the discourse on shareholder value has been challenged by the discourse on 'corporate social responsibility'. The latter focuses on stakeholder management and emphasizes the importance not only of shareholders but also other stakeholders such as customers, employees, suppliers, the environment, and local communities (Donaldson and Preston 1995; Freeman 1984). In short, it is about voluntarily taking greater responsibility for major social and environmental issues in relations with principal stakeholders. The advent of corporate social responsibility as a leading theme in management arose from a crisis of trust arising in an atmosphere of anti-globalization, corporate scandals, and higher volatility of financial markets (Borglund, De Geer, and Hallvarsson 2009; Grafström, Göthberg, and Windell 2008; Windell 2006).

Short-term maximisation of shareholder value at the expense of other stakeholders, investor demands for a quick return and linking executive compensation to short-term increases in share prices are said to be major factors in the corporate scandals in the US around the turn of the millennium (Gray, Frieder, and Clark 2005; Partnoy 2003). Scandals at companies like Enron, WorldCom, and Arthur Andersen fuelled public distrust. (Lorsch, Berlowitz, and Zelleke 2005; Tapscott and Ticoll 2003). When it became evident that some of the companies declaring themselves to be 'shareholder-value' oriented were in fact deceiving stakeholders, including shareholders, the credibility of the discourse on 'shareholder value' was tainted.

In addition, the anti-globalisation movement manifested its criticism at large rallies in connection with meetings of the WTO, EU, and G8, arguing that globalisation was adversely affecting many stakeholders (Klein 2000; Segerstrom 2003). The anti-globalisation movement is described as being directed against capitalism as an idea, against globalisation as a form of imperialism and against global companies exploiting poor countries and poor people (Bhagwati 2004). According to critics, maximisation of shareholder value could then be connected with the misfortune of employees and local communities. If one adds the high volatility of financial markets, for example, the Asian crisis in 1997 and the Internet bubble at the turn of the millennium, one has three sources of the intense distrust that companies and markets needed to overcome. This provided fertile ground for the growth of corporate social responsibility.

From the turn of the millennium on, the discourse on corporate social responsibility has developed rapidly as companies have sought to gain public trust using the concept of corporate social responsibility as a tool (Borglund, De Geer, and Hallvarsson 2009). The issues of social and environmental responsibility had been driven during the 1990s by global non-governmental organizations, or NGOs (Segerlund 2007). Companies now started to address these issues, developing new strategies and enlisting NGOs as partners in managing responsibility in relation to stakeholders. A wave of 'soft regulation' generated new rules and guidelines that companies could follow voluntarily (Crane and Matten 2007; Steurer 2010; Vogel 2005). In total, no less than 100 such 'standards' or guidelines for corporate social responsibility have been established by multi-stakeholder groups, industry organisations, unions and NGOs (Jutterström 2006).

Furthermore, on financial markets investors became increasingly aware of the importance of social and environmental responsibility for corporate valuation, and some institutional investors started to use 'socially responsible investment' criteria in their asset management (Stenström 2008; Vogel 2005). Estimates show that about 10–15 percent of the investment capital managed in the US and Europe is subjected to such criteria (Borglund, De Geer, and Hallvarsson 2009; SOU 2008: 107). Also, those involved in 'investor relations' have become more aware of the importance of corporate social responsibility (Arvidsson 2010; Hockerts and Moir 2004).

In response to these changes, a new market for CSR was formed, including consultants, journalists, academics and other parties involved (Borglund, De Geer, and Hallvarsson 2009; Grafström, Göthberg, and Windell 2008; Windell 2006). Consultants started to offer new services in the field, and the news media reported increasingly on corporate social responsibility. In the Financial Times, for example, such coverage has expanded substantially (Grafström, Göthberg, and Windell 2008; Morsing and Beckman 2006; Windell 2006). Many organizations have started to organize conferences on the topic, and in academia corporate social responsibility has become a more common field of study.

The discourse gained in influence and had a strong impact on company's communication. Of Europe's 150 largest listed companies, 95 percent today have a CSR/Sustainability section on their websites (Borglund, De Geer, and Hallvarsson 2009). Increasingly, companies are using corporate social responsibility as a strategic tool for strengthening their brands and enhancing competitiveness (Kotler and Lee 2005; McElhaney 2009; Porter and Kramer 2006). One example is the Nestlé concept of 'Shared value' developed by Michael Porter and Mark Kramer in accordance with their thinking as set forth in various Harvard Business Review articles (Porter and Kramer 2006; Porter and Kramer 2011).

More than 25 years after Edward Freeman (1984) wrote 'Strategic Management—A stakeholder approach', stakeholder management has revived as a management concept. However, it is still subject to the condition of maximizing financial value. The notion of 'CSR as a business case' is strongly entrenched in the field (Crane and Matten 2007). It is what could be called 'a nodal point' within the discourse, an important argument to which all other arguments must relate (Jörgensen and Phillips 2000). It can be thought of as 'enlightened shareholder value'; by recognizing the needs of the stakeholders, a company will perform better financially (Borglund 2006; Borglund, De Geer, and Hallvarsson 2009; Jensen 2001; Sternberg 1997). Hence, corporate social responsibility has become an influential idea in management, where the business case for stakeholder management is a strong one from a business point of view (Jutterström and Norberg 2011).

The fact that there has been little criticism based on Milton Friedman's (1970) argument that 'the business of business is business' is due in large part to this rationality of the 'business case for CSR'. However, it has been argued that the idea is harmful to profitability and will bring new regulation that hampers trade and economic development (Henderson 2001). In addition, corporate social responsibility has been condemned as a discourse that companies are forced to adopt, not for business reasons but from the pressure of ideology and external expectations (Tullberg 2005). More recent criticism cites the dangers of the growing use of CSR in corporate public relations to build an image of a company inconsistent with its actions in the field (Spence 2007). Moreover, the discourse is said to have failed in actually resolving issues like climate change, corruption and unacceptable working conditions (Visser 2011).

CSR in Connection with Mergers and Acquisitions

Considering the development described above, what are the implications of CSR for mergers and acquisitions? There are several centred on responsibilities in relation to mergers and acquisitions (Crane and Matten 2007). These issues concern corporate responsibility and stakeholder relations, where stakeholder practices change in ways that can be both a strength and a source of worry (Waddock and Graves 2006). The issues can include, for example, diversity, community engagement, human resource practices, environmental responsibility, and product quality.

Mergers and acquisitions may be harmful to non-investor stakeholders such as employees, suppliers, and the local community by reducing the level of innovative shareholder-relations practices (Chase, Burns, and Claypool 1997). With the change in responsibilities towards these stakeholders, they risk being neglected in favour of short-term financial interests (Crane and Matten 2007). The effects on the dynamics of the company's stakeholder relations may weaken the company's position. Some empirical findings suggest that the target firm risks losing the competitive advantage from which it has benefited thanks to strong and trustful stakeholder relations (Waddock and Graves 2006).

On the other hand, there is an argument that M&A transactions can benefit society and stakeholders because they create more efficient markets and improve management performance (Chase et al. 1997). The arguments in favour of a shareholder-value orientation are that it will enhance the creation of financial value and the wealth of society as a whole (Jensen 2000). The restructuring of American business in the 1980s is said to have improved the efficiency, productivity, and competitiveness of American companies (Jensen 1993; Jensen and Chew 1995). However, there is also an issue of social responsibility in regard to the means used to reach this end. According to stakeholder theory, stakeholders have a right to be respected as such, not just as a means to an end (Evan and Freeman 1993).

In addition, deterioration of stakeholder relations might negatively impact shareholder value in the long run. It would be worthwhile investigating whether this lack of CSR might be an explanation in cases of poor financial performance. Considering the perception that many mergers and acquisition do not create financial value for shareholders (Buono and Bowditch 1989; Cartwright and Cooper 1990; Kleppestö 1993; Pritchett 1985; Sirower 1997), this possibility seems worthy of consideration, though it may be questionable, as Annette Risberg notes in Chapter 13 (in this volume). Especially for employees, the risks are high. Because being part of an integration process may cause hardship to employees (Buono and Bowditch 1989; Kleppestö 1993; Schweiger, Ivancevich, and Power 1987), post-merger integration is an issue of social responsibility. Good management of ethical and responsibility issues in a transaction can result in better employee performance (Lin and Wei 2006). Employment security and caring practices can strengthen commitment to the organization and contribute positively to a successful post-merger process. Here the issue of responsible restructuring comes into play (Cascio 2002). There are indications that restructuring in a more socially responsible manner actually enhances financial performance (Zu 2009).

Handling relations with local communities can also be regarded as a CSR issue. For the community as a stakeholder, much is 'at stake'. Loss of jobs, closing of factories, and relocation of headquarters are negative consequences discussed in the debate on globalisation in connection with mergers and acquisitions and the implications for local communities (Collste 2004; Streeten 2001). Globalisation can change the identity and sense of meaning for individuals in local businesses and local communities (Bauman 2000).

Ways of Managing CSR in Mergers and Acquisitions

Increasingly, corporate social responsibility is becoming part of the due diligence process, where social and environmental risk affects the price of the company to be acquired (Knecht and Calenbuhr 2007). The importance of stakeholder briefings is emphasized by Konstantopoulos, Sakas, and Triantafyllopoulos (2009), who conclude that central factor in the successful outcome of a merger is the methodology of briefing stakeholders during both the negotiation and merger process. Stakeholder briefings can deal with issues like stress, resistance to change and cultural change among stakeholders, especially employees. Briefing is about dialogue with major stakeholders like investors, governments, employees, and NGOs. It is about being proactive and identifying sources of distrust among stakeholders that can adversely affect the progress of the transaction. This is especially important if the parties involved depend on support from the state or other stakeholders that are public agents (Konstantopoulos, Sakas, and Triantafyllopoulos 2009).

On a discourse level, one finds statements by leading global consultancies on CSR and mergers and acquisitions. Deloitte, for example, is promoting and offering related services to clients. According to Deloitte (2009), companies with strong corporate responsibility and sustainability programs in place are likely to be rewarded for their efforts, adding that this aspect will become increasingly important in mergers and acquisitions. KPMG (2004) promotes environmental due diligence and notes that is has become an important feature of a growing number of transactions. Concerning health, safety, social, and environmental (HSSE) issues in mergers and acquisitions, KPMG states that 'simply starting to consider HSSE issues can significantly help reduce the risk of unpleasant post acquisition surprises when undertaking a transaction'.

Increasingly, companies are addressing matters of corporate social responsibility related to their transactions. Some Swedish examples are the investment companies of Ratos and Investor. Ratos states on its website, 'In acquisitions the inherent risks and opportunities are always examined as part of the due diligence process. This includes an assessment of the status of the company's CR work' (www.ratos.se). Investor, which has a similar system, states, 'The company's risk and opportunity profile linked to CSR related issues is mostly included in our screening process for new investments. We remain convinced that well-structured processes and clear CSR strategies will be important for risk management and value creation in the coming years' (www.investor.se).

A third example is Assa Abloy, a global company with Swedish origins that makes door locks and provides other security solutions. The company has grown through acquisitions, with over 150 transactions in most recent years. Assa Abloy writes in their Sustainability Report (2009) that sustainability is an aspect of the due diligence process, highlighting three areas with sustainability risks: manufacturing using hazardous substances, significant environmental pollution, and the supplier base of an acquired company.

After this discussion we turn to an example of how corporate social responsibility can influence an acquisition process: Pernod Ricard's acquisition of Vin & Sprit in 2008.

CASE STUDY: THE ACQUISITION OF VIN & SPRIT BY PERNOD RICARD

Vin & Sprit was the state-owned former monopoly on the procurement of alcoholic beverages in Sweden. In addition, Vin & Sprit had their own production of the very famous brand of Absolut Vodka. It was this brand that attracted the buyer, Pernod Ricard, a global company owning many beverage brands. In this case corporate social responsibility played a special role in view of the state ownership and the industry involved.

Through a media analysis some major issues can be identified as important matters of trust that need to be managed in order to win acceptance of the transaction in the public eye and among influential stakeholders. One of these was the question of jobs in Åhus in the Skåne region of southern Sweden, where the main production facility for Absolut Vodka in Sweden has been located. Many of the 2000 employees were employed there, and the union was strong, with good contacts with the media and with local and national politicians. The issue of keeping production in Skåne and Sweden was crucial, especially because the globalisation debate in Sweden had partly concerned the selling of Swedish 'crown jewels' to foreign companies, with the associated risks for the employees and the nation (Borglund 2006).

A related issue was the position of farmers in Skåne. They were major suppliers of grain to Absolut Vodka and would be negatively affected if the production system were changed. In addition, farms were an integral part of the cultural landscape of Skåne, with the open fields of grain crops. The brand of Absolut Vodka was linked to this landscape, to the high-quality grain from the farmers and to the excellence of the production process. The environmental responsibility aspect of the process was still another issue; it primarily concerned handling water in a clean and sustainable way.

Aside from this, there was the issue of responsible use of alcohol. For Vin & Sprit this question was related to the management of the organisation's internal values. The responsible use of alcohol was a part of organisational identity and culture. It was also linked with the national responsibility for alcohol consumption ascribed to Vin & Sprit by other stakeholders, mainly NGOs and politicians. In the past the sales monopoly, Systembolaget, cooperated closely with Vin & Sprit, which held the monopoly on importing alcoholic beverages to Sweden. Though the monopoly was now deregulated, it remained as part of the Vin & Sprit's history of responsibility in regard to alcohol consumption.

How to handle the marketing of beverages was a CSR issue where Vin & Sprit had an advanced method of management. Specific examples include not targeting young people or other vulnerable groups, no alko pops, and restricting product placement in video games. Moreover, the total amount of the marketing budget is in itself an issue, especially in Sweden.

From the above discussion, one can thus identify several 'holders' of 'stakes', who had to be consulted in order to gain greater acceptance of the transaction. One stakeholder was the employee union at Vin & Sprit, with which it was important to have a dialogue on both a local and a national level. The farmers in Skåne were also important, as was the organisation (LRF), which represented the interests of Swedish farmers on a national scale. The local politicians in Skåne constituted a further group, one likely to be concerned with issues of local industry and landscape. They had connections with politicians at a national level in several parties. NGOs are yet another influential stakeholder that could be expected to express concerns; these include environmental organisations seeking to safeguard environmental interests as well as organisations involved in issues related to 'responsible drinking'.

The Acquisition Process

The parties involved in the transaction were interested in 'corporate social responsibility' during the preparation phase of the acquisition. The seller, the Swedish state, did a benchmark study of the bidders and their accomplishments in 'corporate social responsibility' compared to their peers. It was important for the state to choose a buyer that had an advanced approach to 'corporate social responsibility' and was seen as a trustworthy, respectable and responsible company. The transaction would be scrutinized and analysed in the media. To avoid any political embarrassment to the Government, the seller did not want any accusations or insinuations in the media of selling to an irresponsible company. However, the Government had to sell at the highest price. As a representative of the seller explained,

> 'It was important to sell to a company that was advanced in CSR, but it was not the highest priority. There was a strong pressure on us to be business focused and to make sure that the assets that belong to the citizens are managed in the best way financially'.

Pernod Ricard came out well in the benchmark study. Pernod Ricard was highly progressive in issues relating to 'corporate social responsibility', the analysis showed. Thus, from a 'corporate social responsibility' perspective, the transaction had cleared all hurdles. When Pernod Ricard also turned out to be the highest bidder, the outcome was obvious. As expressed by the seller's representative,

> 'It was no problem since the company that made the highest bid was also advanced in CSR. Since both buyer and seller had a good track record in CSR, they had common interests from this point of view'.

From a political perspective, on the other hand, the process was delicate, as noted above. To address sensitive issues, the seller held a stakeholder dialogue at the outset of the sale process with certain influential stakeholders including unions, local politicians, municipalities, and suppliers. The dialogue involved meeting with stakeholders where the seller established a relationship with them, listening to their views. It was a way to prepare for the criticism that might come, but also a way to prepare for the negotiations with the bidders by obtaining further knowledge on sensitive issues for stakeholders. As the seller representative stated,

> 'It was a central part of the process. We wanted to prepare the bidders to address the important societal interests involved in the transaction. It is important to put the company in a societal context and listen to the stakeholders that could be affected adversely. [. . .] Stakeholders have knowledge that might not always have been considered by the owner. These preparations were important in enabling us to understand what we might be criticized for. Issues were raised that we could then discuss with the bidders. So one could handle these worries'.

In addition, the buyers sought to show their responsibility during the bidding stage of the merger. Pernod Ricard contacted major stakeholders to initiate a dialogue, trying to build good relations with them and showing that Pernod Ricard was a responsible and trustworthy company. There was an analysis of 'corporate social responsibility' as part of the due diligence process, where the performance of Vin & Sprit was compared to that of the bidders. Pernod Ricard did not want to buy a company with serious problems of social and environmental responsibility. Thus, 'corporate social responsibility' was given a role in the negotiations, as expressed by one of the executives at Vin & Sprit who worked with 'corporate social responsibility' issues,

> 'CSR was one of three areas of primary importance. These were about the brand and the financial figures in addition to CSR. For our side people from accounting, the legal department and the CSR department were the ones involved in the selling process'.

The topic of 'corporate social responsibility' was not only a question of perceptions; it could also have financial implications. The executive at Vin & Sprit continued:

> 'If there had been major things missing in our CSR work it would have impacted the price. Now that was not the case, so the analysis became more of a confirmation that this was a well-run company. Also, we were ambitious in the area of CSR, and that strengthened the impression of the entire company'.

At Vin & Sprit 'corporate social responsibility' became an issue in the internal discussion on what company would be a good new owner. Vin & Sprit had a good track record in 'corporate social responsibility' and was clear in its communication. Vin & Sprit was viewed favourably in Sweden on issues like alcohol responsibility, the environment, and working conditions. And Pernod Ricard showed an interest in all these aspects. As the executive at Vin & Sprit stated,

> 'They showed great interest in our CSR work at colleague-to-colleague level. Here we could learn from each other. They were impressed by

our work in CSR, especially in regard to supply chain management and environmental communication and reporting'.

The acquisition was announced on March 31, 2008. Press releases were issued, and joint press conferences were held. Even though 'corporate social responsibility' as such was not given a prominent part in the messages of the actors, there were clear stakeholder perspectives in their communication to the public. The focus in the press release from Pernod Ricard, by contrast, was on the industrial effects of the acquisition, on market development, market shares and the new products. For example, financial synergies were mentioned:

> 'This acquisition will reinforce the growth profile of Pernod Ricard and will generate significant value creation for Pernod Ricard's shareholders. [. . .] In addition, Pernod Ricard is strongly committed to a policy of Corporate Social Responsibility and encourages responsible consumption in order to prevent alcohol misuse and abuse'.

The board of Vin & Sprit was also positive, according to a press release, where the emphasis was on the long term view of Pernod Ricard:

> 'Pernod Ricard has a good reputation in the industry, with international brands as well as a strong local presence. They take a long-term industrial view and have expressed their ambition to continue to develop V&S's operations. The Board sees considerable industrial logic in the deal'.

From the seller, the Swedish government, there is also a message of long-term thinking. For example, the minister responsible for the transaction, Mats Odell, said in a press release, 'Vin & Sprit's business in Sweden will continue to develop. The head office will be in Stockholm and decisions will be taken here. Pernod Ricard is an owner that will develop the company'.

As for Swedish media reports on the acquisition, they focused on stakeholder relations, the long-term commitment of Pernod Ricard and the high price that was paid. The transaction was generally interpreted as a success for the Government as seller. The price of about SEK 50 billion was high, jobs were reasonably safeguarded and acquisition was based on a strong industrial logic. There was little discussion about the financial aspects and almost nothing about the stock market in the reporting. The transaction was portrayed more in relation to the future of Vin & Sprit and its stakeholders. The media contained no accusations of making short-term profits on the transaction or any other evidence of distrust connected to financial markets or of short-term thinking.

In the media, executives at Pernod Ricard emphasised the self-governance and organisational freedom of Vin & Sprit in a decentralised Pernod

Ricard structure. The importance of the production facilities in southern Sweden was noted, as was the significant role of Absolut Vodka in the future. Jobs were to remain in Sweden, and the high price was justified by industrial synergies and the long-term benefits envisioned by Pernod Ricard. One statement in the media report was the following:

> 'He [the chairman of Pernod Ricard, Patrick Ricard] can almost guarantee continued production in Sweden with Swedish personnel. To make vodka from Sweden you have to be Swedish, that is how we work, he says'.

A senior union representative at Vin & Sprit was quoted positively in the media, saying,

> 'Pernod Ricard was probably the best alternative. The company has a clear interest in maintaining the local ties of the products and is expected to safeguard long-term ownership'.

The union 'Livs' is said to appreciate Pernod Ricard's contacting the union prior to the bid and discussing the plans for the future. Pernod Ricard was viewed as a company that appreciated dialogue with its employees. The high price paid became a symbol of secure Swedish jobs and preservation of the ties to Sweden. That was the interpretation made by the media, rather than the opposite interpretation that a high price would necessitate cost-cutting in order to finance the deal. One newspaper wrote in the following summary,

> 'The best guarantee for the 2000 Swedish jobs is in the logic of the brands. These are locally based and would have no value if production were moved. It would make no sense for the buyer to pay tens of billions only to move out of the country and destroy the value of the product'.

CONCLUSIONS

The acquisition of Vin & Sprit by Pernod Ricard shows that when an acquisition involves governmental parties and concerns a sensitive industry often in the media debate, corporate social responsibility can make a difference. The case supports the argument in this chapter that corporate social responsibility is playing an increasing role in mergers and acquisitions. One implication is that shareholder interests are balanced to a growing extent by the interests of several other stakeholders. Of course, financial aspects still weigh heavily in the process, but these can to some extent be complemented by CSR issues, where CSR and 'enlightened shareholder value' are regarded as part of business policy (Borglund 2006; Jensen 2001; Sternberg 1997).

By taking into consideration responsibility towards stakeholders, the hope is to build a more competitive and valuable new company by keeping trustful stakeholder relations intact, in accordance with the discussion in Waddock and Graves (2006). Furthermore, following this policy facilitates the transaction process, reducing the risk of criticism in the media by sceptical stakeholders giving air to their concerns in public instead of discussing them with the parties to the acquisition in a stakeholder dialogue.

Comparing the cases in my earlier studies to Pernod Ricard's acquisition of Vin & Sprit, one finds that CSR now plays a greater part in mergers and acquisitions than 5–10 years ago. This tendency is consistent with the development of the discourses on 'corporate social responsibility' and 'shareholder value' laid out in this chapter. Earlier the concept of corporate social responsibility was not sufficiently widespread to have any impact, and it lacked the strategic importance to become an issue in an acquisition as it did in the Vin & Sprit–Pernod Ricard case. Thus, this chapter shows that CSR can have a role to play in mergers and acquisitions, one that will probably increase over time, to judge from the development of the discourses on 'corporate social responsibility' and 'shareholder value'.

Furthermore, this chapter provides an example of how corporate social responsibility can be managed in a transaction process in light of the discussions in Konstantopoulos, Sakas, and Triantafyllopoulos (2009) and Knecht and Calenbuhr (2007), for example. In Pernod Ricard's acquisition of Vin & Sprit, we can observe an actual stakeholder briefing process of the kind that Konstantopoulos, Sakas, and Triantafyllopoulos (2009) discuss. This seems to support the proposition that stakeholder briefings can address issues of distrust, thereby helping to gain support for an acquisition. There seemed to be little public criticism from stakeholders when the Pernod Ricard acquisition was announced; on the contrary, many stakeholders expressed their support in the media. It is likely that the stakeholder dialogues were helpful in this respect, as is discussed by Konstantopoulos, Sakas, and Triantafyllopoulos (2009).

In addition, we can see that a due diligence process including corporate social responsibility was conducted, in line with Knecht and Calenbuhr (2007). This was done by both the seller and the buyer. The seller, as a public agency, needed to manage the risk of being criticized for selling to a company with poor ethical standards. Conducting a CSR analysis of the bidders was one way to address that risk. Moreover, the buyer expanded the required financial due diligence process to include aspects of social and environmental responsibility in order to make sure that Vin & Sprit was capable of handling specific issues of trust. This is also consistent with the discussion in Knecht and Calenbuhr (2007).

As for the change in importance of stakeholders, all the earlier studies showed a shift in favor of shareholders (Borglund 2006). To some extent this change is a natural part of mergers and acquisitions because they entail a change of ownership where issues of importance to shareholders are emphasized. As discussed, shareholder interests are often given priority, especially in public relations (Hellgren et al. 2003; Tainio et al. 2003; Tainio and Lilja 2003). However, it is likely that the growing importance of corporate social responsibility will offset this to some extent, as may be indicated by Pernod Ricard's acquisition of Vin & Sprit.

The earlier studies also cited instances where other stakeholders were accorded less importance. Probably the development of corporate social responsibility will help stakeholders such as employees and local communities to gain influence and reduce the likelihood of being neglected in favour of short-term financial interests, as is discussed by Crane and Matten (2007). In the long term, CSR aspects may contribute to shareholder value by creating new opportunities for trustful stakeholder relations that enhance competitiveness. This would be in line with the 'business case for CSR' (Crane and Matten 2007).

If negative consequences for stakeholders like employees and local communities could be handled by strategies of social responsibility, this could probably facilitate value creation in mergers and acquisitions. As previously noted, a large proportion of M&A transactions are said not to create any financial value (Buono and Bowditch 1989; Cartwright and Cooper 1990; Kleppestö 1993; Pritchett 1985; Sirower 1997). Emphasising corporate social responsibility, nurturing stakeholder relations and responsible integration processes might be a recipe for improvement.

An overall conclusion is that the stakeholder in focus in this chapter, the shareholders, will have to adjust increasingly to the interests of other stakeholders in a merger and acquisition process. The position of shareholders, so highly privileged in the heyday of shareholder value, the 90's, is likely to be accorded somewhat lower priority with the spread of the discourse on 'corporate social responsibility'.

IMPLICATIONS FOR MANAGERS

One practical implication for managers consists of the tools for addressing corporate social responsibility in connection with merger and acquisitions: the stakeholder briefing process and the due diligence process. This case shows that complex and sensitive stakeholder issues can be managed through the use of these tools. The acquisition of Vin & Sprit by Pernod Ricard is an example where stakeholders on the whole were favourable to the transaction; this is not always true, however.

Another implication is the importance of the growing CSR discourse and of being prepared to integrate issues of social and environmental responsibility into business decisions. It is becoming increasingly necessary to understand the new perspectives of responsibility that are applied to companies by stakeholders such as investors, NGOs, and politicians, as well as by the media. For managers dealing with the growing market of socially responsible investors, this has a direct implication, for an increasing number of investors now require that the companies in which they invest meet certain criteria for social and environmental responsibility (Stenström 2008; Vogel 2005). Managing an IPO will need to address these considerations in order to make sure that major institutional shareholders will not boycott the IPO for lack of corporate social responsibility.

Overall, managers need to include issues of corporate social responsibility in their business agenda, and there are a growing number of strategies for doing so (Halme and Laurila 2009; Kotler and Lee 2005; McElhaney 2008; Porter and Kramer 2006). Corporate social responsibility is developing into a tool for competitiveness, and managers need to learn how to utilize this tool strategically and how corporate social responsibility can contribute to maximising the financial value of the company in the long term.

REFERENCES

Alvesson, M. and Kärreman, D. (2000) 'Varieties of discourse: On the study of organizations through discourse analysis', *Human Relations*, 53(9): 1125–49.

Alvesson, M. and Sköldberg, K. (1994) *Tolkning och reflektion—Vetenskapsfilosofi och kvalitativ metod*, Lund: Studentlitteratur.

Aglietta, M. (2000) 'Shareholder value and Corporate Governance: some tricky questions', *Economy and Society*, 29(1): 146–59.

Arvidsson, S. (2010) 'Communication of Corporate Social Responsibility: A Study of the Views of Management Teams in Large Companies', *Journal of Business Ethics*, 67(3): 241–56.

Assa Abloy (2009) Sustainability Report, www.Assaabloy.com.

Bauman, Z. (2000) *Globalisering*, Lund: Studentlitteratur.

Bhagwati, J. (2004) *In defense of globalization*, New York: Oxford University Press.

Borglund, T. (2006) *Aktieägarvärden i fokus—internationell påverkan på intressentrelationer genom förvärv och fusion*, Doctoral Thesis, Stockholm School of Economics.

Borglund, T., De Geer, H., and Hallvarsson, M. (2009) *Värdeskapande CSR—Hur företag tar socialt ansvar*, Stockholm: Norstedts Akademiska Förlag.

Brodin, B., Lundkvist, L., Sjöstrand S.-E., and Östman, L. (2000) *Koncernchefen och ägarna*, EFI, Handelshogskolan i Stockholm.

Buono, A. and Bowditch, J. (1989) *The human side of mergers and acquisitions—Managing collisions between people, culture and organizations*, San Francisco: Jossey-Bass Publishers.

Cartwright, S. and Cooper, C. (1990) 'The impact of mergers and acquisitions on people at work: Existing research and issues', *British Journal of Management*, 1(2): 65–76.

Cascio, W. (2002) 'Strategies for Responsible Restructuring', *The Academy of Management Executive*, 16(3): 80–91.

Chase, D., Burns, D., and Claypool, G. (1997) 'A suggested Ethical Framework for Evaluating Corporate Mergers and Acquisitions', *Journal of Business Ethics*, 16: 1753–63.

Cioffi, J. (2000) 'Governing globalization?—The state, law and structural change in Corporate Governance', *Journal of Law and Society*, 27(4): 572–600.
Collste, G. (2004) *Globalisering och global rättvisa*, Lund: Studentlitteratur.
Crane, A. and Matten, D. (2007) *Business Ethics*, Oxford: Oxford University Press.
Deloitte (2009) 'How green is the deal? The growing role of sustainability in M&A', Deloitte Development LLC.
Denzin, N. and Lincoln Y. (2000) 'Introduction: The discipline and practice of qualitative research', in N. Denzin and Y. Lincoln (eds.) *Handbook of qualitative research*, London: Sage Publications, pp. 1–30.
Donaldson, T. and Preston, L. (1995) 'The stakeholder theory of the corporation: concepts, evidence and implications', *Academy of Management Review*, 20(1): 65–91.
Evan, W. and Freeman, E. (1993) 'A stakeholder theory of the modern corporation: Kantian capitalism', in G. Chryssides and J. Kaler (eds.) *Introduction to Business Ethics*, London: Chapman & Hall, pp. 254–66.
Fligstein, N. (2001) *The architecture of markets—An economic sociology of the twenty first century capitalist societies*, Princeton: Princeton University Press.
Freeman, E. (1984) *Strategic Management—A stakeholder approach*, Marshfield: Pitman Publishing.
Friedman, M. (1970) 'The social responsibility of business is to increase its profits', *The New York Times Magazine*, September 13, in G. Chryssides and J. Kaler (1993) *Introduction to Business Ethics*, London: Chapman & Hall, pp. 249–54.
Froud, J., Haslam, C., Johal, S., and Williams, K. (2000) 'Shareholder value and financialisation: consultancy promises, management moves', *Economy and Society*, 29(1): 80–110.
Gedajlovic, E. and Shapiro, D. (1998) 'Management and ownership effects: Evidence from five countries', *Strategic Management Journal*, 19(6): 533–53.
Grafström, M., Göthberg, P., and Windell, K. (2008) *CSR—Företagsansvar i förändring*, Malmö: Liber.
Gray, K., Frieder, L., and Clark, G. (2005) *Corporate scandals—the many faces of greed*, St Paul: Paragon House.
Halme, M. and Laurila, J. (2009) 'Philanthropy, Integration or Innovation?—Exploring the Financial and Societal Outcomes of Different Types of Corporate Responsibility', *Journal of Business Ethics*, 84: 325–39.
Hellgren, B., Löwstedt, J., Tienari, J., Vaara, E., and Werr, A. (2003) 'Agents of homogenisation: on the roles of management consultants in mergers', Working paper presented at 17th Nordic Conference on Business Studies, Scandinavian Academy of Management, August 14–16, Reykjavik.
Henderson, D. (2001) *Misguided Virtue*, London: The Institute of International Affairs.
Henrekson, M. and Jakobsson, U. (2001) 'The transformation of ownership policy and structure in Sweden: Convergence towards the Anglo-Saxon Model?', Working Paper, IUI, Handelshögskolan i Stockholm.
Hockerts, K. and Moir, L. (2004) 'Communicating Corporate Social Responsibility to investors, the changing role of the investor relations function', *Journal of Business Ethics*, 52(1): 85–98.
Holmström, B. and Kaplan, S. (2001) 'Corporate Governance and merger activity in the United States: Making sense of the 1980s and 1990s, *Journal of Economic Perspectives*, 15(2): 121–44.
Jensen, M. (1993) 'The Modern Industrial Revolution, Exit, and the Failure of Internal Control Systems', *The Journal of Finance*, 48(3): 831–80.

Jensen, M. (2000) *A theory of the firm—Governance, residual claims and organizational forms*, Cambridge: Harvard University Press.
Jensen, M. (2001) 'Value Maximization, Stakeholder Theory, and the Corporate Objective Function', *European Financial Management*, 7(3): 297–317.
Jensen, M. and Chew, D. (1995) 'U.S. Corporate Governance: Lessons from the 1980s', in J.L. Livingstone (ed.) *The Portable MBA in Finance and Accounting*, New York: John Wiley & Sons, pp. 337–404.
Jensen, M. and Meckling, W. (1976) 'Theory of the firm: Managerial behavior, agency costs and ownership culture', *Journal of Financial Economics*, 3: 305–60.
Jörgensen, M. and Philips, L. (2000) *Diskursanalys som teori och metod*, Lund: Studentlitteratur.
Jutterström, M. (2006) *Corporate Social Responsibility—The supply side of CSR standards*, Doctoral Thesis, SCORE, Stockholm University.
Jutterström, M. and Norberg, P. (2011) *Företagsansvar—CSR som management idé*, Lund: Studentlitteratur.
Kennedy, A. (2000) *The end of shareholder value—Corporations at the crossroads*, Cambridge: Perseus Publishing.
Klein, N. (2000) *No Logo*, London: Flamingo.
Kleppestö, S. (1993) *Kultur och identitet vid företagsuppköp och fusioner*, Göteborg: Nerenius & Santerus förlag.
Knecht, F. and Calenbuhr, V. (2007) 'Using capital transaction due diligence to demonstrate CSR assessment in practice', *Corporate Governance*, 7(4): 423–33.
Konstantopoulos, N., Sakas, D., and Triantafyllopoulos, Y. (2009) 'The strategy of stakeholder briefing during merger negotiation in the bank market', *Journal of Management Development*, 28(7): 622–32.
Kotler, P. and Lee, N. (2005) *Corporate Social Responsibility—Doing the most good for your company and your cause*, Hoboken: John Wiley and Sons.
KPMG (2004) 'Impact—A survey on environmental due diligence', KPMG International, UK.
Kristensson Uggla, B. (2002) *Slaget om verkligheten—Filosofi, omvärldsanalys, tolkning*, Stockholm: Brutus Östling Bokförlag Symposium.
Landelius, A. and Treffner, J. (1998) *Fokusera på aktieägarvärdet—Värdeskapande och företagsvärdering i praktiken*, Stockholm: Ekerlids Förlag.
Lazonick, W. and O'Sullivan, M. (2000) 'Maximising shareholder value: a new ideology for Corporate Governance', *Economy & Society*, 29(1): 13–35.
Lin, C. and Wei, Y.-C. (2006) 'The Role of Business Ethics in Merger and Acquisition Success: An Empirical Study', *Journal of Business Ethics*, 69: 95–109.
Lorsch, J., Berlowitz, L., and Zelleke, A. (eds.) (2005) *Restoring trust in American business*, American Academy of Arts and Sciences, Cambridge: MIT Press.
Lyotard, J.-F. (1979) *The postmodern condition: A report on knowledge*, Manchester: Manchester University Press.
McElhaney, K. (2008) *Just Good Business—The strategic guide to aligning corporate responsibility and brand*, San Francisco: Berret–Koehler Publishers.
Merriam, S. (1988) *Fallstudien som forskningsmetod*, Lund: Studentlitteratur.
Morsing, M. and Beckmann, S. (eds.) (2006) *Strategic CSR Communication*, Copenhagen: DJOF Publishing.
Partnoy, F. (2003) *Infectious greed—How deceit and risk corrupted the financial markets*, London: Profile Books.
Pritchett, P. (1985) *After the merger: Managing the shockwaves*, Homewood: Dow Jones-Irwin.
Porter, M. and Kramer M. (2006) 'Strategy & Society: The Link Between Competitive Advantage and Corporate Social Responsibility', *Harvard Business Review*, December: 78–92.

Porter, M. and Kramer, M. (2011) 'Creating Shared Value', *Harvard Business Review*, January–February: 62–77.
Rebérioux, A. (2002) 'European style of corporate governance at the crossroads: The role of worker involvement', *Journal of Common Market Studies*, 40(1): 111–34.
Rhenman, E. (1964) *Företagsdemokrati och företagsorganisation—Om organisationsteorins tillämpbarhet i debatten om arbetslivets demokratisering*, Stockholm: SAF/FFI/Norstedts Förlag.
Risberg, A. (Chapter 13 in this volume) 'The Stake of High Failure Rates in Mergers and Acquisitions'.
Schweiger, D., Ivancevich, J., and Power, F. (1987) 'Executive actions for managing human resources before and after acquisition', *Academy of Management Executive*, 1(2): 127–38.
Segerlund, L. (2007) *Making Corporate Social Responsibility an International Concern—Norm Construction in a Globalizing World*, Doctoral Thesis, Stockholm University.
Segerstrom, P. (2003) 'Naomi Klein and the anti-globalization movement', in M. Lundahl (ed.) *Globalization and its enemies*, EFI Handelshögskolan i Stockholm, pp. 121–40.
Sirower, M. (1997) *The synergy trap—How companies lose the acquisition game*, New York: The Free Press.
SOU 2008:107 (2008) 'Etiken, miljön och pensionerna—Betänkande från kommittén om AP-fondernas etik och miljöansvar', Stockholm.
Spence, C. (2007) 'Social and environmental reporting and hegenomic discourse', *Accounting, Auditing & Accountability Journal*, 20(6): 855–82.
Stenström, E. (2008) *Shareholder influence on Corporate Social Responsibility*, Doctoral Thesis, Stockholm School of Economics.
Sternberg, E. (1997) 'The defects of Stakeholder Theory', *Corporate Governance*, 5(1): 3–10.
Steurer, R. (2010) 'The role of governments in corporate social responsibility: characterising public policies on CSR in Europe', *Policy Sciences*, 43: 49–72.
Streeten, P. (2001) *Globalisation—Threat or opportunity?*, Copenhagen: Copenhagen Business School Press.
Tainio, R., Huolman, M., and Pulkkinen, M. (2001) 'The internationalization of capital markets: How international institutional investors are restructuring Finnish companies', in G. Morgan, P.H. Kristensen and R. Whitley (eds.) *The multinational firm; organizing across institutional and national divides*, Oxford: Oxford University Press, pp. 153–71.
Tainio, R., Huolman, M., Pulkkinen, M., Yrkkö, J., and Ylä-Anttila, P. (2003) 'Global Investors meet Local managers: Shareholder value in the Finnish Context', in M.-L. Djelic and S. Quack (eds.) *Globalisation and institutions: Redefining the rules of the game*, Cheltenham: Edward Elgar, pp. 37–56.
Tainio, R. and Lilja, K. (2003) 'The Finnish business system in transition: Outcomes, actors and influences', in B. Czarniawska and G. Sevon (eds.) *The northern lights—Organisation theory in Scandinavia*, Malmö: Liber, pp. 69–87.
Tapscott, D. and Ticoll, D. (2003) *The naked corporation—How the age of transparency will revolutionize business*, New York: Free Press.
Tullberg, J. (2005) 'Reflections upon the responsive approach to corporate social responsibility', *Business Ethics: A European Review*, 14(3): 261–76.
UNCTAD (2001) 'World investment report 2001—Promoting linkages', United Nations.
Vogel, D. (2005) *The market for virtue—The potential and limits of Corporate Social Responsibility*, Washington D.C.: Brookings Institution Press.

Waddock, S. and Graves, S. (2006) 'The Impact of Mergers and Acquisitions on Corporate Stakeholder Practices', *Journal of Corporate Citizenship*, 22: 91–109.

Windell, K. (2006) *Corporate Social Responsibility under Construction: Ideas, Translations, and Institutional Change*, Doctoral Thesis No. 123, Department of Business Studies, Uppsala University.

Visser, W. (2011) *The age of responsibility—CSR 2.0 and the new DNA of business*, Chichester: John Wiley and Sons.

www.investor.se (01–02–2011).

www.ratos.se (01–02–2011).

Yin, R. (1984) *Case study research—Design and methods*, London: Sage Publications.

Zu, L. (2009) *Corporate Social Responsibility, Corporate Restructuring and Firm's Performance—Empirical Evidence from Chinese Enterprises*, Berlin: Springer-Verlag.

3 Top Managers as Stakeholders

Their Motives and Sense-Making in a 'Hostile' Merger and Acquisition Process

Mona Ericson

INTRODUCTION

Notably lacking in contemporary research on mergers and acquisitions are studies accounting for how motives are formed and made sense of by top managers involved in a merger and acquisition process where an element of hostility is an integral part. Mergers and acquisitions are often examined as rational strategic phenomena and as outcomes of organizational processes. Only a limited number of studies focus on factors that contribute to managerial resistance or cooperation in an acquired firm (Harrison, O'Neill, and Hoskisson 2000). There is an emphasis on the need to plan well in advance while taking into consideration how procedures and human resources affect the resulting outcomes (Seo and Hill 2005). What happens in the course of the merger and acquisition process is a function of strategic objectives driving the process (Schweiger and Very 2003), without concern for surprising events, and a tension-laden relationship between top managers that influence motives and trigger sense-making. Previous research on merger and acquisition motives (e.g., Chatterjee 1986; Goldberg 1983; Hunt 1990; Napier 1989; Steiner 1975; Trautwein 1990; Walter and Barney 1990) has devoted little interest to how motives are formed and made sense of in connection with what is considered to be at stake from a top manager's viewpoint as a merger and acquisition process unfolds.

Recent studies on takeovers tend to focus more on the relationship between, and the investment incentives of, target firm owners and other stakeholders (Chemla 2005); on the reduction of top managers' control and corporate restructuring (Denis and Kruse 2000); and on CEO turnover, stock price, and operating performance (Kini, Kracaw, and Mian 2004). In a review of the literature on takeovers, Limmack (2000) shows that takeover studies further focus on stock price reaction and on measuring the performance of the firms involved. Recent studies also consider the integration of mergers and acquisitions (Schweiger and Very 2003), with an emphasis on motives in association with different kinds of synergies and on sources of value creation. The rationale is to exploit perceived opportunities, securing a greater return on assets (Pitkethly, Faulkner, and Child

2003), promoting market growth and strengthening the firm's competitive position (Chung 2004). A motive is typically viewed as a basis for action, unilaterally governing merger and acquisition activities.

There is thus a need to supplement existing research on mergers and acquisitions with insights into a merger and acquisition process that heightens the urgency and tension in stakeholder interactions while bringing together and interlinking top managers' motives and sense-making. This need brings renewed interest in the so-called *Iggesund case*, which focused on a merger and acquisition process described in the media as the most spectacular power struggle in Swedish business life at the time (Ericson 1991). In the early 1980s, a forest products firm became the target of a takeover bid that its CEO did not welcome and viewed as hostile. According to Goergen and Renneboog (2003: 101), 'A takeover (attempt) is classified as hostile if the potential target rejects the offer for whatever reason'. Although different types of stakeholders affected by a takeover, can be identified, such as creditors, trading partners, and employees (Chemla 2005), this chapter limits its scope to a few top managers: the CEO of the takeover candidate, and the two chairmen and the two CEOs—the bidders—representing the two would-be acquirers. By virtue of their positions, these five top managers had the legitimate power to undertake a merger and acquisition (Jones 1995; Vaara and Tienari 2002).

'Stake' includes an element of risk (Mitchell, Bradley, and Wood 1997). In the Iggesund case, both the CEO of the target firm and the bidders bore some risk as a result of their divergent interests. The CEO feared a takeover where the identity of the firm might be lost and the position of the firm weakened. For the bidders, synergistic gains through the creation of a larger corporation were at stake. Their interest in the target firm was based on expectations of forming a new constellation with enhanced visibility in the forest products industry and increased competitiveness on the international market. The bidders' claim for immediate attention from the CEO of the target firm, together with the lack of reciprocity in the motives of the bidders and those of the target firm's CEO, made reconciliation difficult. Reciprocity refers to the interdependence of people and to their exchanges in a give-and-take situation, entailing, for example, achievement of a shared understanding on what should and should not happen (Watson 2002). Lack of reciprocity heightens the urgency and tension in stakeholder identification (Maitlis 2005; Mitchell, Bradley, and Wood 1997). In other words, the top managers with key roles as stakeholders in this chapter experienced urgency and tension in their interactions.

The aim of this chapter is to provide insights into the interactions of the five identified top managers and in particular to focus on the bidders' motives and on how the CEO of the takeover candidate made sense of the motives that were made present in the unfolding merger and acquisition process. In connection with the hostile takeover bid, the target-firm stakeholder experienced unpredictability and surprise as he tried to make sense of the situation that emerged from the actions taken by the bidder firms' top management. Interlinked with this aim is my intention to assist merger and acquisition scholars, as well as practitioners, in developing greater sensitivity towards the practical complexity of mergers and acquisitions; this would be done by looking into a process that attracted particular interest in Swedish business and in the media years ago.

The remaining part of the chapter is structured as follows: the next section provides a few glimpses into previous and contemporary research on merger and acquisition motives. It underlines the need to facilitate stakeholder interaction, motive formation, and sense-making by applying a process-relational perspective, which is presented thereafter. This is followed by a section that describes the qualitative method used for generating empirical material, and by an empirical illustration that puts the spotlight on the top managers as stakeholders. The concluding discussion brings to the fore the merger and acquisition motives of these stakeholders and their sense-making and also introduces the concept of *reciprocal sense-making.* Finally, managerial implications are discussed.

RESEARCH ON MERGER AND ACQUISITION MOTIVES

Microeconomics, finance, industrial organization, strategic management, and organization theory have contributed to the development of conceptual frameworks for analysing motives, but with little attention to how stakeholders in a merger and acquisition form and make sense of motives. A common way to describe a merger and acquisition is as a rational process with a series of sequences and causal chains (Haspeslagh and Jemison 1991; Hunt 1990; Kitching 1967, 1973; Seo and Hill 2005). Although scholars criticizing mergers and acquisitions as rational processes have emphasized human aspects (Buono and Bowditch 1989; Cartwright and Cooper 1996; Davies 1980; Lindell and Melin 1991; Nahavandi and Malekzadeh 1988), motives have been the subject of far less theoretical effort than the consequences of merger and acquisition processes (Hitt, Hoskisson, and Ireland 1990; Shrivastava 1986; Trautwein 1990). Research raises mainly financial issues while concentrating on the firm level of analysis; thus, little work has been done on individuals' motives in association with sense-making. The merger and acquisition literature is still dominated by finance and market studies, as Cartwright and Schoenberg (2006) observe.

Our understanding of merger and acquisition motives is largely gained from research from the mid-1970s and throughout the 1980s. Comprehensive lists of motives based on managerial goals and referring to accelerated growth, synergistic qualities, and improved competitiveness were compiled. Conceptualized as reasons for mergers and acquisitions, motives were listed in the form of categories and taxonomies. Walter and Barney (1990) presented a taxonomy of twenty motives relating to variables such as growth, synergy, market power, market share, and efficiency. Steiner (1975) identified two categories of motives, namely those *for* and *against* a merger. Napier (1989) categorized merger and acquisition motives as value maximizing or non-value maximizing. Value maximizing motives are based on the assumption that mergers and acquisitions are planned and accomplished by managers who intend to achieve synergistic gains, increase profitability, and shareholder wealth. These motives have received extensive scholarly interest (Allen and Hodgkinson 1989; Appleyard 1980; Ashton and Atkins 1984; Bradely and Korn 1984; Campbell and Luchs 1998; Chatterjee 1986; Giammarino and Heinkel 1986). Non-value maximizing motives refer to increased sales, asset growth and a manager's desire to build an empire by gaining a dominant position on the market (Napier 1989). From the perspective of the manager, growth leads to a more favourable position in terms of increased action space, status, and prestige (Dennis and McConnell 1985; Jemison and Sitkin 1986; Singh and Montgomery 1987; Steiner 1975).

A contemporary trend in research on mergers and acquisitions is the focus on managers' integration activities and value creation, interlinked with the recognition that culture is a factor that influences firm integration and subsequent outcomes (Cartwright and Price 2003; Kavanagh and Ashkanasy 2004; Schweiger and Very 2003; Stahl and Voigt 2004). Goergen and Renneboog (2003) assert that the main motive for a merger and acquisition is value creation, resulting from operational and informational synergies. The motive is described as a reason for a merger and acquisition. The value creation motive is met through achievement of synergies, which in turn is based on achievement of a strategic and cultural fit. Here 'fit' concerns the degree of compatibility between the firms involved in a merger and acquisition (Bower 2001). Operating synergies refer to economies of scale or scope, whereas informational synergies arise when the combined value of the firms' assets exceeds their individual market value. Goergen and Renneboog (2003) focus on short-term shareholder wealth effects in a takeover, reflected in the premium paid for the target's shares, while distinguishing between different means of payment for the bid.

Other scholars identify two broad motives, acquisition of new technological capabilities and gaining access to new markets (Birkinshaw, Bresman, and Håkansson 2000). Concerned with the creation of value through post-acquisition integration, Birkinshaw, Bresman, and Håkansson conceptually distinguish between the management of task integration and of human integration, assessing the impact on the realization of operational synergies and employee satisfaction. Finding appropriate levels of integration in terms of control, communication and strategic approach adopted by the new parent company is further elaborated in contemporary research (Pitkethly, Faulkner, and Child 2003).

Based on the glimpses into previous and contemporary research provided in this section, I note a tendency to conceptualize motive as a reason for a merger and acquisition. The focus of the studies cited centres on motives as given in advance, preceding managerial action and thus without consideration of the formation and sense-making of motives that could take place in the course of managerial interaction. With such a focus, I realize that the idea of purposefulness runs through the research on merger and acquisition motives, with little consideration of a past-oriented background from which present future-oriented motives might emerge and make sense. Associated with the idea of purposefulness are different types of synergies that arise from a strategic and cultural fit between firms, suggesting that the value of the combined and integrated firm must be greater than the sum of the value of the individual firms (Seth, Song, and Richardson Pettit 2002). Fit is regarded as a critical determinant of the subsequent integration process (Stahl and Voigt 2004). As Cartwright and Cooper (1993) pointed out more than a decade ago, much hinges then on the ability to identify a merger and acquisition partner that represents a strategic and cultural fit.

Drawing on Watson (2002), it can be argued that purposefulness, which seems to be a salient feature of merger and acquisition studies, is to a great extent attached to the organizational entity itself. Synergy and fit are assumed to be achieved between organizational entities such as firms, with limited attention devoted to human interaction driven by a multiplicity of possible motives, some of them hidden (Goldberg 1983), that might be at work in a merger and acquisition process and require sense-making.

To further understand mergers and acquisitions, a process-relational perspective is suggested. It entails gaining insight into human interactions involving the top managers, their motives, and their engagement in sense-making, where a firm is viewed as existing in human interactions and relationships, as will be noted in the following section.

THE PROCESS-RELATIONAL PERSPECTIVE

The process-relational perspective brings human interactions and relationships to the fore. According to Watson (2002: 58), the concern of the process-relational perspective, briefly put, is 'with how things happen in practice'. From this perspective, the firm does not have a straightforward objective existence but exists in human interactions and relationships characterized by negotiation, persuasion, manipulation and tension. The process-relational perspective draws on a social constructionist thinking that recognizes that a firm has a 'being' inseparable from how a human being makes sense of it, Watson (2002: 64) clarifies. Sense-making is an essential part of human existence. To speak of a motive as merely preceding subsequent managerial action is to forget about human interaction through which motives form and become subject to sense-making. A process-relational perspective highlights top managers' continual dealings with and sense-making of changing circumstances and unpredictable occurrences in a merger and acquisition process described as 'hostile'. Moreover, it entails moving beyond a concern for a strategic and cultural fit that arguably reifies firms as organizational entities to be combined and integrated.

Sense-making happens when discrepant cues interrupt individuals' activities and 'involves the on-going retrospective development of plausible images that rationalize what people are doing' (Weick, Sutcliffe, and Obstfeld 2005: 409). This means that an individual provides an interpretation on the basis of what is plausible and workable rather than striving for 'accuracy'. To exercise sense-making is an interpretative process driven by plausibility (Yahaya and Abur-Bakar 2007).

Generally, sense-making suggests retrospective construction of a *frame* in which discrepant *cues* noticed in an on-going flow of events could be placed (Starbuck and Milliken 1988). Frames are constructed out of past moments of socialization, and cues are 'found' in present moments of experience. Weick (1995: 111) explains: 'This means that the content of sense-making is to be found in the frames and categories that summarize past experience, in the cues and labels that snare specifics of present experience, and in the ways these two settings of experience are connected'.

The retrospective feature of sense-making suggests that cues are extracted on the basis of previous actions and of things that have already happened. Yet cues could also be prospectively framed (Wright 2005), prompting sense-making to extend beyond the past and be made meaningful in a larger future-oriented context (Boland 1984). As pointed out in this chapter, a motive emerges prospectively as well when one of the top managers faces the future and imagines what is to come, expecting positive synergies to be achieved through cooperating with a business firm that shares his culturally based ideals. Sense-making in reference to merger and acquisition motives is then an element of top managerial action and interaction that brings together past experiences and expectations for the future.

A process-relational perspective, an important aspect of which is sense-making, thus implies that human beings enact reality, while having 'continuously *emergent orientations*' (emphasis original) (Watson 2002: 105) towards various aspects of a merger and acquisition. As Gergen (1999: 11) maintains: 'The world does not produce our concepts, rather our concepts help us engage that world in various ways'. Reality is not formed in a causal sense and or taken for granted, 'out there' surrounding the individual (Collin 1997). From a process-relational perspective, actions and interactions characterize the merger and acquisition process. Individuals come together in an exchange where their motives are formed and made sense of.

Action includes talk and takes place in a social-cultural world from which the human being cannot be separated (Watson 2002). The human being is not a fixed entity that experiences the world from outside, but shares and participates in the world. Nor is motive a fixed entity that merely guides action. Although a merger and acquisition can be the result of a strategic plan governed by a previously given motive, it is likely that a merger and acquisition unfolds as a process of human interaction in which there are different ways of coping with and making sense of occurrences. As Watson (2002: 63) notes: 'Because human beings are not part of one big unified social grouping in which everyone's interests coincide, there will always be a variety of social constructions available for making sense of any particular part of human existence'. Sense-making is an important dimension of the process-relational perspective, and this dimension is highlighted in the continued empirical illustration and discussion in this chapter.

METHOD

The empirical illustration draws on my doctoral thesis, which focuses on rationalities in a merger and acquisition process (Ericson 1991). A qualitative method was used as an approach to interpretation and understanding of a merger and acquisition process as it dynamically unfolded over time. The qualitative method is thus grounded in a view of reality that in accordance with the process-relational perspective interrelates individual and world through the individual's experience of the world. That experience essentially refers to the dialogical way individuals relate to each other and to the social-cultural world.

The empirical material, generated between June 1986 and January 1989, refers to 41 interviews and a rich set of documentary material, including annual reports, press comments, historical monographs, internal letters, minutes, and tapes. Based on this material, the Iggesund 'case' was designed. Lacking a precise starting and ending point, and not confined to occurrences within the closed boundaries of a single firm, it can be referred to as an 'open case'. It implies openness while building on the material presented in interviews and documents that directed attention to people associated with four Swedish forest products firms; Iggesund, Stora, Billerud, and MoDo, and the two largest commercial banks in Sweden, SEB and Handelsbanken. Holmen, another Swedish forest products firm, also figured in the case. Without reference to a representative of its own, Holmen designated a place for a meeting and was also mentioned as a merger partner of MoDo. These industrial firms and banks were all listed on the Stockholm Stock Exchange.

Included in the study are the CEOs, chairmen as well as deputy chairmen of boards, financial managers, directors of strategic planning, and representatives of labour unions, who influenced and were influenced by the takeover bid for the target firm of Iggesund in April 1981. The interviews were semi-structured, with a focus on the takeover bid, why the bid was offered, and what occurred as a consequence of the bid. Each interview lasted 1–2 hours. To gain insight into a sensitive and tension-laden process and to build a trustful relationship in the interview situation, I did not use a tape recorder but took extensive notes while listening intently to what was said. Before the material was published, the interviewees were given the opportunity to check whether the text referring to them was consistent with what they had said during the interviews. It is interesting to note that in the course of the check, some interviewees added material that brought more depth to the discussion of events surrounding the takeover bid. After changes in the manuscript, the interviewees signed an agreement which allowed me to publish the material and openly acknowledge their participation in the process under their full names. In this chapter, references are made to these persons by title only.

Through examination of the interviews, transcripts of meetings, file documentation, and field notes, a merger and acquisition process developed (the Iggesund case). Including events surrounding and resulting from the bid, the process extended throughout the period 1980–1984. As it appeared, the CEO of Iggesund, and the chairmen and the CEOs—the bidders—representing Stora and Billerud, played key roles as stakeholders in the process.

The process refers to both *mergers* and *acquisitions*. A merger is a 'transaction between two parties of roughly equal size, whereas in an acquisition the larger party takes over the smaller one', according to Goergen and Renneboog (2003: 101). Although these terms are often used interchangeably in the merger and acquisition literature, it is important to distinguish between them. The Iggesund case illustrates a takeover bid that clearly relates to an acquisition where the larger constellation consisting of Stora and Billerud was about to acquire the smaller firm of Iggesund. In addition, the case refers to a strategic plan, outlined by the Iggesund CEO, for a merger between Iggesund and Billerud. Further, the case mentions the vision of the so-called New Group. This vision, formed by the chairman and principal owner of MoDo, designates both Iggesund and Holmen as merger partners of MoDo.

Drawing on the Iggesund case, I limit the following presentation to an excerpt that provides interesting and valuable insight into the top managers' interactions with reference to motive and sense-making.

THE IGGESUND CASE

The Iggesund case takes as its point of departure the situation at the time of the takeover bid. This situation constitutes in the interactions among the top managers of the target-firm and the bidder-firms. Primarily on the basis of the Iggesund CEO's interpretation, background events occurring at the time of the takeover bid of it are presented, followed by the interpretation of the bidders' motives, and of what occurred after the takeover bid. The empirical presentation is structured accordingly. The forest products firms, referred to throughout the presentation as Iggesund, Stora, Billerud, and Modo, and the commercial banks of SEB and Handelsbanken, assume the roles of agents through the ways in which the top managers talk about them. These firms and banks are admittedly ascribed as entities of their own as exemplified by expressions such as 'Stora and Billerud offered Iggesund a price', 'MoDo successively increased the voting rights', and 'SEB and Handelsbanken, competitors since the 1920s, used to keep track of each other's interests'. A process-relational perspective, however, reminds us that an industrial 'firm' (or a 'bank') does not exist in isolation, but through human interactions and relationships.

The Takeover Bid

On April 29, 1981, Iggesund became the target of a takeover bid, the architects of which were top managers at Stora and Billerud. From the perspective of the Iggesund CEO, their joint effort to acquire Iggesund was based on a quite generous bid in terms of price, representing a significant increase in the net worth of Iggesund, and with immediate payment in cash and shares of both Stora and Billerud. To the CEO of Iggesund, the approach of the bidding firm to the target firm management was nevertheless highly unconventional and was expressively described as being 'struck by lightning'.

The Iggesund CEO was a member of the board of the Holmen forest products firm. When attending a board meeting at Holmen on April 29, 1981, he received a telephone call summoning him to the nearby airport as quickly as possible. At the airport he met with the deputy chairman of Iggesund and was to his surprise informed about a takeover bid. The deputy chairman of Iggesund had a close relationship of many years with Marcus Wallenberg (presented below) and was Wallenberg's 'natural discussion partner' on matters that concerned restructuring, primarily in the Swedish forest products industry. As it turned out, Marcus Wallenberg had ordered his discussion partner to fly from Stockholm, where they had met, to the Norrköping airport, situated south of Stockholm and near Holmen where the Iggesund CEO was that day. At the airport the CEO of Iggesund was informed about the bid of Stora and Billerud. On the very same day, the takeover bid was on the afternoon radio news.

Stora and Billerud offered Iggesund a price without any written explanation in advance of their reasons for wanting to acquire Iggesund, plainly by-passing the CEO, the principal shareholders and the board of directors of the target firm. This was a highly unorthodox way to approach a target firm and triggered speculation about the bidders' motives. The CEO of Iggesund was given the impression that 'Stora and Billerud were acting under heavy pressure'. He regarded the bid as 'hostile', judging from the actions taken by top managers of Stora and Billerud. He also ascribed a crucial role to Marcus Wallenberg, a well-known investor and shareholder in Swedish companies.

As board member and chairman of dozens of companies, Marcus Wallenberg played a major role in the development of Swedish industry and took an active part in the business operations of Stora and Billerud. Marcus Wallenberg continued the work of earlier generations of the influential Wallenberg family. In 1996, Bartal wrote: 'In no other Western country does a single family enjoy the same degree of influence or authority. The Wallenbergs control a lion's share of their country's top companies, and have done so for decades' (p. 7). In 1856, the grandfather of Marcus, André Oscar Wallenberg, founded Stockholms Enskilda Bank. As the first modern commercial bank in Sweden, it played a pioneering role in the continuing industrialization. In 1972, Stockholms Enskilda Bank merged with Skandinaviska Banken, forming a single new bank, SEB. At the time of the takeover bid, Marcus Wallenberg served as honorary chairman of the SEB board.

Behind the Scenes of the Takeover Bid

Ever since the summer of 1980, MoDo successively increased its voting rights in the Iggesund stock. As Iggesund lacked a dominating owner and could be bought relatively easy, the chairman and principal owner of MoDo referred to Iggesund as 'a floating company'. Sharing this view, representatives of SEB and Handelsbanken and their associated firms in the Swedish forest products industry saw Iggesund as an attractive takeover candidate. In the words of the chairman of Billerud, who was also chairman of SEB, Iggesund was 'a dog without a master'.

As the CEO of Iggesund pointed out, the takeover bid caused a wave of shocked surprise, uncertainty and negative reactions among the employees of Iggesund. There had been no negotiations between the Iggesund CEO and the bidders prior to the bid, and there had not been time for the CEO of Iggesund to inform employees and discuss the bid with them. On April 29, the takeover bid was on the radio news. That same day, outdoors at an airport, the CEO of Iggesund learned about the bid from the deputy chairman of Iggesund, who had been given the role of messenger by Marcus Wallenberg.

Because Marcus Wallenberg, as a result of his close connection with SEB, was involved in preparing and designing the takeover bid, the CEO of Iggesund concluded that the bid inevitably had to do with the long-standing rivalry between the two biggest banks in Sweden, SEB, and Handelsbanken. Based on the relations of each bank with industrial firms in different parts of Sweden, two banking spheres were discernible, the SEB sphere and the Handelsbanken sphere. Underlying the takeover attempt were thought to be the conflicting interests of the SEB sphere, where Marcus Wallenberg played a major role, and the Handelsbanken sphere.

Marcus Wallenberg, interested as he was in structural changes in Swedish industry, had long had an eye on the forest product firms in southern and middle Sweden. In the early 1980s, Iggesund, situated in the north of Sweden, attracted special attention from both Marcus Wallenberg, representing the SEB sphere, and the chairman and principal owner of MoDo, associated with the Handelsbanken sphere. Stora and Billerud were associated with the SEB sphere. Handelsbanken, it turned out, was also engaged in the development of forest product firms, but mainly those situated in northern Sweden. MoDo, located in the north, was one of them. At the time of the takeover bid, Iggesund did not belong to either sphere.

SEB and Handelsbanken, competitors since the 1920s, used to keep track of each other's interests and strategic actions. It seemed as if SEB, rather than Stora and Billerud, intended to acquire Iggesund in a contest with Handelsbanken, further fuelling the antagonism between the banks and their respective spheres. In April 1981, the Handelsbanken sphere controlled over 25 percent of the voting rights in Iggesund. Consequently, the chairman of MoDo and the chairman of Handelsbanken were about to be appointed members of the board of Iggesund. From the viewpoint of Marcus Wallenberg and the members of the SEB sphere, the upcoming appointments were a threat to their restructuring plans. The rapid strategic move by the representatives of the SEB sphere entailed a takeover attempt that was considered necessary to prevent Iggesund from being incorporated into the Handelsbanken sphere.

Although additional top managers can be identified in the context of the rivalry between the banking spheres, the CEOs of Iggesund and the bidders were more visible in the process that was unfolding. Marcus Wallenberg and top managers of SEB and Handelsbanken seem to have prevailed behind the scenes of the takeover bid. In the exchanges that took place between the CEO of Iggesund and the chairmen and the CEOs of Stora and of Billerud, the urgency and tension intensified, aggravating the element of hostility in the merger and acquisition process and increasing the stakes from the viewpoint of these top managers.

The Bidders' Motives

The CEO of Iggesund was in urgent need of information on the bidders' motives, that is, the motives of the chairmen and the CEOs of the two would-be acquirers, Stora and Billerud. He acted rapidly, mobilizing against the threat of being taken over by Stora and Billerud, as Iggesund's survival as an independent business firm was obviously at stake. Almost a week after the announcement of the bid, the Iggesund CEO was informed by Stora and Billerud on the motives for the takeover attempt. According to the financial manager of Stora, the motives were related to profitability, positive synergies and increases in market shares. From the bidders' perspective, there was the promise of an organizational and strategic fit between Stora, Billerud, and Iggesund; in addition, calculations showed that close coordination between the three companies would provide substantial financial and economic benefits. Moreover, corporate renewal would enhance international competitiveness. The synergies cited by the top managers of Stora and Billerud were expected to bring about considerable advantages. On financial grounds there were no doubts that the new combination would be stronger than if the parties were separate, the top managers concluded. It should be noted, though, that one of the bidders, the CEO of Billerud, did not believe that any synergistic gains would be realized between Iggesund and Billerud in 1980—at the time when the Iggesund CEO presented his counterpart at Billerud with a merger plan. In 1980, however, the circumstances under which the advantages of combination were discussed were different.

The merger negotiations with the Billerud management in 1980 add complexity to the motives for the takeover bid, as the CEO of Iggesund remarked. Iggesund planned to merge with Billerud, and the management of Iggesund made strong efforts to convince the CEO and the chairman of Billerud of the advantages of a merger. The plan stated that the presumptive constellation had the potential to become one of the most competitive corporations in Scandinavia. Iggesund and Billerud together were expected to achieve what was far beyond their individual capabilities.

The unwillingness on the part of the Billerud management in 1980 to sacrifice values that had been built up over a long time strongly affected the merger plan, which was never implemented. The CEO of Billerud considered the positive synergies proposed by the CEO of Iggesund to be exaggerated. Fearing negative consequences for the existing production program of Billerud, he resisted merging with Iggesund. At stake were patriotic ideals and strong traditions. Considering the upcoming celebration of the centennial anniversary, he regarded an autonomous position to be of pivotal importance. He did not wish to risk undermining the autonomy and the ideals and traditions maintained over the years by merging with Iggesund. Moreover, the CEO of Billerud concluded that the on-going structural changes in Billerud would be further delayed by a merger, referring to the employees' unpleasant experience of living through several structural changes during the past decade. He was convinced that both the shareholders and the labour unions of Billerud would disapprove of the merger plan and added that Iggesund from a geographical perspective was situated at too great a distance.

At this point one of the bidders is worthy of special attention. As it appears, the CEO of Billerud resisted cooperating with the CEO of Iggesund when presented with the plan that was drawn up by the Iggesund management to merge the two companies. Yet a year later, in association with the top managers at Stora, the Billerud CEO welcomed the formation of a new and larger corporation together with Iggesund. The stakes had obviously changed over time, in different contexts of human interactions and relationships.

Consequences of the Takeover Bid

Inasmuch as Iggesund's autonomous position was at stake, the CEO of Iggesund continued to emphasize the need to mobilize against the threat of domination by new shareholders. The Iggesund CEO disregarded the synergies estimated by the presumptive acquirers as well as the claimed increases in market shares and shareholder wealth. Together with his employees, he acted to prevent the 'intruders' from taking over Iggesund. They all expected the worst: 'being eaten up by big brother'. They were disconcerted at the thought of being incorporated into Stora and Billerud in view of the hostile manner in which the would-be acquirers had approached Iggesund. Besides, being absorbed by a much larger corporation, with a domain extending from the Norwegian border in the west to the Baltic Sea in the east, there was the threat of losing the 'Iggesund identity', as the CEO of Iggesund expressed it. The hostile takeover bid exposed the target firm to the risk of losing the closeness developed in the firm over centuries. This closeness was accompanied by a sense of social responsibility; Iggesund took care of its employees, even outside the workplace and after hours. This indicates a strong feeling of identification or oneness (Thach and Nyman 2001). This sense of unity was shared by the deputy chairman of Iggesund, who served as Marcus Wallenberg's discussion partner and on his order acted as the messenger of the takeover bid. It is noteworthy that the deputy chairman of Iggesund was also very close to the Iggesund CEO and felt like a 'genuine Iggesund inhabitant'. Strongly affected by the local history and the traditions of the Iggesund firm, he gave his sincere support to the strategic actors and employees of Iggesund in their struggle to resist any acquisition attempt.

The CEO of Iggesund was convinced that the company would be able to preserve its autonomy. The calculations by the financial manager of Iggesund were dependent on the continued existence of Iggesund as an independent firm. Comparative analyses of the companies involved in the merger and acquisition process provided the basis for solvency, liquidity and future plans in financial terms. According to calculations, Iggesund would be able to run its business on its own. As the CEO of Iggesund emphasized, however, if radical structural change was inevitable, collaborating with MoDo was preferable because the two firms shared ideals originating from similar historical experience. In relation to MoDo, he did not consider Iggesund's identity to be at stake. At least for a short period, MoDo was regarded as an attractive business partner. The CEO of Iggesund did not fear any loss of autonomy, but he was still unaware of the intentions of the chairman and principal owner of Modo to form the New Group through a merger of MoDo, Iggesund and Holmen. From the perspective of the Iggesund CEO, an optimistic business outlook was associated with the emerging merger motive of cooperation with MoDo.

A Never-Ending Process

In 1988, MoDo merged with Iggesund and Holmen, and the vision of the new corporate group, the third largest in the Swedish forest products industry, materialized. Stora and Svenska Cellulosa AB (SCA) ranked as the first and second corporate owners. The merger resulted in the delisting of Iggesund shares from the Stockholm Stock Exchange. In 1990, SCA purchased 32 percent of the voting rights in MoDo. A strategic alliance was formed with MoDo but was abandoned a few years later, and SCA sold its MoDo shares. MoDo was hit hard by the global recession in the early 1990s. A new strategy to concentrate production on newsprint and magazine paper was adopted, and for this purpose the subsidiaries of Holmen Paper and Iggesund Paperboard in Holmen were formed in 1999. The strategy also included finding an alliance or a merger partner. In agreement with SCA, the 50–50 jointly owned company of MoDo Paper was established. To differentiate itself from MoDo Paper, MoDo changed its name to Holmen (*Holmen AB—Company History* 2011). Today, Iggesund, under the name of Iggesund Paperboard as a subsidiary of Holmen, is the third largest manufacturer of high-quality virgin fibre paperboard in Europe (*Iggesund* 2011).

CONCLUDING DISCUSSION

As illustrated in this chapter, merger and acquisition motives are subjected to sense-making, which has been defined as a process through which actors construct a reasonable and workable interpretation of occurrences (Ifvarsson 2003; Weick 1995). In this case, the takeover bid appeared to make no sense to the CEO of the target firm of Iggesund. As the merger and acquisition process unfolded, no plausible explanation was provided. A whole week elapsed before the motives for the bid were revealed by the bidders. In this unpredictable and surprising situation, it became blatantly clear after several days that the survival of Iggesund as an independent business firm was at stake. This threat seems to have made it especially urgent for the CEO of Iggesund to make sense of the situation by quickly getting information about the motives underlying the bidders' actions. Because hostile takeover bids rarely occurred in the Swedish business community in the early 1980s, there were no socially accepted rules or procedures to follow that would facilitate sense-making and provide legitimacy. The Iggesund CEO was uncomfortable with an offer considered beyond the pale of legitimacy at the time. Legitimacy refers to 'a desirable social good', according to Mitchell, Bradley, and Wood (1997: 867). A takeover bid without previous contacts and negotiations with the takeover candidate would lack legitimacy. The bidders bore the risk of having confronted the target firm in a socially unacceptable way, and the CEO of Iggesund could not rely on past experience in the emerging situation, for at the time of the bid, he seemed to have only arbitrary fragments of relevant experience. Drawing on Weick (1995), it can be argued that because experience provided no cues it was impossible to tie the fragments together in a way that made sense.

In order to make sense of the surprising bid, the CEO of Iggesund traced actions back through the history of the rivalry between the two Swedish banking spheres and of a merger plan that was never realized. The CEO thus brought the SEB and Handelsbanken spheres into the picture. He also ascribed a crucial role to Marcus Wallenberg, who in fact was involved in preparing and designing the takeover bid. A frame was thereby formed from which cues could be extracted from history to help make sense of the takeover bid. From the point of view of the Iggesund CEO, frame refers here to the banking-sphere context. Also in regard to the sphere context, the bidders risked leaving unmet Marcus Wallenberg's expectations of structural changes within the forest products industry and out-competing the Handelsbanken sphere. In reference to the sphere context, the stakes thus become considerably greater.

The underlying motives for the bid were strongly related to the long-standing rivalry of the two spheres, where Stora and Billerud were utilized as pawns in a game orchestrated by Marcus Wallenberg. By adding a retrospective element, the CEO of Iggesund transformed the situation experienced into one that made sense. The history of the two banking spheres cast a long shadow over the confusing flow of events, guiding the CEO in his efforts to find a plausible and workable interpretation of what was going on. When engaging in retrospective sense-making, he reviewed the history of the rival banking spheres and thereby included what was assumed to be the role of Marcus Wallenberg.

Following Weick (1995), it can be argued that the CEO of Iggesund made sense of the motives for the takeover bid by extracting cues from present occurrences and combining them with occurrences from the past. Once he had learned about the past of the two competing spheres and the planned merger with Billerud, the unexpected seemed possible to deal with and talk about. Moments of the past were thus viewed through the lens of the present to help discern motives based on the rivalry between the banking spheres, and on the merger plan. 'Sensemaking is about the enlargement of small cues. It is a search for contexts within which small details fit together and make sense', Weick (1995: 133) purports.

Looking to the future, the bidders constructed a frame where cues in the form of present moments served as a bridge between the present and the future. It seems that the chairmen and the CEOs of Stora and Billerud gained confidence in their assessment of the situation and the future business outlook. Cues were connected by these top managers in the expectation of a financially stronger group, in a manner that increasingly made sense to them, though not to the CEO of Iggesund. At stake, from the viewpoint of the target-firm stakeholder, was the identity of Iggesund and the social position of its employees established over time. The Iggesund CEO did not refer to his own formal leadership position as being at stake, but expressed his sincere concerns in relation to Iggesund and its employees. A general observation in studies on the human aspect of mergers and acquisitions is that employees experience a high degree of anxiety when faced with a possible merger and acquisition. As their jobs might be at risk, it is imperative for the CEO to quickly reduce anxiety through timely and accurate information about the situation (Napier, Simmons, and Stratton 1989).

The target-firm stakeholder also engaged in prospective sense-making. On the basis of an imagined future, the CEO of Iggesund constructed a frame in which expectations were formed about cooperation with the chairman and principal owner of MoDo, who actually shared his culturally oriented understanding of how to manage a forest products business. Sense-making is concerned with interpretation and construction of the meaning of complicated settings (Brown 2000). The CEO of Iggesund made sense prospectively of cooperation with MoDo with little awareness of what might be at stake in regard to Iggesund's continued operations as an independent business firm. The MoDo strategy was to be implemented step-by-step. The fact that the acquisition of Iggesund was the first step of that merger strategy had not yet become known to the Iggesund CEO.

Reciprocal Sense-Making

The empirical illustration also indicates that what is alleged by the buyer, concerning the future, has to be accepted by the seller if a merger and acquisition is to be accomplished. The buyer's motives are questioned until they make sense to the seller, and the seller's motives must likewise make sense to the buyer. This makes merger and acquisition motives an issue of reciprocal sense-making. Here 'reciprocal' refers to exchanges between seller and buyer and can be described as a give-and-take situation characterized by a shared understanding on some matter (Watson 2002). This is exemplified by the interactions between the CEO of Iggesund and the chairman and principal owner of MoDo. These two top managers shared a culturally oriented understanding of how to manage a forest products business which helped them to make sense of proposed cooperation. Lack of reciprocity could lead to tensions and difficulties in reconciling and cooperating (Maitlis 2005; Mitchell, Bradley, and Wood 1997).

Motives for actions taken by top managers of a bidding firm are not always overtly expressed when the bid is made. From the perspective of target-firm top managers, this situation might be experienced as a surprising one that triggers sense-making. Events can be made understandable in the process, facilitating reciprocal sense-making. But when the top managers diverge in their views of what is at stake, sense-making revolves around collision-filled and tension-laden events, leaving little room for the reciprocity that favours reconciliation.

To further explain reciprocal sense-making, an image of a pendulum swinging to and fro between the past and the future can be drawn, bringing to the fore motives that make sense retrospectively and prospectively. The oscillating motion implies that merger and acquisition motives are formed over the course of events, rather than at fixed points. In reciprocal sense-making both past-oriented and future-oriented motives can be found when moments in the present are connected with the past and the future.

The influence of the past and the present on conscious actions explains why it is difficult to assess motives directly from what individuals say and do, McClelland (1985) acknowledges. The Iggesund case focuses on how motives are formed and made sense of in an on-going flow of interactions among top managers. The case makes salient the temporal properties of motives in association with present past-oriented and present future-oriented occurrences. The past is brought to light when expectations for the future and what is at stake are expressed by the top managers in terms of the present, continuously forming and reforming the present and, in turn, shedding new light on the past. In the context of the hostile takeover bid, as viewed by the CEO of Iggesund, expectations of continuing operations in the future as an independent business firm were accompanied by fears of weakening the identity and position developed in the past. From the bidder's perspective, expectations for the future included the formation of a new constellation that would enhance visibility in the forest products industry and competitiveness on the international market. At the same time, the historically established 'power relationship' between the SEB sphere and the Handelsbanken sphere, and the dominating role of Marcus Wallenberg, were also at stake. Still another example relates to the merger negotiations that took place in 1980 between the CEOs of Iggesund and Billerud. From the perspective of Billerud's CEO, expectations of preserved autonomy in the future, as manifested in Billerud's centennial celebration, simultaneously put ideals and tradition developed in Billerud over the years at stake. Expectations for the future helped shape the past, as brought to life in current actions. This gives a view of time that differs from uniformly calibrated clock time. As merger and acquisition motives form in a process, both a retrospective and a prospective view should be included.

As empirically illustrated, the past is not simply followed sequentially by the present and the future. The present is formed and reformed depending on how the past is brought to light when expectations for the future and stakes involved are articulated.[1] Present actions taken with motives linked to synergistic financial gains reflect a historical past that in connection with future-oriented motives and stakes drive a merger and acquisition process forward in an unpredictable direction.

To gain greater sensitivity and understanding in regard to the practical complexity of a merger and acquisition process, it is necessary to put the spotlight on motives as formed and made sense of in human interactions. As the chapter indicates, we need to be open to the nonlinearity that is shown in the interrelatedness of retrospective and prospective sense-making. This directs our attention to reciprocal sense-making. To enhance our understanding of reciprocal sense-making, we also need to focus on merger and acquisition processes where urgency and tension bring about situations where there is little scope for reconciliation among top managers. Diverging views of the stakes, and 'hostility' in the interactions of top managers, add complexity to reciprocal sense-making. As empirically illustrated, conflicting views of what is at stake give rise to unpredictability and surprise, and this triggers sense-making.

'For too long research designs have rested on the spacious assumption of synergy' as Harrison, O'Neill, and Hoskisson (2000: 178) note. It is thus necessary to expand the research domain of concepts and constructs, and for the benefit of both theorists and practitioners include top manager interaction and motives in association with sense-making. That also applies to reciprocal sense-making. From this chapter we realize that relationships among top managers are in constant flux and that identification of these particular stakeholders is in terms of each as a constructed reality, rather than a stable objective reality (Mitchell, Bradley, and Wood 1997). Implied in this view is the notion of *emergence* (Kurtz and Snowdon 2003), suggesting that motives form and reform, and become subject to sense-making in the course of top manager interactions. In connection with a hostile takeover bid, the CEO of a target firm most likely experiences unpredictability and surprise. A variety of social interpretations could be available to this top manager in an attempt to make sense of an unusual and somewhat confusing situation that emerges as a result of a would-be acquirer's bid that could even put the survival and identity of the targeted firm at stake.

Notably lacking in previous research on mergers and acquisitions are studies that focus on top managers' interactions, motives, and sense-making, as pointed out in the introduction to the chapter. Nor is there any prior research with a focus on reciprocal sense-making. Further, there is little exploration of merger and acquisition processes where an element of hostility is present. It is thus important to supplement the existent body of merger and acquisition research with studies on motives and accounting for sense-making, including reciprocal sense-making. Here a process-relational perspective should be employed that brings together and interrelates top managers, motives and sense-making. A process-relational perspective takes a critical stance towards taken-for-granted ways of describing firms and motives. The process-relational perspective highlights the fact that these phenomena are based on human nature and are changing in character (Watson 2002).

Little attention has been paid in the literature on sense-making to top managers' addressing issues concerned with mergers and acquisitions. For this reason also, it is important to supplement research on sense-making. Prior research on sense-making focuses on many other types of contexts such as academia (Gioia and Thomas 1996), the Coffee Company, theater production (Ifvarsson 2000), strategic management control in small firms (Ifvarsson 2003), hospital (Brown 2000), the Arms to Iraq Affair (Brown and Jones 2000), and British symphony orchestras (Maitlis 2005). Sense-making is also linked to storytelling (Berry 2001; Boje 1991; Boyce 1995; Czarniawska 1997), cause-mapping techniques (Weber and Manning 2001), innovation in an IT company (Coopey, Keegan, and Emler 1997), collaborative communication in an American university (Theus

1995), cross-cultural training (Osland et al. 2000), network interaction patterns in relation to employee perceptions (Ibarra and Andrews 1993), and interactive disintegration of role structure in a minimal organization (Weick 1993). It should be noted, in addition, that sense-making studies concentrate on how stakeholders other than top managers, construct their identities, perceive the organization's image and respond to organizational crises, as Maitlis (2005) notes. Scholars have examined sense-making in turbulent and crisis-laden contexts where there is a need to form a plausible interpretation and understanding of occurrences, but with little attention paid to the top manager, to mergers and acquisitions, and to motives.

Managerial Implications

A focus on stakes, motives, and sense-making, including reciprocal sense-making, in a merger and acquisition process also has managerial implications. Top managers' heightened awareness of and sensitivity to how individuals involved in mergers and acquisitions experience and interpret occurrences can bring more clarity to the question of what constitutes 'success' and 'failure' and what factors contribute to 'success' and 'failure'. It is essential for a top manager to gain deeper insight into motives because motives influence the integration of firms and the subsequent outcomes. Sense-making considerations help in the development of an appreciation that motives are formed and interpreted as a merger and acquisition process unfolds.

Owing to lack of reciprocity in top managers' relationships and interactions, tension and hostility may emerge, creating a need to make sense of what is going on by providing a plausible and workable interpretation. Top managers in their role as stakeholders must acknowledge that what comes to light in on-going interactions is just as important as the results produced by their interactions, and that urgency and tension in their interactions spur further sense-making. An enhanced focus on the reciprocal dimension of sense-making could also help managers to enrich their repertoire of action in exchanges with other stakeholders. The reciprocal dimension refers to the interdependence of people and centres on a give-and-take situation characterised by a shared understanding of what should or not should happen.

NOTES

1. For a further elaboration of the future-past relationship in connection with sense-making also with regard to emotions, see Ericson (2010).

REFERENCES

Allen, M. and Hodgkinson, R. (1989) *Buying a Business. A Guide to the Decision*, London: Graham and Trotman.

Appleyard, A. (1980) 'Takeovers: Accounting policy, financial policy and the case against accounting measures of performance', *Journal of Business Finance & Accounting*, 7(4): 541–54.

Ashton, D. and Atkins, D. (1984) 'A partial theory of takeover bids', *Journal of Finance*, 39(1): 167–83.

Bartal, D. (1996) *The Empire—The Rise of the House of Wallenberg*, Stockholm, Sweden: Dagens Industri.

Berry, G.R. (2001) 'Telling stories: Making sense of the environmental behavior of chemical firms', *Journal of Management Inquiry*, 10(1): 58–73.

Birkinshaw, J., Bresman, H., and Håkansson, L. (2000) 'Managing the post-acquisition integration process: How the human integration and task integration processes interact to foster value creation', *Journal of Management Studies*, 37(3): 395–425.

Boje, D.M. (1991) 'The storytelling organization: A study of story performance in an office-supply firm', *Administrative Science Quarterly*, 36, March: 106–26.

Boland, R.J. Jr. (1984) 'Sense-making of accounting data as a technique of organizational diagnosis', *Management Science*, 30: 868–82.

Bower, J.L. (2001) 'Not all M&As are alike and that matters', *Harvard Business Review*, March: 92–101.

Boyce, M. (1995) 'Collective centring and collective sense-making in the stories and storytelling of one organization', *Organization Studies*, 16(1): 107–37.

Bradely, J.W. and Korn, D.H. (1984) 'The changing role of acquisition', *The Journal of Business Strategy*, 12(4): 30–42.

Brown, A.D. (2000) 'Making sense of inquiry sensemaking', *Journal of Management Studies*, 37(1): 45–75.

Brown, A.D. and Jones, M. (2000) 'Honourable members and dishonourable deeds: Sensemaking, impression management and legitimation in the "Arms to Iraq Affair"', *Human Relations*, 53(5): 655–90.

Buono, A.F. and Bowditch, J.L. (1989) *The Human Side of Mergers and Acquisitions*, San Francisco, CA: Jossey-Bass.

Campbell, A. and Luchs, K.S. (1998) *Strategic Synergy*, London: International Thomson Business Press.

Cartwright, S. and Cooper, C.L. (1993) 'The role of culture compatibility in successful organisational marriage', *Academy of Management Executive*, 7(2): 57–70.

Cartwright, S. and Cooper, C.L. (1996) *Managing Mergers, Acquisitions and Strategic Alliances: Integrating People and Cultures*, Oxford: Butterworth-Heinemann.

Cartwright, S. and Price, F. (2003) 'Managerial preferences in international merger and acquisition partners revisited: How are they influenced?', in C. Cooper and A. Gregory (eds.) *Advances in Mergers and Acquisitions*, 2, Elsevier, pp. 81–95.

Cartwright, S. and Schoenberg, R. (2006). 'Thirty years of mergers and acquisitions research: Recent advances and future opportunities', *British Journal of Management*, 17: 1–5.

Chatterjee, S. (1986) 'Types of synergy and economic value: The impact of acquisitions on merging and rival firms', *Strategic Management Journal*, 7(2): 119–39.

Chemla, G. (2005) 'Hold-up, stakeholders and takeover threats', *Journal of Financial Intermediation*, 14: 376–97.

Chung, K.-H. (2004) 'Corporate acquisition decisions under different strategic motivations', *Advances in Management Accounting*, 12: 265–86.

Collin, F. (1997) *Social Reality*, London: Routledge.

Coopey, J., Keegan, O., and Emler, N. (1997) 'Managers' innovations as 'sense-making', *British Journal of Management*, 8: 301–15.

Czarniawska, B. (1997). *Narrating the Organization*, Chicago: The University of Chicago Press.

Davies, Y. (1980) 'Takeovers: It seems everyone's a loser', *Management Accounting*, 58(8): 22–23.

Denis, D.J and Kruse, T.A. (2000) 'Managerial discipline and corporate restructuring following performance declines', *Journal of Financial Economics*, 55(3): 391–424.

Dennis, D. and McConnell, J. (1985) 'Corporate mergers and security returns', *Journal of Financial Economics*, 16: 143–87.

Ericson, M. (1991) *Iggesundsaffären. Rationaliteter i en strategisk förvärvsprocess*, Stockholm, Sweden: Stockholm School of Economics, EFI.

Ericson, M. (2010) 'Toward a *sensed* decision-making approach', *Management Decision*, 48(1): 132–55.

Gergen, K.J. (1999) *An Invitation to Social Construction*, Thousand Oaks, CA: SAGE.

Giammarino, R. and Heinkel, R. (1986) 'A model of dynamic takeover behaviour', *The Journal of Finance*, XLI(2): 465–80.

Gioia, D.A. and Thomas, J.B. (1996) 'Identity, image, and issue interpretation: Sensemaking and strategic change in academia', *Administrative Science Quarterly*, 41(3): 370–87.

Goergen, M. and Renneboog, L. (2003) 'Value creation in large European mergers and acquisitions', *Advances in Mergers and Acquisitions*, 2: 97–146.

Goldberg, W.H. (1983) *Mergers Motives Modes Methods*, New York: Nichols.

Harrison, J.S., O'Neill, H.M., and Hoskisson, R.E. (2000) 'Acquisition strategy and target resistance: A theory of countervailing effects of pre-merger bidding and post-merger integration', in C.L. Cooper and S. Finkelstein (eds.) *Advances in Mergers and Acquisitions*, 3, Elsevier, pp. 157–82.

Haspeslagh, P. and Jemison, D. (1991) *Managing Acquisitions: Creating Value Through Corporate Renewal*, New York: The Free Press.

Hitt, M.A., Hoskisson, R.E., and Ireland, R.D. (1990) 'Mergers and acquisitions and managerial commitment to innovation in M-form firm', *Strategic Management Journal*, 11(4): 29–47.

Holmen AB—Company History (2011) Retrieved June 20, 2011, from http://www.fundinguniverse.com/company-histories/Holmen-AB-Company-History.html.

Hunt, J.W. (1990) 'Changing pattern of acquisition behaviour in takeovers and the consequences for acquisition processes', *Strategic Management Journal*, 13(1): 69–77.

Ibarra, H. and Andrews, S.B. (1993) 'Power, social influence, and sense making: Effects of network centrality and proximity on employee perceptions', *Administrative Science Quarterly*, 38(2): 277–303.

Ifvarsson, C. (2000) *Sensemaking and Management: A Theoretical Discussion with Research Implications*, Licentiate Thesis, Luleå University of Technology.

Ifvarsson, C. (2003) *Sensemaking for Strategic Management Control*, Doctoral thesis, Luleå University of Technology.

Iggesund (2011) Retrieved June 20, 2011, from http://www.iggesund.com/main.aspx.

Jemison, D. and Sitkin, S. (1986) 'Acquisitions: the process can be a problem', *Harvard Business Review*, 64(2): 107–16.

Jones, T.M. (1995) 'Instrumental stakeholder theory: A synthesis of ethics and economics', *Academy of Management Review*, 20(2): 404–37.

Kavanagh, M.H. and Ashkanasy, N.M. (2004) 'Management approaches to merger evoked cultural change and acculturation outcomes', in C.L. Cooper and S. Finkelstein (eds.) *Advances in Mergers and Acquisitions*, 3, Elsevier, pp. 1–33.

Kini, O., Kracaw, W., and Mian, S. (2004) 'The nature of discipline by corporate takeovers', *The Journal of Finance*, LIX(4): 1511–52.

Kitching, J. (1967) 'Why do mergers miscarry?', *Harvard Business Review*, November–December: 84–101.

Kitching, J. (1973) *Acquisitions in Europe: Causes of Corporate Successes and Failures*, Switzerland: Business International S.A.

Kurtz, C.F. and Snowdon, D.J. (2003) 'The new dynamics of strategy: Sense-making in a complex and complicated world', *IBM Systems Journal*, 42(3): 462–83.

Limmack, R.J. (2000) 'Takeovers as a disciplinary mechanism', *Advances in Mergers and Acquisition*, 1: 93–118.

Lindell, M. and Melin, L. 'Internationalization through acquisition: The realization of corporate vision', paper presented at the EAM Conference, Managing in Global Economy IV, 1991.

Maitlis, S. (2005) 'The social processes of organizational sensemaking', *The Academy of Management Journal*, 48(1): 21–49.

McClelland, D.C. (1985) *Human Motivation*, Glenview, IL: Scott, Foresman and Company.

Mitchell, R.K., Bradley, R.A., and Wood, J.D. (1997) 'Toward a theory of stakeholder identification and salience: Defining the principle of who and what really counts', *The Academy of Management Review*, 22(4): 853–86.

Nahavandi, A. and Malekzadeh, A.R. (1988) 'Acculturation in mergers and acquisitions,' *Academy of Management Review*, 13(1): 79–90.

Napier, N.K. (1989) 'Mergers and acquisitions, human resource issues and outcomes: A review and suggested typology', *Journal of Management Studies*, 26(3): 271–89.

Napier, N.K., Simmons, G., and Stratton, K. (1989) 'Communication during a merger: Experience of two banks', *Human Resource Planning*, 12(2): 105–22.

Osland, J., Bird, A., Delano, J., and Jacob, M. (2000) 'Beyond sophisticated stereotyping: Cultural sensemaking in context/executive commentaries', *The Academy of Management Executive*, 14(1): 65–79.

Pitkethly, R., Faulkner, D., and Child, J. (2003) 'Integrating acquisitions', in C. Cooper and A. Gregory (eds.) *Advances in Mergers and Acquisitions*, 2, Elsevier, pp. 27–57.

Schweiger, D.M. and Very, P. (2003) 'Creating value through merger and acquisition integration', in C. Cooper and A. Gregory (eds.) *Advances in Mergers and Acquisitions*, 2, Elsevier, pp.1–26.

Seo, M.-G. and Hill, N.S. (2005) 'Understanding the human side of merger and acquisition: An integrative framework', *The Journal of Applied Behavioral Science*, 41(4): 422–43.

Seth, A., Song, K.P., and Richardson Pettit, R. (2002) 'Value creation and destruction in cross-border acquisitions: An empirical analysis of foreign acquisitions of U.S. firms', *Strategic Management Journal*, 23(10): 921–40.

Shrivastava, P. (1986) 'Postmerger integration', *The Journal of Business Strategy*, 7(1): 65–76.

Singh, H. and Montgomery, C.A. (1987) 'Corporate acquisition strategies and economic performance', *Strategic Management Journal*, 8(4): 377–86.

Stahl, G.K. and Voigt, A. (2004) 'Impact of cultural differences on merger and acquisition performance: A critical research review and an integral model', in C. Cooper and S. Finkelstein (eds.) *Advances in Mergers and Acquisitions*, 4, Emerald, pp. 51–82.

Starbuck, W.H. and Milliken, F.J. (1988) 'Executives' perceptual filters: What they notice and how they make sense', in D.C. Hambrick (ed.) *The Executive Effect: Concepts and Methods for Studying Top Managers*, Greenwich, CT: JAI Press, pp. 35–65.

Steiner, P. (1975) *Mergers, motives, effects, policies*, Canada: University of Michigan Press.
Thach, L. and Nyman, M. (2001) 'Leading in limbo land: the role of a leader during merger and acquisition transition', *Leadership & Organization Development Journal*, 22(4): 146–50.
Theus, K.T. (1995) 'Communication in a power vacuum: Sense-making and enactment during crisis-induced departures', *Human Resource Management*, 34(1): 27–49.
Trautwein, F. (1990) 'Merger motives and merger prescriptions', *Strategic Management Journal*, 11: 283–95.
Vaara, E. and Tienari, J. (2002) 'Justification, legitimization and naturalization of mergers and acquisitions: A critical discourse analysis of media texts', *Organization*, 9(2): 275–304.
Walter, G.A. and Barney, J.B. (1990) 'Management objectives in mergers and acquisitions', *Strategic Management Journal*, January: 79–86.
Watson, T.J. (2002) *Organising and Managing Work. Organisational, Managerial and Strategic Behavior in Theory and Practice*, Harlow, Great Britain: Financial Times/ Prentice Hall.
Weber, P.S. and Manning, M.R. (2001) 'Cause maps, sensemaking, and planned organizational change', *Journal of Applied Behavioral Science*, 37(2): 227–51.
Weick, K.E. (1993) 'The Collapse of sensemaking in organizations: The Mann Gulch disaster', *Administrative Science Quarterly*, 38(4): 628–43.
Weick, K.E. (1995) *Sensemaking in Organizations*, Thousand Oaks, CA: SAGE.
Weick, K.E., Sutcliffe, K.M., and Obstfeld, D. (2005) 'Organizing and the process of sensemaking', *Organization Science*, 16(4): 409–21.
Wright, A. (2005) 'The role of scenarios as prospective sense-making devices', *Management Decision*, 43(1): 86–101.
Yahaya, S.-Y. and Abu-Bakar, N. (2007) 'New product development management issues and decision-making approaches', *Management Decision*, 45(7): 1123–42.

Part II

Middle Managers and Employees

4 The Arranged Marriage Syndrome

Challenges to Subsidiary Managers during the Integration Process between Two Merging Multinational Companies

Roger Schweizer

INTRODUCTION

> 'It is like an arranged marriage. Since the parents negotiate the deal, the subsidiaries do not have much of a choice'.
>
> (Arun Maira, CEO of Innovation Associates, describing a merger between the subsidiaries of two MNCs in Skaria in 1998)

Some of the largest merger and acquisition transactions in business history have taken place since the 1990s,[1] and most of these have been between multinational companies (MNCs) (Schweizer 2005). Remarkably, research has paid comparatively little attention to the subsequent local integration processes in mergers and acquisitions between MNCs, despite their prevalence and importance for international business (ibid.).

Despite an on-going debate between international business scholars and organizational theorists regarding the uniqueness of MNCs, most agree that MNCs face a higher degree of complexity (be it a matter of degree or a matter of kind) than other, simpler types of organizations (Ghoshal and Westney 1993). As Doz and Prahalad (1993) have argued, MNCs not only cover multiple geographical markets with multiple product lines in typically multifunctional activities (i.e., they have to deal with multidimensionality), but they also have to find optimal trade-offs for different businesses, countries, functions, and tasks because of the range of economic and political characteristics that differ between countries (i.e., they face heterogeneity). In other words, MNCs differ in their organizational complexity from simpler organizations in that they operate in many, often dissimilar environments with multiple subunits linked through shared policies or strategies (Prahalad and Doz 1987). Because of this organizational complexity, an integration process between two globally merging MNCs is not a single integration process between two organizations, but a myriad of different, interrelated local integration processes between units of the two MNCs.

This chapter focuses on how the concurrent worldwide consolidation influences the characteristics of the local integration processes when two MNCs merge. How the parent firm coordinates and controls the local integration process and how subsidiaries react towards parental involvement during the local integration process are discussed in Schweizer (2005, 2010). This chapter identifies the conditions managers of merging MNCs' subsidiaries face (hereafter referred to as 'premises') as a result of the merger when combining their local activities, and discusses how these premises influence the nature of those efforts. Hence, the stakeholder on whom this chapter focuses is the local subsidiary manager. Indeed, a global merger or acquisition between MNCs can have dramatic implications for a local manager. For example, a local manager could lose her job to a counterpart joining the firm in a global merger or acquisition. Also, the global merger and subsequent consolidation process might diminish the power of the newly created subsidiary in the MNC.

It is important to note that subsidiary managers are not only worthy of study as stakeholders because they and their local organizations are affected by the global merger decision by their parents, but also because their behaviour affects the overall outcome of the merger. Indeed, subsidiary managers are important stakeholders for the potential success of the local integration process and therefore also for the global integration process because they have to balance the parent firm's requirements and expectations with the reality faced locally. As has been shown in earlier studies, many of the problems encountered during the integration process can be avoided by the early involvement of middle and operating managers, especially those that eventually have to run the actual integration activities (Jemison and Sitkin 1986; Mirvis and Marks 1986; Pritchett 1985).

The particular emphasis in this chapter, which employs a case-study approach, is on human-related integration phenomena. This term includes any human-related feeling, reaction, action, object, fact, occurrence, etc. that can be observed during an integration process. I use the term to distinguish this discussion from the often negative descriptions of intelligible characteristics found in the literature, which uses such words as problems, hinders, barriers, or dysfunctions. As will be discussed in more detail, integrating previously independent firms often has a dramatic impact on the merging firms' employees. For subsidiary managers, it is of utmost importance to manage human-resource-related issues not only circumspectly, but also in a way that is compatible with the norms, values, and laws in the local context and that addresses the expectations of the parent firm. By studying human-related phenomenon during the local integration process of two globally merging MNCs and how they are influenced by the previously sketched premises, this chapter focuses on a critical area for the potential success or failure of the process.

In sum, the chapter proposes a new conceptualization aimed at helping to understand the challenges local subsidiaries face when trying to implement a global merger and/or acquisition decision. Furthermore, by highlighting a stakeholder hitherto neglected in the literature, i.e., subsidiary managers, and how their management of human-related phenomena during the local integration process is influenced by being part of the concurrently on-going global merger, the chapter offers a complementary explanation of why many mergers and acquisitions between MNCs are characterised by severe problems during the post-merger phase.

The chapter continues with a review of the literature on the integration process and the variety of human-related integration phenomena discussed in the literature. Thereafter, the chapter addresses methodological considerations and presents the case studied. Subsequently, I compare the premises of the case to the notion of an arranged marriage. This comparison results in the proposed Arranged Marriage Syndrome, which is defined as the consequences of the premises faced by subsidiary managers, inherent in being part of the concurrent worldwide consolidation, for human-related phenomena during the integration process between two globally merging MNCs' subsidiaries. The chapter concludes with a discussion of broader implications of the Arranged Marriage Syndrome and of future research.

HUMAN-RELATED PHENOMENA DURING THE INTEGRATION PROCESS

Pablo (1994) described the integration process following an acquisition as a process by which inter-firm coordination and system control are achieved through the efficient and effective direction of organizational activities and resources toward the accomplishment of a particular set of common organizational goals. This direction involves adapting the merging firms' value-generating activities in order to realize technical synergies (Schweiger, Csiszar, and Napier 1994). Furthermore, it involves altering bureaucratic mechanisms of authority and control to ensure internal coherence, as well as transforming systems of values, beliefs, and practices to create congruent organizational frames of reference (ibid.). The focus in this chapter is on human-related integration, rather than on procedural or physical integration (cf., Shrivastava 1986), although the three are interrelated.

A merger or acquisition and the subsequent integration process are powerful events that have the potential to dramatically change the situation of employees and managers (Aguilera and Dencker 2004; Ivancevich, Schweiger, and Power 1987; Seo and Hill 2005). Larsson et al. (2001) divided human-related or psychosomatic reactions of employees and managers into reactions and issues stemming from (1) an individual level, (2) an interpersonal level, and/or (3) a collective level.

On an individual level, research has found that employees often experience initial shock, disbelief and grief during an integration process (e.g.,

Marks and Mirvis 1985), as well as a high degree of uncertainty, not least because they often know little about the objectives of the deal (e.g., Ivancevich, Schweiger, and Power 1987; Schweiger, Ivancevich, and Power 1987; Fugate, Kinicki, and Scheck 2002). Marks and Mirvis (1998: 36) summarized these and other psychosomatic reactions of employees and managers with the notion of the 'merger syndrome', which is 'triggered by the unavoidably unsettled conditions in the earliest days and months following the announcement of a deal'. In these early days, people are preoccupied with what the merger means for them, resulting in significant political manoeuvring and an increased focus on maintaining status (e.g., Marks and Mirvis 1998; Schweiger, Ivancevich, and Power 1987; Seo and Hill 2005). In addition, people suffer loss of identity when they can no longer identify themselves with their company (e.g., Schweiger, Ivancevich, and Power 1987; Terry and O'Brien 2001) and are under a high degree of stress (e.g., Ivancevich, Schweiger, and Power 1987; Jemison and Sitkin 1986). Stress is often manifested in other negative effects on employees' psychological and physiological well-being, such as sleeplessness, depression, anxiety, loss of self-esteem, and lower job and life satisfaction (e.g., Buono and Bowditch 1989; Marks and Mirvis 1998; Seo and Hill 2005). However, reactions during a merger and/or an acquisition differ from person to person because individuals cognitively appraise and interpret events differently (Ivancevich, Schweiger, and Power 1987).

On an interpersonal level, the literature has discussed various management styles applied and mechanisms employed to facilitate integration. For example, because managers are often under extreme time pressure during an integration process and have to cope with many complex tasks, including difficult decisions, they often employ a crisis-management mode or a war-room mentality—an authoritative management style with centralized decision making—to create at least an illusion of control (e.g., Marks and Mirvis 1985). At the same time, a leadership vacuum can occur in the sense that there is a 'lack of appropriate leadership to articulate a new purpose of the combined firms' (Haspeslagh and Jemison 1991: 122). Management may become passive (e.g., Schweiger and DeNisi 1991) or hastily promise autonomy and no changes (e.g., Haspeslagh and Jemison 1991), and managers' reactions of course affect employees' reactions (e.g., Buono and Bowditch 1989). Other human-related phenomena on an interpersonal level discussed in the literature are increased turnover among top managers (e.g., Shearer 2004; Walsh 1989), decreased organizational performance (e.g., Haspeslagh and Jemison 1991), insufficient communication (e.g., Napier, Simmons, and Stratton 1989), and reliance on rumours (e.g., Schweiger and DeNisi 1991).

Finally, previous studies have also highlighted collective-level phenomena that occur during the integration of two organizational cultures, such as cultural clashes based on differences in organizational cultures (e.g., Buono and Bowditch 1989; Nahavandi and Malekzadeh 1988) and the 'us-versus-them' syndrome (Marks and Mirvis 1998).

METHODOLOGY

Because of the explorative nature of the study, this chapter uses a case-study approach (Yin 2003). Using Stake's terminology (1994), the instrumental case study provides insight into issues that have been ignored. The case studied is a local merger between the pharmaceutical units of Sandoz India Limited (SIL) and Hindustan Ciba-Geigy (HCG) as a result of their parent companies' global merger in 1997 to create a new pharmaceutical giant, Novartis. I used a theoretical sampling approach (Merriam 1998) when choosing to focus on the pharmaceutical industry (many mergers and acquisitions between MNCs can be found in this industry). Furthermore, I chose to focus on the Indian merger because 'it makes sense to choose cases such as extreme situations' (Pettigrew 1988 in Eisenhardt 1989: 537).[2] Finally, the choice of Novartis was made for convenience (Merriam 1998) because of the ready access to managers at Novartis.

The data used for the case were collected by several means, as is typical in case-study research (Yin 2003). Most important among the methods of data collection are the 39 open-ended interviews with managers involved in the integration process at both the headquarters and the subsidiaries.[3] Articles from international and Indian newspapers, newsletters internal to the global and Indian companies, internal slides, information distributed during the merger, and so forth made up the secondary data. The data collection was part of a broader study (Schweizer 2005) for which local managers and employees were asked to give their merger stories; but the focus here is on the parts of the collected data that relate to the premises local subsidiaries face because the local managers' integration process is part of a global combination process. Inspired by the arranged marriage metaphor and following the step-by-step process described by Merriam (1998), I identified four premises—the mandatory nature of the local merger; lack of local involvement in the global merger decision-making process; the subsidiaries' late involvement in the global merger process; and a local merger based on global conditions—faced by the managers during the coding process. Then I analysed how these premises impact the human-related phenomenon during the integration processes observed in the empirical data in general and how they influenced the managerial capability of the subsidiary managers in particular. Finally, I arrived at the proposed Arranged Marriage Syndrome.

THE CASE

On March 6, 1996, a global merger was announced between Sandoz and Ciba, two Swiss MNCs with their headquarters in Basel (Switzerland). With a market value of $80 billion, it was the largest corporate merger in history to that date. Nine months after the announcement of the merger on an equal partnership basis, Ciba and Sandoz formed Novartis on January 1, 1997.

Because of legal restrictions in India at the time, only 51 percent of the Indian subsidiaries, SIL and HCG, was owned by their parent companies. Both SIL and HCG had multi-divisional organizational structures, among which were the pharmaceuticals divisions. For both subsidiaries, the global merger came at a critical time, not least because the Indian pharmaceutical industry was experiencing dramatic changes. First, the Drug Price Control Order had been liberalized, offering companies increased freedom to set their own prices. Second, India had signed the General Agreement on Tariffs and Trade, which meant that the country also reintroduced a product patent regime that had been replaced by the Indian Patent Act in 1970. The reforms in 1970 had made new drugs available cheaply by encouraging local firms to make copies of imported drugs, resulting in India becoming a non-prioritized market for many MNCs. In addition, the two subsidiaries had recently undergone a critical period of change, with HCG's pharmaceutical unit implementing necessary changes after a last-minute evaluation saved the company from being shut down completely in 1994, and SIL was still implementing its parent's global decision in 1994 to demerge the chemical divisions.

The following sections present the identified premises related to the fact that the merger between SIL and HCG was part of a global merger, and discuss the impact of those premises on the human-related nature of the local integration process.

The Mandatory Nature of the Local Merger

The most obvious and most critical premise of the local merger between SIL and HCG is that they merged only as a result of their parent companies' decision to merge globally. For the two subsidiaries, the merger was a clear mandate: 'The marriage had already taken place . . ., so we had to get along' [HCG 7b]; 'You accept the merger as being mandated. . . . When the managing director announced the global merger, at that point in time, the merger was globally a done deal' [SIL 2b]; 'the merger was a fait accompli when [the parent companies] said that the merger is going to happen. There was no question of fighting the merger because, at the end of the day, we were an affiliate for a multinational company' [HCG 2b]. Despite the fact that neither SIL nor HCG were wholly owned by their parent companies and that another 24 percent from local shareholders was needed to get final clearance for the deal, the parent in Basel stated unequivocally that it did not want to have two different local corporations. When the legal merger in India was delayed as a result of an on-going struggle between the shareholders of SIL and HCG (several of SIL's shareholders were not delighted with the recommended swap-ratio and sought legal recourse), Basel, despite a policy of non-interference in local legal processes, threatened to rename

HCG Novartis India Limited (NIL), and to terminate SIL and transfer its staff and products to NIL.

Another reason for the mandatory nature of the deal was that both SIL and HCG were dependent on their parents for access to products and financial resources, had high levels of trust in their parent organizations and strongly identified with them (cf., Kostova and Roth 2002): 'I was proud to work for Ciba. There was a strong attachment and dependency toward the parent' [HCG manager 1b]; 'We saw ourselves very much as a Swiss company' [SIL manager 5a]; 'I was proud to work for Sandoz' [SIL manager 3b]. Whereas this strong identification with the pre-merger global organizations resulted in the loss of that identity after the merger (cf., Schweiger, Ivancevich, and Power 1987), it helped the employees to understand the global merger idea, which reduced 'not-invented-here feelings' (cf., Kostova and Roth 2002).

Lack of Local Involvement in the Global Merger Decision-Making Process

The second premise identified is that neither SIL nor HCG was involved in the decision-making process leading to the global Novartis merger decision. The global merger announcement made by the boards of Ciba and Sandoz concluded a three-month long negotiation period between the two parent companies, which had taken place in secret and had involved only a few people in order to minimize any concurrent upheaval in the business community or among employees. The managements of SIL and HCG had not been involved when many of the critical decisions of the subsequent global integration process were made, including decisions related to future business units, the group and management structure, the selection of key positions, the overarching strategy of strengthening the new company's strategic core operations by pushing innovation, and Novartis' being structured as a holding company. In view of Hedlund (1981), who argued that the degree of subsidiary autonomy and participation in strategic decision making and implementation depends on the type of decisions to be made, this lack of involvement by management below board level is not surprising considering the strategic importance of the global merger for the two MNCs. In addition, the sensitive nature of the decision-making (Haspeslagh and Jemison 1991) and the perceived necessity for speed (Jemison and Sitkin 1986) may have contributed to the decision to limit involvement. Furthermore, the relatively small size of the Indian pharmaceutical market and the parents' relatively pessimistic view of it contributed to SIL's and HCG's lack of involvement in the decision-making process.

Although SIL's and HCG's non-involvement in the global merger decision is just another example of reality for less important, peripheral subsidiaries (e.g., Jansson, Saqib, and Sharma 1995), their lack of involvement had considerable implications for the human-related integration issues. First, the lack of involvement contributed to the initial shock—local managers and employees were caught completely unaware by the merger announcement—and during the first couple of weeks, they received practically no information about what was going to happen locally. Uncertainty during an integration process is unavoidable (Ivancevich, Schweiger, and Power 1987), as many of the changes evolve during the integration process and are not known in advance (e.g., Jemison and Sitkin 1986; Schweiger and DeNisi 1991); in this case, being far from the centre of decision-making fuelled the uncertainty. As discussed in the literature, uncertainty led to feelings of stress and negatively affected people's well-being, resulting in lower work performance.

Furthermore, especially during the important initial period of the integration process, the lack of involvement of local managers in the decision-making process caused confusion among them, resulting in loss of leadership and in management passivity (cf., Schweiger, Ivancevich, and Power 1987). As Haspeslagh and Jemison (1991) suggested, the initial lack of information from the parent company caused a leadership vacuum because of local managers' uncertainty about the company's future and the objectives of the transaction. Under the circumstances, the managers felt very uncomfortable, and because they could not give their staff proper direction, their feelings of impotence were transferred to their employees, who had turned to their managers for guidance and answers (cf., Mirvis and Marks 1986). Consequently, local management had difficulty motivating their local personnel, who were dealing with stress, loss of motivation, higher management turnover, and decreased well-being.

SIL's and HCG's lack of involvement in the decision-making process had another, more wide-ranging implication for the local integration process. As mentioned here, during the three-month process that preceded the global merger announcement, many important decisions related to the subsequent global integration process were made, including the condition that the merger would be a merger of equals, creating the structure of the future global corporation and its strategic focus. These decisions set out a distinct pathway for the global integration to come, including the Indian integration process. Thus, it was predestined that the Indian integration process, in line with the global consolidation, would be characterized, using Pablo's (1994) terminology, by a high level of integration involving extensive sharing of financial, physical, and human resources. As a result, SIL and HCG managers saw their freedom to implement the global merger locally severely reduced from the start. Among other factors that will be discussed later, this led to an unnecessarily high degree of integration in India, which not only impeded realisation of local synergies (cf., Pablo 1994) but also impacted many of the human-related integration phenomena (not least during the cultural integration process).

SIL's and HCG's Late Involvement in the Global Merger Process

SIL and HCG became involved only late in the overall merger process, which had implications for the local integration. As Jemison and Sitkin (1986) argued, many of the problems that can occur during the integration process can be avoided by involving middle managers and operating managers early, especially those who eventually have to run the integration activities. In the case of SIL and HCG, the Indian management experienced many difficulties in managing the local integration, especially during the first couple of weeks, because they had no access to the information, assumptions and analyses that had been developed before conclusion of the global deal. This type of knowledge would have been especially valuable because the initial communiqués from Basel contained no information about what was going to happen in India.

Furthermore, as Marks and Mirvis (1998) mentioned, the critical success factors for the global merger that the global management did communicate were not perceived as such by the local organizations. Whereas the notion of a merger of equals was important during the negotiating phase and was the guiding principle for the composition of the board of directors and the financial terms of the transaction, the doctrine for the integration in general and for the management selection process in particular was operational excellence and sustainable performance. However, in India, the equal nature of the deal was stressed in many of the decisions made (especially those related to the leadership selection process), which led to feelings of disillusionment and cynicism and to a local schism between SIL and HCG managers and employees when the decisions resulted in perceived inequality. In addition, from Basel's perspective, the merger was a done deal, and the integration process was only a minor problem to be solved: 'Take the Ciba and the Sandoz, merge them, and get on with the business as you think is best' [HCG 1a]. This outcome is in line with Haspeslagh and Jemison's (1991) argument that top management's attention usually peaks at the time of the deal but, when it comes to the actual integration, they typically have moved on to other matters.

Another implication of the late involvement of SIL and HCG in the merger process is that they lacked a courtship period. They did not have the time to get to know each other beforehand (as their parent companies had done during their three-month negotiation period), and when the local management teams eventually met to implement the local merger, they were still not well acquainted. Consequently, the first couple of meetings were 'stormy, with people walking out of the meeting' [SIL 1b] and the participants had to be focused on getting to know each other, because the local management teams still had only a relatively vague idea of what Basel was going to expect. As Pritchett (1985) pointed out, without a courtship period in which companies have the opportunity to get to know each other and work through important differences, the actual integration can turn out to be a long, drawn-out, and gut-wrenching experience. For example, SIL and HCG set about the integration process with very different attitudes about unions. Lohrum (1992) and Haspeslagh and Jemison (1991) highlighted the importance of the initial observation or stage-setting phase, where the two parties observe each other and the situation before continuing the integration process. SIL and HCG were basically thrown directly into the execution phase (Ivancevich, Schweiger and Power 1987), which increased uncertainty and with it the degree of stress and other negative feelings.

A Local Merger Based on Global Conditions

The final premise identified is that the merger decision was based on global industry dynamics. Like most of the other contemporaneous mergers and acquisitions between MNCs active in the pharmaceutical industry, the Novartis merger was a result of the combination of governments' increased price pressures and dissemination of me-too drugs and generic substitutions, resulting in increased pressure on MNCs' R&D efforts. New technological breakthroughs—especially in genomics, combinatorial chemistry, and high throughput screening—offered exciting opportunities to accelerate the development of new drugs. However, because of the high initial investments necessary and the increased risk and cost of bringing new drugs to market, merging with or acquiring another pharmaceutical MNC became attractive. Such deals allowed the merging companies to increase the R&D budget and to spread the risk regarding R&D investments.

Whereas many of SIL's and HCG's managers understood the motives behind the global merger decision ('the stories that were built around the merger made sense' [HCG 1b]), several managers argued that those motives had no bearing on the Indian market; the synergies (50 million Indian rupees) that would eventually be attained were not very impressive. Looking more closely at the situation SIL and HCG faced, one can only concur with local managers' criticism of the global deal's local fit.

Although both SIL and HCG had recently been or were currently involved in reorganizations, the global merger announcement came at a time when the general climate for MNCs in the Indian pharmaceutical industry was changing for the better, as the market was growing. Because the merger resulted in a considerably larger combined sales force, the deal seemed at first glance to meet the prerequisite that firms in the Indian market would need to enlarge their sales forces in order to be successful. However, many firms in India were enlarging their sales forces and extending their reach by establishing well-functioning co-marketing alliances, rather than getting involved with a thorny sales force integration following a merger or acquisition. A second condition for success in India at the time was a large and well-balanced product portfolio to justify the high marketing costs. However, the merger led to a larger combined portfolio that was no better balanced than SIL's and HCG's. In addition, because the newly created subsidiary still lacked products for India's most important and lucrative segments (e.g., antibacterials), 'the merger deepened the portfolio more than broadened it' [HCG 1a].

A positive effect of the merger was that it gave the subsidiaries the opportunity to build a more efficient distribution system and to rationalize and modernize their third-party production—changes that improved the new organization's chances of success and which, considering the strong unions and unionized stockists, would have been more difficult to implement under 'normal' conditions (as a new legal entity, Novartis was not bound by the previous, relatively disadvantageous agreements with HCG's and SIL's stockists any more).

Nevertheless, the local strategic fit of the Novartis merger is at least questionable because most of the positive effect could have been obtained through other, less dramatic changes. For example, at the time of the Novartis merger, Indian pharmaceutical firms increasingly and with great success started to join hands to extend their reach and to reduce marketing costs (e.g., the alliances between Ranbaxy and Glaxo as well as between Ranbaxy and Cipla). Hence, in India, in order to increase sales forces and to achieve better market penetration, it might have been preferable to establish well-functioning co-marketing alliances, rather than to get involved with complicated sales force integration following a merger. In other words, the local merger would most likely suffer from an unnecessarily high degree of integration, or over-integration. This over-integration might partly explain the low degree of local synergies achieved, and the relatively low growth rate in the first years following the merger (which, at 3 percent, was not impressive in Indian terms). As Pablo (1994) mentioned, the level of integration is critical, because under- or over-integration can result in failure to create value, or even in value destruction. As mentioned, over-integration in this case also gave rise to the thorny, difficult, and 'unnecessary' task of combining the two organizations' sales forces, their salary, and allowances systems, and so on. Although only a few people lost their jobs, the merger dramatically impacted career paths; employees whose expected promotions did not materialise showed signs of disillusionment and felt unfairly treated, resulting in negative feelings toward the merger, and the perception that it was the reason for their own personal 'defeat'.

Drawing on the four premises discussed earlier—(1) the mandatory nature of the local merger; (2) the lack of local involvement in the global merger decision-making process; (3) the subsidiaries' late involvement in the global merger process; and (4) the fact that the local merger was based on global conditions—the local merger is compared in the following sections with an arranged marriage, and the implications of the 'arranged' local merger and the subsequent integration process are bundled into the single notion of the Arranged Marriage Syndrome.

THE ARRANGED MARRIAGE SYNDROME

Mergers and acquisitions have long been compared with marriages (e.g., Cartwright and Cooper 1993, 1995; Davis 1968; Dooley and Zimmerman 2003). Dooley and Zimmerman (2003: 56) further used the notion of an arranged marriage when pointing out that '[t]he vast majority of people involved in the mergers are not given a choice about getting married to another organization. Instead, like an arranged marriage, they need to learn to live with a partner not completely of their choosing, but potentially to their liking'.

The situation that SIL and HCG managers faced was analogous to an arranged marriage in several ways, one of which was that the 'marriage' was arranged by their parents who, for a variety of reasons such as imperfect and incomplete information, believed that their subsidiaries could not be relied upon to find suitable partners (Batabyal 2001). Another similarity in the situation managers faced was that, like children whose parents confidently assume they will agree to the proposed marriage, the managers were not consulted for their input before the proposal was finalized. Therefore, the decision may not be influenced by 'the local situation' of the child (his or her feelings for the partner or individual needs) but by the broader dynamics of family or community needs. Thus, the criteria the parents lay down for a match may differ significantly from those important to the child.

Of course, all metaphors are, by definition, only partially true and 'tell us what to see and what not to see as they forcibly focus our attention on certain aspects instead of others' (Boye 1999: 20). Also, the arranged marriage metaphor does not completely fit the local merger studied because Sandoz and Ciba did not look for a specific 'spouse' for each of their subsidiaries. The global Novartis merger would be more appropriately termed an 'arranged mass marriage'.

However, the metaphor makes considerable sense when studying a single local integration process from the perspective of the two subsidiaries because the consequences of the parental merger mandate for SIL's and HCG's local integration process correspond well with commonly cited implications of an arranged marriage's impact on a couple's post-marital life together. As we saw, the immediate reactions of Indian managers were relatively critical toward the local appropriateness of the global merger decision with regard to the timing of the deal, its underlying rationales, the level of integration needed, and the fit between SIL and HCG as merger partners. Although their parent companies did not put SIL and HCG in a non-viable situation, the lack of fit resulted in various complications during the integration process. Similarly, couples in arranged marriages have been found to be consistently less happy than couples in marriages built on love (e.g., Xiaohe and Whyte 1990).

Another negative aspect of the global merger was that the timing of the announcement was far from perfect because SIL and HCG were experiencing critical challenges at the time. Similarly, the timing of arranged marriages is often based on factors other than the readiness or maturity of the children to make such a contract. Like couples in arranged marriages, SIL and HCG met for the first time as marriage partners and had no time or opportunity to get to know each other before negotiations began related to how, not whether, the marriage would proceed. Such prior acquaintance between potential marriage partners allows respect and understanding to grow before the more difficult situations and decisions inherent in a marriage need to be addressed. Finally, as with an arranged marriage, where offspring must struggle to meet their parents' expectations on such issues as having children, taking part in family rituals and traditions, putting up with in-laws, or contributing to family expenses, SIL and HCG had to meet a variety of requirements from their parent companies.

Of course, there is always the other side of the coin: arranged marriages also have positive elements. As Xiaohe and Whyte (1990) argued, love matches typically involve a very intense romantic involvement, accompanied by idealization of the partner and fantasies about wedded paradise before the wedding that quickly fade after the honeymoon, once reality sets in and everyday jobs, child-care burdens, financial anxieties, and ordinary life inevitably lead to a decline in romantic feelings, happiness and satisfaction with the relationship over the years. In contrast, because the partners in an arranged marriage do not know each other well (if at all) and because they do not have any romantic feelings for one another prior to the marriage, they have nowhere to go but up; after the marriage the couple will have the opportunity to get to know one another and forge common bonds. The resulting compatibility and mutual concern are likely to lead to a more mature form of love, providing a more realistic and durable bond that can survive the test of time. In other words, as Xiaohe and Whyte (1990: 710) put it, 'love matches start out hot and grow cold, while arranged marriages start out cold and grow hot'. The partners in an arranged marriage accept the marriage and try their best to make it a success instead of breaking up at the slightest conflict. The spouses get to know one another on a practical level first, looking beyond trivial issues of attraction.

The case presented here reveals several indications of such an optimistic interpretation of an arranged marriage's consequences. Among others, the local management teams showed a clear tendency during the process to focus more on 'hard facts', such as the integration of systems and structures, and less on 'soft issues', such as culture and values. Moreover, the local management endeavoured to follow their parents' wish that they integrate their activities smoothly and successfully. They seemed to try hard to make the partnership work. Thus, there are many analogies between both the premises and consequences of the local merger studied and an arranged marriage.

CONCLUSIONS AND IMPLICATIONS

In conclusion, drawing on the previous discussion and inspired by the 'merger syndrome' (Marks and Mirvis 1998), this chapter argues that managers of subsidiaries of globally merging MNCs must deal with the Arranged Marriage Syndrome when integrating their organizations locally. The Arranged Marriage Syndrome is defined as the consequences of the mandatory premises of the local integration process between two globally merging MNCs' subsidiaries. This mandate is accompanied by the local subsidiaries' non-involvement in the decision-making process leading to the global deal (and thus their late involvement in the overall merger process), and by not considering the local preconditions and of the human-related integration phenomena that will affect the outcome of the local integration process.

The Arranged Marriage Syndrome presented in this study is an initial proposal and needs further research and delimitation. The notion of an arranged marriage offers room for promising further research as well as for a more general use of the Arranged Marriage Syndrome. As Dooley and Zimmerman (2003: 56) argued, 'the question of whether two firms should engage one another is a good question for executives and board of directors, but not a relevant one for the majority of people involved in the merger. For them, a commitment is made and they have to try to make it work as best they can—in this way, the marriage metaphor is appropriate and insightful. The vast majority of people involved in mergers are not given a choice about getting married to another organization. Instead, as in an arranged marriage, they need to learn to live with a partner not completely of their choosing, but potentially to their liking. Their decisions revolve around how to be in the marriage.' Hence, the same premises of 'arranged' partnerships between subsidiaries can be found in most types of mergers and acquisitions. The relationship between a parent company and its subsidiaries is a hierarchical power relationship in which the subsidiary must trust, identify with and depend on the parent to do what is in its overall best interest, even if the subsidiary is not initially in love with the result.

Awareness of the Arranged Marriage Syndrome's existence is also important for practitioners—those making the decisions and those who have to implement them. More specifically, managers on the corporate level should try to minimize subsidiary managers' exposure to the Arranged Marriage Syndrome. As this chapter has shown, subsidiary managers' ability to appropriately handle human-related phenomena locally is negatively impacted by the Arranged Marriage Syndrome. Corporate management should try to involve local management as early as possible in the merger and acquisition process. Furthermore, communication that is transparent, open and effective is important.

NOTES

1. Despite legal differences in the definitions of mergers and acquisitions, research has shown that they share a wide range of issues and problems, not least of which are the challenges of the integration process (Risberg 1999). In line with Macy (1998), who argued that the differences are important for accounting and regulatory purposes but have little economic, organizational, or financial meaning, this study uses the two terms interchangeably.
2. I could reasonably expect that the local preconditions faced by the two Indian pharmaceutical units, and the global considerations on which the Novartis merger decision has been based, would differ considerably (cf., Jansson, Saqib, and Sharma 1995). Hence, I believed the expectations, requirements, and mandates, etc. of the parent company and the expectations, etc. of the subsidiary managers during the local integration process to be very different and to a large degree insurmountable, and therefore the Arranged Marriage Syndrome to be very visible.
3. To guarantee the anonymity of the respondents when using quotes, this chapter refers to them as, for example, HCG (Hindustan Ciba Geigy) XY or SIL (Sandoz India Limited) XY, where X stands for a specific number for each manager (our way of remembering who said what), and Y either for (a) meaning the interview was conducted in 2001, or (b) meaning the interview was conducted in 2003.

REFERENCES

Aguilera, R.V. and Dencker, J.C. (2004) 'The role of human resource management in cross-border mergers and acquisitions', *International Journal of Human Resource Management*, 15(8): 1355–70.

Batabyal, A.A. (2001) 'On the likelihood of finding the right partner in an arranged marriage', *Journal of Socio-Economics*, 30(3): 273–81.

Boye, P. (1999) *Developing transnational industrial platforms—The strategic conception of the Öresund Region*, Doctoral Thesis, School Of Economics and Management, Lund University.

Buono, A.F. and Bowditch, J.L. (1989) *The human side of mergers and acquisitions*, San Francisco: Jossey Bass Publishers.

Cartwright, S. and Cooper, C.L. (1993) 'Of mergers, marriage and divorce—The issues of staff retention', *Journal of Managerial Psychology*, 8(6): 7–10.

Cartwright, S. and Cooper, C.L. (1995) 'Organizational marriage: "Hard" versus "Soft" issues?', *Personnel Review*, 24(3): 32–42.

Davis, R.E. (1986) 'Compatibility in corporate marriages', *Harvard Business Review*, July–August: 86–93.

Dooley, K.J. and Zimmerman, B.J. (2003) 'Merger as marriage: Communication issues in post merger integration', *Health Care Management Review*, 28(1): 56–67.

Doz, Y. and Prahalad, C.K. (1993) 'Managing DMNCs: A search for a new paradigm', in S. Ghoshal and D.E. Westney (eds.) *Organization theory and the multinational corporation*, New York: St Martin's Press, pp. 24–50.

Eisenhardt, K. (1989) 'Building theories from case study research', *Academy of Management Review*, 14(4): 532–50.
Fugate, M., Kinicki, A.J., and Scheck, C.L. (2002) 'Coping with an organizational merger over four stages', *Personnel Psychology*, 55: 905–28.
Ghoshal, S. and Westney, D.E. (1993) 'Introduction and overview', in S. Ghoshal and D.E. Westney (eds.) *Organization theory and the multinational corporation*, New York: St Martin's Press, pp. 1–23.
Haspeslagh, C.P. and Jemison, D.B. (1991) *Managing acquisitions—Creating value through corporate renewal*, New York: The Free Press.
Hedlund, G. (1981) 'Autonomy of subsidiaries and formalization of headquarters—subsidiary relationships in Swedish MNCs', in L. Otterbeck (ed.) *The management of headquarter—subsidiary relationships in multinational corporations*, Aldershot.
Ivancevich, J.M., Schweiger, D.M., and Power, F.R. (1987) 'Strategies for managing human resources during mergers and acquisitions', *Human Resource Planning*, 10(1): 19–35.
Jansson, H., Saqib, M., and Sharma, D.D. (1995) *The state and transnational corporations—A network approach to industrial policy in India*, Aldershot: Edward Elgar Publishing.
Jemison, D.B. and Sitkin, S.B. (1986) 'Corporate acquisitions: A process perspective', *Academy of Management Review*, 11(1): 145–63.
Kostova, T. and Roth, K. (2002) 'Adoption of an organizational practice by subsidiaries of multinational corporations: Institutional and relational effects', *Academy of Management Journal*, 45(1): 215–33.
Larsson, R., Driver, M., Holmqvist, M., and Sweet, P. (2001) 'Career dis-integration and re-integration in mergers and acquisitions: Managing competence and motivational intangibles', *European Management Journal*, 19(6): 609–18.
Lohrum, C. (1992) *Integration av människor och kulturer efter ett företagsköp—En fallstudie*. Research Reports, 27, Swedish School of Economics and Business Administration, Helsinki, Finland.
Macy, A.M. (1998) *The impact of pharmaceutical mergers on economic agents*, Doctoral Thesis, Texas Tech University.
Marks, M.L. and Mirvis, P.H. (1985) 'Merger syndrome: Stress and uncertainty', *Mergers and Acquisitions*, 20: 50–55.
Marks, M.L. and Mirvis, P.H. (1986) 'The Merger syndrome', *Psychology Today*, 26(10): 36–42.
Marks, M.L. and Mirvis, P.H. (1998) *Joining forces—Making one plus one equal three in mergers, Acquisitions and Alliances*, San Francisco: Jossey-Bass Publishers.
Merriam, S.B. (1998) *Qualitative research and case study applications in education*, San Francisco: Jossey-Bass Publishers.
Mirvis, P. and Marks M.L. (1986) 'Merger syndrome: Management by crisis', *Mergers and Acquisitions*, 20: 70–76.
Nahavandi, A. and Malekzadeh, A. (1988) 'Acculturation in mergers and acquisitions', *Academy of Management Review*, 13(1): 79–90.
Napier, N.K., Simmons, G., and Stratton, K. (1989) 'Communication during a merger. The experience of two banks', *Human Resource Planning*, 12(2): 105–22.
Pablo, A.L. (1994) 'Determinants of acquisition integration level: A decision-making perspective', *Academy of Management Journal*, 37(4): 803–36.
Prahalad, C.K. and Doz, Y.L. (1987) *The multinational mission: Balancing local demands and global vision*, New York: The Free Press.
Pritchett, P. (1985) *After the merger: Managing the shockwaves*, Dallas: Dow Jones-Irwin.

Risberg, A. (1999) *Ambiguities thereafter—An interpretive approach to acquisitions*, Doctoral Thesis, Institute of Economic Research, Lund University.

Schweiger, D.M., Csiszar, E.N., and Napier, N.K. (1994) 'A strategic approach to implementing mergers and acquisitions', in G. Von Krogh, A. Sinatra, and H. Singh (eds.) *Managing corporate acquisitions: A comparative analysis*, London: Macmillan Press.

Schweiger, D.M. and DeNisi, A.S. (1991) 'Communication with employees following a merger: A longitudinal field experiment', *Academy of Management Journal*, 34(1): 110–35.

Schweiger, D.M., Ivancevich, J.M., and Power, F.R. (1987) 'Executive actions for managing human resources before and after the acquisition', *Academy of Management Executive*, 12: 127–38.

Schweizer, R. (2005) *An arranged marriage under institutional duality—The local integration process between two globally merging MNCs' subsidiaries*, Kungälv: BAS Publishing.

Schweizer, R. (2010) 'Headquarters-subsidiary relationships during dramatic strategic changes—The local implementation of a global merger between MNCs in India', *Review of Market Integration*, 2(1): 101–34.

Seo, M. and Hill, N.S. (2005) 'Understanding the human side of merger and acquisition: An integrative framework', *Journal of Applied Behavioral Science*, 41(4): 422–43.

Shearer, B. (2004) 'Taking potshots at golden parachutes', *Mergers & Acquisitions*, 39(9): 14–18.

Shrivastava, P. (1986) 'Postmerger integration', *Journal of Business Strategy*, 7: 65–76.

Skaria, G. (1998) 'The odd couple', *India Today*, 1998-11-07.

Stake, R.E. (1994) 'Case studies', in N.K. Denzin and Y.S. Lincoln (eds.) *Handbook of qualitative research*, Thousand Oaks: Sage Publications, pp. 236–47.

Terry, D.J. and O'Brien, A.T. (2001) 'Status, legitimacy, and in-group bias in the context of an organizational merger', *Group Processes & Intergroup Relations*, 4: 271–89.

Walsh, J.P. (1989) 'Doing a deal: Merger and acquisition negotiations and their impact upon target company top management turnover', *Strategic Management Journal*, 10(4): 307–22.

Yin, R. (2003) *Case study research. Design and methods*, 3rd ed. Applied Social Methods Series, London: Sage Publications.

Xiaohe, X. and Whyte, M.K. (1990) 'Love matches and arranged marriages: A Chinese replication', *Journal of Marriage and the Family*, 52(3): 709–72.

5 Internal Legitimacy for Change in Mergers and Acquisitions

Magnus Frostenson

INTRODUCTION

Internal stakeholders such as employees are, more or less by definition, at the core of the firm. Reflecting the multiplicity of internal stakes, this chapter focuses on the internal stakeholders of target firms. The significance of employee-related issues in mergers and acquisitions has been emphasised for at least a couple of decades (Buono and Bowditch 1989). Several researchers blame failed mergers and acquisitions on poor integration and lack of respect for the human values of the target firm (for example, Schweiger and DeNisi 1991; Shrivastava 1986). Usually, the literature sketches a dichotomy where management is contrasted with employees, understood as a relatively uniform collective that needs to be treated gently in order to avoid discontent. Very often, these studies take a managerial stance, focusing on managerial activities said to facilitate or complicate the integration of an acquired firm (see, for example, Haspeslagh and Jemison 1991; Olie 1994). Relatively few studies target employees more directly (with some notable exceptions, like Lohrum 1996; Risberg 1997, 1999, 2001, 2003; Søderberg 2003, 2006). For this reason, employee perceptions and ideas concerning the consequences of mergers and acquisitions are rarely described from an internal company perspective. Even rarer are challenges to the assumption that employees are a uniform group with common interests, an assumption that stakeholder theory has seriously questioned (Freeman 1984).

In this chapter, the concept of internal legitimacy will be used to highlight the conditions for internal acceptance of changes following mergers and acquisitions. Internal legitimacy can be seen as an internally generated managerial licence to operate. The presence or absence of internal legitimacy is an essential aspect to consider in order to gain a deeper understanding of the prerequisites for successful management of newly acquired firms. The purpose of the chapter is to identify the basis of internal legitimacy and to illustrate its significance in mergers and acquisitions.

The chapter builds on my dissertation, published in Swedish in 2006 (Frostenson 2006). It concerns four case studies of Swedish firms that have recently been acquired by or merged with foreign competitors (two to five years before the study). The chapter is structured as follows: first, the concept of internal legitimacy is developed. Then, its general significance in mergers and acquisitions is discussed. A methodology section follows. Then, four case studies illustrate the multifaceted internal realities of organizations. Based on the empirical material, the basis of internal legitimacy in mergers and acquisitions is identified. Finally, the chapter discusses what to learn from the cases and draws general conclusions and formulates managerial implications. This also implies shedding light on the current debate on foreign ownership of traditional crown jewels of Swedish industry like the car manufacturers Volvo and Saab.

INTERNAL LEGITIMACY

According to an often cited definition, legitimacy is 'a generalized perception or assumption that the actions of an entity are desirable, proper, or appropriate within some socially constructed system of norms, values, beliefs, and definitions' (Suchman 1995: 574). Legitimacy is a central concept in organizational research but has rarely been used as an explanatory concept in the internal organizational context. In its extensive use, for example, within neo-institutional theory (DiMaggio and Powell 1983; Meyer and Rowan 1977), it is attributed explanatory power when it comes to understanding why organizational fields and structures develop in certain, often similar, ways. Such structures tend to take shape and develop not only according to purely 'rational' (in a technical sense) considerations, but also from a tendency to conform to 'symbolic myths' (Meyer and Rowan 1977), to which it is necessary to adapt in order to gain societal recognition and to act in accordance with social expectations.

Legitimacy theory tends to view legitimacy as constructed in a social context (Meyer and Rowan 1977). This context is often relatively undefined. Even though institutional factors such as laws and rules play a part in the formation of legitimacy, it is basically a mental concept created in a human setting where norms and values condition the evaluation of a certain organization, structure or activity. Legitimacy is thus constructed in the wider social context of the company.

Along with legitimacy theory, it is possible to see the internal organizational context as a social system where different norms, values, beliefs, and definitions exist and condition managerial action (cf., Ezzamel, Willmott, and Worthington 2001; Moll and Hoque 2011). An implication of this is that legitimacy theory is relevant to use in a more narrow sense, in a specific internal arena where certain activities, structures, and managerial actions are evaluated against certain practical and cognitive frames that the organizational boundaries imply. Internal legitimacy can be defined as an internal managerial licence to operate. This 'licence' (used in a figurative sense) is a form of mandate to lead the organization. It is generated in the internal organizational context for different reasons. The internal organizational context is of course not isolated from the external social system. Employees may share the values, beliefs, and assumptions of the external social system. But internally, organizational activities are evaluated more directly against a specific frame of reference, for example, ideals concerning a well-performed job or the power relationships inside the company.

Internal legitimacy has been characterized as an accumulated 'capital' for management—a prerequisite for authority—based on a relational context. The more such capital there is, the greater the freedom of action for management (Sjöstrand 1997). Such insights are common, for example, in research on charismatic leadership, where subordinates accept and support someone's mandate to lead on emotional rather than traditional or legal grounds. The relationship is upheld by trust (Ekman 2003), not by formal control mechanisms or sanctions. The power conferred by internal legitimacy rests on informal acceptance of the person and her/his capacities and competencies, or so-called referent power (Ciulla 2002). What seems to follow from these studies is that formal hierarchy is not an all-embracing or adequate basis for understanding organizational life (Ezzamel, Willmott, and Worthington 2001; Freeman 1984; Frostenson 2009). As far as stakes or interests are concerned, the hierarchical division between managers and employees is not enough to enable us fully to understand the different stakes of persons within each group (cf., Lohrum 1996).

Researchers that have used the concept of internal legitimacy to understand and explain organizational phenomena include Brown (1997). The organization, he claims, can be a means through which the individual validates himself and gains self-esteem. The more positive the self-image the organization helps to create, the more positively it will be valued by its members. And, as a consequence, it will be seen as desirable, proper and appropriate (cf., Suchman 1995). Important for legitimacy is also organizational correspondence with the norms and values of its members and its ability to convey meaning. At the core of this reasoning, however, Brown (1997) suggests that there is a 'narcissistic' and basically self-centred conception of how individuals perceive themselves and the organizational context to which they belong. According to such a perspective, legitimacy becomes a form of 'reward' granted by the members of the organization. Moll and Hoque (2011), point to the importance of internal legitimacy in a case study concerning the introduction of a new budget system in an academic organization. They claim that implementation met with severe difficulties because the system was inconsistent with the staff's internal values and expectations for the university. For this reason, staff undermined it through patterns of under- and over-spending. Internal constituents of different kinds, they argue, should be seen as significant legitimating agents that condition important change in organizations.

As Moll's and Hoque's (2011) case study suggests, internal legitimacy is not just about relationships between persons. Also power, a new order, procedures, new organizational forms, and so on, may or may not be seen as legitimate. An implication of this is that internal legitimacy for managers is conditioned by the activities that they perform or the arrangements that they instigate. In cases where the distance between the one in power (for example, a new overseas owner) and the legitimating social collective (for example, local employees in the target firm) is substantial, the legitimacy process is more abstract and resembles the development of system trust, where trust is not referable to an individual but to systems or the procedures or structures that a new order creates (cf., Giddens 1991).

As for the basis of legitimacy, Suchman (1995) suggests three different forms of legitimacy, each resting on different sources. Legitimacy—and thus internal legitimacy—may be *moral*. Moral legitimacy is based on the correspondence between the actions of the organization and the values of society. Legitimacy may also be *pragmatic* (in Suchman's terms), which means that it is based on the self-interest of legitimating agents (the organization acts in a way that benefits them). And legitimacy can also be *cognitive*, which means that the basis for legitimacy rests on the fact that legitimating agents understand what the organization does and find its activities meaningful.

In my earlier research (Frostenson 2006) I transferred this model to the internal organizational arena. Internal legitimacy, in this respect, becomes an internal licence to operate. It builds on trust, instrumental calculations and cognitive understanding. In other words, there are some general prerequisites for internal legitimacy. The employees must be able to trust the new owners, to see a potential gain from them, and also to understand their activities and intentions. As I argued in Frostenson (2006), trust is facilitated by perceived value correspondence; instrumental calculations rest on self-interest, whereas cognitive understanding is reached through perceptions of the meaningfulness of the actions taken by the new owner.

In a newly acquired company, evaluations of the new order are made on the basis of such different but co-existing aspects. A positive evaluation on these grounds results in internal legitimacy. The process of actively granting (or denying) legitimacy to a new order is triggered by direct experience of change (cf., Moll and Hoque 2011). Changes may consist of new work procedures, new work content or new organizational forms following a merger or acquisition. The traditional understanding of legitimacy as a concept that refers to power is upheld if one sees changes as expressions of power that are evaluated on moral, self-interest, and cognitive grounds (due to the lack of active relationships between the new owner and the employees of the target firm).

One could of course ask why internal legitimacy is needed at all. Such a question presupposes that formal hierarchy and power of decision are all that is needed to run an organization. The discussion on legitimacy, however, emphasizes that such formal arrangements are not sufficient to lead an organization (Ezzamel, Willmott, and Worthington 2001). One reason for this is that formal power is without force if subordinates do not acknowledge and approve of it. Power requires acceptance in order to be exercised. The previously mentioned informal support structure, or 'capital,' that legitimacy constitutes is also of symbolic kind. To create informal symbolic support structures through formal means is often a hopeless task because formal power does not automatically confer the capacity to create a coherent system of symbols that are understandable to subordinates (Scott 1991). Speaking different languages (figuratively, and frequently also literally) than subordinates is not conducive to making them do what you want them to do.

INTERNAL LEGITIMACY AND MERGERS AND ACQUISITIONS

In the mergers and acquisitions literature, there has been an explicit focus on rhetorical creation of legitimacy for action. Erkama and Vaara (2010), for example, illustrate rhetorical strategies in a shutdown case following an acquisition. By illustrating how management and other stakeholders legitimate or de-legitimate a shutdown, they point to strategic ways of developing an understanding of a controversial issue. As Vaara and Tienari (2002) note, the construction of a legitimate case can be seen as resting on different communicative strategies. Such strategies reflect a need to justify mergers and acquisitions, or managerial action, often through 'rationalistic' discourse referring to the creation of economic value. This need is also reflected in other studies of multinational companies, not necessarily with a focus on mergers and acquisitions, dealing with the need to legitimate action in the eyes of a wider audience (Vaara and Tienari 2008).

Although such studies focus on legitimation strategies for a public audience, through media and public communication, other studies to some extent bring up the issue of legitimation inside multinational enterprises. Kostova and Zaheer (1999) explicitly mention internal legitimacy but define it as the acceptance and approval of an organizational unit by other units within the multinational enterprise, primarily the parent company. Such an understanding of internal legitimacy is best seen as legitimacy for a particular organization within a wider organizational structure. Internal legitimacy as used in this chapter refers to legitimacy within an organization, where internal constituents are seen as significant legitimating agents (Moll and Hoque 2011). For this reason, management studies and merger and acquisition studies with employee perspective, such as those focusing on identity creation and ambiguity, employ a conception of internal legitimacy more relevant to this study.

Though not using the concept of internal legitimacy, Ezzamel, Willmott, and Worthington (2001) touch upon its essence by pointing to the impossibility of implementing change in organizations without understanding that employee resistance cannot be reduced to trade union activity. A broader conceptual understanding of employee resistance requires realizing that employees care not only about job security but also about identification with the new arrangements or practices that are being implemented. In the mergers and acquisitions literature, it has been noted that identity issues are central to target firms (Lohrum 1996; Søderberg 2003). Thus, a new regime that challenges the self-narrative which employees uphold has not understood the symbolic values it threatens through implementing change. As Søderberg (2003) notes, the 'stories' or understandings of the new regime are rejected by the employees unless negotiated and reconciled with the different stories told by the employees.

Lohrum (1996) sees target firms as constituted by group identities that are continuously recreated in the interaction between different employees in different cultural settings. This also means that common perceptions and ideas are more unifying bonds in the organizations than are hierarchical position or formal functions. Identification and securing a position within a certain group becomes a reason for resisting integration measures taken by the new regime. This, however, may also explain why certain groups actually cooperate with the new order and support it. Group identities and loyalties seem to be crucial. Risberg (2001) points to the ambiguity in mergers and acquisitions (see also Risberg 1997, 1999, 2003). The idea of monolithic organizations cannot be upheld, she argues, as it leaves out many other possible representations of the organizations than managers' goals and values. Ambiguity, in the sense of multiple, contradictory and/or inconsistent interpretations, exists in an organization. Multiplicity rather than uniformity characterizes the newly acquired organization. Integration of the target firm in terms of homogenisation becomes a problematic goal reflecting a simplified idea of control and success, according to Risberg (2003). In fact, such an idea may inhibit successful integration, because it is based on wrongful assumptions about the nature of the employee context.

The practical aspects of lacking internal legitimacy are also evident. Low internal legitimacy is harmful to the organization. Practical consequences may include absenteeism, low work motivation and performance or key staff leaving the company. Another effect of low internal legitimacy is that reforms are difficult to implement (Moll and Hoque 2011). High internal legitimacy, on the other hand, tends to foster positive qualities like loyalty, personal drive, and low turnover of staff. Though not using the concept of internal legitimacy, Lohrum (1996) identifies different features of a context where internal legitimacy is missing. Psychological reactions (for example, stress) as well as behavioural reactions (resistance and—if internal legitimacy is present—cooperation) may follow. Through the concept of internal legitimacy, it is possible to acquire a deeper understanding of these reactions. Internal legitimacy, it is fair to claim, signals that the stakes of the employees are respected.

METHODOLOGY

The chapter builds on empirical material from four case studies (see also Frostenson 2006) of Swedish firms that have been either purchased by or merged with foreign competitors. An ambition has been to include companies of different sizes and acquirers of different nationalities, but there is also a merger of equals. The purpose of choosing companies of varying size and cases of varying nature is to provide different contexts of interaction where generalizations can be made that go beyond simple structural explanations (for example, low internal legitimacy because of resentment against the nationality of the acquirer).

Of the four firms in the case studies, two are active in consulting. One is an IT firm acquired by a German competitor, whereas the other is a market research firm taken over by a British company. The third case concerns a firm in the electronics industry that has been acquired by a US industrial group. The last case is a large industrial firm that has merged with a Finnish competitor. Table 5.1 clarifies the picture.

Table 5.1 Case Studies Included in the Sample

Swedish target firm	*No. of employees at the time of acquisition (merger)*	*Former owner*	*Acquirer*	*Size of acquirer compared to Swedish firm*
IT firm	60	Founder of the company and Swedish investment company	German IT firm	Larger
Market research firm	350	Swedish media group	British consulting group	Much larger
Electronics firm	300	Swedish industrial group	US industrial group	Much larger
Industrial firm (merging partner)	20,000	Ownership dispersed but dominated by Swedish industrial group	Finnish industrial firm (merging partner)	Equal

The primary source of information is some sixty interviews with white-collar employees and managers of the four Swedish (target) firms. External as well as internal documents have also been studied. A deliberate choice was to focus on respondents that encounter the new owners in a somewhat more direct way than, for example, blue-collar employees (although blue-collar employees may experience the consequences of the new regime at a later stage, when decisions about, for example, the future location of production facilities have been taken). Another aim was to interview internal stakeholders in different positions and different locations in the firm. In the semi-structured interviews, the respondents were asked to reflect on changes following the acquisitions (and, in one case, the merger). Based on this reflection, it was possible to identify not only which changes these persons considered legitimate and which changes they resented, but also the grounds on which internal legitimacy seems to rest.

THE MULTIFACETED INTERNAL REALITY OF THE ORGANIZATIONS

There are striking differences between the four firms under study in regard to size, profitability, industry, and so on. It is clear in all cases, however, that there is no 'common view' representing all internal stakeholders of a particular firm. In each firm, persons evaluate changes from different vantage points. The multifaceted internal stakeholder context is evident. The internal arena is inhabited by different groups. A primary observation is that internal stakeholders should not be equated with employees in a more narrow sense (blue-collar and white-collar employees). Local managers, for example, also formulate interests or stakes in relation to the new owners.

At the time of the study, the relatively newly founded IT consultant is still permeated by the entrepreneurial spirit and creative Internet culture. Unlike the Internet consultants and communicators active in the company, however, new employees enter the firm without any wish to become part of a 'cultural movement'. Consultants who join the firm aspire to be more like traditional management consultants. Expert knowledge and more 'engineering' ideals are found among IT technicians rather than Internet consultants. After the founding entrepreneurs have logged out, new management takes over and has to create order according to the preferences of the new German owners.

The market research firm is divided between a traditional 'expert' culture and a more business-oriented approach represented mainly by junior consultants who have recently entered the firm. The administrative units are under pressure to live up to the demands of the new British owners. As an example, five CFOs are employed but then leave, voluntarily or involuntarily, during the first couple of years after the acquisition. The field work of market research is done in a local production unit, where the atmosphere and interests are quite different compared to the Stockholm head office.

The electronics firm also has long industrial traditions. It is marked by an engineering culture that is challenged to some extent by the new American owners, even though employees see some resemblance in the new owners' industrial know-how and culture. The differences between the internal stakeholders of the firm are seemingly small and more of a geographical nature, with a division between the production and R&D units. Because no unit is situated in Stockholm, the capital of Sweden, no 'non-capital' identity is constructed, in contrast to the production unit of the market research company. Here, too, however, the administrative units bear the brunt of the burden in terms of the tremendous efforts needed to meet the new reporting and system requirements of the new owners. The employees under constant threat of redundancy, however, are the sales representatives. Duplication of functions—sales personnel from both the buying firm and the target firm—are not needed on different markets.

In the larger industrial firm, the scenario is different. Of course one finds numerous internal stakeholder groups with varying interests and aspirations. But here there is also the formation of a new, more or less international or supranational identity, with the head office of the firm located in London. This feature contrasts with local Swedish management in Stockholm, and in particular with the locally based production unit in a small countryside town, as is highlighted in the study. The local perspective seems to guide both local management and local staff. What happens in the newly formed company is evaluated from a local standpoint with a clear mental heritage of the traditional role that the company has played at the local (and also national) level.

THE BASIS FOR INTERNAL LEGITIMACY IN MERGERS AND ACQUISITIONS

The multifaceted internal stakeholder context illustrated here suggests complex and partly contradictory internal legitimation processes. Referring to the generally experienced changes following the new order, different groups within the firms tend to legitimate or de-legitimate what the acquisition or merger has brought about.

The employees experience changes following the takeover. Changes common to all cases are increased formalisation and administration, requirements of financial reporting, and new financial parameters as part of management control (cf., Roberts 1990). In general, one consequence seems to be a stronger business or sales orientation at the expense of former 'expert cultures' (especially in the market research firm and IT firm, where one central aspect is the ousting of the previous creative Internet age culture). In all case studies, new names and logotypes follow, and in all firms under study, there are reorganizations. More profound structural changes, including downsizing, take place in the IT and market research firms. Being internationalized in a wider sense, implying that you find your everyday work situation affected by the new internationalized ownership, is also common. Certain aspects stand out in different companies, however. The previously mentioned challenge to culture is particularly present in the IT firm and in the larger industrial firm. Increased marginalisation of local units and more internal competition are most evident in the industrial firm, along with the construction of an international giant, which entails relocating top management to London. The electronics firm is appointed a 'centre of excellence' in its new structure because of its competence and advanced products.

Such changes are evaluated by the employees—and also, not to forget, local managers (managers for local subsidiaries of MNCs are studied in Chapter 4 by Schweizer). Perhaps one could infer that tougher measures, such as downsizing, are deemed negative and automatically reduce the internal legitimacy of the new order. This would mean that poor finances automatically lead to de-legitimation of the new owners' efforts to come to terms with the problems. This is not the case, however. Internal legitimacy based on understanding the meaning of the harsh measures taken (cognitive legitimacy) can be found to a greater or lesser degree in all the companies. Such approval is based on understanding and acceptance of the market logic warranting these measures. Going on as before is not an option. And the new owners (in the IT and market research firms) are not necessarily to blame for the financial problems. Acceptance of the market logic can also work as an argument for the acquisition or merger in the first place. The logic is compelling. It had to be done in one way or the other, managers as well as employees seem to think.

Another reason for not automatically de-legitimating the new owners in times of adversity is that employees have few illusions that everything was better before the takeovers. The IT firm is in financial difficulty; the market research firm is 'well-known but wrongly known', as some employees put it; the electronics firm is hampered by a confining ownership structure in a traditional Swedish industrial group where it is not the core business, and the industrial firm lacks opportunities to grow much more organically. In these circumstances, other owners can contribute something new: The IT firm gets financial support; the market research firm provides, among other things, individual career opportunities; the new US ownership of the electronics firm offers new and expanded markets, and at least the top management of the industrial firm find unprecedented individual opportunities when the traditional Swedish company becomes international or even supranational. All these factors contribute to internal legitimacy, based on satisfied self-interest. In other words, pragmatic legitimacy (Suchman 1995) is generated for the new order. Pragmatic legitimacy implies acceptance of a certain order based on self-interest in a broad sense, which may mean career opportunities at the individual level and potential for growth or survival at the company level. Employees may of course also de-legitimate the new order by the same reasoning. For example, one finds no examples of employees that have made a career in Germany as a consequence of the German purchase of the Swedish IT firm.

Although there is little difference between the different internal stakeholder groups when it comes to cognitive and pragmatic legitimacy, the opinions of internal stakeholders about the new order seem to be truly divided when it comes to moral legitimacy. Both identity issues and perceived value correspondence seem to be of considerable importance for moral legitimacy. Here it is evident that employees of the IT firm tend to de-legitimate the new order following the German acquisition (see the following, however). The high status of being a frontrunner in the Internet age or, as one employee puts it, 'part of a cultural movement', has no equivalent under the new German ownership. Being German, getting a new name, not being frontrunner anymore, and so on, are factors that severely challenge the self-perception of the firm in a negative way. Symbolic issues play a vital role in this regard. To some degree the opposite occurs in the market research firm. Being owned by a British giant is at least tolerable from a status point of view. In the electronics firm, other symbolic issues are interpreted in a positive way. Becoming a 'centre of excellence', for example, validates and reinforces the self-image of the firm. In the industrial firm, the loss of national icon status is not easy to bear. After the merger, a new common identity must be constructed.

But apart from the more emotionally based aspects of identity and status, the importance of perceived value correspondence is clear. If the new owner either reflects the values of the acquired firm or at least shows tolerance enough to continue letting them prosper, the employees will look favourably upon the new owner. Perhaps the most striking example is the electronics firm. Employees clearly refer to values that are shared with the new American owner, what they call a 'Nordic heritage', the importance of honesty, fair play, casual behaviour, and so on. They also construct a common engineering culture, where the cornerstones are values like competence, objectivity, and carefulness. There is reciprocity in these values. The Americans share them with the Swedes, who receive self-recognition as well as recognition from the American owners. This recognition includes continued relative autonomy to act as a Swedish company.

It is also evident that employees de-legitimate the new order for basically the same reasons. When they experience challenges to the values that they hold, the reaction is negative. Examples include strong negative reactions to hierarchical management, limitation of personal autonomy or of co-determination in the workplace, lack of competence, unfair treatment, and narrow provincialism (national bias as in the industrial firm, where Swedes find that Finns favour their compatriots). Formalisation and strong quantitative evaluation of work do not find approval, either.

All in all, changes in procedures and structures do not seem to be those to which employees react most negatively. Changes in procedures and structures may give rise to resentment because of negative consequences from a personal point of view, for example, but there is a more profound challenge relating to work content and identity. Here it is evident that one's position within the company—which is not necessarily equivalent to hierarchical position—plays a part. Group identities matter, as noted by Lohrum (1996). The bearers of culture—like the creative Internet communicators of the IT firm—strongly resent the German challenge to their identity. Becoming an 'industrial' subunit of a German firm is not in line with their self-perception. Other parties inside the firm applaud the new regime, which creates at least some stability after the chaos that is said to have prevailed before they entered the scene. Traditional expert researchers of the market research firm strongly dislike being evaluated on the basis of how much they sell, whereas younger people within the company see this as an opportunity. The electronics firm is relatively homogeneous, it seems; the sales representatives, however, feel strongly threatened by the new ownership, and it is quite reasonable for them to de-legitimate the new order from a pragmatic, self-interested view. Because of the size and nature of the industrial firm, internal stakeholders are numerous and the local culture tends to clash not only with the (supra)national but also with the culture of other local units in a form of internal competition.

WHAT TO LEARN FROM THE CASES

As shown, different interests, values, expectations, and ambitions tend to condition internal legitimacy for the new order. For this reason, the integration and optimal utilization of the newly acquired subsidiary are not a simple predictable process where 'employee resistance' is one more or less static component, but a multifaceted phenomenon that may well go hand in hand with 'employee support'. Some employees applaud the new owners and the changes that follow the merger or acquisition, whereas others deplore the new order. In the target firm, different interests, expectations, and constructions of identity shape the reception of the new owners. Depending on who is asked, the answer will vary considerably.

Judging from the cases, a number of factors relevant to the creation of internal legitimacy are obvious. Employees in the firms examined evaluate and—in certain cases legitimate—the new order specifically on perceived grounds of continued autonomy of the firm, competence of the new owner, extent of identification with the new owner, degree to which measures taken seem consistent with market logic, and, finally, the extent to which personal career interests can be satisfied by the new owner. All these factors can be linked to the aspects of legitimacy discussed by Suchman (1995).

The autonomy factor is based on preferences for continued freedom and on the ability to influence the working context. It is clear that employees expect an organizational context where the organization is respected for its worth and competence and where the individual is given space for self-realisation, creativity, and some form of a say in an organizational context. Internal legitimacy seems to be higher if the purchased organization is provided with a sort of free zone where it can maintain and develop its business and activities. It appears common among employees to believe that the organization has been acquired because of what it is perceived to be rather than what the acquirer wants to make of it. A recurrent idea in at least two of the firms, the market research firm and the electronics firm, is that 'we chose who should buy us'. This is hardly an expression of a cry for a radically changed course of action. After a while, however, what really happens seems to be the opposite. Things change, and self-perceptions are challenged. Granting autonomy becomes something of a litmus test of the new owner. If granted, autonomy is viewed as a sign of tolerance and acceptance of the target firm's unique qualities and competence.

Competence is also required of the new owner. It can be regarded instrumentally as something that the target firm needs to do well in order to increase its market potential, or more in terms of trust. Through exhibiting competence, the acquirer proves trustworthy. Competence is a value of high importance, strengthening trust and thereby internal legitimacy. The instrumental aspect seems important as well, however. Transfer of knowledge from the new owner to the target firm becomes a sign of competence in itself and also of good will.

Identification with the acquirer also seems to be of utmost importance (cf., Ezzamel, Willmott, and Worthington 2001). This factor refers to what the target firm considers itself to be, what it aspires to be and what the new owners may help it to become in the future. It is linked to an ideal image cherished by the employees of the target firm. Essential ingredients of identification would seem to include status, recognition of one's own features in the new owner and confirmation of the firm's and the new owners' competence and attractiveness. National borders, on the other hand, are a potential barrier to identification (cf., Risberg, Tienari, and Vaara 2003). Interestingly enough, origin of the acquirer is subjected to a form of status evaluation, where Anglo-Saxon countries seem to find more acceptance than other countries (Finland and Germany), a factor that becomes increasingly prominent the less the employees know about the acquirer as such.

Financial realities may also bring about acceptance of change. This factor refers to market logic and can be linked to cognitive legitimacy. Provided employees understand and accept the rules of the market game—an evolutionary logic where weak finances will not hold up in the long run and unprofitable companies will not last forever—cognitive legitimacy may be generated within the firm.

Not surprisingly, employees evaluate changes on the basis of their personal ambitions and career interests. This instrumental aspect of internal legitimacy seems to be facilitated by clear understanding of the objectives and preferences of individual employees. Gaining insight into what employees are actually seeking and in what position they feel comfortable is highly advisable for companies that acquire competitors. Though seemingly self-evident, this may not be the case, as the owner may lack interest in the cultural asset represented by the newly purchased target firm.

CONCLUSIONS

The chapter claims that internal legitimacy is a central issue for successful mergers and acquisitions. At the same time, the multifaceted internal stakeholder context makes internal legitimacy a form of resource or capital that is unevenly generated within the firm. In terms of stakeholder theory, the presence of internal legitimacy signals that the interests (or stakes) of the employees are respected and acknowledged. On the other hand, there are few crystal-clear cases where internal legitimacy of a particular order or regime is either omnipresent or non-existent. As the cases suggest, different bases for internal legitimacy co-exist. Tendencies towards legitimating a new order in one respect can be counteracted by de-legitimating tendencies in another. For example, the German owners of the IT firm and their measures taken may suggest low internal legitimacy for lack of value correspondence. But at the same time, the new owners may enjoy some internal legitimacy because of the financial support they provide (pragmatic legitimacy) and an understanding of the business logic behind their actions (cognitive legitimacy).

One important aspect of mergers and acquisitions is that the context in which managers gain legitimacy is quite different than in more direct relationships between managers and employees. In mergers and acquisitions the perceived distance to management increases, particularly in international mergers and acquisitions. This means that the relationship between the employees and the manager becomes more diffuse. (Even though local managers of course remain present, they are seen as agents of the owners, who make the actual decisions.) In this blurred relationship, *the internal legitimacy process tends to become indirect and to build more on the symbolic significance of certain actions taken by the new regime*. The acquiring company and its often anonymous managers are evaluated according to the content and symbolism of their perceived actions, activities, and structures under the new ownership (cf., Ezzamel, Willmott, and Worthington 2001). Internal legitimacy in mergers and acquisitions is different from direct acknowledgement of the authority of a charismatic leader (cf., Sjöstrand 1997). It is more a sort of acceptance of a new order—a general licence to operate—than a mandate given to a particular manager.

The apparently strong position of what Suchman (1995) calls moral legitimacy should also be considered in mergers and acquisitions. Value correspondence and symbolic identification can be linked to this form of legitimacy. This calls for *even more thorough consideration of what the acquiring firm stands for, what it represents, and what its actual and symbolic impact on the daily work of employees actually is*. Resolution of such issues seems crucial to lasting internal legitimacy. It is not reached by maintaining or subsidizing a failing target firm financially for any length of time. Such support may of course be needed temporarily, but it is hardly a solid basis for an enduring internal legitimacy. Moral justification and symbolic identification seem to be a stronger basis for internal legitimacy than gaining new market shares for the company or providing career opportunities for individuals.

Another aspect that the internal legitimacy perspective brings into view is that *the relatively simplistic dichotomy between managers and employees loses much of its substance*. Of course, the dichotomy remains in a formal sense. But the interests of employees and local managers in a new setting may well converge, though for different reasons, as in the large industrial firm described earlier. A local manager may identify much more with her or his old firm and its employees than with a position as subordinate manager in the new organizational setting. Employees of the target firm may find links to the new international organization that permit them to bypass the traditional local hierarchical order.

All in all, internal legitimacy seems to be of help when it comes to understanding the dynamics of mergers and acquisitions and the debate on them. It adds a further conceptual basis for understanding, for example, ambiguity (Risberg 1997, 1999, 2001, 2003) and the formation of group identities (Lohrum 1996).

MANAGERIAL IMPLICATIONS

Some managerial implications can be drawn from the study. The different factors important for legitimation in a Scandinavian context should be taken into account by a new regime that acquires a Scandinavian firm. With regard to the autonomy factor, genuine openness to diversity—to giving the Scandinavian firm and employees a satisfactorily large creative space and sufficient freedom to continue and develop their business—is recommended. As for the high valuation of competence—both the target firm's own and the buying firm's—the creation of arenas for dialogue and knowledge transfer is essential. Identification requires an actively created symbolic language with which the employees can identify, while spelling out a clear business logic may enhance cognitive legitimacy for actions taken. Finally, in regard to pragmatic legitimacy, the ability to identify personal aspirations and objectives is necessary. De-legitimating a new order may, as the chapter claims based on the case studies, be a consequence if the owner fails to take the previously mentioned measures. Perhaps this is shown most clearly by the IT firm, where the bearers of culture shun the symbolic language of the new owners, distrust their competence and resent what they consider to be a loss of autonomy. Important culture bearers leave the organization, and motivation dwindles. In fact, the IT firm went bankrupt a few months after the case study was done. By contrast, the new American owners of the electronics firm seem to consider these factors. Internal legitimacy is high because of perceived value correspondence, attractive symbolic language, the new owners' high level of competence, relatively high autonomy and improved market potential. Growth and profits are reported to be steadily increasing.

The study suggests that certain aspects often referred to as typically Swedish or Scandinavian matter, such as resistance to hierarchies based on an ideal of equality or an understanding of freedom in terms of co-determination. It is also vital to have a say and an influence rather than being subject to arbitrary treatment (cf., d'Iribarne 1996/97, 2002). The concentration on the Scandinavian context may of course be seen as a limitation of the study, for strong cultural traits condition what actually creates internal legitimacy. But this hardly reduces the need for internal legitimacy; rather, it calls for studies that identify how internal legitimacy is created in different cultural settings and also in other contexts than mergers and acquisitions.

The current debate on cross-border mergers and acquisitions further illustrates the need to understand the roots, causes, and consequences of internal legitimacy (or the lack of it). Understanding the initially strong scepticism of potential Chinese owners of traditional Swedish icons like Volvo Cars requires an understanding of the factors essential to internal legitimacy. One important factor described earlier is identification, which implies a sort of status valuation on national level. The attractiveness of Chinese acquirers will be dependent on the attractiveness of China and Chinese companies in general. This is not just a matter of liking or disliking, but an identity issue that reflects at a practical and symbolic level what it is like to be a subsidiary of a Chinese firm. At the same time, however, trade unions and others may be aware of and also support what new Chinese owners can achieve and contribute from a financial point of view. Contrasting forces of legitimacy co-exist. The Chinese tradition of acquiring competence when they do not have it themselves may also be well known. This indicates two things: first, as new owners the Chinese acquirers do not have the competence needed to develop the business; second, the acquired firm possesses that competence with its strong engineering culture built on a solid foundation. Both these factors affect internal legitimacy. A self-understanding is explicitly spelled out and contrasted with a perception of 'the other' that is rather diffuse because the employees know relatively little, if anything, about the competitors that are going to acquire their company.

With regard to research, this chapter challenges two tendencies in the literature. First, the dichotomy between management and employees in mergers and acquisitions is questioned. The issue of internal legitimacy is not based on a rift between management and employees, but may involve struggles between local management and the management of the acquirers or, for that matter, local top management and middle management. Another aspect of this is, of course, that employees are not seen as a uniform cadre with common interests and similar processes for legitimation. Rather, legitimation is contested among employees. Even though certain studies (like Ezzamel, Willmott, and Worthington 2001; Lohrum 1996; Risberg 2001, 2003; Søderberg 2003) should be commended for questioning the uniformity of the employee cadre, this chapter adds a conceptual tool, internal legitimacy, to aid in further understanding the basis of this multifaceted employee context. Second, along with this reasoning, the chapter offers arguments for challenging the traditional understanding of employee resistance, prevalent in much of the mergers and acquisitions literature. Where resistance exists, the internal legitimacy concept may clarify why it does. It may also explain how it can exist alongside employee support for change in the organization. With regard to stakeholder theory, internal legitimacy also adds to our understanding of the nature of internal stakes. Identifying different forms of internal legitimacy helps us to differentiate between the different kinds of 'outputs' that internal stakeholders want to receive from the company. An obvious fact, judging from this study, is that when trying to understand the internal nature of mergers and acquisitions, we completely miss the point if we regard such outputs as purely financial or career related in the context of mergers and acquisitions. Future research should take the multifaceted nature of internal stakes into account when exploring the internal or cultural aspects of mergers and acquisitions.

REFERENCES

Brown, A.D. (1997) 'Narcissism, identity and legitimacy', *Academy of Management Review*, 22(3): 643–86.

Buono, A.F. and Bowditch, J.L. (1989) *The Human Side of Mergers and Acquisitions: Managing Collisions Between People, Cultures, and Organizations*, San Francisco: Jossey-Bass Publishers.

Ciulla, J. (2002) *Trust and the Future of Leadership, Companion to Business Ethics Blackwell Guide to Philosophy Series*, Oxford: Blackwell.

Di Maggio, P. and Powell, W. W. (1983) 'The Iron Cage Revisited: Institutional Isomorphism and Collective Rationality in Organizational Fields', *American Sociological Review*, 48: 147–60.

d'Iribarne, P. (1996/1997) 'The Usefulness of an Ethnographic Approach to the International Comparison of Organizations', *International Studies of Management and Organization*, 26(4): 30–47.

d'Iribarne, P. (2002) 'Motivating workers in emerging countries: universal tools and local adaptations', *Journal of Organizational Behavior*, 23: 243–56.

Ekman, G. (2003) *Från prat till resultat—Om vardagens ledarskap*, Malmö: Liber Ekonomi.
Erkama, N. and Vaara, E. (2010) 'Struggles Over Legitimacy in Global Organizational Restructuring: A Rhetorical Perspective on Legitimation Strategies and Dynamics in a Shutdown Case', *Organization Studies*, 31: 813–39.
Ezzamel, M., Willmott, H., and Worthington, F. (2001) 'Power, Control and Resistance in "The Factory that Time Forgot"', *Journal of Management Studies*, 38(8): 1053–79.
Freeman, R.E. (1984) *Strategic Management: A Stakeholder Approach*, Boston: Pitman.
Frostenson, M. (2006) *Legitimationskontrollen—en studie av etiska värderingars roll i gränsöverskridande fusioner och förvärv*, Stockholm: EFI Förlag.
Frostenson, M. (2009) 'Stakeholder Theory and the "Black Box Problem", Internal Clarity or Confusion?', *Philosophy of Management*, 8(3): 37–46.
Giddens, A. (1991) *Modernity and Self-Identity: Self and Society in the Late Modern Age*, Stanford, CA: Stanford University Press.
Haspeslagh, P.C. and Jemison, D.B. (1991) *Managing Acquisitions—Creating Value Through Corporate Renewal*, New York: Free Press.
Kostova, T. and Zaheer, S. (1999) 'Organizational Legitimacy under Conditions of Complexity: The Case of the Multinational Enterprise', *Academy of Management Review*, 24(1): 64–81.
Lohrum, C. (1996) *Post-Acquisition Integration—Towards an Understanding of Employee Reactions*, Helsinki: Hanken School of Business.
Meyer, J.W. and Rowan, B. (1977) 'Institutionalized organizations: Formal structure as myth and ceremony', *American Journal of Sociology*, 83: 340–63.
Moll, J. and Hoque, Z. (2011) 'Budgeting for legitimacy: The case of an Australian university', *Accounting, Organizations and Society*, 36: 86–101.
Olie, R. (1994) 'Shades of Culture and Institutions in International Mergers', *Organization Studies*, 15(3): 381–405.
Risberg, A. (1997) 'Ambiguity and communication in cross-cultural acquisitions: towards a conceptual framework', *Leadership and Organization Development Journal*, 18(5): 257–66.
Risberg, A. (1999) *Ambiguities Thereafter. An Interpretive Approach to Acquisitions*, Lund: Lund University Press.
Risberg, A. (2001) 'Employee experiences of acquisitions', *Journal of World Business*, 36(1): 58–84.
Risberg, A. (2003) 'Notions of Shared and Multiple Realities in Acquisitions. Unfolding and critiquing dominating notions of acquisitions', *Nordiske Organisasjonsstudier*, 5(1): 58–82.
Risberg, A., Tienari, J., and Vaara, E. (2003) 'Making Sense of a Transnational Merger: Media Texts and the (Re)construction of Power Relations', *Culture and Organization*, 9(2): 121–37.
Roberts, J. (1990) 'Strategy and accounting in a U.K. conglomerate', *Accounting, Organizations and Society*, 15(1–2): 107–26.
Schweiger, D.M. and DeNisi, A.S. (1991) 'Communication with Employees Following a Merger: A Longitudinal Field Experiment', *Academy of Management Journal*, 34(1): 110–35.
Scott, W.R. (1991) 'Unpacking Institutional Arguments', in P. Di Maggio and W.W. Powell (eds.) *The New Institutionalism in Organizational Analysis*, Chicago: The University of Chicago Press.
Shrivastava, P. (1986) 'Postmerger Integration', *The Journal of Business Strategy*, 7(1): 65–76.
Sjöstrand, S.-E. (1997) *The Two Faces of Management: The Janus Factor*, London: International Thompson Business Press.

Søderberg, A.-M. (2003) 'Sensegiving and sensemaking in an integration process: A narrative approach to the study of an international acquisition', in B. Czarniawska and P. Gagliardi (eds.) *Narratives We Organize By*, Amsterdam: John Benjamins Publishing Company.
Søderberg, A.-M. (2006) 'Narrative Interviewing and Narrative Analysis in a Study of a Cross-border Merger', *MIR: Management International Review*, 46(4): 397–416.
Suchman, M.C. (1995) 'Managing legitimacy: Strategic and Institutional Approaches', *Academy of Management Review*, 20(3): 571–610.
Vaara, E. and Tienari, J. (2002) 'Justification, Legitimization and Naturalization of Acquisitions: A Critical Discourse Analysis of Media Texts', *Organization*, 9(2): 275–304.
Vaara, E. and Tienari, J. (2008) 'A Discursive Perspective on Legitimation Strategies in Multinational Corporations', *Academy of Management Review*, 33(4): 985–93.

6 The Internal Auditor's Involvement in Acquisitions

Fredrik Nilsson, Nils-Göran Olve, and Olof Arwinge

INTRODUCTION

Senior managers and corporate specialists play an important part in acquisition processes.[1] Through their formal tasks and personal career interests, they may be regarded as stakeholders in the process, in the sense that this term is used by Freeman et al. (2010: 26). To what extent such persons *outside* the executive management team get involved in shaping strategy seems not to have been studied much, although staff members in accounting and finance are reported to have somewhat more influence than other staff (Miller, David, and David 2008). In this chapter, we focus on one such stakeholder: the internal auditor and her/his involvement in acquisitions.

In recent years, internal auditors have been assigned an important role in the overall risk management of organizations (Gramling and Myers 2006; Stokhof 2008). Internal auditors are regarded as risk experts in many large organizations (Allegrini et al. 2006; Hass, Abdolmohammadi, and Burnaby 2006). Through their independent status they provide assurance to the board, but also to other stakeholders such as the executive management team, regarding the adequacy and effectiveness of governance, risk management, and internal control processes (IIA 2011).

The *purpose* of this chapter is to investigate and discuss the involvement of the internal auditor in acquisitions, with a focus on the acquiring firm. In other words: what is the internal auditor's involvement in the risk management process connected to strategy formulation and execution, preceding and following an acquisition?

THE INTERNAL AUDITOR

The duties of the internal auditor include evaluating and contributing to the improvement of risk management processes,[2] governance, and control processes in organizations (IIA 2011: 29). The internal audit provides independent assurance primarily to the board and its audit committee, but there is also a close relationship between the internal auditor and the executive management team as well as others in the organization (IIA 2003).

Acquisitions are among the most risky steps a board can take, where success is dependent on a complex sequence of actions. Whether it is true or not that many acquisitions fail (see Risberg in this volume), weaknesses in strategic logic and/or pre- and post-acquisition processes are often claimed to exist. It is therefore reasonable to expect that risks related to an acquisition initiative would fall within the scope of the internal audit activity, because inadequate risk management both pre- and post-acquisition could compromise firm performance. Such internal audit involvement is touched upon in some normative contributions to the literature, concerning, for example, participation in due diligence activities preceding a major business transaction (Dounis 2008; Tramp 1998). However, few empirical studies examine the involvement of the internal auditor in relation to the management of strategic initiatives and complex non-routine processes, such as an acquisition.

What contributions internal auditors can make will depend on their roles, the respect they enjoy, their abilities and obviously regulations and professional standards. In this chapter, we are interested in ideas about possible contributions, the actual involvement of present-day internal auditors, and the extent to which these ideas and actual involvement are compatible with their role in firms.

The chapter is based on data from five explorative case studies on acquiring companies; the data concern the internal auditors' involvement in the acquisitions. The following three sections discuss the expected type of involvement for the internal auditor and our research design. Then our five cases are presented, followed by a discussion of the results and ending with implications.

CHANGING RISK AND ASSURANCE PROCESSES

Recent years have witnessed an increase in the attention paid by practitioners and scholars to the risk management and internal control practices of firms (Maijoor 2000; Power 2007; Spira and Page 2003). Reports from consultancies and auditing firms (e.g., Grant Thornton, 2009) as well as those issued by regulatory bodies (e.g., The Swedish Financial Supervisory Authority 2011) testify to this increased attention. 'Hot areas' include *reputational risk* and *operational risk* (Power et al. 2009) and how company practices in the financial sector spread and evolve based on the Basel-framework for banks (BIS 2011) and the Solvency-framework for insurance companies (European Union 2009). Today, managing risks that may impair the achievement of goals is a top board and executive priority (Capriotti 2009; Donaldson 2007).

As a consequence, internal processes with an impact on risk and control are changing. New types of risk professionals are emerging, and the rise of the chief risk officer is perhaps the most visible example (Hutter and Power 2005; Mikes 2009). This development is most notable in financial institutions, where it has been driven largely by regulatory frameworks and standards, but is becoming established in other industries as well. Also, internal auditing processes are gradually changing and developing. The control-based focus of audits is changing to a risk-centred focus (Gramling and Myers 2006; Sarens and De Beelde 2006; Spira and Page 2003).

Risk management and internal control practices are thus becoming tied to the strategic agenda of firms, where risks derive from the goal-setting and strategy process, and are dealt with through a variety of risk responses, such as reduce, accept, share, and avoid (COSO 2004). In this way, strategic agendas that include acquisition initiatives can be expected to form part of the analysis and actions taken by the internal auditor, but also other functions such as risk management, compliance, controlling, and legal. A process perspective on such initiatives suggests that risks should be tracked throughout the process of planning, negotiating and integrating assets (Pablo, Sitkin, and Jemison 1996).

The risks arising from acquisitions are partly the same as with other major strategic commitments, and they are related to an analysis of future market prospects and the ability to succeed with new ventures. In addition, the post-acquisition process may present unforeseen difficulties (see, e.g., Beusch 2007). There are also difficulties in predicting market reactions. An acquisition target will be known among its customers, suppliers and other stakeholders for various qualities, imagined or real. Often their reactions to an acquisition are difficult to predict and will determine whether an acquisition is successful (see, e.g., Öberg 2008). Risk may be categorized in a variety of ways, and several regulatory and professional frameworks exist, such as COSO (2004).

Both the board and the executive management team are expected to be deeply involved in the strategy-related process preceding and following an acquisition (Armour 2002; Parke 2007). When an acquisition fails, one may therefore suspect that the board and management of the purchasing firm have been so eager to complete the transaction that they have not adequately considered and managed the risks involved. Not infrequently, post-acquisition analysis is rather one-sided in its focus on the risks of failure that should have been avoided (cf., McNaught 2004). The concept of risk, however, also includes areas related to strategic risk, such as taking advantage of opportunities for creating new business.

EXPECTED GENERIC TYPES OF INTERNAL AUDITOR INVOLVEMENT IN ACQUISITIONS

Acquisition strategy entails assumptions about market reactions and emerging business trends. The due diligence process is intended to evaluate acquisition candidates, but there are obvious limits to the ability to uncover weaknesses (and evaluate potential for improvement); insufficient skill in managing integration may jeopardize acquisition outcomes for years to come. Ideally, all of these risks could fall within the scope of the internal auditor's continuous monitoring and risk analysis, and, if assessed as significant, become part of its audit agenda. Therefore it is reasonable to assume that the internal auditor could be involved in auditing acquisition projects and strategies both pre- and post-acquisition.

With the acquisition process as a point of departure, we anticipate that internal auditor involvement pre- and post-acquisition (cf., Calipha, Tarba, and Brock 2010) will differ along the three dimensions of strategy, risk, and control. Accordingly, these dimensions will be used to describe and analyze internal audit involvement and the way it relates to an overall focus as illustrated in Figure 6.1.

The acquisition *strategy* should affect both pre- and post-acquisition phases and ultimately the outcome of the acquisition (Jemison and Sitkin 1986). Internal auditors are involved in strategy if they focus on the formulation of acquisition strategies and/or the execution of such strategies. Providing assurance for addressing *risk* would generally seem more related to strategic types of risk preceding an acquisition, whereas it may be related mostly to operational types of risk later in the integration process (cf., COSO 2004; IIA 2007). An example of the former is the risk of a strategic misfit (Haspeslagh and Jemison 1991), and an example of the latter is the risk of failed system integration (see Beusch in this volume). Similarly, we argue that providing assurance early on in the process entails more preventive type of *control* (to prevent errors), whereas audits in later stages would typically provide a more detective type of control (to detect errors) (cf., Arwinge 2010; Pickett 2011).

Taken together, the involvement plotted on the left-hand side of the model would generally suggest an internal audit focus on design ('Are the firm's acquisition projects and related strategies appropriately formulated?'),

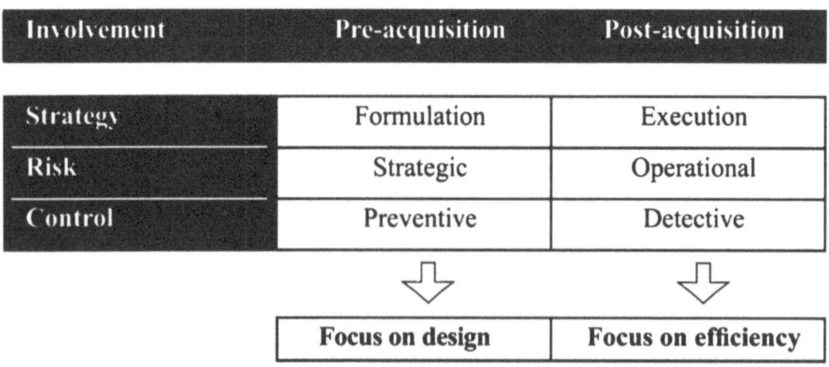

Figure 6.1 Expected generic types of internal auditor involvement in acquisitions.

whilst the right-hand side suggests a focus on efficiency ('Are the firm's acquisition projects and strategies being efficiently executed?') (cf., IIA 2011). The effective handling of strategic acquisitions would benefit from involvement in both columns.[3] The internal auditor may also combine the two columns, in which case there is audit activity in connection with both the formulation and the execution of acquisition initiatives. We will use Figure 6.1 when discussing our findings.[4]

RESEARCH DESIGN

The case study methodology was chosen for the following reasons. First, we focus on the acquisition process and the internal auditor's involvement in that process—especially the strategy-related activity preceding and following an acquisition. By using case studies, it is possible to acquire a tentative understanding of these processes at the chosen firms. This research design also enables us to obtain an overall picture, which can then be used to identify especially interesting aspects to address in greater detail in future studies (cf., Hägg and Hedlund 1979). Second, in our literature review we found surprisingly few empirical studies on how the involvement of the internal auditor relates to strategy, and specifically to acquisitions, despite its obvious relevance for both scholars and practitioners. The study can therefore be characterised as exploratory (cf., Yin 2003).

Because we are concerned primarily with the acquiring firm's internal auditors, we chose firms that we considered to have well-developed internal control and internal auditing. In other words, the firms were expected to put considerable emphasis on evaluating and improving their risk management processes and the principal risks that may significantly impair firm performance (IIA 2007, 2011), such as those that may arise from an acquisition. Because this study is explorative, we were also interested in investigating any differences in the involvement of the internal auditor following an acquisition. Therefore we chose to study the internal audit function at Swedish firms representing different industries, such as manufacturing of industrial products, high-tech security solutions, as well as insurance and banking. These companies and their internal audit function are described in Table 6.1. The interviews took place in the summer of 2010.

Five chief internal audit executives (henceforth referred to as chief audit executives) and one group acquisition process manager were interviewed. They were considered to have a good knowledge of how the acquiring firm handled the strategic risk inherent in acquisitions and especially the involvement of the internal auditors. All have long experience and are familiar with these questions, although it should be noted that some of them have occupied their present positions for only a couple of years. As a result, their knowledge of a specific acquisition activity at the companies studied may

Table 6.1 Basic Data of the Cases

Firm name	*Type of Business*	*International audit function*
Atlas Copco	Stationary compressors, construction and mining equipment, industrial tools, and assembly systems	7 auditors
If	Property and casualty insurance	18 auditors
Saab	Solutions for military defence and civil security	5 auditors
Sandvik	Tools for metal-cutting, mining and construction, products in advanced materials	16 auditors
Skandia	Insurance and bank	15 auditors

be somewhat limited. Some referred to experience in previous positions and with acquisitions in general. However, we do not consider this limitation to be a significant problem in the present study because we are interested in an overall basic understanding of internal auditor involvement in strategy-related activity at these firms.

The interviews were open-ended and lasted for about 90 minutes. As they were not tape-recorded and were conducted in Swedish, the quotations in the text are not exact replications of what was said by the interviewees. However, the quotations, as well as the description of the cases, have been read and approved by the interviewees.

INTERNAL AUDITOR INVOLVEMENT: FIVE CASES ON THE INTERNAL AUDIT FUNCTION

The following sections provide an account of the five cases (i.e., the internal audit function and the internal auditor involvement in acquisitions). They start with a short description of the company and its internal audit function. This is followed by accounts of some acquisition activities and the involvement of the internal auditor.

Atlas Copco

Atlas Copco is a global manufacturer of industrial products. The internal audit function has 7 employees specifically devoted to that function and spread over the world. In addition, 200 people throughout the organisation typically put in 2–3 weeks each on a project basis from time to time during a normal year.

The company has a decentralized structure, where eighteen divisions within three business areas handle their own acquisitions, which however require approval from business area management, group management and the board. There are usually six or seven acquisitions per year, but the number varies considerably if viewed over a longer period. One of their largest acquisitions to date is the Prime Service Corporation in 1997. It represented a new strategy focused on increasing revenues by also providing rental services to equipment users (www.atlascopco.se). However, this strategy was not a success, and the corporation was divested in 2006 (Sundberg 2009).

Partly because of the Acquisition process competence group, formed in 2002–2003, acquisitions are not a major task for the internal auditors. It consists of the Group controller, a legal counsel, and representatives of each of the three business areas, with the Group acquisition process manager as its executive. Its mission is to gather and utilize experience from past acquisitions, to convert it into useful learning and to feed this information back to the Atlas Copco organization in order to improve the quality of the acquisition process.

Before an acquisition project is presented to executive management and the board of directors, the Group acquisition process manager reviews proposals to determine whether they are reasonable. Consistency in financial forecasts is evaluated, as is documentation for assumptions about business growth and other variables that are important for acquisitions to be successful. Calculations are based on historical data (the three previous years), and projections are made for the next five. In a discounted cash flow valuation model, a value at the horizon is used to indicate the acquisition candidate's value at that point in time—as a theoretical sales value—in order to avoid the need for estimating even longer-term data. The strategic benefits must always be present, but there may be occasions when the strategic rationale is allowed to have an even stronger impact than the financial valuation on the decision whether to acquire the unit or not, for example, when a small manufacturer is meant to be used as a bridgehead into a new market. In spite of the acquisition database containing descriptions of the intended acquisition process, personal involvement by the Group acquisition process manager is needed:

> 'The formal responsibility for a particular acquisition project is with operational management, but I will raise a red flag if I sense unwarranted risk-taking. In emergencies I can inform group management and the responsible division management about my doubts. I or others in the Acquisition process competence group also provide coaching at an early stage of each attempted project as well as after closing the deal for the recently acquired unit'.
>
> (Group acquisition process manager)

On occasion, the internal auditors may assist in due diligence, but the existence of the Group acquisition process manager means that it is normally sufficient to involve the auditors only post-acquisition. These audits are made within 24 months after closing. Here the internal auditors may take part, but this mainly post-acquisition audit process is run by the Acquisition process competence group. A summary of each post-acquisition audit is presented to the board of directors. Each division is required to prepare a follow-up report 12 months after closing. This report is called the 'Integration Status Report' and is presented to the board of directors as well. Following acquisitions, the Chief audit executive would like to see early involvement by the internal audit function:

> 'The intention is to perform internal audits of acquired units within 6 months after closing. An internal employee survey is part of the integration follow-up and such surveys are performed 6, 12, 24 and 36 months after closing date. When a firm becomes part of the group, it is also subjected to yearly "control self-assessments" which general managers for all entities within the group are to fill in-although they may delegate some of this task to specialists within their unit. It is a set of approximately 350 questions where the local entity indicates whether they are in compliance or non-compliance with a number of group policies. This process is coordinated by the internal audit function'.
>
> (Chief audit executive)

Summarizing, as from 2004 Atlas Copco has formalized instructions, which are continuously developed for the acquisition process under the responsibility of the Group acquisition process manager. The internal auditors have limited contact with acquisitions until they are at a fairly advanced stage of integration. This arrangement fits well with the small size of this function and the decentralized structure.

If

The property and casualty insurer If P&C Insurance is headquartered in Sweden and active in eight North European countries. It is owned by Finnish group Sampo. The internal audit function in Sampo mostly concerns If, with the Chief audit executive of If also heading Sampo's internal audit function. There are 18 internal auditors at If.

Acquisition activities at If have been limited mainly to extending its presence in neighbouring countries. For instance, they bought the small Russian insurance company SOAO Region a few years ago (www.if.se). As some If customers had business in Russia, If followed them there and opened a representation office. Later they wanted to expand their business in that market through an acquisition. Sampo (the parent company of If) has decided that the internal auditors should concentrate on operational auditing, leaving the audit related to the financial statements solely to the external auditors.

Internal auditors at If thus focus on business processes. These should be consistent and their risks should be identified so that they can be discussed with those responsible. Therefore auditors need to understand the business. 'We must start with the business processes to predict what leads to business results', says the Chief audit executive. But it is not the role of the internal auditors to decide on risk levels or whether processes are acceptable. In these matters, the Chief audit executive refers to The Institute of Internal Auditor's International Professional Practices Framework (IPPF) as

> 'The Bible—but even biblical interpretations may always be discussed. And both our profession's and our companies' propensity to change are constraints. In the financial sector, it has been a tradition for internal auditors to be at the disposal of the external auditors, rather than performing the risk-based audit that is central according to IPPF'.
>
> (Chief audit executive)

The focus on processes means that the internal auditor's involvement in new ventures like acquisitions is limited to asking: Do they follow the project model as they should? There have also been specific checks on whether internal control is practiced as it should be in such projects. Applying these checks requires care, however, because as the Chief audit executive says, 'it is the core business processes and not the internal controls specifically that make the company function.' By focusing on conformity with processes, If's internal auditors must obviously also make sure that these are appropriate, and encourage changes if they are not:

> 'We fairly often suggest changes in processes and regulations. But it's "You might consider," not "Thou shalt". Internal audit does not make that decision!'
>
> (Chief audit executive)

This means that the involvement of internal auditors in acquisitions is very limited—maybe also because there have been too few acquisitions to develop extensive processes that could be audited. The Chief audit executive was informed about the acquisition in Russia and had access to the due diligence study, but did not visit the acquired company until the transaction was completed. It was a small company without any internal audit, and recruiting a local internal auditor and building up its internal audit function required most of her attention and effort, not least because of differences in national cultures.

With its focus on the operational audit, such changes must take into account all kinds of controls and be adapted to the business processes concerned. This implies that if acquisitions occurred more frequently at If, its internal audit function might propose more specific rules and regulations for how to handle them. This would be in line with the general view of the Chief audit executive that there is a growing demand for more explicit identification of risks so that board decisions will be more thoroughly considered.

Saab

Saab AB—unrelated to the car producer Saab Automobile AB—is a manufacturer of high tech security solutions. The internal audit function employs 5 people. They are not connected to any ongoing project or management assignments and report directly to the board.

Since 1999 the Saab group has been involved in several mergers and acquisitions. The most important one is the merger with Celsius in 1999, which temporarily increased Saab's degree of diversification. However, after 2003 the corporation changed from a portfolio strategy to a strategy based on activity-sharing (Nilsson 2010; www.saabgroup.com). This change in strategy could be one explanation why very few acquisitions have been made since 2007.

At Saab an acquisition is treated like any other risk. As the internal auditing function has limited resources, it is selective in taking on assignments. So far auditing has taken place only post-acquisition. Examples of typical questions addressed are: How was the decision to acquire made? Is the business case convincing? Are the contract terms acceptable? This type of analysis can show whether the managers have made decisions that are in the long-term interest of Saab:

> 'If a decision is made to acquire a firm without the proper analysis and preparations, we would criticize that decision. Sometimes I wonder if it is easier to buy a firm for 25 billion than a new machine for 1 million. A merger or an acquisition must be evaluated in relation to the goals of the group'.
>
> (Chief audit executive)

The interviewee stressed several times that the internal auditors help to increase transparency in regard to how decisions are made, as well as the risks and their effects. The auditors help the board to look behind the reports that the board members receive from management and in that way improve analysis and discussion of these reports. Another very important area is ensuring compliance with the law as well as company regulations and policies. The internal auditors have a strong focus on independent follow-up of decisions already made. This clearly affects their role in an acquisition:

> 'We should not become involved until the deal is done. We should not take part in the due diligence process [. . .] The reason is that we should be able to audit transactions without being involved. I must be able to stand in front of the board of directors and criticize the decisions made in the pre-acquisition phase. My integrity cannot be questioned [. . .] I look upon myself as an auditor. It all boils down to the importance of following certain rules and procedures. Of course there is also a more soft and

pro-active side to being an internal auditor. But in many cases it is not self-evident what we should audit'.

(Chief audit executive)

The interviewee considers acquisition decisions to be important and risky for the group, but difficult to audit. One reason seems to be the lack of clear rules and guidelines—especially for the integration process. Even goals and strategies can sometimes be a bit fuzzy. This tends to make the audit more difficult because it is hard to establish whether there is a fit or a misfit between the acquirer and the acquired firm.

On the other hand, when the acquisition process is not well developed, the internal auditor can contribute advice on how the process should be improved. By taking a process view, the auditor can concentrate on the structures and procedures affecting the decision-making, without risk of being involved or connected with the decisions made. It seems that a process view is also a way of standardizing learning, as the experience gained from earlier acquisitions will affect the design and use of processes and in that way institutionalize best practice. The following quote shows the interviewee's belief in the importance of process design and use:

> 'A well-designed process is a prerequisite for all sorts of creative work. It is a myth that great discoveries are the results of coincidence. This is not the case! It is no coincidence that a novel idea is developed. It is the result of a well-designed process'.
>
> (Chief audit executive)

To sum up, the internal audit at Saab is focused strictly on facts: to determine whether a decision was made according to rules and regulations. Because it is difficult to evaluate whether an acquisition was a success or a failure, most decisions prepared and made according to the Group's best practice are accepted. A typical comment in the auditor's report—often the comment is no longer than a few sentences—would be that a decision during the pre-acquisition phase was made by someone who did not have the authority to make that decision.

Sandvik

Sandvik is a global manufacturer of tools for metal-cutting, mining, and construction equipment as well as advanced materials. The internal audit function consists of three groups focusing on financial reporting, IT and compliance. In total the function employs 16 people.

The company has been involved in many acquisitions. Some of these were very large, such as the acquisition of Tamrock. This acquisition was instrumental in developing a strong position in the mining and construction industry. In Sandvik an acquisition should always, as in the case of Tamrock, be strongly related to one of the business areas and their strategies. An acquired firm is expected to contribute to group earnings within two years (www.sandvik.se).

The importance of the strategy and the risk management process was mentioned several times during the interview. In this process possible acquisitions should always be discussed. According to the interviewee, the Sandvik executive management team has a very good knowledge of their businesses and possible acquisition candidates. Sometimes investment banks present novel strategic ideas, but their strength usually lies in valuation and facilitation of a deal. According to the interviewee, the strategy process at Sandvik is the starting point:

> 'An acquisition could be a possible solution to fill an identified "gap" in the strategy. I consider this process to be very important and it is always done in a serious manner and with a long-term outlook. It is not worthwhile to propose an acquisition that does not fit with the long-term strategy'.
>
> (Chief audit executive)

However, the involvement of the internal auditors in this connection has so far been limited. At Sandvik the planning of the audit always starts with an analysis of the business and support processes. Based on a discussion with the business areas, staff functions, and the external auditors, a risk map is produced. The Enterprise risk management process is focused on likelihood and impact of important activities. According to the interviewee, an acquisition is only one of several risks:

> 'Our way of managing risk is working well. We only buy companies that we know very well and that fit our present business. For example, our Mining and Construction business bought three firms in the mineral exploration business. Very soon we had achieved a leading position. Of course we had a very specific goal with these three acquisitions: to diversify up-stream in order to establish contact with our customers in the mining industry at an early stage. Most of our acquisitions follow this pattern'.
>
> (Chief audit executive)

So far some auditing has been done in regard to the integration process. Because Sandvik is a multinational company, pursuing many international acquisitions, the total risk exposure in this respect is considerable. The audits of the integration process have identified some weaknesses which should be avoided in the future. One example is that the cultural differences between the acquirer and the acquired firm can be enormous and are easy to underestimate.

The involvement of the internal auditing function in the pre-acquisition process has so far been non-existent at Sandvik. One reason is that a typical acquisition is a rapid process involving a few people on the board and in top management positions. Another reason is that the internal auditors have focused on scrutinizing the strategy process—especially how goals and strategies at the group level are implemented at lower organizational levels. The interviewee summarizes his view of the involvement of internal auditors in the strategy process as follows:

> 'It would be possible for us to have an opinion about how an acquired firm fits together with the Sandvik group. But to have such an opinion before the deal is closed? For me it is hard to imagine a situation in which Sandvik would acquire a firm that did not fit our strategy, considering all the effort we put into the strategy process. How could an internal auditor audit the risks connected with a certain strategy? You do not talk about strategies in the audit committee! And where is the line drawn between the internal auditor and the controller in this respect? There are many important activities that could (and perhaps should) be audited. For example, how well do we succeed with our R&D-projects? About 4 percent of group sales is invested in these important projects. We have not done much auditing in that area either. Are we really competent to audit R&D?'
>
> (Chief audit executive)

Skandia

Skandia is an insurance and banking company (www.skandia.se). Skandia was acquired by Old Mutual in 2006 (www.oldmutual.com), following a turbulent period in which several top managers were accused of fraud and tax violations. The internal audit function at Skandia is part of the business unit Nordic within the Old Mutual group and employs 15 people. IT auditing is organized as a separate function covering all business units. There is also an independent risk management function.

After the takeover Skandia has not been involved in any acquisition. The primary reason is a strong focus on the process of integrating the large Skandia group into Old Mutual; lack of financial strength is also a factor. Some potential acquisition targets have been subjected to a due diligence process, but the finding was that they did not fit the Skandia and Old Mutual strategies.

At Skandia an acquisition is more or less to be considered as any other risk. The Chief audit executive stresses that during the pre-acquisition phase (e.g., the due diligence) the first priority is to establish whether the target is financially sound. Is the reporting structure designed in such a way that the financial result can be considered credible? The internal auditors must ensure that the board receives reliable and transparent data for their decision-making. This requirement includes not only accounting information, but also the determination whether the target fits the strategic profile of the business:

> 'As internal auditors we must, generally speaking, understand the strategy process. I must therefore maintain close contact with the managing director of Skandia in order to understand company strategies. There are strategies at several levels and I must understand them to be able to perform an audit. We must be one step ahead—to understand the risks and how they can be handled. We do not care about the strategic decisions. If a decision has been taken we must follow it up to see whether it is implemented [. . .] Here you can find the dividing line between an internal auditor and a business controller. The latter has the full responsibility. We can capture what has happened but also identify the risks'.
>
> (Chief audit executive)

To identify risks is also the focus in the integration phase. The interviewee cited the integration between Skandia and Old Mutual as an example. One risk is that subsidiaries will not follow the rules and procedures of the group. At the same time the internal auditors must consider the important differences in business culture between the two firms—for example, in regard to the view of the customer relationship. What is considered a risk in one part of the world is not always a risk in Sweden. Another risk is that the top management will not realize the challenges of integrating a large firm such as Skandia into the group. To begin with, the strategies were somewhat unclear, although there were some very clear goals. This has now changed:

> 'What we have done, and what we can do, is to increase transparency. In a merger or an acquisition the main question is whether it makes sense to own this firm? For us it is natural to always think of the business logic'.
>
> (Chief audit executive)

During the interview, the interviewee returned several times to the role of the internal auditors. She considered it very important that they be pro-active, in other words that they identify and communicate what may happen, not only what has happened. In her view, the internal auditor is in a position to have considerable influence on the decisions made in the organization. In this position, the auditor faces numerous requirements: to be knowledgeable about the business, to have good judgement and to be socially competent. She views such requirements as part of a trend that has grown during the last couple of years. At the same time, she recognizes the importance of the 'tone at the top'. Both in Old Mutual and in Skandia, there is a lot of interest in the internal audit function and a lot of encouragement to be pro-active:

> 'We [the internal auditors] do not have an opinion about strategies, but on the other hand we cannot just silently watch faulty decisions being made.

Imagine, for example, that according to the strategy cost effectiveness must improve. How do you manage such a situation? We cannot limit our role to auditing this in retrospect and finding that it did not work! [. . .] To have an opinion about strategy also increases the demands on the internal auditor. It makes the audit more complicated—we see a lot of risks, but many of them we cannot manage. However, just to be aware of them has significant value. [. . .] We have gone from being an "auditing machine" to becoming much more qualified'.

(Chief audit executive)

DISCUSSION AND CONCLUSIONS

We now turn to the common tendencies that we have identified through comparing the involvement of the internal auditor in acquisitions. The comparison is based on the account of the five cases of internal audit functions. They will be related here to the model (see Figure 6.1) that was introduced earlier in this chapter.

In general, acquisition processes receive little attention from internal auditors, whose primary involvement is post-acquisition—after the acquisition has been decided and most analyses, due diligences and decisions have been made. Integration will then have been going on for several months, and the internal auditor's focus will be on reviewing how the specific acquisition strategy is being implemented. At this stage, the internal auditor's attention is similar to that given to other group businesses; the question is then whether the newly acquired business unit has adopted the group's processes for handling risks. The internal auditor may, however, also view the pre-acquisition phase retrospectively. Saab's interviewee stresses that he should not get involved as an auditor in a due diligence process, but may in retrospect criticize decisions earlier in the process that have been based on inadequate data.

Strategy. In general, the interviewees found it important to understand the strategy process, but they do not regard it as their task to question the outcome (such as an acquisition decision) as long as the process is followed. 'You do not talk about strategies in the audit committee', Sandvik's interviewee commented, and his colleague at Skandia also emphasized that internal auditors should not be concerned with the acquisition decision, but with the underlying strategy process that is set up in order to produce and manage such decisions. Strategy is thus important for internal auditors in at least two ways: to understand the objectives and direction of the business, and for reviewing to determine whether strategy processes have been adequately designed or effectively adhered to. In general, it is our impression that the focus of internal auditors is more on the execution of strategy rather than on the design and content of strategy.

Risk. The interviewees at Saab, Sandvik and Skandia agreed that an acquisition may involve risks, but that these should be treated just like any other risk. The internal auditor should therefore prioritize risks according to likelihood and impact. Strategic risks, such as those concerning decisions related to corporate and business strategy, as well as operational risks, thus fall within the scope of the audit. Overall, however, there was a tendency among the interviewees to focus more on operational risk linked to acquisition initiatives, for example, the risk that an integration process may not be efficiently carried out.

Control. In Figure 6.1 we distinguished between preventive and detective controls. Although it is debatable whether the internal audit represents a form of control, we argue that audits in various ways may be characterized as more preventive or more detective, depending on the general timing and scope of their activities. Preventive audits, for example, may provide control to assure that acquisition candidates conform to group strategy, or that acquisition projects have been set up adequately and according to established group processes. This type of early audit was not discussed much by our interviewees, whereas reviewing integration processes received at least some attention. In this way, it is fair to describe the internal audit involvement in our five cases as more detective than preventive from a control point of view.

We had expected to find some significant differences between the cases, but overall the companies are located on the right hand side of Figure 6.1, where the focus is on reviewing strategy execution during the post-acquisition process. Partly as a consequence, the risks subject to review are more of an operational nature. We also argue that the involvement of the internal auditors in general could be considered more detective than preventive, as it mostly comes into play after critical go/no-go decisions have been made and the acquisition initiatives are being, or have been, carried out. We thus conclude that the internal auditors in our case firms were focused on strategy execution rather than on design in the strategy formulation phase.

We will now extend our discussion about possible reasons why the involvement of internal auditors in acquisitions is so limited. A number of issues may explain this situation and the type of involvement which the case firms exhibit. We will consider three such issues: *the importance of independence; information flows between stakeholders;* and *complex and non-routine processes.* They were identified during our analysis and in our discussions, which were based on the interviews but also on observations in light of our general understanding of mergers and acquisitions, governance and internal control as well as stakeholder theory.

The importance of independence. Objectivity and independence are important for internal auditors (IIA 2011: 16). Any conflicts or potential impairments in regard to such values must be addressed by the internal auditors according to set standards and practice advisories. The interviewees testify to this requirement, which is likely to be a factor tending to limit their involvement early in acquisition processes. If internal auditors were involved when acquisition projects and strategies are established, they might become too closely involved in the decision-making process. The internal auditor must remain objective and independent, as usually prescribed by regulatory texts, and thus not be involved in making business decisions and assuming operational responsibilities. This point is stressed several times in the interviews.

Protecting independence is likely to be more difficult when providing assurance for risks in the pre-acquisition phase—both when auditing the acquisition set-up, and when reviewing the way in which the underlying business case is examined and approved by specialists, the executive management team and the board. With this arm-length's principle, it is not surprising that the internal auditors have limited involvement in the strategy-related activity preceding an acquisition.

Information flows between stakeholders. Another factor limiting the involvement of the internal auditor is decentralized decision-making. Many acquisitions are small and local, and as long as the prescribed processes are followed, local management should be given time to show what they can accomplish. In our study, and perhaps most clearly in Skandia, strategic risks, such as those connected with ineffective acquisition processes and related transactions, are treated like any other risk. Thus, such risks form a part of the risk universe and potentially the audit agenda as well. But they should be managed in a way appropriate to decentralized decision-making, taking into account the information flows between internal stakeholders: all employees from corporate board members to local managers.

In the pre-acquisition phase, few of these managers were involved, and for companies that stressed decentralized responsibilities (in our study, particularly Atlas Copco) it is considered wrong for corporate group functions to step in—except to make sure that intended procedures are followed and that group knowledge is applied. In the post-acquisition phase, normal internal audit practices will sooner or later run their course. But in addition to these, internal auditors might help their firms to learn from acquisitions and perhaps to redirect the continuing processes of integrating acquired firms. Are the intentions for the acquisition being fulfilled? Were pre-acquisition estimates correct? Except for Atlas Copco, which has a special team focused on group learning, we had expected more involvement from internal auditors in answering such questions.

Input regarding significant acquisition risks may typically originate from the board, if not identified by the internal auditor or the business. The process of identifying and approving risks that should be subject to review by audit thus seems based largely on communication and input from the board and executive management. Any shortcomings in the internal auditor's work, specifically related to the pre-acquisition phase, may thus be a result of the earlier risk analysis process and the input provided by stakeholders such as the board, its audit committee and its management.

Complex and non-routine processes. A third issue relates to the inherent complexity of the acquisition processes. Even though these processes may be documented and standardized, they are non-routine compared to 'conventional' core business processes, such as procurement, sales, manufacturing, or accounting. Many auditors may be more used to reviewing compliance with regulations concerning fair treatment of customers in the sales process, or reviewing internal control over payment or accounting processes, than auditing a process that occurs very irregularly, is strategic and complex and thus less standardized. Auditing complex acquisition processes, both pre- and post-acquisition, presents some formidable challenges to any internal auditor.

One aspect of these challenges relates to the kind of data that the internal auditor is capable of reviewing and evaluating. Should the internal auditor limit her-/himself to formal correctness, i.e., compliance with established group policies, processes, and the review of related key controls, or is it possible to go further and consider the content of strategy—in particular the risks entailed? Based on our cases, the answer is apparently to adhere to the first alternative: formal correctness. The testimony of auditors suggests that their focus is on compliance with set policies, processes and related controls without actually taking a position on the content of strategy (i.e., the acquisition-related decisions), but rather limiting their opinion to how decisions were made. There is, however, no clear-cut line between the two, and auditors in fact become involved in strategy in order to understand risks and related controls. Seemingly there is still a distinction between process and content, and any opinions regarding the content of acquisition strategy are out-of-scope for auditors. But the soft character of acquisition-processes and related controls may be difficult enough to audit without having to pay attention to real content, with typical and 'harder' controls replaced by controls that are softer in nature.

Taken together, these three issues—the importance of independence, information flows between stakeholders, and the complexity of non-routine processes—seem to provide good reasons why the internal auditor's involvement in the acquisitions covered by our cases has been concentrated largely in the post-acquisition phase, at least up until now. These reasons do not, however, prove that this situation is desirable for the future. This issue is part of a broader question: how should the expertise available to a firm be accessed and applied in acquisitions in order to handle the associated risks in a well-considered and effective way? Now, in the final section of this chapter, we turn to the implications for internal auditing in this regard.

MANAGERIAL IMPLICATIONS

The study shows that internal auditors are mainly involved post-acquisition, providing assurance for integration, and particularly that the recently acquired firm will adopt the processes of its new corporate group. Should this degree and type of involvement surprise us? Not really, given the three issues that were identified earlier (the importance of independence, information flows between stakeholders, and complex non-routine processes). Should internal auditors increase their involvement? Their professional status as risk experts in large organizations should mean that their competence in matters of risk and control (as well as other areas such as accounting and IT) could be highly useful in significant acquisition projects. As acquisitions are risky, as indicated in the beginning of the chapter, perhaps the board and its audit committee, or the executive management team, could make better use of the internal auditors earlier on in acquisition processes. In addition, as internal auditing is both an independent assurance activity and a consulting activity, there seems to be room for the internal auditor to take on more responsibility as advisors in acquisition projects.

In the opinion of our interviewees, performing credible and useful internal audits seems to involve the recurring application of specified procedures, rather than unique applications of risk-assessment knowledge in one-of-a-kind situations. Internal auditors are surrounded by regulations and standards and are increasingly seen as support for a corporation's board rather than its management, with independence as a key value. This may preclude any strong involvement in individual acquisitions. However, as internal auditors are advising the board on risks, they may well consider extending their involvement to acquisitions, as risks associated with these often have a strong impact on the acquiring corporation's prospects: not only in terms of its forecast profits, but also its possible future growth, reputation, and any legal and workplace problems. In addition, the integration process itself presents risks of unforeseen incompatibilities of systems, processes, and culture (Beusch and Schweizer in this volume). Here we are not marketing an extension of the internal auditor's focus in connection with acquisition initiatives, but just pointing out that in view of the competence of internal auditors as risk and control experts, more extensive (and preventive) auditing may be appropriate earlier in acquisition processes. Following the stakeholder view held in this book, several other risk-related group-wide functions in large firms, such as risk management or compliance, might be considered in a similar way.

We undertook this investigation in order to learn more about the involvement of internal auditors in acquisitions. Obviously the five cases do not provide a sufficient basis for general recommendations. Yet our results furnish some important clues about internal audit activity in acquisition initiatives. In particular, they highlight the fact that who is involved, when and for what purpose, may have received too little attention in the discussion on acquisitions—among both researchers and practitioners. It has long been noted that competence in the area of acquisitions needs to be nurtured and may be a competitive asset, but it usually resides in few people near the corporate apex. A more systematic treatment of risks related to acquisitions may require involvement of a broader group, as well as systematic application of risk management skills.

ACKNOWLEDGEMENTS

The research upon which this chapter is based was partly financed by the Jan Wallander and Tom Hedelius Foundation and the Tore Browaldh Foundation.

NOTES

1. This chapter focuses on acquisitions, but our reasoning could also be applied to mergers.
2. We use the term internal auditor throughout the chapter to include both the individual as well as the function.
3. We see a parallel to the need to distinguish between different 'Value for money audits'. For a recent proposed frame-work for illustrating this distinction, see Grönlund, Svärdsten, and Öhman (2011).
4. A focus on efficient handling of acquisitions—on the right—presupposes that risks have been adequately considered and communicated in the pre-acquisition phase on the left. Given the profession's recent ambitions to support boards and managements with an independent view of major risks, ambitious internal auditors may consider focusing also on the left-hand column. See the section 'Managerial Implications' at the end of this chapter.

REFERENCES

Allegrini, M., D`Onza, G., Paape, L., Melville, R., and Sarens G. (2006) 'The European literature review on internal auditing', *Managerial Auditing Journal*, 21: 845–53.

Armour, E. (2002) 'How boards can improve the odds of M&A success', *Strategy & Leadership*, 30: 13–20.

Arwinge, O. (2010) *Internal Control—A Study of the Concept and Themes of Internal Control*, Licentiate thesis No. 1431, Linköping Studies in Science and Technology, Linköping University.

Bank for International Settlement (BIS)—Basel Committee on Banking Supervision (2011) *Basel III: A global regulatory framework for more resilient banks and banking systems*, December 2010, Rev. June 2011, see www.bis.org, information retrieved January 2012.

Beusch, P. (2007) *Contradicting Management Control Ideologies—A Study of Integration Processes Following Cross-border Acquisitions of Large Multinationals*, Doctoral Thesis, BAS Publishing.

Beusch, P. (Chapter 7 in this volume) 'When the Integration of Management Control Systems Is at Stake—Experience from the Car Industry'.

Calipha, R., Tarba, S., and Brock, D. (2010) 'Mergers and acquisitions: A review of phases, motives, and success factors', *Advances in Mergers and Acquisitions*, 9: 1–24.

Capriotti, P. (2009) 'Economic and social roles of companies in the mass media: The impact media visibility has on businesses' being recognized as economic and social actors', *Business & Society*, 48: 225–42.

COSO (Committee of Sponsoring Organizations of the Treadway Commission) (2004) *Enterprise Risk Management—Integrated Framework, Executive Summary*, New York: AICPA.

Donaldson, T. (2007) 'Closing reflection: "Ethical blowback": the missing piece in the corporate governance puzzle—the risks to a company which fails to understand and respect its social contract', *Corporate Governance*, 7: 534–41.

Dounis, N.P. (2008) 'The auditor's role in mergers and acquisition', *Internal Auditor*, June: 61–63.

European Union (2009) 'Directive 2009/138/EC of the European Parliament and of the Council of 25 November 2009 on the taking-up and pursuit of the business of Insurance and Reinsurance (Solvency II)', *Official Journal of the European Union*, 17.12.2009.

Freeman R.E., Harrison, J.S., Wicks, A.C., Bidhan, L.P., and De Colle S. (2010) *Stakeholder Theory: The State of the Art*, Cambridge: Cambridge University Press.

Grant Thornton (2009) 'Corporate governance series: Enterprise risk management: Creating value in a volatile economy', available at www.grantthornton.com.

Gramling, A.A. and Myers, P.M. (2006) 'Internal auditing's role in ERM', *Internal Auditor*, 63: 52–58.

Grönlund, A., Svärdsten, F., and Öhman, P. (2011) 'Value for money and the rule of law: the (new) performance audit in Sweden', *International Journal of Public Sector Management*, 24: 107–21.

Hägg, I. and Hedlund, G. (1979) 'Case studies' in accounting research', *Accounting, Organizations and Society*, 4: 135–43.

Haspeslagh P.C. and Jemison, D.B. (1991) *Managing Acquisitions: Creating Value through Corporate Renewal*, New York: The Free Press.

Hass, S., Abdolmohammadi, M.J., and Burnaby, P. (2006) 'The Americas literature review on internal auditing', *Managerial Auditing Journal*, 21: 835–44.

Hutter, B. and Power, M. (eds.) (2005) *Organizational Encounters with Risk*, Cambridge: Cambridge University Press.

IIA 2003. The Institute of Internal Auditors (2003) *Internal Audit Reporting Relationships: Serving two Masters*, The IIA Research Foundation.

IIA 2007. The Institute of Internal Auditors (2007) *Internal Auditing: Assurance & Consulting Services*, The IIA Research Foundation.

IIA 2011. The Institute of Internal Auditors (2011) *International Professional Practices Framework (IPPF)*, 2011 Edition, The IIA Research Foundation.

Jemison, D.B. and Sitkin, S.B. (1986) 'Corporate acquisitions: A process perspective', *Academy of Management Review*, 11: 145–63.

Maijoor, S. (2000) 'The internal control explosion', *International Journal of Auditing*, 4: 101–9.

McNaught, T. (2004) 'Most M&As fail! Success lies in asking the right questions', *New Zealand Management*, 51: 41–42.

Mikes, A. (2009) 'Risk management and calculative cultures', *Management Accounting Research*, 20: 18–40.

Miller, S., David, H., and David, W. (2008) 'From strategy to action. Involvement and influence in top level decisions', *Long Range Planning*, 41: 606–28

Nilsson, E.B. (2010) *Strategi, styrning och konkurrenskraft: En longitudinell studie av Saab AB*, Doctoral Thesis No. 1318, Linköping Studies in Science and Technology, Linköping University.

Öberg, C. (2008) *The Importance of Customers in Mergers and Acquisitions*, Doctoral Thesis No. 1193, Linköping University.

Pablo, A.L, Sitkin, S.B., and Jemison, D.B. (1996) 'Acquisition decision-making processes: The central role of risk', *Journal of Management*, 22: 723–46.
Parke, C. (2007) 'Keeping control—A board's role in M&A', *New Zealand Management*, 54: 80–81.
Pickett, K.H.S. (2011) *The Essential Guide to Internal Auditing*, Chichester: Wiley.
Power, M. (2007) *Organized Uncertainty: Designing a World of Risk Management*, Oxford: Oxford University Press.
Power, M., Scheytt, T., Soin, K., and Sahlin, K. (2009) 'Reputational risk as logic of organizing in late modernity', *Organization Studies*, 30: 301–24.
Risberg, A. (Chapter 13 in this volume) 'The Stake of High Failure Rates in Mergers and Acquisitions'.
Sarens, G. and De Beelde, I. (2006) 'Internal auditors´ perceptions about their role in risk management: A comparison between US and Belgian companies', *Managerial Auditing Journal*, 21: 63–80.
Schweizer, R. (Chapter 4 in this volume) 'The Arranged Marriage Syndrome—Challenges to Subsidiary Managers during the Integration Process between Two Merging Multinational Companies'.
Spira, L.F. and Page, M. (2003) 'Risk management: The reinvention of internal control and the changing role of internal audit', *Accounting, Auditing & Accountability Journal*, 16: 640–61.
Stokhof, P. (2008) 'Risk responsibilities', *Internal Auditor*, August: 21–25.
Sundberg, K. (2009) *Atlas Copcos strategi och styrning: Verktyg som ger guld*, Licentiate Thesis No. 48. Department of Business Studies, Uppsala University.
The Swedish Financial Supervisory Authority [Finansinspektionen] (2011) *Risks in the Financial System 2011* [Risker i det finansiella systemet 2011], November 15, 2011.
Tramp, J. (1998) 'Thriving on change: The internal auditors role in mergers and acquisitions', *Journal of Accountancy*, April: 33–36.
www.atlascopco.se, information retrieved during the summer of 2010.
www.if.se, information retrieved during the summer of 2010.
www.oldmutual.com, information retrieved during the summer of 2010.
www.saabgroup.com, information retrieved during the summer of 2010.
www.sandvik.se, information retrieved during the summer of 2010.
www.skandia.se, information retrieved during the summer of 2010.
Yin, R.K. (2003) *Case Study Research: Design and Methods*, Newbury Park: Sage.

7 When the Integration of Management Control Systems Is at Stake

Experience from the Car Industry

Peter Beusch

INTRODUCTION

Mergers and acquisitions have been a strategy in the automobile industry since its earliest days. Growing technological complexity and ever-shortening product life-cycles have long forced automobile producers to enter various kinds of alliances and production networks. During the 1990s and thereafter, limited organic growth potential and industry overcapacity of more than 25 percent worldwide (KPMG 2010) led many car companies to believe that mergers and acquisitions were the only option for realizing their growth targets. During the last decade increased competition among automobile producers has put greater pressure on prices and favoured consumer demand for a wider variety of car models (MacNeill and Chanaron 2005; Orsato and Wells 2007). As a consequence, profit margins for many vehicle manufacturers have dropped, and economies of scale and reaching high plant utilization have become even more crucial in the new millennium.

Automobile firms have typically tried to bundle rather than destroy brands, a possible reason why consolidation issues in the car industry may not have been as obvious to customers as in many other industries. In 2005, for example, the three car companies of General Motors, Ford, and DaimlerChrysler alone accounted for some 30 different brands (www.OICA.net). Thus, it has been and still is essential for acquirers to integrate operations and processes across brands so that customers would not notice if anything negative happened to their favoured brand. As a result of shrinking margins, the striving for economies of scale across different car brands within the same company, achieved with the aid of common features and parts, has become an increasingly important strategic weapon in recent decades.

The new millennium, however, also revealed a new trend after several large car companies, which had collected some of the finest car brands and incorporated them into their consolidated financial structure, had to sell some of their brands, which were often well-known, usually at a heavy loss and to almost unknown car manufacturers in the Orient or to capital investment firms. In most recent years alone, several unsuccessful partnerships were formed, of which the following are only examples: BMW sold off the MG Rover Group at a large loss in 2000. GM, on the other hand, had to buy its way out of the 'put' option held by Fiat in 2005, and DaimlerChrysler divested its interests in Hyundai and Mitsubishi before they separated in a remarkable reverse of fortune in 2007. Most notable might have been Ford's last few major business deals, with the sale of Aston Martin in 2007, Jaguar and Land Rover in 2008, and finally Volvo Cars in March 2010 in what has been called 'China's biggest overseas auto deal' (Kinnander and Naughton 2010).

These cases exemplify that merged multi-brand car companies rather often fail to realise the intended cost savings and economies of scale. Value was destroyed rather than created, often because of miscarried and inappropriate integration of largely technology-based automobile consolidations. Managing product variety at the same time as achieving economies of scale and scope with different brands after mergers and acquisitions is a complex task that can magnify human error and thus heighten the risk of negative system performance (Hu et al. 2008) or even the risk of irreparable brand corrosion (Strach and Everett 2006).

The principal explanation for the break-up of the DaimlerChrysler marriage in 2007, for example, was that top management overestimated the synergies attainable between Mercedes' premium position cars and Chrysler's more mainstream models (Badrtalei and Bates 2007; Blasko, Netter, and Sinkey 2000; Bradford 2007; Krebs 2007). According to the authors, there was simply too little overlap to permit scale economies. Additional factors contributing to the divorce were that the two companies were not equals, as proposed in the beginning, and that intercultural communication was heavily underscored by management.

Similar reasons may explain the break-up of the Ford brand family that was built up mainly during the 1990s. In 2010, the American car producer, which only three years earlier was the proud owner of the four premium brands with a European heritage—Aston Martin, Jaguar, Land Rover, and Volvo—was left with its 'almost presidential' Lincoln premium brand after the phase-out of Mercury. In both cases, aligning and integrating brands with different strategic positions (cost leadership versus differentiation), together with the often different cultural heritage of important stakeholder groups, seem to have been major obstacles to success.

THE AIM AND METHOD OF THIS CHAPTER

Volvo Cars (from now on called *VOLVO*) was acquired in 1999 by *FORD*, the American car manufacturer and about ten times larger than *VOLVO*. The acquisition was the starting point for a long series of projects in the management control area,[1] mainly at *VOLVO*, for the purpose of integrating the accounting and finance functions of the two companies. By extension, this was supposed to lead to better accounting and calculation methods, primarily to support and improve brand integration and common product development, but also to find the optimum level of product variety in the two brands.

The aim of this chapter is to illustrate some of the complexity involved when management control systems were supposed to be integrated by actors with different perspectives and cultural heritages and to highlight the difficulties that arose in trying to achieve economies of scale and scope. These difficulties were due to the complicated balancing act of *VOLVO* managers as they tried to adjust to the new owner's strategy and at the same time achieve the situational adaptation that *VOLVO*'s own brand strategy was designed to bring about.[2]

The focus is on the experience of two different stakeholder groups: management control system designers who represent their respective former owners, *VOLVO* and *FORD*, with each applying particular mindsets and logic. The material in this chapter emerged from interviews with 31 key designers of management control systems, 22 of them Swedish and 'old' *VOLVO* employees and nine expatriates sent to Sweden by *FORD*, all of Anglo-Saxon origin.[3] All 31 interviewed actors, except one head of HR, were responsible for integrating financial and business control issues. All belonged to 'middle' or upper management, depending on the point of view (the entire *FORD* sphere or only *VOLVO*). Included were a CFO and a chief controller, some accounting heads and some project managers charged with integrating accounting and finance issues. Most interviewees were members of the 'Finance Leadership Team' and hence responsible for designing and implementing a management control system at *VOLVO* that was supposed to be 'as integrated as possible' into *FORD*.

The interviews were conducted between 2003 and 2006. Each interview lasted between 45 minutes and two hours, and all were tape recorded and transcribed. Loosely structured interview techniques were used, mostly to ask about the interviewees' experience of what was and had been going on in regard to the acquisition and the post-acquisition processes. This approach was combined with follow-up and probing but also specifying questions intended to reduce misunderstandings and to help comprehend the complex social phenomenon under study (e.g., Qu and Dumay 2011).

In addition to conducting the interviews, company reports and other written materials were studied to capture the explicitly stated aims and tasks but also corporate values and ideologies that normally appear in such documents (Schein 2001).

Prior empirical merger and acquisition research has focused strongly on issues related to system integration (e.g., Brown, Clancy, and Scholer 2003; Carlsson and Henningsson 2007; Granlund 2003) or human and cultural integration (e.g., documented in Cartwright and Schoenberg 2006; Shimizu et al. 2004). The diversity of problems involved when both areas (systems and people) are studied simultaneously has habitually been overlooked, though (Beusch 2007). This chapter is therefore intended to demonstrate that sharing parts after acquisitions, above all when the companies pursue different major strategies (cost leadership versus differentiation), entails not only benefits associated with product development costs and life-cycle time reductions, but also enormous challenges in form of finding a common way to deal with product variety and costs of complexity.

The reasons for this are mainly connected to the fact that rather rationally planned and considered areas, such as product development, actually involve very little technique but a lot of communication (Bragd 2002: 2). This is the case because the built-in product logic is often the result of the interaction between different generations of actors, some outside but most inside the organization. These personnel may be car designers and engineers, but for most questions they were financial and accounting managers, the particular group reported on in this chapter, because they were responsible for the design of the management control system at *VOLVO*.

The content of the chapter is based on the assumption that reality combines (at least) four aspects, namely, 'facts, possibilities, values and communication,' which need to be integrated in order to address validity (Norreklit, Norreklit, and Israelsen 2006: 42). Hence, this chapter is built on the presumption that reality is an integrated construct when applied pragmatically in organizations or other social settings and when dealing with situationally relevant activities, problems, thoughts, and actions, such as the work of integration after acquisitions, referred to by Norreklit, Norreklit, and Israelsen (2006: 42) as a 'pragmatic constructive approach'. The essence of this approach is to gain a better understanding of the distinction between physical and social phenomena, but also the connection in-between the two, and to be able to describe human action, organizational activity, and social relationships as something in which individuals are actively involved.[4]

All organizational practices include elements of communication and applying certain logics and value schemes (e.g., Vaara 2001, 2002). Therefore, two interconnected communication issues are presented in this chapter. The first has to do with the inherent logic of the two brands' different Part Number Systems and the communication required between these systems in order to generate common accounting and financial data. The Part Number System is a way to describe and identify the different raw materials, parts and products with codes containing numbers and letters, often between 6 and 36 digits long.[5] A typical car consists of more than 30,000 parts; thus, part numbers are seen as the key to all flows of materials from production to distribution and as a component essential for brand integration and optimal product variety.

The second issue deals with the communication between the management control system designers, who include the Swedish *VOLVO* managers and the newly arrived expatriates from the old *FORD* sphere. Ultimately, this case is also about different managers' ways of viewing and describing the reality experienced during the integration attempts, a factor that has a fundamental impact on all decision making and thus on the outcome of mergers and acquisitions.

The remainder of this chapter is organized as follows: the next section begins by introducing some issues related to the two companies' different business strategies and simultaneous attempts to achieve product variety and commonality, resulting in high complexity. Complexity is also the main reason why further problems arise. There is a need for a common Part Number System for *FORD* and *VOLVO*, as will be illustrated in the section thereafter. Then the real system alignment and the Part Number System solutions chosen follow in the subsequent section. A more detailed discussion and analysis of the integration, with the aid of the reality construct of Norreklit, Norreklit, and Israelsen (2006), introduced earlier, will be provided thereafter, before the concluding section with final comments on what happened to product variety and the brand alignment work at *VOLVO*.

BUSINESS STRATEGY, PRODUCT VARIETY, COMMONALITY, AND COMPLEXITY

FORD and *VOLVO* are both old companies founded back in the beginning of the last century. Historically, *VOLVO* was a Swedish enterprise that started with a European distribution channel. From the 1970s onward, the channel became a global network of highly decentralised marketing and sales companies. Management at *VOLVO* was firmly rooted in Sweden, and the company's historical background had promoted certain types of behaviour while discouraging others. Delegating power to the marketing and sales companies, where business was conducted, and entrusting them with broad freedom of action, was an important factor in the control philosophy of *VOLVO*.

Output control, or controlling ends rather than means, was the philosophy at *VOLVO*, and as long as managers 'brought home the money', the situation was accepted, because this tolerance was thought to engender a feeling of 'doing good business' and 'being good businessmen' in most places. Because the *VOLVO* brand was supposed to be perceived as part of the premium segment, the core strategy was to maintain a premium price position. The role of finance and accounting was to support and to 'sell' solutions to business areas only. The accounting and finance managers were seen as financial business partners with other functions, but not as representing much of a function themselves.

In stark contrast, *FORD* was a typical American company that had revolutionized the way cars were manufactured back in the years around and right after the First World War. Particularly through centralization of all areas and functions, with rigorous standardization and above all with assembly lines, mass production was adopted throughout the industry. *FORD* became one of the world's largest manufacturers and had achieved a global presence by the end of the Second World War. Moreover, *FORD's* cost leadership strategy resulted in management control functions that up to the present remained strongly formalized and centralized. Consequently, the data used needed to be as standardized as possible.

For all these reasons, accounting and finance in general, and issues of information technology and systems in particular, seemed to play a much stronger role in *FORD* than *VOLVO*. Hence, product ideas at *FORD* were perceived as the result of financial and infrastructure (i.e., IT and systems) capabilities. At *VOLVO*, on the other hand, Swedish managers felt that the characteristics of the products manufactured (quality, safety, and care for the environment) were the core issue and that the infrastructure, which included finance and IT, had to adapt to these core characteristics.

After the acquisition, the goal of *FORD* and *VOLVO* was to share components and production processes across families of products while at the same time finding the 'optimum' or 'appropriate' level of product variety for increasing market shares by better serving heterogeneous market segments. Although this objective seems to be central in the auto industry in general (Scavarda et al. 2009) it meant something very particular at *FORD* and *VOLVO*, which followed different business strategies. Whereas commonality is primarily the essential approach for mass producers, product variety is about offering the customer a greater range of different products and is largely a feature of a differentiation strategy. Finding the right mix of the right products thus seemed to be the main challenge for both organizations, and this view had a considerable impact on the designers of the management control system.

The principal way to achieve cost savings at *FORD* and *VOLVO* after the acquisition was to cut down on the number of platforms and to adopt modular assembly. Basically, a platform is the floor of a vehicle along with some major components such as suspension sets. When a car model uses a different platform, dedicated engineering, general tooling, and different assembly elements are required.

Variety, on the other hand, is characterized by a number of different designs of a part, system or product, and the greater the complexity, the higher, in general, the total cost of managing it. Product complexity affects all company functions and activities from R&D to after-sales and even recycling, which also form the entire chain of costs. Therefore, to facilitate achievement of economies of scale and scope with help of common features, but also of the right product variety, *FORD* and *VOLVO* needed first to find out which parts added customer value and which did not.

In order to optimize commonality among the different articles that were parts of different variants of cars produced, both *VOLVO* and *FORD* system designers in different areas had for decades been developing sophisticated models that fit the particular organization and its structures. One such model, the article governance model, developed primarily during the 1990s at *VOLVO*, had the principal purpose of increasing the use of part number management, hence the measurability and accountability of parts in order to achieve optimal commonality and cost effectiveness. Parts and articles, which were supply units with their own classification numbers in particular coding systems, were structured in groups according to whether they were 'common, similar, or unique'. 'Similar parts' were considered most dangerous because they added little customer value but entailed significant additional costs because of their high complexity.

To assign costs to different parts, products, and ultimately entire cars at *VOLVO*, system technicians mapped out 'system footprints' for each system, which was separated into some 50 different domains (i.e., engine, tank, cooling, etc.). As a result of this mapping, four areas could be observed, representing four combinations of customer need for variety (high and low) and cost of complexity (high and low). Later, after the status of variety offered for each product was included, the result was the variety-complexity table illustrated in Figure 7.1.

The area with low complexity cost and low customer value, called *Minor Proliferation* in Figure 7.1, included systems with low potential for further cost saving through variant reduction (ex: Battery, Fuel Tank, and Insulation). Despite low complexity costs, systems in the *Profitable Proliferation* area offered high customer value and were therefore profitable to the manufacturer because the customer was willing to pay for special options (ex: Wheels, Radio, Lighting). Systems with high complexity costs but low customer value had high potential for variant reduction; hence *Commonality* was a must for these systems (ex: Wiring Harness, Tailgate). Finally, the potential for cost reduction, despite high complexity costs, was relatively low for systems in the *Platform Strategy* area because these systems offered

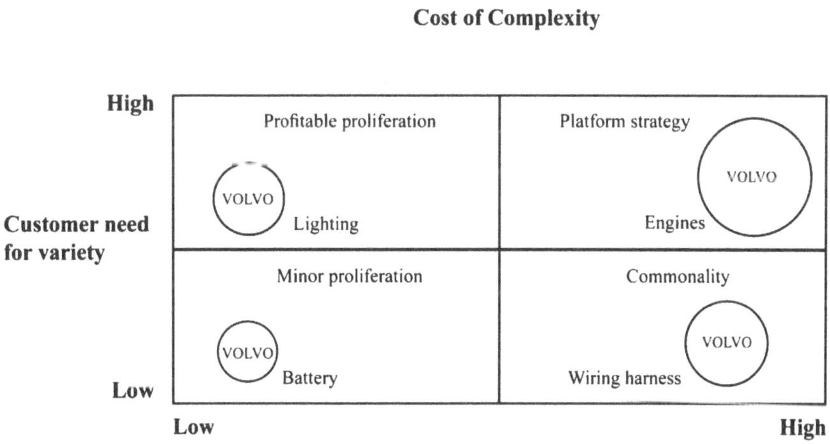

Figure 7.1 System portfolio including costs of product variety and complexity at VOLVO.

high customer value and therefore had substantial strategic implications (ex: Engines, Seats, Body-In-White).

As described earlier, complexity drives costs, and at *VOLVO* and *FORD* it significantly correlated above all with the degree of product customization, the number of parts handled, the products manufactured in small batches, and the through-put time needed. Legal requirements on different markets, but above all questions of design and choice of property, determined which of the different parts and articles to use and thus the part complexity as well.

Other important determinants of complexity cost included the overall number of system variants and parts, as well as sales volumes and number of production plants. In addition, the required spare part strategy determined the level of service to customers. This factor in turn affected the number and geographical dispersion of storage depots, and it had an enormous impact on flow complexity and thus on overall complexity. Therefore, the total product variety costs, or complexity costs, could be viewed as the sum of the costs of all systems, markets, and plants.

Part number management, and thus dealing with all different parts through their numbers, was then viewed primarily from a value-chain perspective in order to determine which activities in the handling of parts added customer value and where in the organization costs occurred. Compared to *VOLVO*, *FORD* had historically focused more strongly on cost-cutting centred on the production function as a consequence of their overall 'cost leadership strategy' and size. *FORD* has thus applied a similar system for production more or less globally. *VOLVO*, on the other hand, had different systems within different production facilities, mostly in order to focus on the downstream parts of the value chain that were closer to the customer. As this focus was connected with the differentiation strategy, the sequences differed to a significant extent.

Swedish financial managers at *VOLVO* estimated that 20 to 30 percent of the total cost of *VOLVO* cars was attributable to complexity, and they assumed that there existed, at least in theory, an optimum variant scenario with a maximum profit, i.e., a maximum difference between revenue and costs. Comparable numbers at *FORD* seemed to be lower, but comparison of the value chains at *VOLVO* and *FORD* was difficult and appeared unfair in view of significant differences in business strategy (cost leadership versus differentiation).

The main challenge arose from a difference between two sorts of complexity: internal and external. Internal complexity, at least at *VOLVO*, included what customers did not really perceive (e.g., different designs of exhaust systems). This area was where it was easiest to achieve economies of scale among different brands. It was also here that engineering, planning, and production processes were core functions of the manufacturer. For this reason, internal complexity, or internal efficiency or, as a Swedish *VOLVO* manager put it, 'the financial logic', was the area where mass-production systems (e.g., *FORD*) were superior to premium brand systems. In this sphere, the greatest value was produced at the beginning of the value chain.

External complexity, on the other hand, could be recognized by customers in instrument panels, engines, and the like. Within this area, market needs, company strategy, design, styling, and image issues were more central, providing a competitive advantage for premium car producers (e.g., *VOLVO*). This area was referred to by a manager as the sphere of 'market logic', and measures here showed how 'effective' an organization actually was.

It was also considered important to know how parts management internally and externally affected suppliers' and customers' costs and how activities and links could be better managed. There was a major difference between the two companies in this respect: *VOLVO* produced and delivered car models primarily on a global basis, whereas *FORD* of Europe, which was seen as the new standard for *VOLVO*, manufactured and delivered their particular products on a European scale only. This difference was the reason why coordination later became difficult and why the first common platforms under development were for Europe only, rather than the whole world. This limitation was viewed as a major drawback by Swedish *VOLVO* managers.

THE NEED FOR A COMMON PART NUMBER SYSTEM

In most cost comparisons made to determine optimal product variety and brand integration, one major drawback was evident at *VOLVO* in the form of the two noncompliant Part Number Systems. The more *FORD* and *VOLVO* started to work together on building common platforms, the bigger the problems became, not only in terms of calculation, but also in production. The reason, according to a Swedish financial manager in manufacturing, was that '*FORD* factories are built for *FORD* products'. The different Part Number Systems remained a major obstacle for a long time as they were the basis for the information put into most other systems, including production.

As soon as a new part number was created for a common *VOLVO* and *FORD* product, the new number would have to be integrated into the old Part Number System in order to make sense; this requirement was impossible to meet as these systems differed in their design logic. Not only were *VOLVO*'s product codes and their 'product development language' different from *FORD*'s, but even within *FORD* of Europe, there were some nine different ways to describe vehicles. At *FORD* of Europe, for example, the situation was functionally different (e.g., marketing and sales had a different language and a whole set of different codes than the warranty people) because these systems had developed differently in different functions.

For the consolidated reporting, on the other hand, *VOLVO* needed to use the global code of the acquirer's suppliers; thus, they needed to convert all information into *FORD* format. In this case, there were around 1,000 suppliers to 6–8 business units, together with 40–50 manufacturing facilities and approximately 40 shipment entities. Therefore, when they attempted joint programs, they had massive conversion problems and consequently high costs as well:

> 'There are approximately a hundred people in FORD of Europe whose entire job is to convert between these languages. All they do, day in and day out, is to translate and decode data from one system into another so that the process keeps moving. And that is extremely inefficient. If we reorganize and we re-engineer so that we only are using one set of codes and one language, then those jobs can go away and we will have a lot more accuracy and a lot fewer problems caused by all this inefficiency'.
>
> (Swedish Financial Integration Project Mgr. at VOLVO)

Hence, either a total change in the Part Number System or a continuous translation was unavoidable in the long run, most managers on both sides agreed, and a former *FORD* accounting head with good system knowledge emphasised that here lay the key to success for the entire car industry:

> 'We have to find a way to have common part numbers, a common structure! Here is where the real difficulties are in the car business, in getting the two car companies to use common product development systems, etc. That is where the opportunity is for the business'.
>
> (Accounting Mgr., formerly at FORD)

Adopting a common part coding structure after an acquisition might seem like a good idea. Between the Part Number Systems of *FORD* and *VOLVO*, however, there were still enormous differences in 2005 that gave rise to the following statement:

> 'The part numbering system, [. . .] that is a very fundamental issue, a building block, based on fundamentally different concepts. The difference is so fundamental that it gets into everything, and it is enormous. So I am not sure if we can really comprehend what it takes to change it. And of course, the FORD guys say Volvo should just do it. But if you walked into Dearborn [HQ of FORD] and said, yeah well, we would like you to change the part numbering system; people would be jumping out of windows and all sorts of things. It is so fundamental'.
>
> (Top Financial Mgr. at VOLVO, formerly at FORD)

Almost from the very beginning, *FORD* wanted to establish common systems and processes both overall and within the area of Part Numbers, because they believed this to be a business necessity. Sharing the Part Number System, they supposed, would enhance, for example, the ability to retain historical data and provide forecasts and enable faster transmission of information. In addition, it was simply considered necessary for integrated supply and all sorts of inventory reduction programs. Most of all, however, it seemed essential as a means of determining optimal product variety in the development of future common products. Swedish managers, by contrast, were not as convinced of the need for commonality:

> 'Common systems and processes are easily considered necessary. They [expatriates] wanted us to do it, but we asked why. We questioned things, we have different attitudes'.
>
> (Swedish Financial Integration Project Mgr. at VOLVO)

Seemingly, Swedish system designers expected explanations and sound reasons, whereas former *FORD* managers at *VOLVO* expected more cooperation. Non-Swedes at *VOLVO* were surprised at the Swedes' reluctance and wondered whether they 'forgot that they are wholly owned by FORD'. Many former *FORD* managers at *VOLVO* felt that for about the first three years their initiatives had been generally rejected, almost regardless of their potential impact. As a consequence, there was little change overall. The problem of different perspectives appeared to be a major source of conflicts. What might be best from the viewpoint of the entire *FORD* enterprise on the subject of Part Number System integration might not be best for *VOLVO* only, as former *FORD* managers admitted:

> '. . . [Part Number System change] is a huge step because the difference in system language is so fundamental that it would lead to changes in all other systems within VOLVO. So if we change that, a lot of other systems downstream will have to change, and the cost would be huge. VOLVO does the math and they say: Well, we don't think there is a good payback on that. It costs too much, there is not enough product improvement, so why should we do it. But FORD does the math from the standpoint of the entire enterprise and finds that actually it will be a lot more efficient in terms of communication across brands. So for the entire enterprise such an investment makes sense. But it doesn't if you just put on your VOLVO hat'.
>
> (Head of Finance, Expatriate formerly at FORD)

Because of size differences, *FORD* managers at *VOLVO* generally assumed that *VOLVO*, more or less mechanically and despite different principal strategies, should adapt to the *FORD* system applications.

Former *FORD* managers at *VOLVO* had difficulty in understanding why Swedish control system designers believed that there could be another way than simply to align their systems with the *FORD* systems. It was more or less 'impossible to think in other terms' because 'the tail simply cannot wag the dog'. However, as *VOLVO* was a large organization itself, the situation was not as clear-cut to some as it appeared to others. A Swedish IT manager in finance even questioned such 'predetermined physical laws':

> 'It is not easier to change a system in an organization with 30.000 employees than in an organization with 300.000. Exactly the same job must be done. So it costs the same amount of money to change at VOLVO as it costs to change at FORD, because it is the same job and involves the same obstacles'.
>
> (Swedish IT manager in Finance at VOLVO)

For many Swedish *VOLVO* managers, ownership or company size was not reason enough to require changes in the information system. Rather, they preferred to evaluate the quality features of the two systems as a basis for negotiations in accordance with their conviction that *VOLVO* had superior systems in many respects. The general belief of Swedish managers was that their organization's system applications overall were strongly cross-function-oriented and therefore superior because they integrated functions far better than the *FORD* systems did. They observed that this was a major reason why *FORD* had not changed the systems during the first years following the acquisition. Their attitude was 'yes, you are big, so what? we are good', an attitude that generally permeated most discussions at *VOLVO* and led to missing some of the work of integration:

> 'I mean, you do not like to change your company's [system solutions] for the worse. When you are changing one thing at the time, then you at least want to be at the same level afterwards or preferably at a higher level. That is something an acquired organization has to guard against'.
>
> (Swedish Project Mgr. with a large change project at VOLVO)

Whereas Swedish managers generally felt that they did not want to change for the worse, they recognized they had to make some changes. But these had to be in the right order, 'piece by piece' or 'the way this is done in Sweden', rather than all at once, which was considered to be the usual approach of Americans. A 'grand solution' was not viable as the organization had to keep going during the changes:

> 'It is like doing a jigsaw puzzle, so to speak. It's about knowing which way is the smartest one for completing the puzzle, which piece to take first. Of course, you would like to take everything at once and simply go from here to there. But that would mean that a company would have

to take time out for a year, and that of course is not possible. That is why we have to work piece by piece'.

(Swedish Project Mgr. with a large change project at VOLVO)

Several Swedish but also a couple of Anglo-Saxon managers at *VOLVO* found that because of insufficient knowledge in different areas—due mostly to high staff turnover—people often did not know what to do. Therefore, for at least a quarter of a year, the organization almost did not know where they were financially. Moreover, systems were interconnected, and when the chain broke in the wrong way, substantial risks and financial dangers seemed to follow:

'If you pull on one end there is a great risk that the whole house will fall apart, the entire block [. . .] There are lots of consequences for product development, purchasing, etc. [. . .] If we changed all systems we use at VOLVO to the FORD systems, it would cost many hundred millions of dollars, and everything would be in transition for several years'.

(Swedish Project Mgr. with a large change project at VOLVO)

Also from a practical view, some managers believed that faster changes were simply not possible:

'It never gets easier the longer one waits. It only becomes more difficult and more expensive. But the tactic of VOLVO so far has still been to take one step at a time and to change systems when it fits the car programs and when the financial situation allows it. But of course, FORD would have liked to do the changes much faster'.

(Swedish Project Mgr. with another large change project at VOLVO)

The problem appeared to be to determine what system solutions were better or worse, who was to decide at the bitter end, and on what basis such decisions would be considered and made. The narratives also illustrated that managers' preferences for certain features of particular 'system-technical' support tools at *VOLVO* often seemed exaggerated; less desirable characteristics, however, were left out in order to highlight the superiority of the favoured system.

Another problem was that most, if not all, managers of management control system integration on both sides, *FORD* and *VOLVO*, argued for their preferred system only as it existed in its original setting. This was predictable because they had worked only with their own systems. It was also argued that as systems normally were designed to fit a certain setting, the major problem was how to evaluate functionality of various systems in different environments and with different principal strategies. When such evaluations were made, 'culture' became a problem in dealing with 'system-technical' issues:

> 'culture comes into the picture when people judge whether different systems are superior or not; that it is where culture comes in, when you have to evaluate, from both points of view [VOLVO and FORD]. I mean, we are looking at the question objectively—what do we have, what do our colleagues have, and which one is better. But of course there is always the subjective aspect that one's own system is better in one's own environment. One always arrives at that conclusion in the end'.
>
> (Swedish IT manager in finance at VOLVO)

Time passed, but things were not moving as *FORD* expected because acceptance by all key financial and accounting managers at *VOLVO* was required before moving on. In many cases these managers in 2006 were still the original Swedes, who felt satisfied and proud that they had won some 'battles' by being able to keep things the way they were earlier. But these Swedes also acknowledged defeats:

> 'certain things simply must be done. That is the way it is as you never can win all battles, that is never possible in any dialogue. Nonetheless, you must try to keep some fixed points unwaveringly'.
>
> (Swedish Head of Finance at VOLVO)

Apparently, these 'battles' were normally fought with groups of 'three to five people on each side': there were always some with about 'the same ideas when it came to four or five certain core things'. This way of 'fighting battles' was viewed, by Swedish managers at least, as a good negotiation process because the two sides were then able to achieve a balance among these different core ideas. Another reason was that this kind of consensus helped to convince the 'other team' and resulted in ten core ideas that 'were probably good for everyone', as expressed by a Swedish head of Finance. *FORD* expatriates at *VOLVO*, however, often ran into trouble with *FORD* headquarters, where people could not understand why things were taking so long. What they could not see was that their 'agents' had to spend considerable time 'sitting down with people and simply discussing matters with them, reasoning with them to get them to understand that this is the way we are going to do it, an approach not very common in an American setting.

THE PART NUMBER SYSTEM SOLUTION

During 2006, management control system integration managers on both sides experienced a 'crossroad', but in rather different directions. To *FORD* managers at *VOLVO*, it was imperative to implement real changes and to become truly integrated in many more areas than was the case so far. This meant simply that Swedish managers would have to accept most proposed changes. Swedish managers, on the other hand, considered that the last possible moment had come to return to their roots by doing what they did best, namely focusing more on processes and streamlining them further.

Apparently, Swedish integration managers had succeeded to some extent in explaining the danger of eroding the *VOLVO* uniqueness. A new organization, called 'Process and Operations Excellence', was therefore created within *VOLVO* for the purpose of recapturing and strengthening this process view. Finding ways to 'converge' the different mind-sets and ways of working was the goal of the new organization. Notably, from then on the word 'convergence' had replaced the word 'integration' in most illustrations on internal documents but also in the narratives provided by the interviewees. The guiding concept, moreover, was that *VOLVO* and *FORD* should meet somewhere in between.

Up to that point, many thought that the change process overall had been difficult. One major problem was that numerous Swedish key managers had left the company (five out of eight key IT and business managers involved with finance and accounting issues had departed); this missing competence was difficult to replace. Partly as a consequence, the workload was enormous during certain periods, and the morale of the remaining staff was low:

> 'We went through one quarter of absolute pain [late 2004], anxiety, criticism from operating management, etc. It was really painful. It was horrible [. . .] The hours were ridiculous, the morale was low, and we still suffer a bit from that today [end of 2005 and beginning of 2006]. We have recovered somewhat, but we have lost a lot of people in my department because during the really busy period people worked an awful lot of overtime. Since we loosened up a little, they relaxed a little, and they thought, oh well, let's try something else. But we lost a lot of good people at the company who just thought, oh hang on, that is not the way I want to live my life, with the workload, stress and pressure the way a North American company expects. And they think, hey, we are going to go back and work for a Swedish company'.
>
> (Accounting Mgr., FORD expatriate at VOLVO)

By the end of 2006, when the last interviews were held at *VOLVO*, the overall integration process, had taken around seven years. Yet the *VOLVO* management control system still looked about the same in many areas as it did prior to the acquisition, particularly the system and technology parts. System-technical changes had not yet been realized to the degree *FORD* had hoped, owing mostly to the complexity of the different Part Number Systems, and plans for the next four to five years had to be made to align them further and to facilitate other integration tasks.

In 2006, the two organizations agreed, after long discussions and evaluations, that the only solution was to align the systems in two steps. The first step would align different processes and practices within the entire sphere of *FORD* and *VOLVO*. The second step would then de-fragment and consolidate information technology solutions within the entire sphere. In this second step, two more steps would be needed. First, collecting all systems within *VOLVO*, mostly in a newly implemented system solution, and second, aligning with *FORD*. Once all these steps were accomplished, the entire data structure, including the Part Number System, was supposed to be in a format that could be aligned with the *FORD* system if, but only if, they implemented new system applications in several areas.

Implementing the changes was planned to last at least until 2010, but there were changes on both sides simply because a one-sided approach appeared 'system-technically', and even more from a human perspective, impossible to follow. Moreover, the planned changes would take time, to some extent because the changes started as late as they did, but more likely 'because issues of this complexity and importance simply take a long time'. Several integration managers from both sides also believed that it was not even possible to grasp what all this would mean, and that in an earlier stage of the process, no one would have understood it anyway. Basically, therefore, there was no other option.

DISCUSSION OF THE 'SUPPOSED' INTEGRATION

As mentioned earlier, research on integration after mergers and acquisitions has generally focused either on system-technical issues or on socio-ideological issues, whereas this study has tried to shed light on the subject from both perspectives. Internal documents and the narratives of management control integration managers illustrate that complexity in practice increases considerably when companies with different business strategies and, in addition, a different cultural heritage, merge.

The reason for this is that the change of simple transaction-oriented systems (e.g., Part Number Systems) to achieve synergies and save costs is not possible because meaning is normally attached to each field in the number chain. Hence, the system is logically linked in most cases to certain products, particular processes and specific organizational structures. In addition, these systems are closely tied to each other and often understood only by particular stakeholders with specific preferences.

The different Part Number Systems at *FORD* and *VOLVO* generated many problems in most areas where different actions might have solved the problems. Typically, historical data and experiences were mentioned by managers seeking to discuss necessary changes. Such data were often presented in the form of empirical evidence, like the 'facts' mentioned in Norreklit, Norreklit, and Israelsen (2006). *FORD* managers, for example, provided the empirical 'fact' that *FORD* of Europe employed around a hundred people every day to translate and decode data from one system into another, a costly, time-consuming procedure. This was also a 'fact', or an epistemologically objective statement (Searle 1995: 8).

'A hundred people' was information that was probably recognized as a 'fact' by most managers on both sides, no matter who had to pay, because the evidence seemed rather obvious. In many other cases, however, there may have been long, in-depth discussions about the validity of certain facts. Mistrust of facts seems to be very common after mergers and acquisitions, as trust needs to be established before integration can take place (e.g., Tomkins 2001).

Moreover, the 'facts' presented were generated by different accounting techniques and different arrangements that resulted from dissimilar costing methods. The difference was made not by the facts themselves, but by what lay behind them. Thus, the same numbers did not automatically mean the same thing, as they had been produced by different systems and different actors.

Therefore, one great challenge in these post-acquisition processes was that facts always needed to be recognized and established first by the different managers from the different sides in order to be considered as facts. This challenge could be one of the most daunting after mergers and acquisitions because lack of trust in people, and in numbers as well, might be the rule rather than the exception.

'Facts' are formed by the past (and the present) and have a relatively straightforward 'appearance'; some therefore believe that facts by themselves constitute reality. The past and present alone are never reality, however, nor do facts alone constitute reality (Norreklit, Norreklit, and Israelsen 2006). Thus, it is not really helpful knowing that we have spent a certain amount of money or time doing something in the past (such as a hundred people working on translation of the Part Number System) without having some idea why this information is relevant and useful for the future. Hence, 'facts' have to be brought into contact with possibilities, a meeting that cannot be accounted for empirically. 'Logic' comes into play here as people start to reflect systematically upon what should be done and what the possible options are.

In this study, it appeared as if most *VOLVO* managers from both sides had agreed on the future action that was needed. Most faced a crossroads simply because the problems of having different product and system languages were obvious to them. These managers then started to construct certain possibilities that were based on the 'facts'. These 'factual possibilities' were derived from the real facts through reflection and logical operations. Factual possibilities are probably what Searle (1995: 8) would categorize as 'epistemologically subjective matters', as they are already dependent upon managers' attitudes, feelings, and values.

In the case of the Part Number Systems, one possible alternative, in short, was to align them quickly to those of *FORD* of Europe. This alternative was favoured by former *FORD* managers because it was quite logical; only 20 percent had to change in order to fit into the other 80 percent. A different logic, however, seemed possible from an IT standpoint, as apparently the same effort was required to change systems and processes for organizations employing 30,000 people as for ones employing 300,000. This view was probably a 'fact' to the knowledgeable manager (IT expert) who expressed it, but less so to the others, who might not accept it as true.

Another alternative was to align with the *VOLVO* systems. Their Part Number System had considerable advantages because it was apparently more process-oriented than that of *FORD* of Europe. This solution seemed most logical if *FORD*, as an entire enterprise, intended to become more process-oriented in the future. Further logical support for this alternative was provided by the argument, often advanced by Swedish managers, that you did not normally change to something worse. It made no sense to change to an inferior alternative, they believed, illustrating the similarities between logic and sense-making. In the long term, however, this logic was faulty, particularly to *FORD* managers, who reasoned that you had to give up a small part now in order to get back something larger in the future (provided there was a future together).

Even though most managers felt that some action was required, the alternative of doing nothing and continuing with the problems unsolved was nevertheless logical because new problems would arise as changes were made when fitting together the pieces of the jigsaw puzzle. Not doing anything was logically valid as change projects of this kind required enormous amounts of money, 'probably hundreds of millions of dollars', and of time. At *VOLVO*, several managers believed that they were forced by such a change project to put all production on hold. Everyone in the *FORD* sphere feared expenses, more than ever when the financial situation, it seemed, was progressively deteriorating. This choice also appeared logical as neither *FORD* nor *VOLVO* knew for certain how long their relationship would last or what the pay-back period would be.[6]

These few alternatives, and there would be many more, demonstrated that opportunities arose through constructive use of logical operations and the recognition that such possibilities were then largely automatic and the result of previous learning (Norreklit, Norreklit, and Israelsen 2006). The alternatives also showed that the application of certain logic seemed to be strongly in line with the positions and perspectives of the particular actors involved, in this instance, as a manager of either the acquired or the acquiring unit. The logic that appeared strongest was the socio-economic one, where particular managers simply wanted the financially best solution for their favoured entity, represented by their brands and related to the particular strategy and situation but not standardized. For the *FORD* expatriates at *VOLVO*, however, this entity was *FORD* and not *VOLVO*, for the integration mission, in the narratives of the managers, was more evident than some newly gained brand loyalty.

The case study exemplified clearly the different values of managers and what was at stake for them when they needed to choose between the different possibilities. 'Values' were the motivating force that gave these managers the energy to search for 'new facts' in order to make stronger arguments for, and better evaluations of, the different possibilities (e.g., Norreklit, Norreklit, and Israelsen 2006; Searle 1995). The managers made further use of these arguments afterwards as they 'finely honed' them in order to position themselves for 'winning the battles' later on, as often had been the case at *VOLVO* during the period after 2003.

Different issues were involved for different managers. In this respect, *VOLVO* managers clearly preferred to consider their Part Number System as process-oriented; their system therefore played a fundamental role in delivering products that in the end were supposed to satisfy customers. This structure had to be defended at almost all costs because a change for the worse could jeopardize the entire differentiation strategy, they believed. Overall, the values of *VOLVO* managers were closely tied to the process that resulted in particular product characteristics in most aspects, following the premium brand strategy described earlier.

Most *FORD* managers, on the other hand, applied their value scheme more directly to financial technicalities and costing techniques, consistently with a cost leadership strategy. In taking such a pragmatic view, former *FORD* managers at *VOLVO* therefore could not really understand all these 'value-laden' arguments of the Swedish *VOLVO* managers. The Part Number System was then mostly about achieving the same numbers, which of course was difficult, but it had very little to do with customer issues or different ways of controlling and managing processes and ultimately the company.

Nevertheless, values themselves, like facts and logic, did not represent reality unless interrelated with other managers' values, facts, and logic (Norreklit, Norreklit, and Israelsen 2006). Here the last of the four elements of reality came into play most strongly, namely, 'communication'. This took place when managers used language and communication tools in general, or other kinds of support tools, in order to package and deliver a message or idea to other individuals and groups with the intention of establishing some sort of inter-subjective reality.

At *VOLVO* it appeared, from around 2003 on, that three or four influential senior managers in finance and accounting needed to share this inter-subjective reality if they were to have any chance of 'winning battles'. Individual reality was not enough; it was necessary to move to a higher level, to common reality in groups, in order to influence the integration process in regard to this question (i.e., Part Number Systems) and many, if not most, other questions as well.

Apparently, to achieve real change, inter-subjective reality was required at *VOLVO* because formal power (as owner) in many matters was not legitimate enough to effect change. In many cases inter-subjective reality in groups of three to four managers was needed to execute the actions desired, but also—and this was even more obvious at *VOLVO* during the years between 2002 and 2004—to prevent unwanted actions. Language and communication as such had the unique ability to generate functions with new status or other new institutional facts.

CONCLUSION AND PRINCIPAL IMPLICATIONS

The interview period lasted only until 2006. Inside knowledge about the real outcome of the investments in brand alignment and product variety, but also the integration of the Part Number Systems, cannot be provided in this chapter. It can be concluded, though, that the failure of Part Number System integration illustrated a typical 'Catch 22' situation: Whatever moves the managers, and thus the designers of the management control system at *VOLVO*, might have chosen to make, there would have been trouble. Part Number Systems, because of a set of inherently logical rules and conditions, apparently work between two organizations in a way that often is illogical. Therefore, a desired integration outcome or solution is difficult to achieve after mergers and acquisitions.

The years after 2005 have been tumultuous, mostly for *FORD*, as sales plummeted and the financial situation began to worsen further (it became even poorer during the financial crisis in 2008/2009). In 2006, *FORD* announced *The Way Forward*, which included the closure of seven vehicle assembly plants and seven parts plants by 2012, the loss of around 30,000 more jobs, and a reduction in material costs of at least $6 billion by 2010.

In 2010, the car corporation *VOLVO* became part of the Chinese company Geely, to which it was sold by *FORD* for $1.8 billion, or around $4.6 billion less than they paid for it in 1999. Internal and external memoranda at both *VOLVO* and *FORD* document the substantial achievements during their 11 years together. *FORD* and *VOLVO* have apparently helped each other to grow in different ways. *VOLVO*, it is noted, was given a different (better?) styling; but above all, the company's vehicle line-up has grown from seven models to 10. The increase was mostly within the bigger-car segments and thus on more profitable markets. This result might be due to good cooperation in product variety planning, but perhaps also to better costing methods. *FORD*, on the other hand, gives the impression of having profited most from the platform sharing strategies, as the company seem to have improved its safety standards considerably.

The previous discussion indicates that it is not easy to determine whether an acquisition of this magnitude and character has been successful. In the final analysis, however, it is often the bottom line that counts. In this case, the bottom line for *FORD* was a loss of $4.6 billion. That number, however, might have been heavily influenced by bad timing as well, as *FORD* was forced to sell *VOLVO* during a deep recession. Thus, this chapter seems to be another story of somewhat miscarried and inappropriate integration that destroyed rather than created value.

Clearly there are many interrelated reasons for this destruction of value, but one of the principal ones is obviously underestimation of the complexity involved in trying to achieve economies of scale and scope at the same time as product variety is at stake. Integrating two brands with different primary strategies and bringing together key system designers (possibly in production systems as well as in control systems), with different customs and traditions as well as interests in different brands, is no easy task, particularly when these designers and the systems involved use 'different' languages.

The most important implication of this case for practitioners is a warning not to overestimate the benefits of scale or underestimate the complexity of brand variety and brand integration after mergers and acquisitions. As rational as system issues appear to be in theory, in reality they involve very little technique but a lot of communication. This finding implies that there is a need for a better understanding of the multifaceted relationship between physical and social phenomena.

NOTES

1. Broadly defined, management control is 'everything managers do to help ensure that their organization's strategies and plans are carried out or, if conditions warrant, that they are modified' (Merchant 1998: xi). Thus, it is a logical integration of different management accounting tools used to gather and report data and to evaluate performance (Horngren, Sundem, and Stratton 1996).
2. System and process integration with *FORD* was a goal at *VOLVO* that seems extraordinary today as people, in and outside the company, now in 2011 are working on the de-coupling of structures and processes. The reason for this is that *VOLVO* is already part of the Chinese manufacturer Geely, a curious fact that might add a particular flavour to this study.
3. 25 interviewees were selected in a single conversation with two integration managers, a *FORD* expatriate and a Swede, based on the criteria that they would have key knowledge and responsibility in management control related issues and in the acquisition. The other six were proposed along the way.
4. The opposite view is the one of more mechanical and passive stakeholders, neglecting the aspect that people have a free will and want to be motivated intrinsically rather than extrinsically (Jakobsen, Johansson, and Nørreklit 2011).
5. As an example, the *FORD* Part Number System for a trunk weather strip is D0AZ-6543720-A. The prefix is D0AZ, the basic part number is 6543720, and the suffix is A. To decode the prefix, D0AZ, the first letter represents the decade of the part; in this case D stands for the 70s. The letter A is used for the 40s, the letter B for the 30s, etc. In this way all letters and numbers in the entire chain have a meaning.
6. With this uncertainty thereafter, mergers and acquisitions always seem to be at a disadvantage compared to investments in organic growth; a sense of not really belonging to the family appears to be part of everyday life for many actors following a merger or acquisition.

REFERENCES

Badrtalei, J. and Bates, D. (2007) 'Effect of organizational cultures on mergers and acquisitions: the case of DaimlerChrysler', *International Journal of Management*, 24(2): 303–17.

Beusch, P. (2007) Contradicting Management Control Ideologies—A study of integration processes following cross-border acquisitions of large multinationals, Doctoral Thesis, Göteborg: Bokförlaget BAS.

Blasko, M., Netter, J.M., and Sinkey, J.F. (2000) 'Value creation and challenges of an international transaction—The Daimler Chrysler merger', *Internal Review of Financial Analysis*, 9(1): 77–102.

Bradford, W. (2007) 'DCX purchasing chief retires', *Automotive News*, 6/18/2007.

Bragd, A. (2002) *Knowing Management—An ethnographic study of tinkering with a new car*, Göteborg: BAS Publisher.

Brown, C., Clancy, G., and Scholer, R. (2003) 'A Post-Merger IT Integration Success Story: Sallie Mae', *MIS Quarterly Executive*, 2(1): 15–27.

Carlsson, S.A. and Henningsson, S. (2007) 'Managing information systems integration in corporate mergers and acquisitions', in M.M. Cunha, G.D. Putnik, and B.C. Cortes (eds.) *Adaptive technologies and business integration: Social, managerial and organizational dimensions*, Hershey, PA: Idea Group Inc., pp. 172–86.

Cartwright, S. and Schoenberg, R. (2006) 'Thirty years of mergers and acquisitions research: Recent advances and future opportunities', *British Journal of Management*, 17: 1–5.

Granlund, M. (2003) 'Management accounting system integration in corporate mergers—A case study', *Accounting, Auditing & Accountability Journal*, 16(2): 208–43.

Horngren, C.T., Sundem, G.L., and Stratton, W.O. (1996) *Introduction to management accounting*, 10th edition, London: Prentice-Hall.

Hu, S.J., Zhu, X., Wang, H., and Koren, Y. (2008) 'Product variety and manufacturing complexity in assembly systems and supply chains', *CIRP Annals—Manufacturing Technology*, 57: 45–48.

Jakobsen, M., Johansson, I.L., and Nørreklit, H. (2011) *An Actor's Approach to Management: conceptual framework and company practice*, Copenhagen: DJØF Publishing.

Kinannder, O. and Naughton, K. (2010) 'Ford sells Volvo to Geely in China's biggest overseas auto deal', *Bloomberg Businessweek*, March 29, 2010.

KPMG (2010) *KPMG Global Auto Executive Survey 2010*.

Krebs, M. (2007) 'Daimler-Chrysler: Why the marriage failed', *Auto Observer*, May 17, 2007.

MacNeill, S. and Chanaron, J.J. (2005) 'Trends and drivers of change in the European automotive industry: (I) mapping the current situation', *Int. J. Automotive Technology and Management*, 5(1): 83–106.

Merchant, K.A. (1998) *Modern management control systems: text and cases*, Upper Saddle River, NJ: Prentice Hall.

Norreklit, L., Norreklit, H., and Israelsen, P. (2006) 'The validity of management control topoi: Towards constructivist pragmatism', *Management Accounting Research*, 17(1): 42–71.

Orsato, R.J. and Wells, P. (2007) 'U-turn: the rise and demise of the automobile industry', *Journal of Cleaner Production*, 15: 994–1006.

Qu, S. and Dumay, J. (2011) 'The qualitative research interview', *Qualitative Research in Accounting & Management*, 8(3): 238–64.

Scavarda, L.F., Schaffer, J., Scavarda, A.J., Reis, A., and Schleich, H. (2009) 'Product variety: an auto industry analysis and a benchmarketing study', *Benchmarking: An International Journal*, 16(3): 387–400.

Schein, L. (2001) *Managing culture in mergers and acquisitions*, New York: The Board.

Searle, J. R. (1995) *The construction of social reality*, New York: The Free Press.

Shimizu, K., Hitt, M.A., Vaidyanath, D., and Pisano, V. (2004) 'Theoretical foundations of cross-border mergers and acquisitions: A review of current research and recommendations for the future', *Journal of International Management*, 10(3): 307–53.

Strach, P. and Everett, A. (2006) 'Brand corrosion: mass-marketing's threat to luxury automobile brands after merger and acquisition', *Journal of Product & Brand Management*, 15(2): 106–20.

Tomkins, C. (2001) 'Interdependencies, trust and information in relationships, alliances and networks', *Accounting, Organization and Society*, 26: 161–91.

www.OICA.net (International Organization of Motor Vehicle Manufacturers), http://oica.net/category/about-us/ (accessed November 10, 2010).

Vaara, E. (2001) 'Role-bound actors in corporate combinations: a sociopolitical perspective on post-merger change processes', *Scandinavian Journal of Management*, 17(4): 481–509.

Vaara, E. (2002) 'On the Discursive Construction of Success/Failure in Narratives of Post-merger Integration', *Organization Studies*, 23(2): 211–48.

Part III

Suppliers and Customers

8 Managing the Influence of External Competitive Change during Integration

Svante Schriber

INTRODUCTION

Acquisitions are often regarded as a means for increasing the competitiveness and performance of the participating firms (Porter 1987). One of the most often cited motives for acquisitions is synergy (Trautwein 1990). When realized through organizational integration, synergies can improve performance of the involved firms in several ways. Common examples include economies of scale and scope in operations, logistics, or administration (Häkkinen 2005), reaching new customers (Lee and Lieberman 2010), or improved innovative capability (Al-Laham, Schweizer, and Amburgey 2010). In all, these and similar synergies can make acquisitions an attractive strategic option for the firms involved.

But what is beneficial for firms involved *in* an acquisition is not necessarily beneficial for organizations *outside* it. As the distribution of profits is typically contested on competitive markets, external stakeholders—surrounding organizations whose interests are affected by and thus with a stake in an acquisition—can find their interests at risk. For instance, an acquisition offering economies of scale in production to the merged firms is likely to mean reduced demand for and hence lower sales for suppliers to those firms. Similarly, competitors can see their market share at risk when the acquiring firm attempts to reach new customers. And for customers an acquisition among suppliers leads to a concentration of available procurement alternatives, often followed by increasing prices. Thus, from the perspective of external stakeholders, the announcement of an acquisition might be viewed with concern or even disapproval.

A possible reaction from external stakeholders perceiving an acquisition as potentially harmful would be to try to prevent that harm. Outside stakeholders could react by attempting to keep the acquisition from attaining its goals. This is particularly likely in the integration phase after an acquisition has been made public. At this time potential synergies are to be realized through organizational integration between the merged firms (Larsson and Finkelstein 1999), a process that can last many years (Barkema and Schijven 2008). External stakeholders are thus left with ample time to mount a strategic response and interfere with a process which will determine whether the acquisition creates value or not (Haspeslagh and Jemison 1991). In sum, during the integration phase acquisitions on competitive markets face the risk of antagonistic reactions aimed at reducing or preventing synergy realization, thereby threatening the success of the acquisition.

Despite this risk, research on acquisitions has paid relatively little attention to whether or how managers in acquisitions are required to manage or mediate the influence of outside stakeholders during integration. Instead, the literature on strategic management has mainly studied the impact on acquisition performance, focusing on factors inside the organizations involved. These factors would include whether experience from previous acquisitions lead to higher performance in subsequent deals (Chatterjee 2009; Zollo and Singh 2004), or how performance is influenced by the degree of similarity between the involved firms (Kim and Finkelstein 2009; Makri, Hitt, and Lane 2009; Shelton 1988), and by gaining access to specific resources, such as technical knowledge (Graebner 2004; Uhlenbruck, Hitt, and Semadeni 2006). Whereas this undoubtedly matters for the outcome of an acquisition, the focus on the relationships between the involved firms and their resources has diverted attention from the relationship between acquisitions and their competitive environment.

Also, integration management studies of acquisitions tend to have an internal focus (Schriber 2008). With an empirical emphasis on the post-acquisition phase, common topics include how employees react to announcements of acquisitions (Schweiger and Goulet 2000), how to manage language differences in multinational acquisitions (Vaara et al. 2005), problems arising from differences in organizational or national cultures (Schoenberg 2000), and the impact of acquisitions on organizational identity (Seo and Hill 2005). The consequence is that with few exceptions (e.g., Anderson, Havila, and Salmi 2001) post-integration literature has been limited to issues internal to the acquisition. In sum, even if several external stakeholders such as governmental bodies, consultants, competitors, suppliers, and customers can influence acquisitions (Parvinen and Tikkanen 2007), neither the strategic nor the integration management literature has focused on the external strategic challenges that may face managers of post-acquisition integration processes.

To help fill this gap, the present chapter addresses the question how external stakeholders are handled during the integration phase. I thereby view acquisitions as processes, including target selection, negotiation, and integration, and as being mainly the responsibility of the managers at the firms involved (e.g., Haspeslagh and Jemison 1991). Consequently, a management perspective is taken, with specific attention to managers of integration, that is, those managers at various levels and from both of the involved firms who are responsible for integration. Further, the view is taken that those external stakeholders who find their interests negatively affected by an acquisition may act to defend their interests, thus making it more difficult for integration managers to achieve the goals of the acquisition. In light of this discussion, the present study seeks to contribute to the literature on acquisitions by explaining how and why certain external stakeholders can influence acquisitions during the integration process, thereby adding new knowledge on how poor performance of acquisitions (e.g., King et al. 2004) can be improved.[1]

A Resource Dependence Perspective on Synergy Realization

A common starting point in strategic management literature is that firm performance depends on competitiveness, that is, on the relationship between the firm and its business environment (Amit and Schoemaker 1993; Ansoff 1965; Helfat et al. 2007). Traditional views ascribe strategic management a relatively high degree of discretion in influencing firm competitiveness, as in selecting its industry or strategy (Porter 1980). According to other perspectives, by contrast, a critical challenge for management is posed by the limits to managerial discretion imposed by the environment of an organization.

One example of the latter view, which can be helpful in analysing the management of acquisitions, is the resource dependence perspective (Pfeffer and Salancik 1978). In essence this perspective regards inter-organizational relations between stakeholders as characterized by different, and often conflicting, interests. Here stakeholders with greater external power are more likely to reach their objectives than less powerful stakeholders. Power has been defined as 'the extent [to which A] can get B to do something that B would not otherwise do' (Dahl 1957: 202–3). External power, then, relates to the ability of one organizational party to influence another. According to the resource dependence perspective, external power is derived from controlling resources on which others are dependent. More formally: the power which one organizational party can exert upon another is proportional to the degree to which the other party perceives her/himself as dependent on resources controlled by the first (Emerson 1962). Power and dependence are thus two sides of the same coin. As stakeholders can be, and often are, mutually dependent, the power which can be exerted is measured by 'net' dependence. If for instance a customer firm is more dependent on products from a supplier than the supplier is on selling to that particular customer, then the supplier can exert power over the customer. An important qualification is that decision makers are unlikely to have a perfectly accurate impression of the 'real' dependence. Because power and dependence are invisible, there is room for misinterpretation of dependence, for bluffing (Kuhn 1964), and for other attempts to appear as controlling more resources and hence as more powerful than is actually the case (Pfeffer and Salancik 1978).

A resource, in turn, is defined as anything that is needed; for a firm it might be materials, financing, or access to a harbour. The degree to which power can be exerted over another party is determined by three factors

(Pfeffer and Salancik 1978). The first is the importance of that resource to the other stakeholder. Even if both iron ore and paper clips are needed by a steel producer, the ore is obviously more important to the steel producer than the clips. Controlling the iron ore thus offers greater possibilities for exerting external power than controlling the paper clips. Secondly, the tighter the control of a resource, the more power can be exerted. For instance, as patents are more protected on some markets than others, proprietary knowledge is controlled to different degrees, providing more or less of a basis for power over others. Finally, the number, quality, and price of available alternatives modify the dependence on a certain resource, where scarcity increases dependence. For instance, managers in acquisitions have been found to pay extra attention to an employee with important and scarce competence (Ranft and Lord 2002), as they are forced to do by that employee's power, based on the company's dependence on the knowledge resources controlled by the employee.

The resource dependence perspective thereby offers potential for new insights into the management of acquisitions. Firstly, this perspective highlights the external limits to managerial discretion in realizing synergies, enriching the academic literature on synergy realization and value creation in acquisitions. Secondly, as in analyses of bargaining power in industries (Porter 1980), resource dependency helps to explain, though in a somewhat innovative way, how profits are likely to be distributed. This original approach offers a clear theoretical foundation for power over others by focusing on organizations rather than industries, and by analysing power relations in dyads or networks that potentially supersede predefined categories of industry position. Thirdly, power relations can change and be changed. This makes it possible to view the interplay between synergy realization and external stakeholder resistance as an integral aspect of integration management and, further, to consider acquisitions as a means of altering the status quo in power relationships.

METHOD

This study is based on a broader investigation of integration management (Schriber 2008). During the process of the research, it became increasingly apparent that managers continuously re-considered their initial goals in adjusting to, as well as attempting to influence, external organizational parties in the competitive environment of the acquisition. The present chapter focuses on data from one acquisition. Specifically, it develops conclusions on how resource dependence on external stakeholders during the integration phase affects the chances of reaching acquisition targets.

The study focuses on the process of realizing synergies on the Swedish fresh bread market during the integration between the bakery firms of Skogaholm and Schulstad. Although this horizontal acquisition took place in a traditional and mature industry, it turned out to require several adjustments during integration because of changing circumstances. In line with the focus on integration management, the study is based on 32 interviews with employees from both firms, including managing directors, specialists, and bakery personnel, but with an emphasis on middle management responsible for realization of synergies.

Data collection took place during the integration process and continued for a year. The semi-structured interviews lasted between one and two hours and resulted in 250 pages of interview data that were summarized in a case description. Interviewees read shorter summaries of the data in order to enhance validity. Alongside the results of the realization efforts, there was a growing recognition that market conditions were changing during integration, thus requiring a change in synergy goals as well. This necessity suggested that it might be appropriate to take a more dynamic view of synergy realization, leading in turn to a review and new analysis of the data while searching for fruitful concepts to describe the forces behind those changes.

INTEGRATION BETWEEN SKOGAHOLM AND SCHULSTAD

Early in 2003 the Federation of Swedish Farmers, the owner of Skogaholm, almost doubled its Swedish bakery capacity by acquiring Schulstad. Although both firms were international, synergies between Skogaholm and Schulstad were expected mainly on the Swedish fresh-bread market. Schulstad, originally a Danish bakery company, had entered the Swedish market via an acquisition in 1999 and attempted aggressively to grow since then. At the time of the acquisition, Schulstad was the third largest producer of fresh bread and closing in on Skogaholm, the second largest. Together they would reinforce their second place behind Pågen, the market leader. The industry was plagued by overcapacity, and in 2002 both Skogaholm and Schulstad had gone through a process of drastically reducing the number of bakeries, leaving Skogaholm with around 550 employees in six bakeries and Schulstad with four bakeries and around 400 employees.

One reason for both the staff reductions and the acquisition was mounting pressure from the three dominating retail chains: ICA, the largest, with a market share of around 50 percent; KF, and Axfood, an aggressive newcomer. At that time, retail chains were centralizing procurement from separate local sources in Sweden, Denmark, and Norway to the Nordic level. This made it harder for bakery firms to cultivate good, long-lasting relations with local store owners. Instead, it required them to bid on large central purchases four times a year, administered by the purchasing functions of retailers. This transition also meant that historic ties were dissolved, further increasing competition. For example, ICA re-evaluated its choice of Skogaholm as preferred supplier, and KF no longer honoured the tradition of buying mainly from Schulstad. Retailers also demanded more new products, adding to the pressure on bakeries. During 2002, market conditions combined with the financial burden of aggressive growth made Schulstad's situation financially untenable. Skogaholm's CEO approached the principal owner of Schulstad, and on New Year's Eve, in the final hours of 2002, the contract was signed for the acquisition of Schulstad by Lantmännen, which already owned Skogaholm. Given its size in terms of market share, the acquisition had to await acceptance by the Swedish Competition Authority until April, when integration was initiated.[2]

Initial Synergies Envisioned

The potential synergies envisioned by Skogaholm top management reflected the situation on the market and included more efficient use of bakeries and logistics to lower costs, as well as the opportunity to increase brand awareness and develop new products to appeal to consumers. In total, four areas where synergies were expected were specifically identified:

- Reducing costs in production
- Reducing costs in logistics
- Reducing costs in IT and administration
- Increasing margins through launching new products and building brand loyalty among consumers.

Early Accomplishments

The actual efforts to realize synergies started almost nine months after the signing of the contract. Integration would not be legal until the acquisition was approved by the Competition Authority in April 2003. In accordance with the Skogaholm culture, managers were given considerable freedom to form their own organizations. Starting from the top, each manager appointed her or his subordinates, a cascading process that was more or less finished by late June. As summer vacations immediately followed, all substantial efforts to realize synergies had to wait until September.

Once integration had started, several achievements could soon be noted. Efforts were directed at the four areas of intended synergies, and in a process of continuous feedback, top management were promptly informed about these successes. Schulstad's IT department was soon closed and Schulstad's head office drastically reduced. Being considered superior in these areas, Schulstad units were given responsibility for product development and marketing, including Skogaholm products. The logistics systems including re-loading hubs, routes, subcontracted transports, timetables, and loading, were checked for overcapacity. As could be expected, several integration problems arose, but there were also achievements. In March 2004 the number of trucks in one of three market regions had been reduced by some 30 percent. A logistics planner observed, 'We set the goals, such as "we need to save this much in logistics in mid-Sweden". All those goals were reached. It proved easier than expected to reach our logistics goals!' Production cutbacks also proceeded as planned. Idle production lines and some entire bakeries, such as one in Varberg on the west cost of Sweden, were closed.

Random External Influence on Integration

Integration managers soon realized, however, that the market conditions prevailing at the outset of the integration process were about to change. For instance, there was a trend among the retail chains ICA, KF, and Axfood of moving from negotiating locally towards centralized procurement at a Nordic level and standardizing product ranges. This tendency had implications for integration. Suppliers were presented with opportunities to win large contracts for predetermined quantities, qualities, and prices. For managers at Skogaholm-Schulstad, this meant that sales could potentially fluctuate considerably, depending on whether contracts were lost or won. As production levels thereby became more uncertain, the potential for cost-cutting and synergies in production also became less predictable. As a manager at Skogaholm described the situation a year after approval by the Competition Authority, 'You don't decide [production levels] once and for all. We live in a new world. We don't have control of everything anymore because we don't know what the customers will buy'. As a consequence, integration managers had to adjust to shifting circumstances by being more careful when realizing synergies.

Managers responsible for synergy realization had to take other external changes into account as well, including seemingly random instability. In one such instance, the launch of the new, common Skogaholm-Schulstad product range was interrupted. During autumn 2003 marketing staff from both firms were working intensely on merging the product ranges of Skogaholm and Schulstad; introducing new, high-margin products and discontinuing less profitable ones, while reducing the overall number of products. The presentation of the new assortment was planned for early 2004. Just before then, however, ICA called a halt; ICA's new electronic ordering system was not operating correctly. This suspension forced ICA to resort to its old system, which was capable of ordering only old products, requiring hectic adjustments at Skogaholm-Schulstad. In haste, ingredients, advertising, and packaging material for the old products had to be ordered, and production rearranged as previously, before it was finally possible to reinstate the new system and the new products. During this period, integration managers were dependent on good relations with retailers and thus forced to adapt to changing circumstances, despite the inconvenience.

Deliberate External Attempts to Influence Integration

Both the centralization and order system examples described earlier illustrate how changes which were not intentionally directed against the acquisition nevertheless impacted the management of synergy realization. At other times integration managers also faced deliberate attempts to influence synergy realization. Before the acquisition the customers of Skogaholm and Schulstad—ICA, KF, and Axfood—had asked for more new products. The expanded product range would benefit the three retailers by attracting more consumers to their stores. Integration managers hoped that new products would be to the advantage of Skogaholm and Schulstad as well; apart from potentially increased sales volume, newer products also created an opportunity for higher margins. The integration process at Skogaholm-Schulstad mirrored this ambition; by integrating and centralizing much of product development to Schulstad, the number of new products more than doubled in one year. But although all retailers had demanded more new products, one of them—KF—suddenly announcement publicly in spring 2004 that it would accept no new products from their 100 largest suppliers until further notice. A member of Skogaholm's top management team analysed the situation as follows:

> 'Just read the papers: KF wants to part with 25 percent of their suppliers all at once. We don't want to be one of those; we want to be a major supplier to KF Nordic. This came all of a sudden and made us realize that the outside world doesn't stand still'.

That specific action took integration management by surprise. The underlying intention, however, was all too familiar to managers at Skogaholm-Schulstad, who viewed it as an attempt by KF to increase its dominance over suppliers in preparation for pressuring them to lower prices. Another Skogaholm manager put it this way: 'Retail chains decide at headquarters, "We want these products from this supplier, those from that one". And as for us who have similar products, we get played off against each other so that we will lower prices'. Additionally, integration managers were convinced that the timing was no coincidence and that KF was taking advantage of supplier weakness during the process of integrating product ranges; when all products were being negotiated at once, Skogaholm-Schulstad was in a very vulnerable position, for no agreement would mean no sales. The chains did not wait to exploit this situation, as was clearly recognized by a member of Skogaholm's top management: 'Of course the retailers are taking advantage of us. They know we are changing, they know we want to reach a contract. They know a lot of things, and of course they use it against us'.

Thus, the influence of parties not directly involved in the acquisition was no coincidence. These organizations—the retail chains, which held a stake in how the acquisition developed—actively intervened to influence the synergy realization process and the synergistic benefits which integration managers could achieve. By controlling the marketing channel to consumers, retail chains could effectively bar Skogaholm-Schulstad from the market. Of course, the chains would thereby suffer some inconvenience. But in terms of net dependence in the short run, the bakeries were at a disadvantage. There were only limited sales channels outside of the retail chains, such as petrol stations and convenience stores, whereas several bakeries competed to supply bread to the retailers. The three conditions for external power (Pfeffer and Salancik 1978) over the acquisition were thus fulfilled: high importance for maintaining Skogaholm-Schulstad sales, which would otherwise plummet; lack of alternative sales channels, and tight control of the critical resource—access to consumers—by the retail chains. Integration managers faced an overall situation where retail chains were aware of their external power and took advantage of it to make the goals of the acquisition more difficult to reach.

Influence of External Third Parties on Integration

The synergy realization process was also influenced by relations to organizational parties with which Skogaholm-Schulstad had no direct contact. One motive for the acquisition was to increase the capacity to fulfil the central purchasing contracts required by retail chains. These contracts were the basis for more detailed calculations of required production levels and hence of synergy potential. But during integration, in spring 2004, several ICA stores started deviating from the central contracts. This change reflected a more relaxed attitude at ICA towards the central contracts, with the result for Skogaholm-Schulstad that actual sales did not match planned production.

The reason for ICA's change of policy soon became apparent: ICA was under examination by the Swedish Competition Authority for its dominating position on the Swedish retail market. In that situation, any further attempts at centralization risked confirming the Competition Authority's suspicions. ICA quickly responded by abandoning the centralization project and presenting itself as a coalition of many stores, stressing the local and entrepreneurial nature of the firm. A manager at Skogaholm remarked, 'We can clearly see that the Competition Authority is scrutinizing ICA and that centralization efforts have decreased. ICA is not as intent on implementing central orders as before'.

The effect for Skogaholm-Schulstad was that synergy potential changed. Synergy potential had previously been calculated on the assumption of central contracts. When those contracts were not followed, the production and transport planning of integration managers was rendered obsolete. Until the situation stabilized, it was necessary to reschedule and postpone synergy realization efforts to see which synergies would last and which would be subject to further change.

This development illustrates that the acquisition was influenced by powerful external stakeholders whose actions created repercussions that spread via other stakeholders. In this case the power of the Competition Authority to limit ICA's profits forced the latter to adopt a new approach that affected the benefits available to its suppliers. Put differently, the synergies achievable in the acquisition were not only the result of integration processes, or of a tug of war with retailers, but tokens in a competitive game in the industry. In this game, synergies were challenged, changed, and created as relations between the acquisition and its environment evolved.

Integration Efforts to Influence the External Environment

If the situations described earlier portray managers in the acquisition as reactive to the external power of customers or authorities, reality was more balanced. A part of synergy realization was directed towards influencing the environment around the acquisition. For instance, suppliers to the acquisition soon came under pressure. Integration of purchasing functions in Skogaholm-Schulstad, comparison of prices, and demands for larger discounts paved the way for more favourable conditions and prices, such as for ingredients, logistics subcontracting, and IT services.

Efforts were made to influence customers as well. For the first time Skogaholm products were advertised on national TV. The advertisement was organized by Schulstad's marketing department, and hence a result of integration. The direct purpose was to strengthen the brand in the minds of the consumers. Advertising was intended to boost demand for Skogaholm-Schulstad products among consumers, increasing volumes and the prices which consumers were willing to pay. A desired indirect effect was to see that these products accounted for a larger share of retailers' profits, thus making retailers more dependent on Skogaholm-Schulstad. From a resource dependence perspective, integration managers attempted to manipulate consumer purchasing, a resource on which retailers were dependent, in order to offset the disadvantage of integration managers in terms of power.

But higher sales of bread were also in the interest of retailers. Increasing the volume of bread sales to customers would benefit Skogaholm-Schulstad through higher sales to retail chains and retailers through higher sales to consumers. This shared interest opened the way for a certain degree of collaboration that was visible in several of the efforts to realize synergy. For instance, all product introductions and campaigns, such as free tasting samples in stores, were coordinated with central functions of retail chains and booked weeks in advance. An even clearer example of cooperation was the hiring of 'Space Management Consultants', paid for by Skogaholm-Schulstad to help retail stores. Half a dozen of these consultants were hired in one of Skogaholm-Schulstad's market regions shortly after the acquisition; their task was to improve bread section layout and design in retail stores. A sales manager at Skogaholm describes the role of these Space Management Consultants as follows:

> 'We try to help the store to increase its profits. The Space Management Consultant gathers the facts and data needed, and then suggests how we think they should build their bread section. Then the Consultant

physically builds the section, follows up, of course, what the store earned today and lets them know what we aim for tomorrow'.

One obvious reason for assuming the costs of rebuilding stores owned by retailers was to give Skogaholm-Schulstad products a better presentation in the racks at the expense of competitors' products. But the longer-term purpose was to develop more cooperative relations with retailers. The hiring and paying of personnel to assist retail stores was an attempt by integration managers to influence the environment of the acquisition. It was also an illustration that dependencies between participating firms and external stakeholders, which could generally be described as competitive, also had symbiotic elements. Both retailers and Skogaholm-Schulstad benefited from the work of the Space Management Consultants, opening the way for a certain measure of collaboration between integration managers and external stakeholders.

Contested Distribution of Benefits

But even if integration managers and retailers agreed to cooperate on certain issues, some underlying tension remained. This was illustrated when the project to realize synergies in logistics was implemented late in 2003. Some of the cost synergies in logistics were to be obtained through reducing the number of hubs, or warehouses to which products from different specialized Skogaholm-Schulstad bakeries were transported. After mixing and reloading the products according to customer order specifications, products were distributed to the stores. As several hubs were not fully utilized and the two firms had hubs in the same towns, reducing the number of hubs was a relatively easy way to achieve substantial savings.

Simultaneously, a far more ambitious plan was being discussed in the bakery industry. It meant adopting a system already in place in Denmark, where the entire bakery industry—even competitors—shared hubs and distribution to stores. This offered a further opportunity for optimization that would lower costs for the entire industry. These discussions made it necessary to put the realization of logistics synergies on hold in order to avoid costly integration of Skogaholm's and Schulstad's logistics organizations, followed by subsequent adaptation to the new, industry-wide system. Officially Skogaholm-Schulstad was strongly in favour of the Danish system, and its managers were active in contacting competitors and industry organizations to advocate the change. Moreover, retail chains supported this development as they saw an opportunity to share in the gains. As a member of Skogaholm's top management team explained, 'That's their incentive: they see that they can cut costs for the system as a whole, for all bread suppliers, and that they can lower their purchasing price'. Even though the Danish system was eventually delayed and integration managers instead proceeded alone with integrating Skogaholm-Schulstad hubs, the discussion of the Danish solution reveals a second and slightly more subtle way in which retail chains used their external power; they allowed integration managers relative freedom, or even provided support, for undertaking actions that would lower costs, but waited eagerly for the gains to appear, so that the chains could then wrest them out of the hands of integration managers. The external power of retailers in this situation was used to support the symbiotic goal of realizing synergies, but with to the intention of assuming a more competitive position when it came to distribution of benefits.

DISCUSSION

In contrast to representations of integration processes in the literature on acquisitions, synergy realization efforts in the Skogaholm-Schulstad acquisition do not appear isolated from events outside of Skogaholm-Schulstad. This chapter has brought to the fore several instances where integration managers interacted with external stakeholders. The presentation of data has deliberately highlighted instances of conflict between the goals of integration managers and powerful external stakeholders. It is hardly surprising that retail chains were the stakeholders to appear most often in the data; at the time of the acquisition, they used a strong external power position to dictate business conditions to their suppliers, including Skogaholm-Schulstad. Retailers themselves, however, were not invulnerable to external power, as was shown when the Competition Authority forced ICA to change its behaviour regarding centralization, which in turn affected synergy realization at Skogaholm-Schulstad. At the same time, integration managers attempted to influence the environment of the acquisition. The events in and around the acquisition can thus be described as the result of an ongoing interplay of power relations, changing the potential profits, both in day-to-day business and in terms of synergies present in the acquisition. The fact that the acquisition in this chapter took place in a relatively stable industry suggests that these effects are also likely to appear in other industries, and potentially to an even greater extent in immature and dynamic industries. As the preceding discussion suggests, the Skogaholm-Schulstad case permits some cautious generalizations about possible contributions to the literature on acquisitions.

The Two Dimensions of Synergy

A first question is the following: if external influence is more widespread than just in this acquisition, why has it been discussed relatively little in the literature? One possible explanation relates to the terminology used for synergies in acquisition literature. Results from this study illustrate that synergies create value in acquisitions under two conditions: that the integration between the merging firms is successful, and that positive effects are consequently achievable in relation to the external environment. Put differently, value creation from synergies can fruitfully be analysed in two dimensions: firstly, in an *internal* dimension between the firms in the acquisition; secondly, in an *external* dimension between the two firms and their environment. The concepts used to represent synergies in the literature on acquisitions are applied overwhelmingly in the first of these dimensions, as in clarifying the effect on the input-output ratio, for instance, in terms of economies of scale or scope (Panzar and Willig 1981), or in how synergies are realized, as through cross learning (Greenberg and Guinan 2004) or bundling of products (Brush 1996). The terms 'strategic fit' and 'relatedness', which are among the most frequently used for describing potential synergies (Brush 1996; Makri, Hitt, and Lane 2009; Shelton 1988), also focus on the internal dimension. For instance Pablo, Sitkin, and Jemison (1996: 728) suggest that strategic fit can be conceptualized 'in terms of similarity or complementarity of core organizational competencies', focusing on the internal dimension between the merging firms but offering little guidance regarding the external dimension and thus leaving unanswered the question how the acquisition is to create value in its competitive environment. A possible explanation why there has been little academic interest so far in the influence of external stakeholders on acquisitions in general, and on synergies in particular, is that the concepts in use are most readily applicable in discussions on the internal dimension of synergies. The results of this study suggest including in these discussions the external dimension of synergy, which may be highly relevant to the development of acquisitions.

The changes which powerful external stakeholders can create in the external dimension, between the environment and the merged firms, have consequences for the internal dimension, and for perceived stability of synergies. If the value of synergy depends on the external dimension, which can be altered by outside forces, then it also has repercussions on the internal dimension and can affect the kind of integration that will lead to changes in value creation. Highlighting the two dimensions—the internal and the external—and how they relate to each other shows that synergies can arise and disappear. Consequently, as a result of external change, different efforts to achieve integration may be required, or the value of synergies already realized and appropriated may change. Synergies, then, are more dynamic than they are often portrayed to be in academic literature, thus posing additional challenges to integration managers.

Consequences for Valuation of an Acquisition and Integration of a Two-Dimensional View

Including external power in analyses of integration also has consequences for valuation of the acquisition. Change in the external dimension with consequences for the realization of synergies alters the limit to the size of the price premium for the acquisition, where a price above this limit could be an overpayment (Sirower 1997). For example, the synergy potential in an acquisition, where the initial aim was to cross-sell the products of one firm through the sales channels of another, can change if a competitor launches a major marketing campaign at that same market, forcing integration managers to reconsider which integration efforts are likely to be rewarded with value creation, and hence what price is financially justified. Moreover, societal or economic change without any intention to influence a particular acquisition can require changes in the process of integration. For instance, what used to be potential cost synergies can turn into a bottleneck if demand suddenly and sharply increases (Löwstedt et al. 2003; Shaver 2006), a possibility already worth consideration at the time of valuation for an acquisition.

This dynamism in the external dimension of synergy also can be expected to influence how the challenges of integration previously identified in acquisition literature can fruitfully be conceptualized. For instance, the degree to which employees react negatively to stress (Schweiger and Goulet 2000) or cultural shocks (Schoenberg 2000) could be expected to depend not only on internal factors, such as integration management (Larsson and Finkelstein 1999), but also on how these employees view their chances of finding a job outside of the acquisition. A competitor advertising new jobs, or the announcement of dramatic cutbacks in the industry at large, could lead employees in acquisitions to react very differently to acquisition-related stress or cultural shocks. Put another way, even well-known challenges to integration management can look different once the interests of external stakeholders are included in the picture.

External Power as Means and Ends of Acquisitions

The situations discussed in the Skogaholm-Schulstad acquisition focused mainly on problems or challenges for managers responsible for integration; these problems were explained by strong external power, primarily in the hands of the retail chains ICA, KF, and Axfood. As mentioned, however, there were some situations where integration managers had the upper hand. One example is that of synergy realization in logistics systems, which proved easier than expected; here customers had the upper hand over suppliers. A more theoretical explanation, however, is that the outcome is determined by power relationships based on resource dependence. These relationships may, though not necessarily, overlap with positions in the value system. Thus, integration managers who can apply greater external power—be it backward or forward in the value system, over competitors, or over other stakeholders—are likely to create more profits through synergy realization than integration managers who are subject to domination and forced to adapt by external stakeholders.

The analysis can be taken a step further. If, as has been suggested here, the chances for integration managers to realize potential benefits in acquisitions depend on their power relative to external stakeholders, then this implies that power and profits are very closely related. As high relative power can be translated into profits, attempts to increase one's relative external power through acquisitions can thereby be seen as an economically rational end in itself, an objective which can be added to the most commonly mentioned motives for acquisitions (Trautwein 1990). Consequently, external power appears as a source of value creation; thus analyses of 'strategic fit' (Pablo, Sitkin, and Jemison 1996) could be fruitfully complemented with assessments of the power situation in which an acquisition takes place. Moreover, through adoption of a resource dependence perspective, several goals already mentioned in the literature on acquisitions can be considered to possess an external power dimension. For instance, acquisitions aimed at entering new markets (Lee and Lieberman 2010) can be seen as a way to reduce dependence on stakeholders in previous markets. Similarly, acquisitions to enhance the capability to develop unique innovations (Al-Laham, Schweizer, and Amburgey 2010) potentially increase the dependence of customers. The chance of increasing external power for its own sake, therefore, can be seen as one motive among others for pursuing acquisitions.

As vividly shown in the Skogaholm-Schulstad case, external power is also required for realizing the benefits of acquisitions. Failure to appreciate fully the potential negative influence of strong external stakeholders, or mismanagement of direct or indirect relations with these stakeholders during integration, jeopardizes value creation in acquisitions. Not only can integration be obstructed, but even the benefits of successful integration may be appropriated by powerful external stakeholders. This danger emphasizes that the degree to which potential benefits can be realized depends on the skills of integration managers in navigating in and manipulating the network of external power and resource dependencies surrounding the integration process. An example would be through carefully managing information about synergy goals, or even bluffing (Kuhn 1964). The resource dependence perspective suggests that both the benefits of acquisitions and the chances that an acquisition will be successful can be expressed in terms of external power. An acquisition can be used to increase power over external stakeholders, and thereby increase profits, if it allows the merging firms to gain control over resources in high demand by those external stakeholders, but achieving that objective requires at least a minimum of managerial skills in handling the external power situation in the integration process.

CONCLUSIONS

This chapter has taken a resource dependence perspective in an attempt to contribute to the literature on acquisitions. The approach has been to analyse how integration managers handle external stakeholders during the integration process. The analysis showed that integration processes involve far more parties than just the two merging firms. Instead, they appear to be elements in an on-going competitive and interactive process, where stakeholders outside the acquisition attempt to interfere with synergy realization, and integration managers try to thwart these attempts and to influence the situation outside of the firms involved. In the processes which develop, external power through control over resources of importance to others appears as both a goal of acquisitions and as a necessary condition for realizing these goals during integration. Acquisitions are particularly sensitive to external stakeholders with both motive and ability to prevent synergies from being realized, or to squeeze the financial benefits out of synergies already realized.

As a first result of the analysis, a change in synergy terminology has been suggested; from a focus on the internal dimension and integration, the emphasis has shifted to the external dimension of synergy. In terms of resource dependence, the benefits of an acquisition should be expressed in a manner that highlights how these benefits help to increase the external power of the firms involved over stakeholders outside of the acquisition. In common strategic parlance, this would mean describing synergies so as to clarify not only their internal effects, but also their contribution to the competitiveness of the merging firms in relation to the external environment. This bridging of the internal-external boundary in acquisitions calls attention to further results of relevance for the literature on acquisitions. Second, ex ante valuation of synergies in acquisitions could fruitfully clarify whether an acquisition offers an opportunity to gain control over critical resources, either right away or gradually, and hence which synergies are likely to be realized and to offer financial benefits. Third, by stressing the on-going power game following acquisitions, and in line with Mintzberg (1978), this boundary-transcending approach gives rise to the notion that as environments change, strategies might change as well. For instance, the aim of a cost leadership position initially sought by realizing certain synergies might later be changed, possibly with repercussions on what type of integration between the firms would offer additional value. This change, fourth and lastly, emphasizes that integration managers might need greater flexibility during integration than is often emphasised in existing literature on acquisitions.

IMPLICATIONS FOR PRACTITIONERS

In this chapter I have suggested that powerful external stakeholders are unlikely to remain passive towards acquisitions which they perceive as threats, a view consistent with much of strategy research but largely neglected in research on acquisitions. This view has several implications for managers planning, valuating, and integrating acquisitions. The first is that before an acquisition, managers should consider the external power situation in order to assess which synergistic gains can realistically be exploited, and in what instances realization might be hindered by powerful external stakeholders. These stakeholders typically exercise tight control over resources, broadly defined, which are important to the success of the acquisition and for which there are no obvious alternatives. Therefore, mapping the power network *surrounding* an acquisition can be fruitfully added to ex ante analyses of strategic fit *between* the merging firms. This view is also relevant after an acquisition, during integration. Response and retaliation from external stakeholders might change the industry, and thus influence which integration efforts will have effects that are valuable to the merging firms. This comment may be taken as a recommendation to view synergies and synergy realization as closely connected to strategy, which in turn can be dynamic and shifting as the conditions surrounding the acquisition change. One consequence is that integration managers should retain a certain degree of flexibility and readiness to respond to external changes. Such flexibility can be an asset both when positive potential disappears or even turn negative, and when environmental change gives strategic value to new connections between the firms in the form of novel positive synergy potential. This flexibility could also reduce the risk that integration efforts planned early and implemented later, under changed circumstances, will have been made in vain, or even leave the merging firms worse off than before the integration.

NOTES

1. As pointed out in the chapter by Risberg in this volume, the success of acquisitions is often problematized by researchers who refer to the problematization of other researchers, rather than to empirical studies. However, even if measuring acquisition performance is far from a trivial matter (see Schoenberg 2006), it seems fair to argue that studies based on empirical data suggest that there is room for improvement.
2. Based on marketing strategy, it was decided that both firm names should remain as brands. However, for purposes of clarity, the firm names are used to indicate the two merging entities, and Skogaholm-Schulstad to denote the merged firm

REFERENCES

Al-Laham, A., Schweizer, L., and Amburgey, T.L. (2010) 'Dating before Marriage? Analyzing the Influence of Pre-Acquisition Experience and Target Familiarity on Acquisition Success in the "M&A as R&D" type of acquisition', *Scandinavian Journal of Management*, 26: 25–37.

Amit, R. and Schoemaker, P.J.H. (1993) 'Strategic Assets and Organizational Rent', *Strategic Management Journal*, 14: 33–46.

Anderson, H., Havila, V., and Salmi, A. (2001) 'Can You Buy A Business Relationship? On The Importance of Customer and Supplier Relationships in Acquisitions', *Industrial Marketing Management*, 30: 575–86.

Ansoff, I.H. (1965) *Corporate Strategy. An Analytic Approach to Business Policy for Growth and Expansion*, New York: McGraw-Hill Book Company.
Barkema, H.G. and Schijven, M. (2008) 'Toward Unlocking the Full Potential of Acquisitions: The Role of Organizational Restructuring', *Academy of Management Journal*, 51: 696–722.
Brush, T.H. (1996) 'Predicted Change in Operational Synergy and Post-Acquisition Performance of Acquired Businesses', *Strategic Management Journal*, 17: 1–24.
Chatterjee, S. (2009) 'The Keys to Successful Acquisition Programmes', *Long Range Planning*, 42: 137–63.
Dahl, R.A. (1957) 'The Concept of Power', *Behavioral Science*, 2: 201–15.
Emerson, R.M. (1962) 'Power-Dependence Relations', *American Sociological Review*, 27: 31–41.
Graebner, M.E. (2004) 'Momentum and Serendipity: How Acquired Leaders Create Value in the Integration of Technology Firms', *Strategic Management Journal*, 25: 751–77.
Greenberg, D. and Guinan, P.J. (2004) 'Mergers and Acquisitions in Technology-Intensive Industries: The Emergent Process of Knowledge Transfer', in A.L. Pablo and M. Javidan (eds.) *Mergers and Acquisitions. Creating Integrative Knowledge*, Malden, MA: Blackwell Publishing Ltd.
Häkkinen, L. (2005) *Operations Integration and Value Creation in Horizontal Cross-Border Acquisitions*, Doctoral Thesis, Turku School of Economics and Business Administration.
Haspeslagh, P.C. and Jemison, D.B. (1991) *Managing Acquisitions: Creating Value through Corporate Renewal*, New York: The Free Press.
Helfat, C.E., Finkelstein, S., Mitchell, W., Peteraf, M., Singh, H., Teece, D., and Winter, S. (2007) *Dynamic Capabilities: Understanding Strategic Change in Organizations*, London: Blackwell.
Kim, J.-Y.J. and Finkelstein, S. (2009). 'The Effects of Strategic and Market Complementarity on Acquisition Performance: Evidence from the U.S. Commercial Banking Industry, 1989–2001', *Strategic Management Journal*, 30: 617–46.
King, D.R., Dalton, D.R., Daily, C.M., and Covin, J.G. (2004) 'Meta-Analyses of Post-Acquisition Performance: Indications of Unidentified Moderators', *Strategic Management Journal*, 25: 187–200.
Kuhn, A. (1964) 'Bargaining Power in Transactions: A Basic Model of Interpersonal Relationships', *American Journal of Economics and Sociology*, 23: 49–63.
Larsson, R. and Finkelstein, S. (1999) 'Integrating Strategic, Organizational, and Human Resource Perspectives on Mergers and Acquisitions: A Case Study of Synergy Realization', *Organization Science*, 10: 1–26.
Lee, G.K. and Lieberman, M.B. (2010) 'Acquisition vs. internal development as modes of market entry', *Strategic Management Journal*, 31: 140–58.
Löwstedt, J., Schilling, A., Tomicic, M., and Werr, A. (2003) 'Managing Differences in Post-Merger Integration: The Case of a Professional Service Firm', *Nordiske Organisasjonsstudier*, 5: 11–36.
Makri, M., Hitt, M.A., and Lane, P.J. (2009) 'Complementary technologies, knowledge relatedness, and invention outcomes in high technology mergers and acquisitions', *Strategic Management Journal*, 31: 602–28.
Mintzberg, H. (1978) 'Patterns in Strategy Formation', *Management Science*, 24: 934–48.
Pablo, A.L., Sitkin, S.B., and Jemison, D.B. (1996) 'Acquisition Decision-Making Processes: The Central Role of Risk', *Journal of Management*, 22: 723–46.
Panzar, J.C. and Willig, R.D. (1981) 'Economies of Scope', *American Economic Review*, 71: 268–72.
Parvinen, P. and Tikkanen, H. (2007) 'Incentive Asymmetries in the Mergers and Acquisition Process', *Journal of Management Studies*, 44: 759–87.

Pfeffer, J. and Salancik, G.R. (1978) *The External Control of Organizations. A Resource Dependence Perspective*, New York: Harper & Row Publishers.
Porter, M.E. (1980) *Competitive Strategy. Techniques for Analyzing Industries and Competitors*, New York: The Free Press.
Porter, M.E. (1987) 'From Competitive Advantage to Corporate Strategy', *Harvard Business Review*, May–June: 43–59.
Ranft, A.L. and Lord, M.D. (2002) 'Acquiring New Technologies and Capabilities: A Grounded Model of Acquisition Implementation', *Organization Science*, 13: 420–41.
Schoenberg, R. (2000) 'The Influence of Cultural Compatibility within Cross-Border Acquisitions: A Review', in C. Cooper and A. Gregory (eds.) *Advances in Mergers and Acquisitions*, Greenwich, Connecticut: Elsevier Science Inc., pp. 43–59.
Schoenberg, R. (2006) 'Measuring the Performance of Corporate Acquisitions: An Empirical Comparison of Alternative Metrics', *British Journal of Management*, 17: 361–70.
Schriber, S. (2008) *Ledning av synergirealisering i fusioner och förvärv*, Doctoral Thesis, Stockholm School of Economics.
Schweiger, D.M. and Goulet, P.K. (2000) 'Integrating Mergers and Acquisitions: An International Research Review', in C.L. Cooper and A. Gregory (eds.) *Advances in Mergers and Acquisitions*, Amsterdam: JAI, pp. 61–91.
Seo, M.-G. and Hill, N.S. (2005) 'Understanding the Human Side of Merger and Acquisition', *The Journal of Applied Behavioral Science*, 41: 422–43.
Shaver, M.J. (2006) 'A Paradox of Synergy: Contagion and Capacity Effects in Mergers and Acquisitions', *Academy of Management Review*, 31: 962–76.
Shelton, L.M. (1988) 'Strategic Business Fits and Corporate Acquisition: Empirical Evidence', *Strategic Management Journal*, 9: 297–87.
Sirower, M. (1997) *The Synergy Trap—How Companies Lose the Acquisition Game*, New York: The Free Press.
Trautwein, F. (1990) 'Merger Motives and Merger Prescriptions', *Strategic Management Journal*, 11: 283–95.
Uhlenbruck, K., Hitt, M.A., and Semadeni, M. (2006) 'Market Value Effects of Acquisitions Involving Internet Firms: A Resource-Based Analysis', *Strategic Management Journal*, 27: 899–913.
Vaara, E., Tienari, J., Piekkari, R., and Säntti, R. (2005) 'Language and the Circuits of Power in a Merging Multinational Corporation', *Journal of Management Studies*, 42: 595–623.
Zollo, M. and Singh, H. (2004) 'Deliberate Learning in Corporate Acquisitions: Post-Acquisition Strategies and Integration Capability in U.S. Bank Mergers', *Strategic Management Journal*, 25: 1233–56.

9 Supplier Relationships at Stake in Mergers and Acquisitions

Johan Holtström

INTRODUCTION

The relationships of companies with their suppliers are important (Cowley 1988; Håkansson 1989), and they tend to be long-lasting (Håkansson 1990, 2006). Companies with long-lasting business relationships rarely terminate these relationships (Powell, Koput, and Smith-Doerr 1996), and there are indications of increased collaboration between manufacturers and suppliers (Oh and Rhee 2008). One of the main reasons for long-lasting relationships is that they become a '. . . framework for joint development of technologies. . .' (Håkansson 2006: 153). Thus, companies become dependent on suppliers, and a merger or acquisition may jeopardize the relationship, as earlier research has shown that business relationships may be affected by mergers and acquisitions (Anderson, Havila, and Salmi 2001; Havila and Salmi 2002). Thus, the integration process initiated by the merger or acquisition will also impact the supplier relationships of the integrating companies (Holtström 2003; Öberg and Holtström 2006), sometimes in a disruptive way (Anderson, Havila, and Salmi 2001). This chapter focuses on supplier relationships in the horizontal integration following a merger or an acquisition. The purpose of this chapter is to explain and discuss *the importance of supplier relationships in mergers and acquisitions.*

In treating different forms of supplier relationships in mergers and acquisitions, the following section presents different types of suppliers and different kinds of dependence in supplier relationships. Methodological considerations are followed by four cases of horizontal mergers and acquisitions. The next part is a discussion of the supplier relationships at stake in mergers and acquisitions. Finally, conclusions and managerial implications are presented.

DIFFERENT FORMS OF SUPPLIER RELATIONSHIPS

Supplier relationships may range from a potential business relationship between a supplier and the merging companies to deep and long-lasting relationships between a supplier and one or both of the integrating companies. The nature of these relationships depends on the kind of transactions concerned, that is, what is delivered, the degree of product development, the frequency of interaction, and the degree to which the same supplier provides each component or system used, etc. Supplier relationships may change according to the type of goods and services delivered between the companies concerned.

Depending on the type of goods or services delivered, suppliers may be categorised as follows (Holtström 2003, 2009): (i) product-related supply (direct material), (ii) nonproduct-related supply (indirect material), and (iii) equipment supply (investments). Direct material consists of systems, components, and services used in production by the receiving company. This subgroup includes suppliers of raw-materials, commodities, strategic systems, and components. Indirect material consists of goods and services that support the company's operations. This subgroup includes suppliers of general services, office supply, and IS/IT-systems. Equipment supply is the provision of equipment and other installations to maintain, develop, and/or expand the company's operations. This subgroup includes suppliers of new machine equipment for a new production plant or replacement of old equipment.

The strength of the relationships between suppliers and merging and acquiring companies can be gauged by the degree of dependence between suppliers and their customers, ranging from independence to interdependence (Cox, Sanderson, and Watson 2000; Emerson 1962; Ritter, Wilkinson, and Johnston 2004). The degree of dependence between customer and supplier is a measure of the ability to influence the behaviour of a supplier in a way contrary to its interests, for instance (Ritter and Gemünden 2002; Wilkinson and Young 2002). The possibility of switching to another supplier is another indication of the degree of dependence between customers and suppliers (Johanson and Mattsson 1987).

The different kinds of dependence in the relationship between suppliers and their customers could have various implications for supplier relationships following a merger and/or an acquisition. If there is little dependence on suppliers, the relationship may well be viewed 'atomistically'. There may even be no relationship to manage, in which case there is independence between the integrating companies and the supplier. This situation prevails in a perfectly competitive market, where there are many options and switching costs are negligible (Ritter, Wilkinson, and Johnston 2004).

On the other hand, if one company is dependent on another, the other will be dominant, and the relationship will be one of power dominance. The scarcity and utility of the resources concerned are important factors in this type of relationship; thus, a supplier has power over the customer if the resources offered are relatively scarce and are of great utility to the customer. In such a case, the customer needs to review its options, considering the number of alternative suppliers and the substitutability of products.

Another form of dependence between customers and suppliers is interdependence, a relationship of mutual dependence where both the customer and the supplier are important to each other but neither is dominant over the other. Interdependence can take various forms, change over time, and concern different issues (Ritter, Wilkinson, and Johnston 2004). These different customer and supplier dependencies affect the consequences of mergers and acquisitions for business relationships with suppliers.

In a situation where the integrating company has a relationship with a dominant supplier (Cox, Sanderson, and Watson 2000; Emerson 1962; Ritter, Wilkinson, and Johnston 2004), the conditions for the supplier may remain unchanged after the merger or acquisition. For some suppliers, however, a merger or an acquisition may result in losing business with the integrating companies. For other suppliers, by contrast, it may enhance business opportunities. The strength and character of a relationship will determine whether and when a change will result from a merger or an acquisition. This means that numerous factors will determine the potential consequences of a merger or an acquisition on business relationships with suppliers: the type of customer-supplier relationship, the uniqueness of the supplier's business, the number of potential suppliers, the substitutability of products and components offered by suppliers, and the type of merger or acquisition are all important in this regard.

METHOD

This section will highlight supplier relationships in horizontal mergers and acquisitions taken from a broader study on mergers and acquisitions (Holtström 2003, 2009). Four cases are used as a basis for discussing the importance of supplier relationships in mergers and acquisitions. The cases describe different types of supplier relationships in industry, where the merging and acquiring companies represent diverse kinds of manufacturing firms with different lines of business. The cases do not provide a comprehensive picture, but each case is intended to show a potential change in a supplier relationship that could put the relationship at stake in a merger or acquisition. In this study, a collective case study is used in the same way as instrumental case studies; to understand phenomena on a more general level (Stake 2003). Thus, the case illustrations are helpful in finding patterns in the stake of the supplier relationship in mergers and acquisitions.

The data for the cases has been collected primarily from interviews with persons at the corporate and middle-management level, that is, mainly CEOs, purchasing directors, and purchasing managers but also managers in other functions such as sales, distribution, and production. The interviews were held during 2000 for the forest products industry case and during 2001 for the welding industry and automotive industry cases. Finally, interviews for the forklift industry case were held during 2003–2004. The length of the interviews varied from 1.5 to 3 hours, and the total number of interviews for all the cases was 27. The interviews followed the pattern for a non-standardised and non-structured interview. A questionnaire was used as a guide to help the interviewer/s to follow what was discussed during the interviews and to make sure that the interviews covered the areas of interest.

The four cases involve the following companies: ESAB (the welding industry case) is a producer of welding equipment and components; ESAB acquired a number of other welding companies during the 1980s. Stora Enso (the forest products industry case) is a processing industry producing different qualities of paper and raw material for paper production. The company was formed after a merger between Stora and Enso in 1999. In the automotive industry case, a producer of vehicles acquires another automotive producer. Finally, BT Industries (the forklift industry) is a manufacturer of material handling equipment and acquired The Raymond Corporation in 1997. Together, the cases show examples of the different types of suppliers discussed earlier. The following section elaborates on the aspects of central interest in this chapter.

SUPPLIER RELATIONSHIPS IN HORIZONTAL INTEGRATION IN DIFFERENT INDUSTRIES

The Welding Industry—ESAB

In the welding industry the case includes a number of acquisitions by ESAB during the 1980s. ESAB produces welding equipment and welding products. During the period of acquisitions by ESAB, the industry needed structural change. ESAB took an active role in bringing about structural change by acquiring several other independent welding companies and parts of larger firms. The principal suppliers discussed in the case are those furnishing raw materials and standard components to welding manufacturers.

Some important aspects of the relationships with the suppliers should be highlighted. During the process of integrating the acquired companies, the various welding companies proved to be paying widely differing prices for raw materials purchased. ESAB promoted co ordination through joint purchasing in order to reduce price levels in general on the goods purchased. The network of suppliers brought in from the acquired companies, together with ESAB's previous supplier network, formed a new supplier network and thus affected the structure of the integrating company's supplier relationships. In some cases the price reduction achieved was 30–40 percent on goods purchased by ESAB. These types of suppliers, mostly providers of raw materials, are quite easily replaceable by other suppliers. The explanation, according to the acquirer, is the low degree of product complexity and the substantial number of available suppliers. For the suppliers, the business relationship with ESAB and with the companies acquired by ESAB was at stake.

The Forest Products Industry—Stora Enso

When Stora and Enso merged in 1999, both companies were in the forest products industry, with the production of paper and pulp as their primary business. This merger was between 'equals', as the two companies not only produced similar products, but were also about the same size. An interesting aspect of the Stora Enso merger is the dimension of the investment equipment supplier. The supplier concerned, a producer of paper-making machinery and related equipment, held a very strong position on its market as one of the few remaining firms within its business niche. The market for paper-making machinery is decreasing, however, with possible long-term implications for suppliers.

The on-going restructuring process in the forest products industry has led to a diminishing number of available suppliers and greater dependence on some of them. The trend of concentration among suppliers is an obstacle to realising the desired synergy effects of the merger. In addition, fewer supplier options make it difficult to change supplier. There is also a trend among suppliers to strive for growth. In some cases suppliers have sought growth to be able to take on larger orders or delivery projects; this is a reaction to the concentration trend resulting from integration of merged or acquired customers. Thus, when merging companies demand more extensive involvement of their suppliers, the suppliers also need to grow. Increased growth at different levels of the supplier structure also makes the companies more interdependent. Suppliers have an interest in determining the degree to which their dependence on the merged companies will increase and whether this change represents an advantage or an increased risk.

In the integration between Stora and Enso, there were several organisational changes, one being centralisation of investment decisions. This development had consequences for the supplier of investment equipment, leading to changes in its organisation to match the new hierarchical structure of the merged company. The supplier of investment equipment also noticed changes in investment decisions, for example, decisions on new investments were postponed or delayed.

The Automotive Industry

In the automotive industry case, a major automotive producer acquires another automotive producer toward the end of the 1990s. The integrating companies manufacture similar types of products. The supplier relationships described in the automotive industry case are with consultants in product development and with manufacturers of components or parts of components. It is normally not possible to substitute suppliers of these components before a new product is developed. Thus, relationships between customer and supplier are long term and interdependent. Some consultants prove to be key resources for product development. In the automotive industry case some suppliers have a direct relationship with the integrating companies, whereas others maintain contact through tiers of suppliers. Both the manufacturers and the consultants can be described as suppliers of product-related material/services, and the automotive producers are in a dominant power position. However, the relationship has some characteristics of mutual dependence because there are long lead times for product development and long production runs. At stake for suppliers in mergers and acquisitions is their long-term customer relationship, in other words, whether they will continue to serve as suppliers to the new integrated company in connection with future product models.

During the on-going production of a particular type of products, suppliers will normally not be changed. Any substitution that is nevertheless made is regarded as a response to an extreme situation, such as bankruptcy. A change of a supplier is almost only possible for the next generation of products. An important reason for retaining suppliers during on-going production is that changes are very costly and time-consuming. This factor, in combination with a single-source strategy for components, heightens the importance of relationships with suppliers. The relationship for the supplier is therefore not vulnerable until it is time for the next generation of products.

In the acquisition process, the joint resources of the combined companies were reviewed to obtain an overall picture of the potential of these resources and to determine possible needs for new investments. From the standpoint of the consultants, projects were brought to a standstill for a time—a temporary negative consequence of the acquisition for the suppliers. Consequently, supplier relationships not directly bound by contract to the length of the product series may be at risk earlier in a process of integration between merging companies.

After the acquisition in this case, the acquirer began to specialise product development. Development of certain types of components and systems was concentrated in one specific development unit of the integrated company. This concentration on different areas of know-how enhanced opportunities for suppliers with previous involvement in the specific unit area but limited opportunities for suppliers without such involvement. Some supplier relationships could therefore be in jeopardy as a result of internal restructuring following a merger.

The case also shows concentration trends among suppliers in the automotive industry. If an automotive producer has the ambition of reducing the number of suppliers with which it has direct contact, this signals a change in the relationship structure for the suppliers. For example, a supplier previously in direct contact with the integrating company may subsequently have to contact a first-tier supplier and may even become a second-tier supplier. Although this change might not directly threaten the supplier's business, it may subject the relationship to change, forcing the supplier to develop new relationships in order to continue doing business with the customer.

The Forklift Industry—BT Industries

BT Industries is a provider of system solutions for material handling and manufactures forklifts. In addition to the production of material handling equipment, the after-sales market is also important. The company is a major competitor in service and solutions for operating the equipment as well as in financial solutions. Toyota acquired BT industries in the year 2000, but in this chapter the acquisition of The Raymond Corporation by BT Industries in 1997 is described. The acquired company was about the same size as the acquirer, and its principal operations were located in the North American market. The acquisition could be seen as a horizontal one with a 'new' geographical market. The suppliers discussed in this case provide direct material (e.g., components) and services as well as indirect material (e.g., office supplies).

Relationships with some categories of suppliers to BT Industries are relatively stable. This stability is due to the type of products and components delivered. If the components are of low value and transportation costs are high, there will be little or no change in the supplier relationship as a consequence of the acquisition. This relationship is characterized by dependence on the supplier.

Achieving synergies in purchasing was not the initial purpose of BT Industries' acquisition of Raymond. Furthermore, even though the products of the merged companies are used for exactly the same type of operations, there are differences in product standards and safety regulations on different product markets. In view of this factor, together with high cost of changing current products in favour of joint purchasing, the choice was to compare purchased volumes and see whether potential benefits could be achieved without changing the products. Thus, the potential effects on the supplier relationships with the integrating companies were not as dramatic as could be expected in cases of horizontal integration. There are other parameters besides product similarities to take into account when integrating two similar companies. However, a relationship with a dominant supplier of electric components changed from one of dominance to one of more interdependence. With the combined purchasing volumes of the integrated company, it was considered by the supplier to be a more important customer.

After the acquisition, co-ordination of purchasing activities was initiated. The acquisition of Raymond made it possible to lower the costs of administrative infrastructure and support activities, for example, legal and financial services. Thus, suppliers of such services were affected by fewer orders from the acquired company. The acquisition increased the combined company's negotiating power by virtue of a higher volume of purchases. This development affected suppliers differently. Owing to the varying duration of contracts, it could in some cases take time before changes occurred; in other cases voluntary price adjustments were made, and in some instances co-ordination led to renegotiated contracts.

MERGERS, ACQUISITIONS, AND SUPPLIER RELATIONSHIPS

Studies of mergers and acquisitions often illustrate the benefits of consolidation (Larsson and Finkelstein 1999; Rumelt 1974; Wells 1984). As the cases show, these gains might be due to a changed buying pattern of the merging and acquiring companies, that is, to buy more from fewer suppliers. These companies may want more favourable prices and apply pressure on prices with their increased purchasing power. Other aspects relate to changes in organisation. In the forest products industry case, the supplier of investment equipment changed its organisation so as better to reflect developments in the organisation of the merging companies. In this case, the supplier adjusted to the internal power shift of the integrating companies, which had centralised certain decision-making from the subsidiary to the headquarter level. This adjustment shows that supplier relationships are not static and that companies adapt to changes in their relationships (Axelsson 1992; Håkansson and Snehota 1989). Reactions to changes also indicate the existence of dependencies between customers and their suppliers (Johanson and Mattsson 1987). Further, a merger or acquisition may alter the balance between the merging and acquiring companies and their suppliers. As described previously, dependence appears in different forms (Cox, Sanderson, and Watson 2000; Emerson 1962; Ritter, Wilkinson, and Johnston 2004), and a merger or an acquisition may initiate changes in dependence between the companies involved. To restore balance with the merging and acquiring companies, their suppliers may also merge and acquire in response to changes initiated by the original merger or acquisition; these cases are referred to as parallel M&A's (Öberg and Holtström 2006). This section discusses how the supplier relationship may be at stake in cases of horizontal integration.

One necessity in mergers and acquisitions is co-ordination of the purchasing function between the integrating companies. Why is this so important? Purchasing is related to costs, and the cost of purchased components and services is equivalent to a major part of the value added by a company. This makes suppliers important stakeholders. Savings, or cost reductions, in purchasing have a direct impact on overall corporate profitability. After an overview of cost-generating activities, quick cost reductions can often be made. Cost-cutting by the integrating companies may mean less revenue for suppliers and may jeopardise their business operations. However, what is wanted and what is possible may differ depending on the type of supply that can be affected.

The cases show that when the integrating companies initiate joint purchasing, one aim is to reduce the cost of purchased materials. These joint purchasing activities are initiated in the early phases of integration. In horizontal mergers and acquisitions the companies probably have much in common in regard to the potential effects of joint purchasing. It can quite likely be assumed that the products and their components will be very similar. Consequently, suppliers to such integrating companies will be subject to changes in terms of renegotiated contracts, combined volumes and also pressure to lower prices. Sometimes a request may be made for a 'positive' price development in view of the increased efficiency that will generate potential for decreasing price levels over time. The acquisition in the forklift industry may be characterised as horizontal as their products are similar. However, there is a difference because the products were developed for separate markets with different standards. At first glance, these two integrating companies would seem to offer potential through joint purchasing arrangements. Although potential benefits from joint purchasing arrangements are present, the benefits realised could be higher.

Supply of Direct Material

Suppliers of direct material and services (Holtström 2003, 2009) may experience varying changes in their business relationships with integrating companies. In the welding industry case much of the goods purchased were raw materials and components with standardised specifications, for which many alternative suppliers were available. The suppliers could thus be categorised as delivering 'off-the-shelf products'. The customer-supplier exchange can be seen as a discrete transaction (Dwyer, Schurr, and Oh 1987), even though there is a long relationship between customer and supplier, as these types of products are easily substitutable and can readily be provided by other suppliers. Products of this kind may have a volume/price relationship. In a merger or acquisition this means that there will be contacts with more/new suppliers of the same type of components. This situation presents an opportunity to restructure the entire supplier base of the integrating company. In such a case, the economies of scale are obvious, and the relationship between customer and supplier may not be as important as in cases where the suppliers furnish items of greater strategic value.

With a substantial number of suppliers to choose from in the welding industry case, the procurement situation was very favourable for the welding company. As for the suppliers, their relationship was at stake, with the following potential consequences: a larger volume of sales to integrating companies; lower prices owing to economies of scale; little or no volume of sales to the integrating companies. If the relationship is vulnerable as a result of integration, there may be opportunities for restructuring among the suppliers themselves, creating a larger supplier to meet increased demand (Holtström 2003; Öberg and Holtström 2006). Other factors of importance in supplier relationships are the volumes purchased by the acquirer, how large a portion of the supplier's sales and earnings is affected and whether it is possible for the suppliers to find other customers for their products. One positive effect is the new business opportunities for the suppliers selected by the integrating companies, although these suppliers could also face pressure on price levels from the integrating companies, with their negotiating power.

The distinction between more volume-oriented items of purchase and strategic items raises the question whether there are any differences in this regard that depend on the nature of the business relationship. With strategic items there is more of a relational exchange between customer and supplier (Dwyer, Schurr, and Oh 1987), in contrast to the more volume-oriented items in discrete transactions as discussed earlier. The cases studied show that there are close relationships between the merging companies and their suppliers. This finding is consistent with earlier research (Håkansson 1990, 2006). The importance of the relationship is attested by its long duration for product development where suppliers are involved. Thus, there is a mutual commitment between the customer and supplier (Doney and Cannon 1997; Hallén, Johanson, and Seyed-Mohamed 1991; Håkansson and Snehota 1995; Morgan and Hunt 1994). This situation is present in the automotive industry case. The importance of the customer-supplier relationships is also demonstrated by the fact that suppliers are encouraged to seek co-operative alliances in order to compete on larger projects. In the automotive industry case the supplier relationship is not at stake until it is time for a new generation of products. As long as production is on-going, the situation of suppliers is rather stable, with some degree of dependence in the relationship with the integrating companies.

For strategic components the cases show difficulties in exchanging suppliers. Consequently, the relationship between a customer and a supplier may not necessarily be put at stake by a merger or an acquisition. Even suppliers of components with low value and high transportation costs may show relatively stable relationships after a merger or an acquisition; an example would be a supplier of steel components in the forklift industry case. Is it then complicated or not to switch suppliers? As discussed earlier, suppliers of more standardised products may be easily changed as there are many alternative suppliers and low switching costs. In other circumstances, as in the automotive industry case, it might only be possible to change suppliers in the long run. The reasons mentioned are related to product complexity and the high cost of product development. Thus, there are ties of dependence between customer and supplier (Johanson and Mattsson 1987). For a supplier of strategic components, the relationship with the purchaser could be fairly stable, a possible indication that a merger or acquisition might have little effect on the supplied items. Stable relationships could also be a consequence of the fact that changing suppliers is a costly, time-consuming process. In the cases studied the time horizons for changing to another supplier vary from six months up to several years. Time horizons may be extremely distant in cases where product development is concerned and/or quality/functional tests are required for approval of products from new suppliers. The cases also identify another reason why changing suppliers may be difficult; there may be problems in finding other potential suppliers, either because very few suppliers are available or because those who are available lack the necessary capacity or cannot deliver the right quality.

The type and complexity of the purchased goods are related to the possible effects on suppliers in connection with a merger or an acquisition (Anderson, Havila, and Salmi 2001; Havila and Salmi 2002; Holtström 2003; Öberg 2008; Öberg and Holtström 2006). For a supplier of strategic and/or other critical resources, like some of the suppliers in the cases, changing the relationship with their customer appears to be difficult and complex. The critical issue for such a supplier in a merger or acquisition may not be directly relational, but may concern to a greater extent what is exchanged in the relationship. It also seems as if the structural change entailed by a merger or an acquisition will not necessarily affect business relationships with suppliers. One consequence of a merger or acquisition might be a strengthened position for the supplier if the available alternatives are few. Thus, the relationship is subject to change, but in a positive way for the supplier. Suppliers of non-critical items, however, may have a different experience: no change, a stronger position, or a weaker one. This indicates that the consequences for a supplier in its relationship with the merging and acquiring companies depend on the direction in which the relationship develops.

As described in the forklift industry case, a pre-acquisition supplier relationship—considered as one of dominance by the customer (acquirer)—changed to a relationship of greater interdependence. The 'new' forklift company (BT Industries and Raymond), almost twice the size of the independent companies, was considered a more important customer by this supplier. Thus, the supplier relationship, while perhaps not in jeopardy, changed in a more favourable direction for the integrating companies.

Supply of Indirect Material

Supply of indirect material can be found in all cases studied, although earlier studies (Holtström 2003, 2009) show that this type of supply is given more attention where the product similarities between integrating companies are less or not directly obvious. Examples of indirect material like office supplies and computers may be worth investigating for possible synergy. In the forklift industry case there were some similarities in administrative infrastructure, such as solutions for customer financing and co-ordination of legal and auditing services. There may be greater potential for this kind of synergies in integration where products are less similar than in cases of horizontal integration as described in this chapter. However, the explicit focus of integration seems to be primarily on areas related to production. Although indirect material has been given less attention, supplier relationships in that area may also be subject to change in mergers and acquisitions, though it is not clear to what degree. Relevant factors in this regard may include speed of integration, interest in finding and realising synergies in all areas of operation and the type of integration concerned.

Equipment Supply

For suppliers of equipment for investments in machinery, as in the Stora Enso case (Holtström 2003, 2009), a merger or an acquisition means that business opportunities may be jeopardised, for example, through delay or postponement of business projects. A review of the integrating companies' assets in the integration process reveals what capacities and what potential restructuring opportunities there are. The outcome of the integration process may affect business relationships with suppliers. An example can be found in the forest products industry case, where the supplier of machinery and equipment received no orders for new machinery from the merged enterprise for the first four years after the merger. In addition, the market for new machinery and equipment was decreasing, and instead of investing in new machines, companies were upgrading the existing ones. This situation forced the supplier in the case to broaden the scope of its business to include service, operations, and maintenance. Thus, the nature of the supplier's business has been at stake, and it must adapt to the current situation. This case illustrates a situation of possible change in the customer-supplier relationship and a need to adjust to changing market conditions (Axelsson 1992; Hallén, Johanson, and Seyed-Mohamed 1991; Håkansson and Snehota 1989). Mergers and acquisitions tend in such a case to increase interdependence between customer and supplier, as there are fewer alternate entities left to do business with in a decreasing market. Thus, there is a change in the degree of mutual dependence between the companies (Cox, Sanderson, and Watson 2000; Emerson 1962; Ritter, Wilkinson, and Johnston 2004). Also in the automotive industry case, projects were brought to a standstill during a review following the acquisition. In this phase of the integration process, the integrating companies carefully reviewed their investment needs before continuing to invest. Such a review may thus affect supplier relationships if it means that the integrating companies do not place any new orders.

CONCLUDING DISCUSSION

This study on supplier relationships in mergers and acquisitions suggests that suppliers are important stakeholders in mergers and acquisitions because they will be affected by changes initiated by the merging parties. This finding can be illustrated for different types of supply: direct material, indirect material and equipment. Table 9.1 summarises the stakes of potential suppliers in mergers and acquisitions. For suppliers, co-ordination of purchasing activities by the integrating companies is of importance to the supplier relationship, so that the relationship in itself is subject to change. After a merger or acquisition integrating companies will continue to need the resources provided through relationships with their suppliers (Håkansson and Ford 2002). The strategic importance of these supply sources is reflected in their importance to the relationship at stake. The more strategic components were supplied to the merging companies, the less the potential negative effects for the suppliers. Consequently, the supplier's relationship with the integrating companies may not be at stake after all, or at least the risk of changes may be reduced. By contrast, if the components supplied are of less strategic value, the risk of changes in the relationship may be more substantial for the supplier. If in addition the integrating companies have a large selection of potential suppliers to choose from, the risk of changes in the supplier relationship may even be greater for the supplier.

Håkansson (1990) found close collaboration between customers and suppliers in technological development. If there is high degree of joint product development by merging companies, the potential changes in these product development projects pose a risk to the supplier following the merger or acquisition. However, if suppliers are extensively involved in the development projects, the potential change from such collaboration will be more limited the more complex the products are.

Another issue for the supplier in the relationship with an integrating company is whether to continue as a supplier after a merger or acquisition. The nature and extent of the dependence between customer and supplier are important in this regard (Cox, Sanderson, and Watson 2000; Emerson 1962; Ritter, Wilkinson, and Johnston 2004). Extensive dependence between the companies accentuates the importance of the relationship and thus limits the potential for effects like a change of supplier. For suppliers it is therefore essential to understand the complexity of their products as well as the strategic importance of the component in their customers' final product. For suppliers of indirect material, the potential effects are similar to those for suppliers of direct material and thus dependent on the strategic importance of the products supplied. However, the primary interest in determining the consequences of the merger or acquisition for the integrating companies seems to be more associated with direct material. For suppliers of equipment, the cases suggest a temporal dimension in the relationship, the question being how the internal resources of the integrating companies affect the supplier relationship over time. The supplier will then have an interest in determining the timing and extent of new investments by the integrating company.

A relationship of greater dependence between the supplier and the integrating companies may mean that the supplier's organisation need not be of the same proportions as before, or retain previous kinds of competence in some areas, such as marketing, sales, and project management. If the supplier organisation is thus 'downsized', this step will tend to augment the supplier's dependence on the customer. The supplier will be in a more vulnerable position if the business relationship is changed in a way that calls for developing and establishing new ways of doing business. Such a change may then take longer than if the organisation had not been trimmed down. On the other hand, the supplier will benefit from the lower cost of a reduced organisation due to partnership. With increased concentration among companies in an industry, and thus closer relationships between customers and suppliers, it may become more attractive to downsize the organisation in order to cut costs.

Table 9.1 Summary of Possible Supplier Stakes in Mergers and Acquisitions

Type of supplier	*Possible stakes*
Direct material (product related)	Co-ordination of purchasing may affect suppliers but depends on: • Complexity of supplied component—dimension of strategic importance of products; the more strategic the components supplied, the less the potential effect on the supplier relationship, and vice versa. • Product development—high involvement in product development between the supplier and the integrators implies less effect on the business relationship, and vice versa. • Changing suppliers—highly complex components imply greater difficulty in changing suppliers than with less complex components.
Indirect material (non-product related)	Coordinating effects in indirect material may be greater than indicated in horizontal integrations, where integration efforts focus more on direct material. Coordination of indirect material has potential for greater importance, especially when product similarities in the horizontal integration are limited.
Equipment (investment)	Suppliers of equipment may be affected by the integrating companies' review of their investment needs, with a temporary effect of no new investments. Changes in the organisational structure of the integrating companies may affect how the supplier chooses to rearrange its organisation as a consequence of the merger.

MANAGERIAL IMPLICATIONS

First, it is crucial for both the integrating companies and the suppliers to understand the nature of their business relationship. For suppliers it will affect how easy or complicated it is to be replaced as a supplier to companies involved in a merger or an acquisition. Thus, the supplier structure (of current, potential and available suppliers) and the different types of business relationships established between the supplier and the merging companies are relevant when possible changes in their relationship are considered. For the integrating companies these factors are relevant for understanding how to manage supplier relationships in a manner that will help to achieve the intended effects of the merger or acquisition.

Second, the type of products or service (complexity) provided by the supplier is a central determinant of the potential effects of a merger or an acquisition on supplier relationships. A merger or an acquisition represents a structural change in an industry. However, such a change does not necessarily impact supplier relationships, which may be more important than the structural change itself. The purpose of the merger or the acquisition makes a difference, though, in regard to potential changes in relationships with suppliers. Suppliers of more off-the-shelf components may be more easily replaced by suppliers of substitutable alternatives than suppliers of more strategic components.

Third, it is essential to understand the type of relationship that exists between suppliers and their customers in order to identify the potential changes in supplier relationships following a merger or an acquisition. The nature and extent of the dependence between the integrating companies and the suppliers will determine whether and when a change will occur as a consequence of a merger or an acquisition. The typology of different customer-supplier relationships is based on what is supplied in the relationship, that is, direct material, indirect material, and equipment.

Finally, it is important for the companies involved, both the merging companies and the suppliers, to analyse the situation and the potential effects of integration on their relationships. One relevant consideration is the portion of the supplier's turnover potentially affected by the merger or acquisition. In other words, does the merger involve the supplier's principal customer or a less critical one? For the supplier such an analysis would probably be helpful in exploring the possible consequences of a merger or an acquisition for its customers.

REFERENCES

Anderson, H., Havila, V., and Salmi, A. (2001) 'Can you buy a business relationship? On the importance of customer and supplier relationships in acquisitions', *Industrial Marketing Management*, 30: 575–86.

Axelsson, B. (1992) 'Corporate Strategy Models and Networks—Diverging Perspectives', in B. Axelsson and G. Easton (eds.) *Industrial Networks—A New View of Reality*, London: Routledge.

Cowley, P.R. (1988) 'Market Structure and Business Performance: An Evaluation of Buyer/Seller Power in the PIMS Database', *Strategic Management Journal*, 9(3): 271–78.

Cox, A., Sanderson, J., and Watson, G. (2000) *Power Regimes—Mapping the DNA of business and supply chain relationships*, Erlsgate Press.

Doney, P.M. and Cannon, J.P. (1997) 'An examination of the Nature of Trust in Buyer-Seller Relationships', *Journal of Marketing*, 61(April): 35–51.

Dwyer, F.R., Schurr, P.H., and Oh, S. (1987) 'Developing Buyer-Seller Relationships', *Journal of Marketing*, 51(2): 11–27.

Emerson, R.M. (1962) 'Power-Dependence Relations', *American Sociological Review*, 27(February): 31–41.

Håkansson, H. (1989) *Corporate Technological Behaviour: Co-operation and Networks*, London: Routledge.

Håkansson, H. (1990) 'Technological Collaboration in Industrial Networks,' *European Management Journal*, 8(3): 371–79.

Håkansson, H. (2006) 'Business relationships and networks: consequences for economic policy', *The Antitrust Bulletin*, 51(1): 142–63.

Håkansson, H. and Ford, D. (2002) 'How should companies interact in business networks?', *Journal of Business Research*, 55: 133–39.

Håkansson, H. and Snehota, I. (1989) 'No Business Is an Island—The Network Concept of Business Strategy', *Scandinavian Journal of Management*, 5(3): 187–200.

Håkansson, H. and Snehota, I. (eds.) (1995) *Developing Relationships in Business Networks*, London: Routledge.

Hallén, L., Johanson, J., and Seyed-Mohamed, N. (1991) 'Interfirm Adaptation in Business Relationships', *Journal of Marketing*, 55 (April): 29–37.

Havila, V. and Salmi, A. (2002) 'Network Perspective on International Mergers and Acquisitions: What more do we see?', in V. Havila, M. Forsgren, and H. Håkansson (eds.) *Critical Perspectives on Internationalisation*, Oxford: Elsevier Science Ltd.

Holtström, J. (2003) *Suppliers in Mergers and Acquisitions—A study of relationship changes and synergy realisation*, Licentiate Thesis No. 1012, Linköping Studies in Science and Technology, Linköping University.

Holtström, J. (2009) *Synergi?—En studie av några industriföretag*, Doctoral Thesis No. 1232, Linköping Studies in Science and Technology, Linköping University.

Johanson, J. and Mattsson, L.-G. (1987) 'Interorganizational Relations in Industrial Systems: A Network Approach Compared with the Transaction-Cost Approach', *International Studies of Management and Organisations*, 17: 34–48.

Larsson, R. and Finkelstein, S. (1999) 'Integrating Strategic, Organizational, and Human Resource Perspectives on Mergers and Acquisitions: A Case Survey of Synergy Realization', *Organization Science*, 10(1): 1–26.

Morgan, R.M. and Hunt, S.D. (1994) 'The Commitment-Trust Theory of Relationship Marketing', *Journal of Marketing*, 58: 20–38.

Öberg, C. (2008) *The Importance of Customers in Mergers and Acquisitions*, Doctoral Thesis No. 1193, Linköping Studies in Science and Technology, Linköping University.

Öberg, C. and Holtström, J. (2006) 'Are Mergers and Acquisitions Contagious?', *Journal of Business Research*, 59: 1267–75.

Oh, J. and Rhee, S.-K. (2008) 'The influence of supplier capabilities and technology uncertainty on manufacturer-supplier collaboration', *International Journal of Operations and Production Management*, 28(6): 490–517.

Powell, W.W., Koput, K.W., and Smith-Doerr, L. (1996) 'Interorganizational Collaboration and the Locus of Innovation: Network of Learning in Biotechnology', *Administrative Science Quarterly*, 41: 116–45.

Ritter, T. and Gemünden, H.G. (2003) 'Interorganizational relationships and networks: An overview', *Journal of Business Research*, 56: 691–97.
Ritter, T., Wilkinson, I.F., and Johnston, W.J. (2004) 'Managing in complex business networks', *Industrial Marketing Management*, 33: 175–83.
Rumelt, R.P. (1974) *Strategy, Structure and Economic Performance*, Cambridge, MA: Harvard University Press.
Stake, R. (2003) 'Case studies', in N.K. Denzin and Y.S. Lincoln (eds.) *Strategies of qualitative inquiry*, Thousand Oaks, CA: Sage, pp. 134–64.
Wells, J.R. (1984) *In search of synergy*, Harvard University, Graduate School of Business Administration.
Wilkinson, I. and Young, L. (2002) 'On Cooperating Firms, relations and networks', *Journal of Business Research*, 55: 123–32.

10 Why Do Customers Dissolve Their Business Relationships with the Acquired Party Following an Acquisition?

Christina Öberg

INTRODUCTION

The stakeholders described in this chapter are the acquired party's (the target's) customers. The chapter takes their perspective in business-to-business settings and focuses on why they may decide to dissolve their business relationships with the target following the acquisition, that is, in the post-acquisition phase. Dissolution refers here to the customer's active choice to terminate its relationship with the acquired party. The risk of dissolution is important to consider, because customers would affect the value of an acquired party, and because, as described in this chapter, the acquirer may affect the degree of customer losses by resisting integration in customer interfaces (such as product and sales staff integration).

Researchers have drawn attention to the limited amount of literature on the marketing consequences of mergers and acquisitions (Homburg and Bucerius 2005; Mazur 2001), and also stressed the need to consider effects of mergers and acquisitions on business relationships (Anderson, Havila, and Salmi 2001; Holtström 2008). Whereas scholars such as Capron and Hulland (1999), Homburg and Bucerius (2005), and Weber and Dholakia (2000) have researched the marketing dimension, they have done so from the acquiring or merging firm's perspective. The customer perspective on such endeavours is rarely taken. Yet customers are often central in the motives to merge or acquire, such as an aim to strengthen a position, increase sales per customer, or possibly take over specific customer relationships of the target (Kelly, Cook, and Spitzer 2003; Walter and Barney 1990). From a customer perspective, however, the acquisition may be perceived quite differently (Öberg, Henneberg, and Mouzas 2007). Research results indicate that the loss of customers following a merger or acquisition may be severe (Rydén 1972). Certainly, any strategic activity may lead to reactions among customers (Ford and Håkansson 2006). What seems to be the case, though, is that dissolution of customer relationships (Hocutt 1998; Strandvik and Holmlund 2000), initiated by the customer, is particularly prevalent following a merger or acquisition.

Rydén (1972), for instance, found that between 25 and 50 percent of the target's customers may be lost following an acquisition, and as is indicted in this chapter, the figure may be even higher (cf., Öberg 2008). It is also evident from Rydén's (1972) study and the acquisitions presented here that there are substantial differences between various studies, and thereby also between different acquisitions.

The purpose of this chapter is *to describe and discuss customers' reasons for dissolving their business relationships with acquired parties following an acquisition*. The chapter's theoretical point of departure is taken from research on business relationship dissolution. Its empirical part is based on interviews with customers of acquired parties in relation to three sequences of acquisitions. A sequence of acquisitions denotes a succession of several acquisitions that involve the same company as acquirer or acquired party. Hence, for each sequence, the acquirer or target firm overlaps, as do the customers as well. The sequences studied involved the following companies as acquirers or acquired parties: Verimation (acquired by ADB Gruppen Mandator, NetSys, and Nexus), Structurit/Momentum Doc (acquired by Momentum and later BasWare), and BT Industries, (acquirer of Raymond and Cesab, later acquired and presently part of Toyota Industries). In these three sequences of acquisitions, dissolved customer relationships are highlighted, but also treated are acquisitions where such relationships subsequently continued. With the inclusion of both acquisitions resulting in dissolved relationships and those where relationships are continued, it is possible to form an opinion on why the relationships were dissolved based on contrasting characteristics of the acquisitions. Hence, the comparison between the number of dissolved relationships and the acquisition, its integration and the parties to it, helps in determining what forces drive dissolutions. In the analysis section, customer reactions are related to different items covered by the acquisition. The chapter ends with a concluding discussion and suggestions of theoretical and managerial implications.

THEORETICAL CONSIDERATIONS

Customer relationships refer to repeated purchases between two specific parties acting as supplier and customer (Grönroos 2000; Halinen 1996). In such business relationships, customer and supplier often adjust to each other (Hallén, Johanson, and Seyed-Mohamed 1991), implying that value is built into their relationship, in turn interlinking individual episodes of exchange (Håkansson 1982). The benefits to the supplier in terms of decreased marketing costs and increased predictability and per customer revenue (Dwyer, Schurr, and Oh 1987) may be easy to understand, but what are customers' reasons to participate in long-term business relationships with a specific supplier? O'Malley (2003) refers to the following customer arguments: reduced uncertainty and risks because the customer can more easily anticipate quality and other attributes of supply, enhanced value and probability of goal attainment as the supplier knows the customer's preferences, and avoiding the additional cost of constantly searching for alternatives (cf., Pfeffer and Salancik 1978; Williamson 1979). It could thus be suggested that when something interferes with the stability created, reduces value, or raises the costs associated with the relationship, the customer would be increasingly inclined to dissolve its relationship with the supplier.

Dissolution, or as often described in consumer research, termination of relationships, entails the cessation of business agreements between firms (Hocutt 1998). Research on the development of relationships refers to dissolutions as the last (and perhaps inevitable) phase of a relationship (Dwyer, Schurr, and Oh 1987; Ford, 1980). Literature specifically focusing on dissolutions emphasised early on the importance of single so-called critical events (cf., Flanagan 1954) as reasons for relationships to end (Keaveney 1995). Critical events include delivery failures (Balachandra, Brockhoff, and Pearson 1996), bankruptcy (Sutton 1987), key personnel leaving the relationship (Hocutt 1998), strategy changes in regard to the customer (Giller and Matear 2001; Havila and Salmi 2002), and dissatisfaction (Holmlund and Strandvik 1999; Keaveney 1995; Seabright, Levinthal, and Fichman 1992; Tähtinen and Halinen 2002). These different critical incidents or factors imply that changes may occur with the supplier or the customer, or in their relationship, that eventually lead it to dissolve. In other words, any party to the relationship, but also a circumstance external to it, may cause dissolution. In the case of a merger or acquisition, the changes studied in this chapter would relate to the supplier, whereas the reactions are those of customers. Here it is thus the customer that decides to dissolve its relationship with the acquired supplier; in other cases dissolution decisions may well be taken by the acquirer or acquired party, or any of their other business partners.

More recent studies on relationship dissolution have added the current state of the relationship as a variable for termination (Giller and Matear, 2001; Tähtinen and Halinen, 2002). Halinen and Tähtinen (2002) describe dissolutions as processes 'where several explaining factors and events can be intertwined and influential simultaneously' (p. 11). Small failures may add up to grounds for dissolution, and according to Peng and Shenkar (2002) a dissolution process may start to live a life of its own, making it increasingly difficult to repair earlier mistakes. However, the literature still suggests a need for a trigger, one or several incidents, to start the dissolution. A merger or acquisition may well be such a trigger (Halinen, Salmi, and Havila 1999; Havila and Salmi 2002; Hocutt 1998; Seabright, Levinthal, and Fichman 1992), yet the literature has not explained to any significant degree why this would be the case. Mergers and acquisitions encompass a broad spectrum of business transactions, all including a transfer of ownership (Hagedoorn and Duysters 2002); as a result, companies may be integrated to a varying extent (Haspeslagh and Jemison 1991). Consequently, though it may be ownership that initiates the dissolution of customer relationships, what actually drives dissolutions may be differences in degree of integration. If this is so, it would help to explain the great variety in number of dissolved relationships provided by different studies (Rydén 1972; Öberg 2008). Thus, rather than referring to a merger or acquisition as the trigger for dissolution, this chapter searches for the real reasons, in terms of such items as integration and characteristics of the acquirer in the merger or acquisition, when customers dissolve their relationships with the target.

METHOD

The main data source for this chapter is 33 interviews with representatives of 18 different companies, each of which was a customer of one or more companies involved in eight different acquisitions. These interviews were supplemented by an additional 28 interviews with representatives of acquirers and targets. The interviews were conducted between 2003 and 2007. The eight acquisitions were part of three different sequences of acquisitions (involving Verimation, Structurit/Momentum Doc, and BT Industries). They represent different degrees of integration in marketing (integration of sales activities and/or products, Capron and Hulland 1999). Thus, customers were subjected to changes to differing degrees, and they also decided to a varying extent to dissolve their business relationships with the acquired parties. For the study, customers were chosen to represent companies of various sizes (from small family-owned firms to large multinationals) and different industries (consumer goods and services to high-tech industries), as well as customers that had remained with the target and, when applicable those that had dissolved their relationships with it. Table 10.1 describes the customers interviewed for each sequence of acquisitions. In the presentation of the results of the study, the acquisitions are described in terms of the three sequences of acquisitions. The reasons for this choice are that it allows study of several events leading to final dissolution (Halinen and Tähtinen 2002; Peng and Shenkar 2002) and that the customers are the same in each sequence of acquisitions, so that the customer relationship may have gone through one or more of the acquisitions in the sequence.

In the data collection procedure, customers were interviewed with an open-ended question approach (McCracken 1988). The interviews covered, without being limited to, the following areas: the business relationship with the acquired party; its length and content, and the reasons for it; and the acquisition(s)—how they were perceived by the customer, changes related to them and the reactions to these changes. The interviews with representatives of the acquiring and acquired parties also made it possible to capture what happened with other customer

Table 10.1 Customers Interviewed—Numbers of Interviews

Sequence	*Verimation: 3 acquisitions*	*Structurit/ Momentum Doc: 2 acquisitions*	*BT Industries: 3 acquisitions*
Acquirers/ acquired parties (1st name = acquirer; 2nd = acquired party)	ADB Gruppen Mandator/ Verimation NetSys/Verimation Nexus/Verimation	Momentum/Structurit BasWare/Momentum Doc	BT Industries/ Raymond BT Industries/Cesab Toyota Industries/ BT Industries
Number of interviews (customer companies)*	5 interviews (Ericsson; IKEA; InfoData)**	14 interviews (Fakturatjänst; HSB; Kopparstaden; Saab; Scania; Örebrobostäder; two anonymous companies)***	14 interviews (Beslag & Metall, Comau; DFDS Transport; DHL; FläktWoods; Saab; Servera; Volvo Group)

* While there are some overlaps between customer companies in the various sequences (e.g., Saab in the BT Industries and Momentum Doc/Structurit acquisitions), different representatives of the customer company were interviewed for each sequence, a result of differences between products offered by the parties in different sequences (e.g., trucks and IT-systems).

** One interview with representative of company that dissolved its relationship with the acquired party following the 2nd acquisition; two interviews with a representative of company that dissolved its relationship with the acquired party following the 3rd acquisition. In the remaining interviews the customer was interviewed regarding all acquisitions in the sequence.

*** Six interviews with representatives of companies that dissolved their business relationship with the acquired party following the 2nd acquisition.

relationships than those for which interviews were held. Data presented on number of relationships dissolved refer to the entire customer base of the acquired parties, not just customers interviewed, whereas the reasons for the dissolutions are taken from the customer interviews. The interviews lasted between 30 minutes and three hours and were transcribed. In the analysis procedure, each customer was classified based on whether it remained with the supplier or dissolved the relationship following the acquisition. Reasons for remaining as well as reasons for dissolving relationships were categorised based on comparisons between the acquisitions studied (cf., Pratt 2009). These reasons were in turn compared to previous literature on relationship dissolution. It was thus possible to review the findings in the light of existing research and to develop the findings further from the acquisitions studied (cf., Dubois and Gadde 2002; Kirkeby 1994).

THREE SEQUENCES OF ACQUISITIONS

This section describes the three sequences of acquisitions.

Verimation: Decreased Focus on Acquired Party and Attempted Product Replacement

The first sequence of acquisitions describes three acquisitions of the same acquired party: Verimation. The company had early on established a strong position in a product niche, e-mail solutions, where it had become a fore-runner through developing such solutions back in the 1980s. The company was founded by Volvo and Ericsson, helping it to furnish its system to other large companies as well and to establish a strong customer base. In the first acquisition, Verimation was acquired by ADB Gruppen Mandator, a company engaged in IT consultancy and hence an actor in a related business area. ADB Gruppen Mandator intended to sell consultancy services to Verimation's customers. Although few customers responded positively to this idea, the cross-selling attempts and subsequent financial problems of ADB Gruppen Mandator meant that less focus was placed on developing Verimation's product. To come to terms with financial difficulties, ADB Gruppen Mandator divested Verimation by introducing it on the stock exchange. New acquisition attempts were directed at Verimation, one of which fell through when Verimation showed losses. Problems in reaching consensus among board members on the strategy of Verimation led to continual cutbacks in product development. An active search for a new partner followed, with the result that Verimation was acquired again and delisted from the stock exchange. The new acquirer, NetSys, which had held the lease to sell a Canadian IT-system on the Nordic market, soon decided to replace Verimation's product with its own, and a price increase by a full 300 percent put pressure on customers. The product was never replaced. Further challenges arose with a scandal at NetSys related to the company's attempt to sell its leased system outside agreed markets, with a law-suit against the Canadian company and subsequent attempts to acquire it through manipulating the media image of the company. In the end NetSys, and thereby also Verimation, was declared bankrupt. As those managing the bankruptcy estate believed that there was potential future value in Verimation, it was separated from the estate and sold to another new acquirer, Nexus, a listed company specializing in IT security. Nexus saw an opportunity to benefit from the customer relationships of Verimation, to cross-sell its product to these customers, and to integrate security solutions into Verimation's product. Although the original product of Verimation was retained, little attention was paid to developing it further, thus causing it to lose competitive attractiveness.

The customer aspect of this sequence of acquisitions includes an ever-shrinking customer base. Even by the time of the first acquisition, customers had started to question the future of Verimation's system. This course of events was driven by limited product development as well as the appearance of competing alternatives on the market:

> 'What future does the company have? Of course, you do not dare to build solutions on something that may not last. During the second half of the 1990s we realised that this [Verimation's product] could not last forever. We compared the company with IBM's Lotus and Microsoft and made a simple guess as to which solution would last the longest? The answer was quite simple; Microsoft'.
>
> (Jan Fagerström, Manager, Hewlett Packard, previously Ericsson)

Most customers, however, remained for a short period. As a result of greatly increased prices and also the scandal following NetSys' acquisition, many customers decided to dissolve their relationship with Verimation. Customers like Volvo and Ericsson left at about that time. The attempted product replacement triggered further departures, but in that case, customers and Verimation made a combined effort to make the replacement fail. Following the last acquisition, customer losses continued. Most of these customers had made their decisions during the ownership of NetSys but had not managed to find an appropriate new supplier at the time; others remained sceptical of the company and at last found a reason to dissolve their relationships when the final acquirer started to show losses. Decisions by other customers also encouraged companies to dissolve their business relationships with Verimation. One customer that continued to use Verimation's product, but went through several cycles of questioning the company, was IKEA:

> 'There were lay-offs of staff, and at the same time many of the large companies in Sweden left Verimation, including Ericsson and Volvo, and some others. The discussions started again. This was one of the reasons why things were not going well for them. Many others changed to different systems'.
>
> (Tord Åkesson, IT Manager, IKEA)

During the three acquisitions, and based on estimates by representatives of Verimation, almost 70 percent of Verimation's customers dissolved their relationships with the company. Those customers that remained with Verimation did so because they considered that they had good relationships with the sales representatives of the acquired party, who remained the same through all the acquisitions. Some customers stayed because they used the product in their own offerings, relying on it in their own customer relationships.

Thus, the sequence of acquisitions involving Verimation as a target suggests that continuity in sales and service staff, as well as the continued existence of the product, may actually lead customers to stay on, even when much else points to dissolution of the business relationship. The sequence further indicates that acquirers focusing on their own sales and products may negatively impact the development of the target's product and be a reason for dissolution. Sharp price increases and a scandal may also impact dissolution decisions. Havila and Salmi (2000) have previously described how the reputation of an acquirer may cause business partners to dissolve their relationship with it, and Peng and Shenkar (2002) refer to how small failures may add up, leading to a decision to dissolve. These factors are illustrated here by the continuously decreasing focus on product development and the other issues that negatively impacted customer relationships.

Structurit/Momentum Doc: Various Integration Strategies

The second sequence of acquisitions consists of two: Momentum's acquisition of Structurit and BasWare's acquisition of Momentum Doc (Structurit, renamed following the first acquisition). Structurit was a small, innovative Swedish firm that was acquired by a party in a related business area, Momentum. Structurit had developed an electronic invoice-processing system, and much of its customer base consisted of real estate companies. Momentum focused on real estate systems (IT solutions for track maintenance, repair costs, and tenant income in rented estates). The two companies shared the same local markets and in part the same customers as well. The aim of the acquisition was to channel the two companies' respective products to each other's customers; predominately, Structurit's product would be sold to Momentum's customers. Following the acquisition, sales staff were kept as previously, and the two companies also continued to develop and market their own products to customers. Thus additional products were offered, whereas it was still possible to obtain previous products under the same conditions as before. Some years following the first acquisition, Structurit, by the time renamed Momentum Doc, was acquired by another company, BasWare, which was active in the same business area as Momentum Doc, electronic invoice-processing systems. However, whereas Momentum Doc mainly served the Swedish market, BasWare's principal focus had been in Finland. BasWare had started to expand internationally, and this factor, along with a wish to prevent any competitor from attaining a strong position on the Swedish market, was the principal reason for the acquisition. Following the acquisition, the development of Momentum Doc's system was cut back, and eventually a decision was reached to replace it with BasWare's system. This step caused staff that had previously worked with development in Momentum Doc to leave the company; in addition, sales staff decided to depart from the company as they found it difficult to market the BasWare's system to customers to whom they had previously offered the Momentum Doc solution.

In terms of customers, the first acquisition, Momentum's takeover of Structurit, which had allowed Structurit's customers to obtain Momentum's product, entailed no major changes. Customers continued to buy the existing product from the acquired party, and in those cases where customers had also bought the acquirer's product prior to the acquisition, they continued to do so afterwards. Some additional customers began buying Structurit's product, but mostly, the situation remained as before. As a representative of customer put it:

> 'Saab mostly thought of it as a change of name. There was some kind of ownership change, but we did not see that change. From our point of view, it was to be regarded as just a change of names'.
>
> (Lars Gullqvist, Manager Accounting Systems, Saab)

Following BasWare's acquisition of Momentum Doc, the decreased focus on product development meant that customers distanced themselves from the acquired party, yet continued to buy and use its product. As Momentum Doc's product was replaced, and as a consequence of changes in product-development and sales staff, customers began to reconsider their relationship with the acquired party. Typical customer sentiment was expressed the following way by a representative of Kopparstaden, a public housing company that had been a customer of both Momentum and Structurit since before the first acquisition:

> 'Initially we thought, and so we were told, that they would continue with [Momentum Doc's product], use it and develop it. Then we learned that they would transfer customers to BasWare's own system and discontinue [Momentum Doc's product]. And we realised that we should check the market for options'.
>
> (Pär Nyberg, CEO, Kopparstaden)

Kopparstaden and also other customers dissolved their relationships with Momentum Doc following the product replacement. Evaluations were conducted for all customers interviewed, but the result of their evaluations differed between individual customers. Based on approximations by Momentum Doc staff, 20 percent of the customers dissolved their business relationships with the company, 20 percent awaited how things would develop, and the remaining 60 percent decided to continue and thereby shift to BasWare's system. Among the customers deciding to remain with the company, a number shared a common affiliation, dominated by various HSB associations (tenants' savings and building society associations), and were also associated by belonging to the same industry. These customers based their decision partly on whether other customers in the association and the industry made the same choice. They believed that their association and the choice of the same product would strengthen their negotiating power with the supplier. In addition, in the industry scenario customers regarded it as an advantage to have the same product within the industry, allowing industry-specific adaptations.

This sequence of acquisitions thus reveals that changes in the acquired party increased the risk that customers would dissolve their relationship with the acquired party. The first acquisition entailed no actual changes because customers could continue to buy the same products as previously through the same sales personnel as before. They also continued with the same service staff as before. The second acquisition led to changes in the product offered, and as a consequence, changes in terms of service and sales staff. Hocutt (1998) has previously described how key personnel leaving a firm may trigger dissolution, and this factor was one trigger for dissolutions in the case. As in Halinen and Tähtinen (2002), BasWare's acquisition also shows how several triggering factors may be intertwined; here this point is illustrated by the staff departures following replacement of the product, with both changes causing customers to reconsider their current relationship. Apart from key personnel leaving and the product replacement, the sequence provides insight into customer motives for remaining with the company; they base their decisions on what other customers do.

BT Industries: A Sequence of Non-Integration Acquisitions

The third sequence of acquisitions consists of three between companies in closely related product niches. BT Industries was a Swedish manufacturer of warehouse trucks that acquired a US counterpart, Raymond, and thereafter an Italian counterbalance-truck manufacturer called Cesab. BT Industries was shortly afterward acquired by a world-wide counterbalance-truck producer, Toyota Industries. The warehouse and counterbalance-truck market could be divided largely between these two types of trucks, suppliers of which had become increasingly integrated in terms of customer offerings. Before the acquisitions, BT Industries was the third largest supplier of warehouse trucks on the European market and aimed at reaching the counterbalance-truck niche as well as broadening its geographical scope. The acquisition of Raymond, the leading manufacturer of warehouse trucks in the US, meant that BT Industries could now serve the US market. Their intention was to start providing global solutions to increasingly internationalised customers, but the continents remained largely separate markets following the acquisition. Products, sales channels, and individual representatives in the marketing organizations continued as previously. Impelled by developments in the industry, BT Industries found it important to extend its scope of business to the related counterbalance-truck niche. This was done through the second acquisition, that of the family-owned company Cesab, which operated mainly in the European market, the geographical market also served by BT Industries. Following that acquisition, BT Industries started its own line of branded counterbalanced trucks, which were sold through BT Industries' sales channels. At the same time, Cesab continued to sell counterbalanced trucks under its own name through the sales channels (independent dealers) that it had previously used. Thus, BT Industries' customers were offered additional and related products through their existing relationships with BT Industries, while Cesab's customers could continue to buy previous products through their existing relationships with the acquired party.

Soon after this second acquisition, BT Industries was itself acquired by the industry conglomerate, Toyota Industries. Toyota's principal truck business was in the same product area as Cesab (counterbalanced trucks). BT Industries had previously provided warehouse trucks to Toyota and continued to do so following the acquisition. There was no further integration (up to the time of the data collection), and BT Industries continued to sell its trucks under its own brand through its existing sales channels.

From the customers' perspective, basically no customer relationship dissolutions followed the acquisitions. Each acquired party continued to sell its products through existing sales channels; individual contacts remained the same; and brands were kept as before the acquisitions. Customers thus considered themselves unaffected by the acquisitions. Customers emphasised that this was possible because they could continue to buy existing products from established sales representatives, and also because the maintenance staff remained unchanged. Among the customers interviewed, no one saw any reason to change the relationship with BT Industries following the acquisitions, as was corroborated by BT Industries for other customers. Similar patterns were observed in the various companies; Raymond continued to provide trucks in the US; Cesab continued to sell through its independent dealers; and BT Industries maintained its relationships with customers, though it was less successful in providing additional products to them. Volvo is one customer that meets BT Industries on various markets and also maintains a preferred supplier arrangement with Toyota (see Öberg 2010 for details on this particular relationship). A representative of the company reported that no changes were seen on the US market or in Europe with regard to post-acquisition integration:

> 'Raymond does not feel as if it is part of BT. [. . .] It feels that Toyota has not done that much. It is mostly BT, who knows Volvo from before, that pushes things forward. Since Toyota has independent dealers, they do not have the power'.
>
> (Jan Söderlund, Purchasing Manager at Volvo Group)

Hence, the acquisitions described in this sequence reflect how the acquired parties were allowed to continue as before the acquisitions. Non-integration was the policy, and sales channels and products were largely kept as they were before the acquisitions, sometimes supplemented by additional products channelled through existing sales representatives. Moreover, the acquisitions did not lead to dissolution of any business relationships by the acquired party's customers. Continuity of products and sales representatives were indicated as reasons for this outcome.

ANALYSIS

Returning to the reasons for dissolution described in the theory section, three groups of theoretical reasons can be found: explanations in terms of single critical events (Keaveney 1995), those based on the present state of the relationship (Giller and Matear 2001), and those viewing dissolution as a process of several events (Halinen and Tähtinen 2002; Peng and Shenkar 2002). Mergers and acquisitions have been treated as reasons for dissolution of business relationships (Halinen, Salmi, and Havila 1999; Seabright, Levinthal, and Fichman 1992), but also to some extent considered a choice made by the acquirer. Key personnel leaving a company (Hocutt 1998), dissatisfaction and delivery failures in terms of customer requirements (Balachandra, Brockhoff, and Pearson 1996; Seabright, Levinthal, and Fichman 1992) are other reasons similar to those in the acquisitions presented here. The chapter specifically refers to situations where the acquirer makes changes but the customers make the decision to dissolve their business relationships.

In the various acquisitions studied, and also considering reasons for customers to remain with the acquired party, the following reasons for dissolution are suggested: product replacement, staff leaving the acquired party, bad reputation and financial difficulties of the acquirer, less attractive business conditions, and a process of several events occurring at the same time or in a series. Product replacement is illustrated in BasWare's acquisition of Momentum Doc and was also attempted following NetSys' acquisition of Verimation, whereas the other acquisitions, which resulted in fewer or no dissolutions of customer relationships, did not include any product replacements. The impact of staff leaving the acquired party is illustrated by BasWare's acquisition; following the decision to replace the product, sales and development staff decided to leave the acquired party, thus linking key staff leaving a company to product replacement. Issues of reputation are illustrated by NetSys' acquisition of Verimation, whereas financial difficulties were evident both following Momentum's acquisition of Structurit and for all acquirers in the Verimation sequence of acquisitions. How other parties react and thereby affect dissolution decisions could also be described in terms of reputation. This was implicitly the case in the Verimation acquisitions, where decreasing revenue made the company less attractive. Less attractive business conditions resulted following NetSys' acquisition of Verimation, when the acquirer decided to raise prices while at the same time turning its focus away from developing the product. A decreased focus on product development, as illustrated in the Structurit/Momentum Doc and Verimation acquisition sequences, resulted in conditions less favourable than before the acquisitions, and caused relationships to be dissolved. The case of several incidents leading to dissolution is illustrated in the Verimation acquisitions. Price increases, a scandal, cutbacks in product development, and threats of product replacement coincided in this case.

The acquisitions studied also show how dissolution decisions were countered by reasons to stay with the acquired party: the previous product remained, staff stayed, and other customers decided to continue with the company. The sequence of acquisitions including BT Industries, and also following Momentum's acquisition of Structurit, indicate how product continuity limited customer losses to a very few. Continuity of staff was observed in the acquisitions, including BT Industries, while how such continuity decreased the risk of customer relationship dissolution could be studied in the Verimation sequence of acquisitions. Continuity of staff was important for those customers that decided to continue with Verimation despite all the problems occurring under various owners. How other parties affected the decisions to stay or leave was seen in how various parties based their decisions on those of other parties in an association or in the same industry, as illustrated in BasWare's acquisition of Momentum Doc. Table 10.2 summarises the reasons for dissolution in the three sequences of acquisitions, along with reasons for continuity that countered the dissolution decisions.

Table 10.2 Reasons for Dissolution and Continuity

	Reason for dissolution	*Reason for remaining with the acquired party*	*Sequence involving Verimation 3 acquisitions*	*Sequence involving Structurit/ Momentum Doc 2 acquisitions*	*Sequence involving BT Industries 3 acquisitions*
Product replacement/ continuity	Product replacement	Previous products remain	Attempt to replace product following 2nd acquisition (NetSys) not realised	Product replaced following 2nd acquisition (BasWare)	Products continued in all acquisitions
Staff	Staff leaving the acquired party	Staff staying with the acquired party	Staff remained	Staff left following 2nd acquisition (BasWare)	Staff remained
Reputation	Bad reputation and financial difficulties of acquirer	Other customer deciding to remain with the acquired party	Financial difficulties in all acquisitions, bad reputation in 2nd acquisition (NetSys)	Financial issues with 1st acquirer (Momentum) became evident before the 2nd acquisition. Other customers as reason to remain seen in 2nd acquisition	No reputation or financial issues
Inferiority	Less attractive business conditions	—	Price raises and decreased focus on product development	BasWare's product less customised and advanced than Momentum Doc's	No such issues experienced by customers
Process	Several events occuring at the same time, or a series of events, interrelated or over time	—	Price raise, scandal and attempted product replacement following 2nd acquisition (NetSys). Repeated financial difficulties and decreased product development between all acquisitions.	Product replacement led to staff leaving, both factors causing dissolution.	No such issues experienced by customers.

Whereas this chapter focuses on customers' reasons for dissolving their business relationships with the target company, certainly the acquirer or the target may also plan to dissolve relationships with non-profitable customers. Price increases could be one method of achieving this objective, but none of the acquirers or acquired parties interviewed suggested that such attempts were made by them; hence, the dissolutions presented here were all initiated by the customers in reaction to acquisition or integration. The customers that dissolved their business relationships primarily represented large and in terms of prestige important customers to the targets. Verimation lost Ericsson, Volvo, Skanska, and some other customers, while IKEA continued as a customer. Momentum Doc lost many of its early collaboration partners such as Kopparstaden and Örebrobostäder, whereas the initiator of the system that Momentum Doc provided, HSB, remained with the target. Both Verimation and Structurit/Momentum Doc had mainly large customers because of the systems that they provided, and each such customer lost represented both a financial loss and a loss of prestige for the target.

CONCLUSIONS

The purpose of this chapter was to describe and discuss customers' reasons for dissolving their relationships with acquired parties following an acquisition. The chapter notes that factors within the scope of an acquisition may cause customers to dissolve their relationships with the acquired party. This in turn helps to explain the differences in frequency of dissolution between various studies, and it underscores that customer relationships may risk dissolution following a merger or acquisition. Based on the sequences of acquisitions presented, continuity in terms of products decreases the risk of relationship dissolution, while product replacement increases it. This means that an important aspect of retaining customers would be to continue with the products that the target originally offered. Similarly, changes in key staff, including maintenance staff, product developers, and sales staff, may lead to dissolution of customer relationships, whereas continuity of staff lowers such risks. Continuity of staff may also positively counteract consequences of product replacement, thus illustrating how different reasons for dissolution may neutralise one another. On the other hand, if several reasons for dissolution are present in the same acquisition, the risk of dissolution increases. Product replacement, reorganizing sales, maintenance organizations, or integrating product development departments are all means to achieve cost synergies. But this chapter indicates that measures intended to reduce costs may prove very costly to the acquirer and the acquired party in terms of lost customers. The steps that may prevent customer relationship dissolution relate closely to maintaining the target as an autonomous entity following the acquisition by allowing it to continue selling its present products and serving its present customers through existing sales staff and customer interaction.

In additions to items that relate to integration, the reputation and financial weakness of the acquirer may lead customers to dissolve their relationship with the acquired party. In this respect also, decisions to dissolve or remain with the acquired party may be affected by how other customers perceive the acquirer. Departure of other customers increases the risk of dissolution, whereas the risk is decreased when other customers remain with the acquired party and when different customers can act as a common unit or take advantage of other customer relationships. Factors like reputation and financial weaknesses, along with reactions of other customers, are largely beyond the control of the acquirer. By contrast, such reasons as offering customers less favourable business conditions than before, in terms of sharp price raises for instance, are based on decisions by the acquirer or the target. In the present case, these changes were a way for the acquirer to deal with a financially difficult situation, but inferior conditions may also be used to prompt customers to leave the target. A risk associated with such treatment of some customers is that other customers, with whom the acquirer and target wanted to continue their business relationships, may also leave. Whereas different terms of business may well be offered to profitable and unprofitable customers, the effect of some customers' leaving on decisions of other, more profitable customers should be taken into account. In the studied sequences of acquisitions, there was nothing to indicate that only unprofitable customers departed. On the contrary, the large and prestigious customers were the ones that dissolved their relationships with the targets. These customers had often been active in developing the target company's product, and hence, in addition to losing an important source of revenue, and a company vital for keeping other customers, the target also lost an essential contributor to continued development.

In addition to single reasons of product replacement, staff departure, reputation, and inferior business conditions, the dissolution of a customer relationship may eventually result from several incidents in succession. Various triggers may affect one another, producing a chain reaction in the acquired firm. This may also result from increased tension overtime arising from several events in series.

In sum, the following items may lead customers to dissolve their business relationships with the acquired party in a merger or acquisition:

- Product replacement
- Changes in key staff
- Unfavourable reputation, loss of other customers, and financial weakness of the acquirer
- Inferior conditions of business.

Whether a relationship will continue depends heavily on *ties of continuity*, and this chapter also indicates that processes involving several acquisitions may weaken customer relationships to the breaking point.

This chapter thus focuses on *what factors* within the scope of an acquisition may lead to dissolution of customer relationships. Previous research has emphasised in addition the current state of the relationship as an explanation for dissolutions (Giller and Matear 2001; Halinen and Tähtinen 2002). For the relationships and acquisitions studied, this factor may also explain differences between various relationships within the same acquisition. This chapter has regarded customer relationships more as aggregates, even though individual relationships were the sources of the data collected. In further research, differences between individual relationships could be studied and compared on a cross-relationship, cross-acquisition basis.

IMPLICATIONS

This chapter provides a customer perspective on acquisitions and deals with dissolution decisions related to their business relationships with the acquired party. It highlights the risk of customer relationship dissolution following an acquisition. Whereas some statements on number of lost customers have been presented in previous research (Rydén 1972; Öberg 2008), little attention has been paid to risks of dissolution following mergers or acquisitions. For researchers, it is important to consider how such external parties as customers may impact achievement of intentions in acquisitions. The chapter indicates how various events may drive one another and thereby add to the risks of customer relationship dissolution. Dissolution processes thus not only describe the process of dissolving relationships or several events adding up, but also incorporate several parties and reactions, as well as linking triggers to one another. The chapter also indicates that decision of other parties on dissolution may impact the tendency to dissolve a relationship or remain with an existing party.

For managers, it is important to consider what consequences a merger or acquisition may have on the company's customer relationships. This applies to both the acquirer and the acquired party. If the acquired party is valued on the basis of future cash flows or expectations of synergies related to customers, it is important as well to estimate the effect of customer relationship dissolution when calculating such cash flows. Also important to consider when planning the integration of companies is how it would affect existing relationships. Dissolutions following product replacement, for instance, may well outweigh expected cost synergies.

REFERENCES

Anderson, H., Havila, V., and Salmi, A. (2001) 'Can you buy a business relationship?—On the importance of customer and supplier relationships in acquisitions', *Industrial Marketing Management*, 30(7): 575–86.

Balachandra, R., Brockhoff, K.K., and Pearson, A.W. (1996) 'R&D project termination decisions: Processes, communication, and personnel changes', *Journal of Product Innovation Management*, 13: 245–56.

Capron, L. and Hulland, J. (1999) 'Redeployment of brands, sales forces, and general marketing management expertise following horizontal acquisitions: a resource-based view', *Journal of Marketing*, 63(2): 41–54.

Dubois, A. and Gadde, L.-E. (2002) 'Systematic combining: an abductive approach to case research', *Journal of Business Research*, 55(7): 553–60.

Dwyer, F.R., Schurr, P.H., and Oh, S. (1987) 'Developing buyer-seller relationships', *Journal of Marketing*, 51: 11–27.

Flanagan, J.C. (1954) 'The critical incident technique', *Psychological Bulletin*, 51: 327–58.

Ford, D. (1980) 'The development of buyer-seller relationships in industrial markets', *European Journal of Marketing*, 14(5/6): 339–54.

Ford, D. and Håkansson, H. (2006) 'The idea of interaction', *The IMP Journal*, 1(1): 4–27.

Giller, C. and Matear, S. (2001) 'The termination of inter-firm relationships', *The Journal of Business and Industrial Marketing*, 16(2): 94–112.

Grönroos, C. (2000) *Service Management and Marketing: A Customer Relationship Management Approach*, Chichester: John Wiley & Sons.

Hagedoorn, J. and Duysters, G. (2002) 'The effect of mergers and acquisitions on the technological performance of companies in a high-tech environment', *Technology Analysis & Strategic Management*, 14(1): 67–85.

Håkansson, H. (ed.) (1982) *International Marketing and Purchasing of Industrial Goods—An Interaction Approach*, London: John Wiley & Sons Ltd.

Halinen, A. (1996) 'The temporal dimension in buyer-seller relationship models', in P. Tuominen (ed.) *Emerging Perspectives in Marketing*, Turku: Turku school of economics and business administration, pp. 47–72.

Halinen, A., Salmi, A., and Havila, V. (1999) 'From dyadic change to changing business networks: an analytical framework', *The Journal of Management Studies*, 36(6): 779–94.

Halinen, A. and Tähtinen, J. (2002) 'A process theory of relationship ending', *International Journal of Service Industry Management*, 13(2): 163–80.

Hallén, L., Johanson, J., and Seyed-Mohamed, N. (1991) 'Interfirm adaptation in business relationships', *Journal of Marketing*, 55: 29–37.

Haspeslagh, P.C. and Jemison, D.B. (1991) *Managing Acquisitions: Creating Value through Corporate Renewal*, New York: Free Press.

Havila, V. and Salmi, A. (2000) 'Spread of change in business networks: an empirical study of mergers and acquisitions in the graphic industry', *Journal of Strategic Marketing*, 8(2): 105–19.

Havila, V. and Salmi, A. (2002) 'Network perspective on international mergers and acquisitions: What more do we see?', in V. Havila, M. Forsgren, and H. Håkansson (eds.) *Critical Perspectives on Internationalisation*, Oxford: Pergamon.

Hocutt, M.A. (1998) 'Relationship dissolution model: antecedents of relationship commitment and the likelihood of dissolving a relationship', *International Journal of Service Industry Management*, 9(2): 189–200.

Holmlund, M. and Strandvik, T. (1999) 'Perception configurations in business relationships', *Management Decision*, 37(9): 686–96.

Holtström, J. (2008) *Synergi?—En studie av några industriföretag*, Doctoral Thesis No. 1232, Linköping Studies in Science and Technology, Linköping University.

Homburg, C. and Bucerius, M. (2005) 'A marketing perspective on mergers and acquisitions: How marketing integration affects postmerger performance', *Journal of Marketing*, 69: 95–113.

Keaveney, S.M. (1995) 'Customer switching behavior in service industries: An exploratory study', *Journal of Marketing*, 59: 71–82.

Kelly, J., Cook, C., and Spitzer, D. (2003) *Unlocking Shareholder Value: The Keys to Success—Mergers and Acquisitions: A Global Research Report*, London: KPMG.

Kirkeby, O. (1994) 'Abduktion', in H. Andersen (ed.) *Videnskabsteori og Metodelaere*, Frederiksberg: Samfundslitteratur, pp. 122–52.

Mazur, L. (2001) 'Does this acquisition create customer value', *Market Leader*, 13: 1–11.

McCracken, G. (1988) *The Long Interview*, Newbury Park: Sage Publications.

O'Malley, L. (2003) 'Relationship marketing', in S. Hart, *Marketing Changes*, London: International Thomson Business Press, pp. 125–46.

Öberg, C. (2008) *The Importance of Customers in Mergers and Acquisitions*, Doctoral Thesis No. 1193, Linköping Studies in Science and Technology, Linköping University.

Öberg, C. (2010) 'What happened with the grandiose plans? Strategic plans and network realities in B2B interaction', *Industrial Marketing Management*, 39: 963–74.

Öberg, C., Henneberg, S.C., and Mouzas, S. (2007) 'Changing network pictures: The evidence from mergers and acquisitions', *Industrial Marketing Management*, 36(7): 926–40.

Peng, M.W. and Shenkar, O. (2002) 'Joint venture dissolution as corporate divorce', *Academy of Management Executive*, 16(2): 92–105.

Pfeffer, J. and Salancik, G.R. (1978) *The External Control of Organizations—A Resource Dependence Perspective*, New York: Harper & Row.

Pratt, M.G. (2009) 'From the editors: For the lack of boilerplate: tips on writing up (and reviewing) qualitative research', *Academy of Management Journal*, 52(5): 856–62.

Rydén, B. (1972) *Mergers in Swedish Industry—An Empirical Analysis of Corporate Mergers in Swedish Industry, 1946–1969*, Uppsala: Almqvist & Wiksell.

Seabright, M.A., Levinthal, D.A., and Fichman, M. (1992) 'Role of individual attachments in the dissolution of interorganizational relationships', *Academy of Management Journal*, 35(1): 122–29.

Strandvik, T. and Holmlund, M. (2000) 'Customer Relationship Dissolution—What do We Know and What do We Need to Know?', Working Papers 434, Helsinki: Swedish School of Economics and Business Administration.

Sutton, I.R. (1987) 'The process of organizational death: Disbanding and reconnecting', *Administrative Science Quarterly*, 32: 542–69.

Tähtinen, J. and Halinen, A. (2002) 'Research on ending exchange relationships: a categorization, assessment and outlook', *Marketing Theory*, 2: 165–88.

Walter, G. and Barney, J. (1990) 'Research notes and communications: Management objectives in mergers and acquisitions', *Strategic Management Journal*, 11(1): 79–86.

Weber, J.A. and Dholakia, U.M. (2000) 'Including synergy in acquisition analysis: A step-wise approach', *Industrial Marketing Management*, 29(2): 157–77.

Williamson, O. (1979) 'Transaction cost economics: The governance of contractual relations', *Journal of Law and Economics*, 22: 233–61.

Part IV

Public Bodies, Other Parties of Public Interest, and Scholars

11 Mergers in Central Government
Role Ambiguities and Blame-Avoidance

Louise Bringselius

INTRODUCTION

Like some other Western countries, Sweden is currently experiencing a trend towards fewer and larger authorities under the central government, resulting in a wave of mergers (The Swedish Agency for Public Management 2010). However, mergers in the public sector have attracted surprisingly little attention in the international body of literature on mergers and acquisitions. Instead of expanding the empirical horizon of these lines of research, it is assumed that conclusions based on a private context are valid for *any* societal context (Bringselius 2008, 2010). The case is similar in the social sciences in general. This nonrecognition of differences between the private and public sectors has led to many inaccurate generalisations (Perry and Rainey 1988). One reason for the inattention to the sphere of public administration in the literature on mergers, as well as in the social sciences in general, may be that such studies require knowledge found in a wider body of literature.

The wave of mergers currently sweeping over the public sector partly reflects a set of ideas normally referred to as New Public Management (NPM) and frequently cited in the literature on public management since its introduction in 1991 by Hood. A central notion in the New Public Management is that the private sector ought to serve as a role model for the public sector, in order for the latter to become more efficient (Hood 1991, 1995; Pollitt and Bouckaert 2011). Hence, with this set of ideas, traditional public administration theory has moved towards a more neo-liberal ideology (Heeks 1999). Partly as a consequence, many scholars (starting with Osborne and Gaebler 1992; Osborne 1993) have called for 're-invention of government', that is, re-structuring the public administration in a way that enables its agencies to do more with smaller budgets. Mergers are examples of such reforms in administration, whereas the New Public Management has resulted in the opposite in the social services sector, where numerous parties are encouraged to compete on a deregulated market.

One consequence of the New Public Management is that central government in many countries has taken a step back in relation to their authorities. Instead of hands-on *government*, they try to find means for successful *governance* at a distance (Rhodes 1996), sometimes referred to as *agencification* (e.g., Pollitt et al. 2004; van Thiel and Yesilkagit 2011). By providing more autonomy to authorities, as well as service providers, political decision-making should be separated from policy implementation, it is held. In mergers of authorities under central government, this development is interesting because it creates ambiguities in terms of the principal-agent relationship. The distance that many countries have established between central government and its authorities (normally referred to as agencies), which are given extensive autonomy, allows central government to function *both* as a co-responsible principal and as an external stakeholder. However, central government may choose to recognise only the stakeholder role, avoiding responsibility and thus any blame. This tendency to avoid responsibility has been pointed out in previous research (e.g., Hood 2002, 2007; Weaver 1986). Rather than accepting blame for failure to govern authorities successfully, central governments can blame the management team at the authority in question, and argue that this team is responsible for operations. Kelman (2005: 968) holds that the public sector is characterised by 'greater sensitivity of resource providers in the political system to avoiding scandals as opposed to creating results'. Consequently, citizen confidence is questioned, in central government as well as the authority concerned. By blaming the authority when problems occur, central government is able to minimise political risk, as political appointees seek to do (Althaus 2008).

This chapter explores the consequences of role ambiguities pertaining to central government in mergers of authorities under its administration, and what happens when blame-avoidance and political risk become central factors in these mergers. By (partisan) political risk, I mean the risk that the party (or parties) in office will lose citizens' confidence, and thus votes in general elections. In order to avoid confusion regarding the concept of agency, I will refer to governmental *authorities* instead of governmental *agencies*, which is the traditional construct. The chapter is organised as follows. First, the existing literature on mergers and central government is reviewed. A section explaining the research method follows. Findings from a case study of the merger of 22 organisations in the social insurance administration in Sweden are reported and thereafter discussed. Finally, there is a section where conclusions are presented.

MERGERS IN CENTRAL GOVERNMENT

I have briefly introduced the ideas and the contemporary aim of the New Public Management to 're-invent' government. The shift from government to governance of complex networks in public administration has followed a growing trend toward privatisation, where it became increasingly common practice to outsource services to private or semi-private (hybrid) organisations. One consequence, however, has been a weakened central government capability to control its administration and service providers (Peters and Pierre 1998). It has even been argued (e.g., Frederickson 1996; Smith 1999) that the state has been 'hollowed out' by the increasing complexity and fragmentation in which it operates. The 'hollow state' can be understood as a metaphor for a government that increasingly uses third parties to deliver social services and generally to act in the name of the state (Milward and Provan 2000). In a review of the literature on the hollow state, Milward and Provan (2000) point out that principals (e.g., central governments) can very well intervene to help authorities cope with problems, but in order to create stability in networks, governments also need to adopt a long-term perspective and allow managers of its authorities to learn from their mistakes. This long-term perspective is often lacking in public management, they argue. Also in mergers, efforts to achieve quick realisation of synergy may hamper the change process.

Agencification is part of a tradition sometimes referred to as the 'Anglo-School of Governance' (Rhodes 1997; Rhodes and Marsh 1992), and it is meant to enhance the capability of government to exert control over public authorities (Marinetto 2003). An example of agencification, i.e., central governments' taking a step back in relation to their authorities, is the 'Next Step' executive agencies in the UK. These were invented in the 1980s because Prime Minister Thatcher wished to improve efficiency in public administration. The agencies are autonomous bodies within central government departments and thus are typically exposed to the role ambiguities (principal/agent) explored in this study. By 1997, three out of four civil servants in the UK worked at a 'Next Step' executive authority (Next Steps report 1997). A review in 2002 (the Prime Minister's Office of Public Services Reform), while pointing out that the reform was basically successful, revealed that it had also led to several important problems. For example, these authorities had become increasingly distanced from the intentions of ministers, a serious problem from a democratic perspective. There have been similar reforms in the US and the Netherlands. In the US, the National Performance Review (NPR) has aimed to create more flexible, entrepreneurial, and efficient agencies (Gore 1994; Thompson 2000). In the Netherlands, 630 autonomous administrative bodies called ZBOs have been formed (van Thiel and Yesilkagit 2011). Sweden and Finland have also regulated the autonomy of public authorities, but in the National Constitution (for Swedish legislation, see Myndighetsförordningen & Regeringsformen, Chapter 12 §2).

In Sweden, this system is no recent invention; it goes far back in history (SOU 1983: 39; SOU 2008: 119). One reason why the system is so highly appreciated, it has been noted (Pierre 1995), is that it is convenient for political decision-makers. It allows them considerable influence over their authorities, but without a corresponding degree of accountability—it thus enables them to choose whether to assume the role of principal or the role of a stakeholder.

One motive for agencification (for overviews, see Pollitt and Bouckaert 2011; van Thiel 2004) has been to give the policy commitment of central government greater credibility. By separating policy implementation from politics, implementation can also be made more neutral. However, as van Thiel and Yesilkagit (2011: 785) point out, 'Less interference also implies less liability or accountability for the principal, which is appealing to principals, politicians and bureaucrats alike, as they can shift the blame in case of poor performance'. These ambiguities pertaining to accountability may seriously impede a merger process.

In exploring the consequences of such ambiguities, we use a stakeholder approach in this study. Although this approach was developed primarily for the private sector, it is also useful in a public context (Post, Preston, and Sachs 2002). In applying the stakeholder approach to this context, it can be developed and refined (Phillips, Freeman, and Wicks 2003). When a descriptive stakeholder approach is adopted (as compared to an instrumental or normative approach, see Donaldson and Preston 1995), the importance of considering non-economic interests in an organisation is highlighted (Post, Preston, and Sachs 2002). According to Freeman and Reed (1983), stakeholder theory was actually developed in reaction to a one-sided focus on shareholder interest—specifically, financial goals. Traditionally, financial estimates have been given lower priority in public sector concern for justice and the rights of the citizens (Nutt and Backoff 1993), but with the advent of New Public Management, this sector has focused considerably more on performance measurement and efficiency. Another reason for this development may be the growing pressure on national financial budgets as welfare systems become increasingly costly. In public sector mergers, the ultimate principal would be the citizen, but in a parliamentary system, this role is passed on to the elected politicians, in particular the central government. With agencification, yet another principal-agent relationship is introduced, as accountability is delegated. van Thiel and Yesilkagit (2011: 784) describe this shift as follows.

> 'voters (principals) elect politicians (agents) to act on their behalf, politicians (principals) charge bureaucrats (agents) with implementation of their decisions and bureaucrats (principals) delegate this task to the new executive agents'.

By 'new executive agents', the authors mean the autonomous public authorities. In this chapter, we define central government as the principal, together with its ministries (bureaucrats).

What do we know about mergers—in general and in a public sector context? The existing body of literature focused specifically on public sector mergers is limited. However, mergers in central public administration (under the central government or Parliament) appear to be (Bringselius 2008, 2010) characterised by a higher degree of vertical resistance

(resistance between management and employees) as opposed to horizontal resistance (resistance between employees from the merging organisations). One explanation may be found in professionalism. Public administration often recruits well-educated individuals to conduct work that is constrained by rules and formal bureaucratic structures. Some of them are often united by their professional background, for example, judges and police officers, who share a professional identity as well as an (implicit or explicit) code of ethical conduct (Sharma 1997). Thus, professions have a unifying function that may override inter-organisational conflicts in mergers.

Many of the problems typical of mergers and acquisitions relate to the employee and her or his reactions. Consequently, for more than 30 years, the literature on mergers and acquisitions has paid special attention to the human aspects (for some of the early works, see Blake and Mouton 1985; Buono, Bowditch, and Lewis 1985; Marks 1982), addressing a wide range of socio-cultural and human resources issues. In particular, there is today a growing interest in matters of ethics in the literature on mergers and acquisitions (e.g., Chun 2010; Lin and Wei 2006; Syrjälä and Takala 2008), including perceived justice (e.g., Ellis, Reus, and Lamont 2009; Lipponen, Olkkonen, and Moilanen, 2004; Meyer and Altenborg 2007) and issues of trust (e.g., Bringselius 2008; Stahl and Sitkin 2005, 2010), in the literature on mergers and acquisitions. Stahl and Sitkin (2010) maintain that the perceived trustworthiness of the management team will be important to the outcome of the merger. Trust and ethics are also emphasized in public sector reform, and it has been established that maintaining trust in management is imperative for success in public sector reform (Cho and Ringquist 2011). Like mergers in the private sector, many public sector reforms fail to achieve their goals (although these findings may be contested, see Chapter 13 by Risberg in this volume). Czarniawska-Joerges (1989) questions why new reforms are constantly being introduced despite this unfavourable record, and argues that they may be successful in other respects, for example, in terms of regaining legitimacy and re-socialising organisation members. Similarly, it has been noted that New Public Management reforms are often seen as means to 'modernise' government, regardless of outcome (Broadbent and Guthrie 2008; English and Skaerbek, 2007; Lapsley 1999, 2001; Lapsley and Pong 2000).

After mergers, a period of extensive organisational change often follows. Buono and Bowditch (1989: 81) contend that a 'pillage and plunder' strategy is sometimes adopted in this phase, with an instrumental approach to the individual employee. Furthermore, in order to gain legitimacy for a planned change, a sense of crisis is often created (Cortell and Peterson 1999), leading to an unnecessarily centralised and radical approach to change (Boin and t'Hart 2003). This problem is particularly common in a public sector context, where many stakeholders typically need to be involved in the planning process, and where policy-makers must always be able to present new directives and regulations, without considering organisational issues at the authority in charge of policy implementation.

METHOD

In order to explore the role of central government and the importance of political risk in mergers of governmental authorities, a case study has been conducted. The case study method makes it possible to collect rich data material for the purpose of gaining an in-depth understanding of complex phenomena and of formulating proposals for future research. This chapter is based on material from a longitudinal case study on the merger of 22 organisations: 21 local and semi-independent social insurance agencies and the *National Social Insurance Agency* (in Swedish: Riksförsäkringsverket) under the central government. They joined to form the Swedish Social Insurance Agency (SSIA) on January 1, 2005.

The public system of social insurance is meant to provide financial security for people in need, whether because of illness, parenthood or aging. It is therefore imperative that applications for these benefits be handled in a timely and correct manner. Moreover, social insurance policy is an area of politics that attracts considerable attention in public debate. Thus, in this respect as well, it is an important field that extends beyond the merger itself.

In the case study, a total of 125 semi-open interviews were conducted during 2008–2011, covering a wide range of issues. Interviews were conducted with personnel at all levels of the organisational hierarchy, as well as with external stakeholders. For example, interviews were held with the SSIA chief of staff, the SSIA safety supervisor, the Minister of Health and Social Affairs, local union representatives, and the Assistant Undersecretary at the Ministry of Health and Social Affairs. These interviews have contributed to a more thorough understanding of the merger process and of the authority involved. Given the complexity of the authority's operations, I have considered this understanding important. The SSIA has circa 12,000 employees and handles applications for all types of benefits, for example, allowances for childcare and sickness leave.

In fall 2008, the SSIA experienced a major financial and administrative crisis. This study is focused in particular on the time before, and after, this crisis. Because I sought to understand how the central government and SSIA management handled citizen confidence, as related to political risk and blame in connection with the crisis, it was important to study statements in the media. What was said in interviews was not necessarily communicated to the public; I therefore considered communication through the media as particularly important in this study, which is focused on a review of the role of the media. Special attention has been directed at *Dagens Nyheter*, the largest daily journal in Sweden, with national coverage. Press releases with references to the SSIA were also scrutinised. In addition, a qualitative text analysis, as outlined by Altheide (1996), was conducted. The analysis was used to organise text into two categories: one category where the central government was blamed for the SSIA crisis and one where the SSIA management team was given the blame. However, the analysis was also open for combinations of approach, and arguments for various standpoints were noted.

A MERGER WITHIN THE SWEDISH SOCIAL INSURANCE ADMINISTRATION

The first social insurance offices in Sweden were established in the 1940s, as a result of individual initiatives to secure the social welfare and personal finances of workers who became ill. In 1963, the insurance offices were transformed into *public* social insurance authorities (Lindquist 1990). However, because of their history, these offices were organised only as 'semi-governmental' authorities; each was basically independent of the other—with its own regional office, its own board and its own practices. The National Social Insurance Agency, under the central government, conducted evaluations and provided standardised procedures, but they could not override the local offices. These local offices had a shared industry organisation for the purpose of asserting their interests. This common organisation was called the Confederation of Social Insurance Offices (in Swedish: *Försäkringskasseförbundet).*

Because they were not formally placed under central government, the regional offices were difficult to oversee, despite government funding. The public social insurance system could be used by local politicians to adjust unemployment figures. For example, one study (Ericsson et al. 2008) showed that a practice had developed where 'difficult-to-place individuals' with problems in entering the labour market were referred to the public sickness insurance system and sometimes offered a disability pension for their retirement. The risk that the social insurance system would be used as a tool in regional politics was one of the reasons why a reform was recommended after the institutional arrangements in the public social insurance administration had been investigated (SOU 2003: 63). Moreover, the cost of sickness benefits and disability pensions had soared over the years. In 2006, a total of 640,000 citizens (out of 9 million inhabitants in Sweden) had received sickness benefits for at least a year or had been given early retirement because of sickness (figures from the SSIA). This situation had to be changed. The administrative reform (the merger) was therefore supplemented by a political reform of the sickness insurance system, which took effect in July 2008.

The merger was consummated on January 1, 2005. Because of the geographical spread of offices, the National Social Insurance Agency was remoulded, with a head office in Stockholm, the Swedish capital. The group in charge of the integration process was given a central position at the head office, reporting directly to the SSIA Director-General. At the core of this group, called *the Change Program* (in Swedish: *Förändringsprogrammet*), were a number of hired management consultants, who focused on standardisation of work procedures. Employees and managers felt that they had little chance of influencing what was decided or discussed in the Change Program, which was outside the chain of command as a staff function reporting only to the Director-General. The development of a new IT system was also commenced.

The post-merger integration process was accompanied by extensive budget cuts, and the SSIA work force was reduced by thousands during the years following the merger. In the beginning of 2007, it became evident that the SSIA had severe problems with efficiency, administration, employee dissatisfaction and citizen confidence. In a debate article (Malmborg and Efraimsson 2007), the Director-General and the Chairman of the SSIA board admitted that they had 'not been able to provide efficient and service-minded operations' for Swedish citizens. They explained that they had planned a major re-organisation, which would be challenging and costly, and asked the Government and Parliament for 'patience', adding that 'experience shows consistently that changes cost money in the short term, but that this outlay is paid back many times over in the long run'. Gradually, the new organisation was put in place throughout the country, starting in November 2007.

The situation at the SSIA became increasingly chaotic. Four months after the debate article by the Director-General and the Chairman of the SSIA board (Malmborg and Efraimsson 2007), it became clear that the SSIA would not be able to disburse benefit payments on time to all who were entitled to them, and that benefit applications could not be processed within the allotted time, either. Managers at the SSIA explained in an article that they did not stand a chance of meeting deadlines with the reduced work force still available (Dagens Nyheter, July 24, 2007). The Minister of Health and Social Affairs responded that she expected the SSIA to be able to run its operations successfully within the budget available, adding that they had already received additional funding. Both the SSIA management team and the Minister expressed their surprise at the signals from SSIA offices around the country, in an interview in Dagens Nyheter (July 24, 2007):

> 'Both the Minister of Health and Social Affairs and SSIA management are surprised at the warning signals from SSIA offices, since reports show that the time required to process benefit applications has actually been shortened this year compared to last year'.

The organisational change at the SSIA in 2007–2008 was intended to deal with these problems. Specifically, by processing more benefit applications over the Internet or by telephone, they hoped to increase efficiency. Many offices were dismantled or merged. Since the merger in 2005, the number of employees had decreased rapidly, and the workload for the remaining employees had increased substantially. Unions and the SSIA safety supervisor (in Swedish: *skyddsombud*) protested against this development.

In August 2008, the media reported on the rising costs of the new information technology system (development of new computer software) at the SSIA

(Computer Sweden, August 21, 2007; Dagens Nyheter, August 21, 2008). The budget for the development of a new information technology system was exceeded by millions of Swedish Krona each year (one million Swedish Krona equals circa 100,000 Euro), according to internal documents that had leaked out. It soon became clear that there would be a major deficit of almost one billion Swedish Krona (circa 100 Million Euro) for the coming year—and that the Director-General had not informed either the central government or the SSIA board about it. At the same time, benefit applications and payments were not handled on time, and employees complained about constant overtime and a highly stressful work situation. A large number of employees had left the authority. In 2008, many citizens filed complaints against the SSIA for late payment of benefits. Finally, the Parliamentary Ombudsman (*Justitieombudsmannen* in Swedish) conducted an investigation at the SSIA and published a highly critical report on the way that the SSIA had managed contacts with its clients, and in general, the organisational change at the authority. The Parliamentary Ombudsman (January 26, 2009) stated:

> 'The Swedish Social Insurance Agency has apparently neglected, in its organizational change, to consider sufficiently the legal requirements for the processing of applications. It is clear, moreover, that the Swedish Social Insurance Agency was not well prepared for the problems that such an extensive organisational change could reasonably be expected to entail'.

The crisis at the SSIA in 2008 received considerable attention in the media. According to a new employee attitude survey, there was a financial crisis, an administrative crisis and a crisis in terms of employee confidence in the SSIA management. A journal summarised 'the four catastrophes' at the authority in 2008 as follows (Aftonbladet, December 19, 2008).

1. Policy implementation ('the rules')

   'In the past few years, the SSIA has started applying regulations more strictly, resulting in a number of remarkable cases where very sick people were forced back to work'.

2. Payment delays

   'This past summer, 140,000 people did not receive their payments in time. [. . .] Many families with small children had to borrow from friends or seek help from the social welfare authorities'.

3. IT system

   'The SSIA invests 2 billion Swedish Krona each year in a new IT system that does not work'.

4. Organisational change

   'Out of 13,000 employees, 10,000 have had their duties changed this year. Employee turnover is enormous; 2,500 employees left the SSIA last year, and 2,000 employees have left this year. Employee confidence in management has fallen by 50 percent in one year'.

As for the financial problems at the SSIA, the Chief of Staff explained in 2009 that according to forecasts in April 2008 the authority would incur a serious financial deficit towards the end of the year. He had explained this to the Ministry but had received no response: 'I told the Ministry that they could see just by looking at the forecast that meeting the budget would be totally impossible'. The Ministry would later deny that these conversations had taken place, and they were not documented anywhere. In an interview, the (now former) Minister of Health and Social Affairs confirmed that she had been informed that the situation was difficult but under control. In a newspaper article (Svenska Dagbladet, January 26, 2009), the former Director-General responded that he had not concealed any information, adding that it was not fair to make him 'a scapegoat'.

In 2007 the Chairman of the SSIA board resigned in protest. Subsequently she (Efraimsson 2009) claimed that the Government had simply blamed the SSIA for problems that would not actually have occurred if the Government and its Minister had exercised proper oversight of the authority. She maintained that the reforms and financial constraints imposed by the Government on the authority were totally unrealistic. In a newspaper interview (Svenska Dagbladet, December 9, 2009), the chairman of the largest union at the SSIA expressed the same argument and explained, 'We [personnel] are singled out as hounding sick people, but in our opinion the Government is asking for this'. Whereas the Government claimed that the SSIA was responsible for implementation of public policy and had extensive autonomy to interpret the rules strictly or not, employees contended that this autonomy was in fact very limited.

In December 2008, the SSIA Director-General resigned and was replaced by a new Director-General as from January 1, 2009. Her mission was to restore confidence in the authority, to gain control over its finances and to improve its operations. One of the political parties in office issued a press release requesting that the SSIA pay interest to citizens who had to wait for their benefits. In another press release, in January 2009, the political opposition demanded a public debate with the Government on the situation at the SSIA, and claimed that the current problems were due to budget cuts and other actions of the Government.

In 2008, a ranking of citizen confidence showed the SSIA at the bottom of all public agencies in Sweden (Företagarna 2009). The Minister of Health and Social Affairs explained (Ministry of Health and Social Affairs 2009) that she wanted the SSIA to make a formal commitment to provide services to Swedish citizens according to certain standards. In January 2009, a Member of Parliament filed a complaint to the parliamentary Committee on the Constitution against the Minister of Health and Social Affairs in 2002–2006. According to the complaint, the reform (merger) in 2005 was the primary reason for the current crisis at the SSIA.

More funding was granted to the SSIA by the Minister of Health and Social Affairs, but problems still remained. The opposition contended that the current government was responsible for the authority's problems with delayed payments and delays in responding to benefit applications (Dagens Nyheter, September 10, 2009), and so did the unions (Fackförbundet ST, September 16, 2010). In a debate article with the heading 'Pathetic of the Government to blame personnel' (Efraimsson 2009), the former Chairman of the SSIA board (years 2005–2007) claimed that the Government had not given the authority a chance to succeed with its tasks. In another debate article (Carnhede 2010), the Chairman of the principal SSIA union demanded on behalf of the employees at the authority that the Government apologise for blaming them and the authority for the present chaos.

SSIA management was critical of the Government's funding of the authority's operations. In an analysis submitted to the Ministry of Health and Social Affairs (Försäkringskassan 2009, dnr 42291–2009), they singled out two factors as central to developments in 2005–2008. These factors were the internal management culture and the systems of control. The management culture was one where people were afraid to express their opinions. Because the post-merger process was managed through a central 'change program', reporting only to the Director-General, it was hard to obtain reliable information on the progress of the work and the probable savings. An additional factor, according to this analysis, was 'the structural underfunding' of the authority. This factor was considered highly important by many. Could the authority even operate on the financial budget that the Government had allocated?

In an interview 2009, the SSIA Chief of Staff called special attention to the merger process and the way that it had been concentrated in a single division reporting directly to the Director-General. This division, called The Change Program, consisted of circa 25 consultants from a major management consultancy. It was very difficult to obtain any information about what was happening in this division and to influence what was decided there. He also noted the importance of the Director-General, in terms of both leadership and competence, and was critical of the way that the Director-General had concentrated all decision-making authority in himself and two other directors. He added that there had been cut-backs in the administrative functions, and that there had been an excessive focus on production at the offices around the country, without understanding that the administrative functions at SSIA headquarters also had an important task in providing the Government with information. This criticism was presented in a letter from the SSIA to the Ministry (Försäkringskassan 2009).

The Minister for Health and Social Affairs later claimed that SSIA management had implemented the organisational change in 2007 too rapidly, and suggested that this may have been one of the reasons for the crisis in 2008. She also emphasised that she was not allowed to intervene in operational matters and that decisions such as those concerning organisational change were only up to SSIA management:

> 'Organizational changes and how to implement them, how to establish the different departments—these matters are for the SSIA to decide. This became a problem in 2008, when they realized that changes were not proceeding at the expected rate. They then stepped up the pace of the re-organisation and took a decision. I believe this was rather unfortunate, partly because as Minister, and like all politicians, I have no say in such matters. I can govern through financial measures, formal letters, follow-ups, evaluations and temporary assignments but in reality, I am not allowed to interfere and have no intention to do so. This situation may be difficult to explain to the Swedish people, who sometimes think that as a politician I can go in and change decisions or affect operations. This matter of knowledge has been a problem in the debate. Speeding up the organisational change made employees feel insecure and worry, 'Will I be lose my job or need to move?' At the same time, the SSIA totally lost its grip on its finances'.

In spring 2011, a former director at the SSIA (before the merger) wrote a debate article holding 'the poor leadership' at the SSIA to blame for the continued problems at the authority (Hamilton 2011). Thus, three years after the initial crisis, it still could not be determined whom to hold accountable for the problems at the authority, and the debate continues.

This case study shows how the authority in question encountered serious problems following the merger, and how the management of the authority and the Government (with the Ministry) engaged in a 'blame game', where each sought to preserve citizen confidence at the expense of the other. (For more on the changes at the SSIA, see Andersson et al. 2011.) I will now discuss what role the ambiguities played for the Government in this situation, in terms of principal or stakeholder, and what we can learn about mergers under central governments (in particular those in similar contexts) in this regard.

DISCUSSION

The role of central government, as a stakeholder or as a principal, in relation to its authorities was the subject of negotiation in the SSIA case. Avoiding blame became crucial. Because central government is the principal in relation to its authorities, it is always co-responsible for what happens at the authority. The distance between central government and governmental authorities may be guaranteed in the Constitution, but there are always other instruments at hand if central government should wish to influence the decisions of management at the authority. In Sweden, the Government has the power to appoint the director general and to remove and replace this person. In the case study reported here, the minister in question referred to legislation in explaining why in her opinion central government and its ministry were not responsible for the crisis that occurred.

When central government interprets its position as that of a stakeholder, it does not consider itself to be bound by the responsibilities of the authority, and adopting this outsider perspective allows it to criticise—to blame—the authority without concern for its own accountability. The distinction between the position of stakeholder and that of a principal is thus based on whether central government interprets itself as part of the system or as an external stakeholder that is not. Ambiguities such as these may have relevance for many stakeholders. In the introduction to this chapter, I noted Kelman's (2005) assertion that political decision-makers in the public sector were focused more on avoiding negative media coverage than on achieving results. Case study observations indicate that this focus on blame and partisan political risk arises to some extent from the ambiguities of the central government's role in public sector reform. In the SSIA merger, as a consequence of these ambiguities and of the focus on blame-avoidance (at the authorities concerned as well as central government and its ministry), citizens lost trust in both central government and the authority following the merger. The Government argued that authority management was responsible for the situation by forcing through overly extensive and overly rapid organisational changes in 2007–2008. Major organisational changes had in fact been implemented over a short period and with a centralised approach similar to the one described by Buono and Bowditch (1989) as a consequence of many mergers. Boin and t'Hart (2003) see this approach as problematic, partly given the need for governmental authorities always to be responsive to policy changes.

SSIA management, on the other hand, claimed that the crisis was due partly to the excessive speed and scope of political reforms (policy changes), which they were forced to implement while the authority was already undergoing extensive organisational change. The question is why the Government and its ministry did not object earlier to the rapid organisational changes, back when these were being planned, in the regular dialogue with representatives of SSIA management? I have found no formal documents showing that such objections were ever expressed.

Politicians strive to minimise political risk (Althaus 2008). This goal can be achieved by taking advantage of the ambiguities that arise when the central government takes a step back from its agencies—from government (on an operative level) to governance (primarily on a strategic level). These ambiguities make it difficult to establish who is accountable when a crisis follows a merger, as in the SSIA case. Public authorities are dependent upon citizen trust and societal legitimacy. Trust and legitimacy are eroded when no one is prepared to take the blame and to set a new course after a failure, especially in cases where the citizens must bear the consequences. As a principal, the central government could be expected to support and advise its authorities in the merger process, rather than criticise them in public debate.

An alternative approach would have been to view political risk as shared by the authority and central government. Then, they would not have felt a need to blame each other in various media, but could have focused on what could be done to improve the outcome of the merger. Risk sharing is a known problem in agency theory (Eisenhardt 1989), and in the SSIA case, central government chose to minimise their exposure to risk. This choice can be understood as part of a strategy of central government and its ministries for preserving citizen confidence not only in their political party, but also in their administration.

The ambiguity in the role assumed by central government affected the trust of personnel in the merger process as well as society's trust in the authority. This erosion of trust hampered the merger process and put the authority's management team in a difficult and vulnerable position. The authority could not easily place the blame on central government, because it still needed to maintain good relations with its principal. Thus, it may be hard for management teams to succeed in mergers under central government. The difficulty is due partly to the approach to change often adopted after mergers, when changes are radical and centralised (Boin and t'Hart 2003). Part of the explanation can be found in the role ambiguities that allow the central government to make the management team a scapegoat for what is considered a failure.

Finally, role ambiguities may tend to encourage central government to neglect the 'soft' issues under their control. One such soft matter was the management culture at the SSIA, which later (Försäkringskassan 2009) was identified as a crucial factor in the crisis of 2008. The ministries under central government focused primarily on financial and quantifiable measures. I have explained how the degree to which the Ministry was informed of the problems at the SSIA depended on whom one asked, for this information was seldom, if ever, transmitted through informal channels and was neither measured nor formally documented.

CONCLUSIONS

Like the private sector, the central public administration (the central government office and the authorities under central government) in countries around the world is constantly undergoing structural change, with mergers as an important component. These mergers have become increasingly common during recent decades, following trends such as the New Public Management and attempts at 'reinventing government'. In this chapter, I have explained how central government can serve both as an external stakeholder and as a co-responsible principal in mergers of governmental agencies. This ambiguity results in an uncertain relationship between authority management and central government, where establishing accountability becomes difficult. Not only will this factor impede a merger process, but it will also affect the authority's prospects of establishing a trustful relationship with the client (the citizen). Political risk and blame-avoidance strategies are central when the parties decide what role to assume. In order to minimise (partisan) political risk, central government may be inclined to blame the authority when the merger process does not proceed as expected, but to enjoy the benefits if the merger process is successful. The findings in regard to the blame-avoidance strategy in these mergers are supported by several previous studies of governmental strategies pertaining to accountability and blame (e.g., Hood 2002, 2007; Kelman 2005; van Thiel and Yesilkagit 2011; Weaver 1986).

Ambiguities concerning the role of central government, as a principal or as a stakeholder, may also affect the likelihood that central government will react to *informal* alarms, because there will be a strong focus on what is documented when blame is later debated. This may lead central government to focus primarily on financial measures in order to inform itself about its agencies, rather than on 'softer measures'. Soft measures may concern, for example, culture and leadership, and responding to alerts in these areas would be more difficult for the ministry (the central government). This is especially unfortunate in a situation such as a merger, where human-relations aspects, with trust and perceived justice as central issues, have a strong impact on the outcome of a merger. Agencification does not relieve central governments from all responsibility for the performance of their authorities. A strategy more focused on cooperation in order to achieve shared goals, than on blame-avoidance, is likely to benefit all parties in mergers in central government. Mergers in central government, just like mergers in the private sector, represent substantial investments in time and effort, and all parties have an interest in making them work.

REFERENCES

Aftonbladet (December 19, 2008) 'Han avgör efter kaoset'.

Althaus, C. (2008) *Calculating political risk*, London: Earthscan.

Altheide, D.L. (1996) *Qualitative media analysis. Qualitative Research Methods Series 38*, Thousand Oaks: Sage.

Andersson, F., Bergström, T., Bringselius, L., Dackehag, M., Karlsson, T., Melander, S., and Paulsson, G. (2011) 'Crossroads for organizations: A study of recent changes at The Swedish Social Insurance Agency', *Nordiske Organisasjonsstudier*, 13(4): 53–76.

Blake, R.R. and Mouton, J.S. (1985) *The managerial grid III*, Houston: Gulf Publishing Company.

Boin, A. and t'Hart, P. (2003) 'Public leadership in times of crisis: Mission impossible?', *Public Administration Review*, 63(5): 544–53.

Bringselius, L. (2008) *Personnel resistance in public professional service mergers: The merging of two national audit institutions*, Doctoral Thesis, Lund Institute of Economic Research, Lund University.

Bringselius, L. (2010) 'Resistance to change in public sector mergers', *Nordiske Organisasjonsstudier*, 12(4): 30–51.

Broadbent, J. and Guthrie, J. (2008) 'Public Sector to Public Services: Twenty Years of "Contextual" Accounting Research', *Accounting, Auditing and Accountability Journal*, 21(2): 129–69.

Buono, A.F. and Bowditch, J.L. (1989) *The human side of mergers and acquisitions: Managing collisions between people, cultures, and organizations*, Washington, DC: Beardbooks.

Buono, A.F., Bowditch, J.L., and Lewis III, J.W. (1985) 'When Cultures Collide: The Anatomy of a Merger', *Human Relations*, 38(5): 477–500.

Carnhede, A. (2010), Chairman of the union Fackförbundet ST, 'Ansvaret är ditt, Odell', *Aftonbladet*, September 16.

Cho, Y.J. and Ringquist, E.J. (2011) 'Managerial Trustworthiness and Organizational Outcomes', *Journal of Public Administration Research and Theory*, 21(1): 53–86.

Chun, R. (2010) 'Organizational virtue, CSR, and performance', in M. Schminke (ed.) *Managerial ethics: Managing the psychology of morality*, Routledge, pp. 53–68.

Computer Sweden (August 21, 2007), 'Försäkringskassan blöder hundratals miljoner'.

Cortell, A.P. and Peterson, S. (1999) 'Altered states: explaining domestic institutional change', *British Journal of Political Science*, 29(1): 177–203.

Czarniawska-Joerges, B. (1989) 'The Wonderland of Public Administration Reforms', *Organization Studies*, 10(4): 531–48.

Dagens Nyheter (July 24, 2007), 'Tusentals utan pengar när Försäkringskassan sparar'.

Dagens Nyheter (August 21, 2008), 'Försäkringskassans datasystem spränger budget'.

Dagens Nyheter (September 10, 2009), 'Försäkringskassan åter riksdagsfråga'.

Donaldson, T. and Preston, L.E. (1995) 'The stakeholder theory of the corporation: Concepts, evidence and implications', *The Academy of Management Review*, 20(1): 65–91.

Efraimsson, I. (2009) 'Ynkligt av regeringen att skylla på personalen', *Aftonbladet*, May 18.

Eisenhardt, K.M. (1989) 'Agency theory: An assessment and review', *The Academy of Management Review*, 14(1): 57–74.

Ellis, K.M., Reus, T.H., and Lamont, B.T. (2009) 'The effects of procedural and informational justice in the integration of related acquisitions', *Strategic Management Journal*, 30(2): 137–61.

English, L. and Skærbæk, P. (2007) 'Performance auditing and the modernisation of the public sector', *Financial Accountability & Management*, 23(3): 239–41.

Ericsson, U.B., Engström, L.-G., Starrin, B., and Janson, S. (2008) 'Falling between two stools; how a weak co-operation between the social security and the unemployment agencies obstructs rehabilitation of unemployed sick-listed persons', *Disability and Rehabilitation*, 30(8): 569–76.

Fackförbundet ST (16 September, 2010) Chairman Annette Carnhede, 'Ansvaret är ditt, Odell', *Aftonbladet* [Article by Chairman of local union at the SSIA].

Frederickson, H.G. (1996) *The Spirit of Public Administration*, San Francisco: Jossey-Bass.

Freeman, R.E. and Reed, D.L. (1983) 'Stockholders and stakeholders: A new perspective on corporate governance', *California Management Review*, 25(3): 88–106.

Företagarna (2009) 'Myndighetsrankning 2008: Småföretagen gillar Bolagsverket bäst', press release, January 13.

Försäkringskassan, 2009, dnr 42291–2009, 'Åtgärder för effektiviserad ledning och styrning inom Försäkringskassan' [Response to a request by the Government].

Gore, A. (1994) Creating a government that works better and costs less: Report of the National Performance Review, Al Gore National Performance Review Summit, Silicon Press.

Hamilton, E. (2011) 'Brist på gott ledarskap i Försäkringskassan'. *Dagens Nyheter*, March 2.

Heeks, R. (1999) 'Reinventing government in the information age', in R. Heeks (ed.) *Reinventing government in the information age: international practice in IT-enabled public sector reform*, London: Routledge.

Hood, C. (1991) 'A Public Management for All Seasons', *Public Administration*, 6(3): 3–19.

Hood, C. (1995) 'The "New Public Management" in the 1980s: Variations on a Theme', *Accounting Organisations and Society*, 20(2/3): 93–109.

Hood, C. (2002) 'The Risk Game and the Blame Game', *Government and Opposition*, 37: 15–37.

Hood, C. (2007) 'What happens when transparency meets blame-avoidance?', *Public Management Review*, 9(2): 191–210.

Kelman, S. (2005) 'Public management needs help!', *Academy of Management Journal*, 48(6): 967–69.

Lapsley, I. (1999) 'Accounting and the New Public Management: Instruments of Substantive Efficiency or a Rationalizing Modernity?', *Financial Accountability and Management*, 15(3–4): 201–7.

Lapsley, I. (2001) 'Accounting, Modernization and the State', *Financial Accountability and Management*, 17(4): 299–302.

Lapsley, I. and Pong, C.K.M. (2000) 'Modernisation versus Problematisation: Value for Money Audit in Public Services', *European Accounting Review*, 9(4): 541–67.

Lin, C.Y.-Y. and Wei, Y.-C. (2006) 'The Role of Business Ethics in Merger and Acquisition Success: An Empirical Study', *Journal of Business Ethics*, 69(1): 95–109.

Lindquist, R. (1990) *Från Folkrörelse till välfärdsbyråkrati*, Lund: Arkiv förlag.

Lipponen, J., Olkkonen, M.-E., and Moilanen, M. (2004) 'Perceived procedural justice and employee responses to an organizational merger', *European Journal of Work and Organizational Psychology*, 13(3): 391–413.

Malmborg, C. and Efraimsson, I. (2007) 'Försäkringskassan måste göras om från grunden', *Dagens Nyheter*, March 19.

Marinetto, M. (2003) 'Governing beyond the Centre: A Critique of the Anglo-Governance School', *Political Studies*, 51(3): 592–608.

Marks, M.L. (1982) 'Merging human resources: A review of current research', Mergers and Acquisitions, 17(2): 38–44.

Meyer, C.B. and Altenborg, E. (2007) 'The disintegrating effects of equality: a study of a failed international merger', *British Journal of Management*, 18(3): 257–71.

Milward, H.B. and Provan, K.G. (2000) 'Governing the Hollow State', *Journal of Public Administration Research and Theory*, 10(2): 359–79.

Ministry of Health and Social Affairs (2009) 'Cristina Husmark Pehrsson utlovar serviceåtagande', press release, January 28.

Myndighetsförordningen (2007) [Swedish Law].

Next steps report (1997) Cabinet Office, Office of Public Service. *http://www.archive.official-documents.co.uk/document/cm38/3889/3889.htm.*

Nutt, P.C. and Backoff, R.W. (1993) 'Organizational publicness and its implications for strategic management', *Journal of Public Administration Research and Theory*, 3(2): 209–31.

Osborne, D. (1993) 'Reinventing Government', *Public Productivity and Management Review*, 16(4): 349–56.

Osborne, D. and Gaebler, T. (eds.) (1992) *Reinventing government: How the entrepreneurial spirit is transforming the public sector*, Reading, MA: Addison-Wesley Publishing.

The Parliamentary Ombudsman [in Swedish Justitieombudsmannen] (January 26, 2009) Initiativärende och anmälan mot Försäkringskassan om långa handläggningstider och svårigheter att få kontakt med myndigheten m.m. Beslut. Diarienummer: 4346–2008, 5359–2008.

Perry, J.L. and Rainey, H.G. (1988) 'The Public-Private Distinction in Organization Theory: A Critique and Research Strategy', *Academy of Management Review*, 13(2): 182–201.

Peters, B.G. and Pierre, J. (1998) 'Governance without government? Rethinking public administration', *Journal of Public Administration Research and Theory*, 8(2): 223–43.

Phillips, R., Freeman, R.E., and Wicks, A.C. (2003) 'What stakeholder theory is not', *Business Ethics Quarterly*, 13(4): 479–502.

Pierre, J. (1995) 'Governing the welfare state: public administration, the state and society in Sweden', in J. Pierre (ed.) *Bureaucracy in the modern state: an introduction to comparative public administration*, Aldershot: Elgar.

Pollitt, C. and Bouckaert, G. (2011) *Public management reform: a comparative analysis. New public management, governance, and the neo-Weberian state*, third edition, Oxford: Oxford University Press.

Pollitt, C., Talbot, C., Caulfield, J., and Smullen, A. (2004) *Agencies: How governments do things through semi-autonomous organizations*, Basingstoke: Palgrave Macmillan.

Post, J.E., Preston, L.E., and Sachs, S. (2002) *Redefining the corporation: Stakeholder management and organizational wealth*, Stanford, CA: Stanford University Press.

The Prime Minister's Office of Public Services Reform (2002) Better Government Services: Executive Agencies in the 21st Century, The agency policy review: Report and recommendations, United Kingdom.

Regeringsformen [The Swedish Constitution].

Rhodes, R.A.W. (1996) 'The New Governance: Governing without Government', *Political Studies*, 44(4): 652–67.

Rhodes, R.A.W. (1997) *Understanding governance: Policy networks, governance, reflexivity and accountability*, Buckingham: Open University Press.

Rhodes, R.A.W. and Marsh, D. (1992) 'Policy networks in British politics: A critique of existing approaches', in D. Marsh & R.A.W. Rhodes (eds.) *Policy Networks in British Government*, Oxford: Clarendon Press.

Sharma, A. (1997) 'Professional as agent: Knowledge asymmetry in agency exchange', *The Academy of Management Review*, 22(3): 758–98.

Smith, M.J. (1999) *The core executive in Britain*, New York: St Martin's Press.

SOU 1983:39, Politisk styrning—administrativ självständighet [Government report].

SOU 2003:63, 21+1—1. En sammanhållen administration av socialförsäkringen [Government report].

SOU 2008:118, Styra och ställa: förslag till en effektivare statsförvaltning. Slutbetänkande från 2006 års förvaltningskommitté [Government report].

SOU 2008:119, Differentierad styrning [Government report].

Stahl, G.K. and Sitkin, S.B. (2005) 'Trust in mergers and acquisitions', in G.K. Stahl and M.E. Mendenhall (eds.) *Mergers and acquisitions: managing culture and human resources*, Stanford, CA: Stanford University Press.

Stahl, G.K. and Sitkin, S.B. (2010) 'Trust dynamics in acquisitions: The role of relationship history, interfirm distance, and acquirer's integration approach', in

S. Finkelstein and C.L. Cooper (eds.) *Advances in mergers and acquisitions*, 9: 51–82.

Svenska Dagbladet (January 26, 2009) 'Försäkringskassans kris växer'.

Svenska Dagbladet (December 9, 2009) 'Försäkringskassans anställda kräver ursäkt'.

The Swedish Agency for Public Management [in Swedish Statskontoret] (2010) Färre men större: statliga myndigheter åren 2007–2010.

Syrjälä, J. and Takala, T. (2008) 'Ethical Aspects in Nordic Business Mergers: The Case of Electro-Business', *Journal of Business Ethics*, 80(3): 531–45.

Thompson, J.R. (2000) 'Reinvention As Reform: Assessing the National Performance Review', *Public Administration Review*, 60(6): 508–21.

van Thiel, S. (2004) 'Trends in the public sector: Explaining the increased use of quasi-autonomous bodies in policy implementation', *Journal of Theoretical Politics*, 16(2): 175–201.

van Thiel, S. and Yesilkagit, K. (2011) 'Good neighbours or distant friends? Trust between Dutch ministries and their executive agencies', *Public Management Review*, 13(6): 783–802.

Weaver, R.K. (1986) 'The Politics of Blame Avoidance', *Journal of Public Policy*, 6: 371–98.

12 Bank Mergers in Sweden

The Interplay between Bank Owners, Bank Management, and the State, 1910–2009

Sven Jungerhem and Mats Larsson

INTRODUCTION

In this chapter we present a longitudinal study of mergers within Swedish banking over the last 100 years. One principal reason for this long time span is the fluctuation in merger activities and a desire to study the impact of political priorities—codified in regulatory regimes—on these mergers. The stakeholders—*owners*, *managers*, and *the state*—are the focus of this chapter.[1] It is obvious that not only managers and owners but also states play important roles in promoting or restricting mergers between banks in favour of the citizens and the public interest. This study focuses on the role of these stakeholders in the merger process and on the interplay between them. Thus, our intention is to analyze not only the relationship between managers and owners, but also and foremost the role of the state as a stakeholder. The stability of the banking market and of its participants has been of vital importance to the development of the economy and therefore of interest to the state. But during the latter decades of the twentieth century, banks—as suppliers of capital—have become a vital part of Government financial policy. In this analysis we will concentrate on how well the interests of managers and owners correspond to the changing interests of the state, and on how representatives of the banks have engaged in lobbying or negotiating with state representatives in order to influence 'the rules of the game'.

The study covers mergers that involve at least one Swedish commercial bank in the period 1910–2009. Commercial banks are defined as banks with primarily equity ownership, to distinguish them from savings banks and co-operative banks, for example. The limitation to Swedish commercial banks excludes a few mergers involving foreign banks operating on the Swedish market. In our presentation we have not differentiated between mergers and acquisitions, but use the term 'mergers' to describe all types of intercompany union. Because the purpose of our study is to discuss the relationship between the state and privately owned banks, the distinction between mergers and acquisitions is of minor importance.

THE DIFFERENT ROLES OF THE STATE

The state is not a monolith. From a theoretical point of view it can be an institution as well as an organisation acting on a market where the state has established the rules. In order to understand the complexity of the state, it is important to distinguish its different activities. We can identify five different roles for the state on the financial market.

The role of *regulator* is probably the best-known activity of the state. One of the main purposes of regulatory measures is to increase the efficiency of financial markets and make transactions easier to perform. Another important aspect of legislation is the reduction of risk on financial markets—both for banks and for their customers. Closely connected with legislation is the role as *lender of last resort*. This function is seldom discussed openly or even recognized, but in a financial crisis the state has a responsibility to support the financial system—these activities are often performed by the central bank (*Riksbanken*) or by organizations closely connected with it. The third role of the state—*controller* of the financial system—is also dependent on legislation. Control is often exercised by the Bank Inspection Board, but this task can also be performed by *Riksbanken*. (Larsson 1998: 29, 32–33)

These three state activities are of a general character and are intended to stabilize the banking system. In addition, the state serves other functions which are not connected with creation and maintenance of institutional foundations. The state is also both a *supplier* and a *purchaser* of banking services, two roles which have often been interconnected. As the sphere of state activities has grown, the need for financial services has increased. Some of these services have been performed either by the state itself or through state-owned parties operating directly on the market—as a state-owned commercial bank, for example. In a 50-year perspective we can see the growing importance of the state as a customer for financial services in Sweden as well as other West European countries. On the other hand, it has become less involved as an owner of banks and other financial organizations as a consequence of a growing preference for market solutions. (Larsson 1998: 30–31)

This brief discussion illustrates the complexity of the state as a stakeholder and the fact that state interests may sometimes collide with one another or with the interest of other parties on the market. For example, if the state has a political interest in owning and operating a commercial bank, that bank might receive more favourable treatment than private banks. The different roles of the state and of market interests have had, as we shall see, a strong impact on the structure of the Swedish banking system.

THE APPROACH OF THE FINANCIAL REGULATORY REGIME

Since the nineteenth century, the financial market has been the focus of considerable interest on the part of state organizations and authorities. The reason is obvious. The financial market holds the key to general economic development and is thus of paramount importance for private companies as well as local communities and governments. This is another reason why financial markets have been subjected to regulation and control.

Bank legislation and similar regulations for other parties on the financial market are significant elements of the financial regulatory regime. The financial regulatory regime is also connected to other measures for the financial sector such as the currency regulation. The regulations for the currency as well as other financial activities are closely related to general economic policy—together these policy goals and regulations form the financial regulatory regime. This indicates that the financial regulatory regime is a mixture of macro and micro measures—activities exercised by the state in different roles.

Looking at Western European economic development during the twentieth century, it is possible to identify periods when economic policy and regulations are closely correlated between countries. Forsyth and Notermans (1997) distinguish three major financial regulatory periods with this feature: The first period was that of the gold standard, which began in the late nineteenth century and ended in the early 1930s. During this period stable currencies and a restrictive monetary policy were—with some exceptions—given priority in the economic policy of the West European countries. The importance of stability also affected the regulation of commercial bank operations during the late nineteenth and early twentieth centuries. However these regulatory measures were seldom far-reaching, but left room for commercial banks to develop new business activities.

In the second period—between early 1930s and the 1970s—regulation was guided primarily by political goals for growth and employment. In order to reach these goals, economic policy had to be adjusted to specific national economic problems. For the financial market the consequences included a cheap money policy and credit control. Because of this more active economic policy, the financial market was subjected to more extensive regulation.

The third period began in the 1970s and was marked by growing fluctuations in exchange rates and increasing economic internationalisation. Curtailing inflation became the dominant political goal in most West European countries. At the same time, state restrictions were repealed, giving way to market forces as the prime mover for the financial sector. However, with a global financial market and less far-reaching regulation, the risk of failures in the financial sector increased.

Even though these three periods were more or less common to all the Western European economies, the transitional phases between different financial regulatory regimes varied both in length and in timing. As in all development processes, there were forerunners and latecomers. The homogenisation of economic policy after the onset of a new period has taken around 15 years. Thus the periods of 1931–1947 and 1973–1990 were turbulent ones as economic policy was adjusted to new goals and new financial regulatory regimes (Forsyth and Notermans 1997).

The design of the financial regulatory regime has had a considerable impact on both bank owners and managers. The financial regulatory regime provides the framework for all stakeholder activities when it comes to business and structural development. The composition of regulatory measures reflects the aims and wishes of the state, but it might not always be totally consistent with the legislation. Regulatory measures could encourage new business activities in some cases while hampering others. In the same way, regulatory measures might be designed either to promote structural changes such as mergers and acquisitions, or to hamper them (Llewellyn 2001). Underlying the choice of regulation is the overall structure of the financial regulatory regime.

State activities thus can play a major role for mergers in the banking sector. This means that mergers can be a response to stimuli from the market as well as an effect of state promotion of mergers. For this reason the state should be regarded as a stakeholder with own interests in the development of mergers and acquisitions in the banking industry.

SWEDEN'S FINANCIAL REGULATORY REGIMES AND CHANGES IN REGULATION

As noted earlier, previous international research has identified three regulatory regimes during the twentieth century—each with its own special political aims and measures. We will now turn to developments in Sweden, analyzing the changes in national financial regulatory regimes, their consequences for financial regulation, and their potential effects on the merger activities of banks.

After an initial period of strong influence by free banking in the nineteenth century, the financial system underwent a change of regime in the early twentieth century. In 1903 and 1911 new banking legislation was passed, with measures that increased governmental control of the commercial banks' financial stability. At the same time, the larger commercial banks were given the right to own and trade in shares. As the smaller banks were denied this opportunity, larger banks had a competitive advantage. Even though the right of commercial banks to own and trade in shares was limited in the 1920s and totally abolished in the 1930s, these rules were extremely significant. They enabled the largest banks to establish and consolidate groups of controlled and affiliated companies. Thus, a sizable part of Sweden's industry came under the control of one of the three largest banks. (Berglöf and Sjögren 1995; Lindgren 1988)

The smaller banks experienced another problem as well. When capital requirements for commercial banks were increased in 1903 and 1911, smaller banks were forced either to enlarge their own capital or to merge with bigger banks. This effect was sought by the Swedish Bank Inspection Board, which even in the early twentieth century expressed a need for larger banks in order to stabilise the banking sector and finance major investments (Larsson 1998; Söderlund 1978).

The financial regulatory regime established in the early twentieth century resulted in clearer and more detailed regulation compared to the nineteenth century. At the same time, it offered greater opportunities, as became evident when severe banking crises hit the Swedish economy in the early 1920s and early 1930s. The crises resulted not only in the liquidation or merger of several banks, but also in a better understanding of the risks connected with banking, possibly leading to new formal regulations as well as affecting the activities of market participants. In spite of such problems, this financial regulatory regime was maintained until the mid-1940s, when the role of public economic policy gradually expanded.

In the early 1950s new measures were introduced by the Government and *Riksbanken*, which embodied a change in the Swedish financial regulatory regime. This change marked a different economic policy established by the Social Democratic government, which—as in several other countries—was intended to promote economic growth and counteract unemployment while at the same time controlling the allocation of wealth and other resources.

For the Government the overall goal was to make it possible to control Sweden's structural transition from a country with a large share (25 percent) of employment in the agricultural sector to an industrial society. This meant that considerable capital had to be allocated to three different areas: agricultural transformation, production of urban housing and development of the electric-power generation sector. (SOU 1949:13: 16–24)

These changes in the economy were similar to those in other European countries at the time. But what made the Swedish transformation special was the central role of the state in controlling the financing of these changes and making them socially acceptable. In order to manage these changes, it was vital to control capital flows. If the financial market had been free, most capital would probably have been allocated to industry and trade, which could pay a higher interest rate than building companies, for example. Therefore, in the early 1950s the Government, with the help of the politically controlled *Riksbank*, introduced a number of measures to regulate the financial market (Larsson 1998; Werin 1993). In summary, these measures were taken in three basic areas (Prop 1949: 151):

- Control of bank lending limited credit to industry while giving priority to construction of new housing
- Control of interest rates allowed interest rates for savings as well as loans to vary within a limited range in order to lower the cost of borrowing for customers given priority by the state

- Control of the new bond issues, which restricted capital flows to industrial companies.

These measures considerably reduced competition on the lending market and created a financial regulatory regime with strong state governance for the following three decades. Financial control was reinforced by *Riksbanken* through measures to affect bank liquidity, which with the aid of restrictions on lending and interest rates could easily be adjusted to the macroeconomic situation. Gradually these measures were also used by *Riksbanken* to counteract fluctuations in business activity—an extension of Keynesian economic policy. (Werin 1993).

These regulations were cornerstones of the economic policy adopted by the Social Democratic Party, and it was not radically questioned by stakeholders on the market—owners and leadership of the commercial banks—until the late 1970s, when the financial regulatory regime changed and deregulation became an international phenomenon. In Sweden the old financial regulatory regime survived until the mid-1980s, when it was replaced by a more market-adapted and 'liberal' regime, influenced by developments in the US and Western Europe.

With the globalisation of the economy in general and of financial transactions in particular, it had become increasingly difficult to uphold a national financial regulatory regime. During the first half of the 1980s, all politically motivated measures for the financial market in Sweden (which had been introduced in the 1950s) were repealed, allowing banks and other financial intermediaries to compete more freely. At the same time, foreign banks were given the right to establish themselves in Sweden, whilst the previously strict boundaries between banks and other financial actors were gradually erased. The deregulation of the Swedish financial market was accompanied by the introduction of new financial instruments. From the early 1980s Stockholm became an important centre for trade in certificates, options and derivatives. (Nyberg, Viotti, and Wissén 2006: 252–263; Werin 1993)

A number of changes thus formed the basis of the new financial regulatory regime in Sweden. This regime, which was strongly affected by prevailing political ideas, was aimed at strengthening the links between Sweden and Western Europe, especially the European Union. As this new financial regulatory regime was obviously intended to bring about changes in the *functioning* of the financial system, extensive transformations took place in both the structure of the market and the activities of banks.

From a business perspective one may categorize bank mergers according to whether they are motivated by geographical considerations or by a wish to expand the banks' scope of business. This perspective will allow us to distinguish four different types of mergers combining changes in geographical markets with changes in business scope (Jungerhem 1992:

73). Over time, the state has intervened by promoting as well as restricting the merger activities of Swedish banks. If the state promotes market concentration, the result will probably be a greater number of overlapping mergers. On the other hand, a desire to open the market for new financial instruments may result in a larger number of complementary or scope-expanding mergers. Thus both market and political conditions have cleared the way for banks to expand in new directions.

AN OVERVIEW OF MERGERS IN SWEDISH COMMERCIAL BANKING, 1910–2009

The Swedish banking sector consisted of 117 banks in 2009 (Svenska Bankföreningen). There were 32 Swedish commercial banks, 30 foreign banks, 53 independent savings banks, and 2 member banks. The deregulation in the 1980s made it possible for new market participants like foreign banks and new specialized banks to enter the Swedish market. The financial industry has, as noted, been strongly regulated throughout history, and Sweden has been no exception. The existing regulation is intended to prevent financial crises, ensure consumer protection and promote efficiency within the system (Herring and Santomero 2000).

Despite more tolerant rules to facilitate competition, the market is dominated by four banks with roots dating back to the late nineteenth century: *Nordea, SEB, Svenska Handelsbanken,* and *Swedbank*. Depending on which part of the market is studied, these four banks hold a strong or very strong market position. Together they controlled around 70 percent of the nearly 2000 bank branches and over 75 percent of all deposits in Sweden in 2009 (annual reports of *Nordea, SEB, Svenska Handelsbanken*, and *Swedbank* 2009). In number of employees in Sweden, these banks are more or less equal in size.

Mergers have played an important part in the development of banking over the last 100 years (see Figure 12.1). During the period studied, there were a total of 136 different mergers involving commercial banks (savings banks excluded). This development resembles the situation in other countries (Revell 1987: 134).

In accordance with the differences in financial regulatory regimes, there are three distinct periods in the development of mergers: 1910–1944, 1945–1984, and 1985–2009. The first two are similar in that the only mergers then were between Swedish banks, and all took place within Sweden's borders, whereas in the last period there were also mergers between banks of different national origin as well as between banks and insurance companies.

We will analyse the three separate merger periods (financial regulatory regimes) in order to identify the driving forces behind the development of mergers in general and the role of the state in particular.

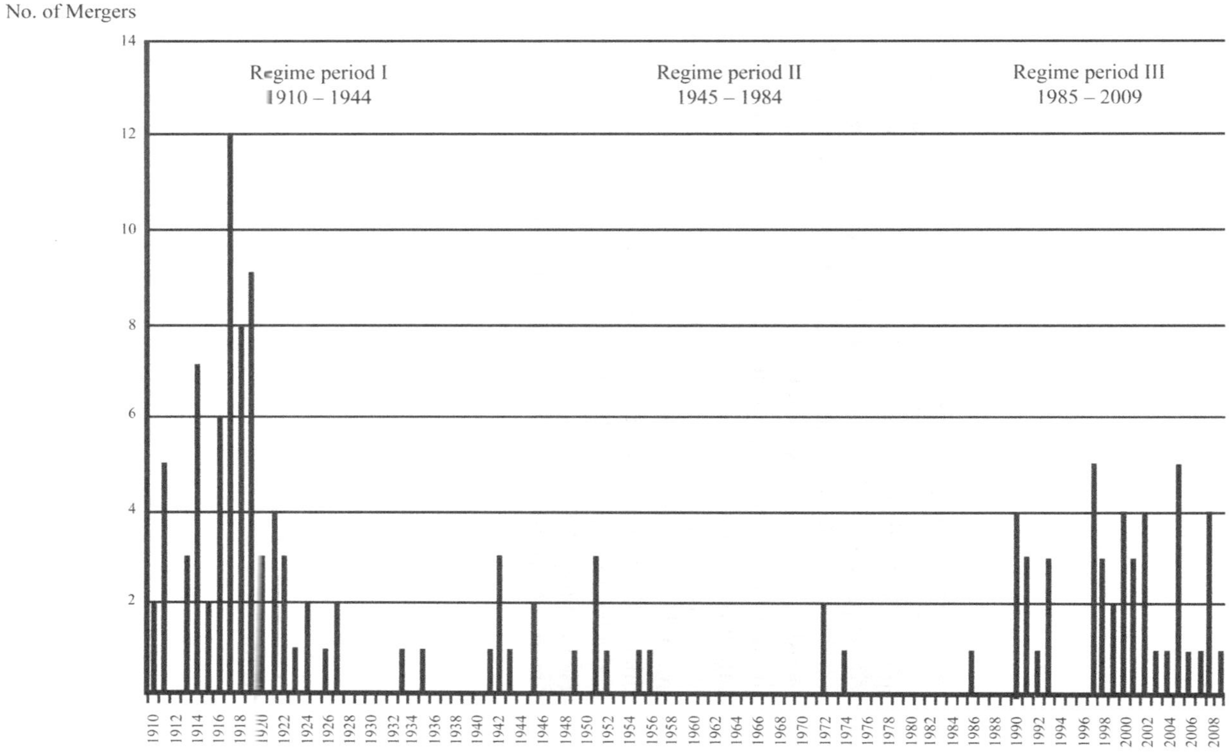

Figure 12.1 Bank mergers in Sweden, 1910–2009.

Source: SOS, uppgifter om bankerna 1913-1991, Jungerhem, 1992, Wallerstedt, 1995 & Svenska Bankföreningen.

INCREASING MARKETS AND COMPLEMENTARITIES—BANK MERGERS IN THE PERIOD 1910–1944

The number of commercial banks in Sweden reached a peak in 1908. But under the pressure of an international economic downturn, several smaller and middle-sized banks were forced to merge with larger competitors. Thus, structural changes had begun even before the banking legislation increased capital requirements in 1911. However, these new measures further encouraged smaller banks to merge with larger ones. If this was a 'push' effect of the new legislation, institutional changes on the market had a strong 'pull' effect. The right to own and trade in shares was of special interest to the larger banks and stimulated their expansion. (Larsson 1998)

These new business opportunities appeared at the same time as the First World War increased general demand for products and stimulated inflation. The development of the financial sector during the latter 1910s can best be characterized as 'speculation'. In a longer-term perspective, however, the banks' ownership interests in industrial companies, in addition to increased lending, led to higher risk levels for banks. (Hildebrand 1971; Söderlund 1978)

These changes in business opportunities, together with the increased capital requirements for commercial banks imposed by regulation, promoted merger activities in the banking sector. The fear of being left behind and not being able to compete made small and medium-sized banks as well as large banks interested in mergers. From a macro perspective the merger activities in the banking sector culminated in 1917, when 12 mergers were registered (see Figure 12.1). But in 1918 and 1919 there were also a large number of mergers. An important reason for the continued merger activities—in spite of the economic stagnation in 1918 and 1919—was that the establishment of new bank branches was subject to approval by the Bank Inspection Board. It was thus easier to reach new geographical markets through mergers with other banks. (Söderlund 1978)

A comparison with merger activities on the Stockholm Stock Exchange suggests that the period 1916–1919 was quite special. The highest number of mergers, 80, was registered in 1918. That same year a total of 160 companies were listed on the stock exchange. These mergers were concentrated in the industrial sector, especially the engineering industry. (Larsson 2002)

It seems clear that the latter 1910s were a merger period in the Swedish economy. In fact, the highest merger rates in the entire twentieth century were recorded in these years. Considering international demand and inflation, this is hardly surprising. During this period mergers, specialization, and organisational changes became somewhat of a substitute for technical development. The question, however, is in what way this general period of mergers influenced attitudes towards mergers. Was there a lack of alternative scenarios? Although these questions have not been thoroughly scrutinized, it is possible to obtain an approximate answer by discussing some examples of Swedish commercial banks at the time.

In 1910 *Skandinaviska Banken* merged with its largest competitor, *Skånes Enskilda Bank*, which was of equal size. For *Skandinaviska Banken* this merger was of the utmost strategic importance since it opened up the market of southern Sweden. The merger thereby increased the value of the bank considerably. It also changed the distribution of market shares, and during the ten years that followed, other banks sought to restore the previous market balance among the banks.

Competition between the largest commercial banks was especially intense. With the merger in 1910, *Skandinaviska Banken* had become by far the largest bank, followed by *Svenska Handelsbanken* and *Göteborgs Bank*. The three largest banks all had strong management traditions, with the owners involved in decisions on policy and strategy. In the majority of mergers carried out by *Skandinaviska Banken* and *Svenska Handelsbanken*, close contact was maintained between the board of directors and the managing director.[2] It seems that owners and management were in agreement on the merger policy that was followed. (Hildebrand 1971; Söderlund 1978)

However, one of the largest banks stands out with a strategy of its own: *Stockholms Enskilda Bank*, which was controlled by the Wallenberg family—probably the most influential private owners in Swedish banking and industry. Whereas the other large banks to a greater or lesser extent were involved in mergers, *Stockholms Enskilda Ban*k did not undertake a single merger during the 1910s and 1920s. This was a deliberate choice of the Wallenberg family, who not only were the controlling owners at the time, but also constituted the banks' management (Hildebrand 1971; Lundström 1998).

In the 1910s and during the interwar period, the two commercial banks *Skandinaviska Banken* and *Svenska Handelsbanken* were the principal competitors on the banking market. This affected their interest in mergers with other banks. For *Svenska Handelsbanken* it was especially important to increase deposits in order to compete, and this objective was probably one of the principal reasons why *Svenska Handelsbanken* was involved directly or indirectly in 19 banking mergers, or more than 1/3 of the total, between 1913 and 1926.

A quick look at two mergers carried out by *Svenska Handelsbanken* in the 1910s reveals more closely the driving forces behind these activities. *Bank AB Norra Sverige* was created in 1908 through the reorganisation of an old bank with financial problems. With new equity capital and 40 branches in Sweden—the largest number for all commercial banks—it was an interesting merger partner for *Svenska Handelsbanken*. In 1914 these two banks were joined together. Though they were equally large, *Svenska Handelsbanken* was obviously the stronger party. This merger enlarged the network of offices and thus increased deposits, but it was especially important as a complement to *Svenska Handelsbanken's* operations in northern Sweden. With this merger *Svenska Handelsbanken* consolidated its position as the second largest bank in Sweden and as a financier for the Swedish paper and wood industry. (Hildebrand 1971: 99–107)

After this merger it was no longer essential to increase the number of offices in northern Sweden. But when *Skandinaviska Banken* in 1917 started a discussion with representatives of another bank in northern Sweden—*Norrlandsbanken*—the management of *Svenska Handelsbanken* decided to act promptly. In order to stop *Skandinaviska Banken's* takeover, *Svenska Handelsbanken* presented an offer that *Norrlandsbanken* could not turn down. A similar strategy was adopted in 1926, when *Svenska Handelsbanken*, through the takeover of *Mälarbanken*, prevented other banks from merging (Hildebrand 1971: 118–21, 204–10).

These examples illustrate that the background of decisions to merge or acquire banks could be quite complex. A general objective of increasing deposits was combined with a specific need to consolidate in new geographical areas or reach new industrial customers. Another important reason for the great merger wave in the 1910s and 1920s was the competitive situation. It was vital to grow in order to avoid hostile takeovers; at the same time, bank mergers made it possible to oppose the strategies of competitors. Both managers and owners seem to have shared the same basic outlook in this regard, and with a state policy promoting mergers and larger banks, it is hardly surprising that this period witnessed the greatest number of bank mergers. For the winners—especially the two largest banks, *Skandinaviska Banken* and *Svenska Handelsbanken*—their already strong positions were reinforced, increasing their financial value.

The number of mergers fell sharply during the latter half of the 1920s and 1930s. Financial problems in the banking sector connected to the deflation crisis in the early 1920s, as well as the general depression in the early 1930s, probably hampered the concentration process. In addition, a shortage of attractive borrowing customers in the 1930s limited the banks' interest in increased lending—one of the central driving forces behind the mergers in the 1910s. Thus, the need for larger banks was no longer as pronounced. By 1930 the number of commercial banks, which was 80 in 1910, had been reduced to 30. However, there were still some relatively small banks on the market, a couple of which merged with larger banks in the 1930s and 1940s. These changes were not very significant. Of supreme importance for the banking structure, on the other hand, was the creation of a new state-owned commercial bank in 1949/1950.

UNDER GOVERNMENTAL CONTROL—BANK MERGERS IN THE PERIOD 1945–1984

The events leading up to the establishment of a Swedish state-owned commercial bank are quite interesting and in a longer-term perspective connected to economic problems. It all began in the 1920s. *Svenska Lantmännens Bank* specialized in agricultural lending and developed rapidly in the 1910s, but the growing problems of the agricultural sector after World

War I seriously undermined the bank's finances. Because no other banks were interested in acquiring *Lantmännens Bank*, the state considered it necessary to step in as an owner in order to avoid more widespread bank liquidations. In 1923 the new state-owned *Jordbrukarbanken* was established to take over the former bank's operations. This was the first step by the state in assuming a role as an owner of commercial banks and as a supplier of capital on the banking market.

However, an agricultural bank was hardly a substitute for a fully developed commercial bank, even though it acquired additional branches from other banks in crisis. In the late 1940s the Social Democratic Party—the governing party at the time—initiated an official enquiry into the establishment of a state-owned commercial bank. The investigating committee found several reasons for such an establishment. Among other things, it would enable the state to govern banking activities more effectively; moreover, a state-controlled commercial bank would help to stimulate competition on a market with oligopolistic tendencies (Prop 1949:151; SOU 1949:13). In March 1950 the new bank, *Sveriges Kreditbank,* started operations based on the activities of *Jordbrukarbanken* and the recently acquired *Sundsvalls Kreditbank*. Compared to this acquisition, other bank mergers in the 1950s were of lesser importance. This larger-scale merger reflects the state's interest as owner and stakeholder on the banking market, while also illustrating the mixture of roles that the state assumed during the decades after the Second World War.

The establishment of a state-owned commercial bank was a vital part of the new government policy for financial markets based on the priorities developed by the Social Democratic Party. With the sweeping regulation imposed in the early 1950s, the business activities of banks were hampered, and competition was given little consideration. In principle, *Sveriges Kreditbank* was supposed to promote efficiency in the banking sector and to increase competition. In fact, however, there is little to indicate that this was the result. Instead, state-owned companies were requested to use the state-owned bank for all their transactions, whereas private companies still utilized private commercial banks for their banking relationships (Anell et al. 1992). A reduction in the number of banks would hardly promote competition, and in order to maintain the structure of the banking industry and to hinder mergers, the Bank Inspection Board was more accommodating to requests from established banks to open new branches.

No bank mergers were registered in the 1960s, but in the early 1970s two strategic mergers were carried out. One of them, the merger between *Skandinaviska Banken* and *Stockholms Enskilda Bank* in 1972, is probably the best-known bank merger in Swedish history. The managers played a central role at *Skandinaviska Banken,* whereas *Stockholms Enskilda Bank* was directly run by the Wallenberg family as both managers and owners. Although antagonism within the Wallenberg family threatened the merger, it was finally brought to a successful conclusion by Marcus Wallenberg. (Lindgren 2007)

The new bank, *Skandinaviska Enskilda banken (SEB),* became the largest Swedish commercial bank, with strong ties to a sizable part of Swedish industry. For this reason the Government was sceptical about the merger. When *Smålands Enskilda Bank* and *Göteborgs Bank* merged to form the new *Götabanken* in the same year, the state decided to intervene through the Bank Inspection Board. At the initiative of the Bank Inspection Board, the remaining commercial banks agreed to avoid merging with other Swedish banks. This agreement was only informal, but the banks kept their promise, and there were no further mergers between privately owned commercial banks until after the deregulation of the banking market in the 1980s. It might seem surprising that banks accepted this agreement, but because it did not directly threaten the operations of existing banks, it could be tolerated.

There was one other important merger in the 1970s. The creation of *SEB* obviously irritated both the Government and the managers of the state-owned *Sveriges Kreditbank.* By the late 1960s, some were urging that the state-owned commercial bank assume a more active role. Certain representatives of the governing Social Democratic Party were even advocating socialisation of the entire banking sector. However, this suggestion was never acted upon, and in 1970 *Sveriges Kreditbank* began to cooperate more closely with the Postal Savings Bank, which was likewise state-owned. With the establishment of *SEB*, voices were raised once again for a more active state bank, especially because the collaboration between *Sveriges Kreditbank* and the Postal Savings Bank was not functioning very well. From a political point of view, it was also considered important to counterbalance the concentration of private capital that *SEB* represented. After a speedy inquiry and with the strong and active support of the Social Democratic government, *Sveriges Kreditbank* and the Postal Savings Bank merged in January 1974. (Anell et al. 1992)

The regulatory regime during 1945–1984 was thus characterized by extensive and diversified governmental activity. The banking market was subjected not only to the traditional banking legislation, but also to special measures by *Riksbanken*, governmental ownership on the banking market, 'voluntary' agreements between banks and the Bank Inspection Board and finally the threat of nationalisation of the banking sector. Thus, the state was more or less active in all different of its roles—except as lender of last resort. From a public perspective, bank mergers became more of an issue for the financial system than for individual banks. Obviously these measures limited the possibilities for commercial banks to merge with other banks. However, the need for mergers was limited, as mergers ran counter to competition and market discipline. As a stakeholder the state was both active and reactive. It was active in the sense that the state was responsible for the general regulations which banks were obliged to follow, and reactive in taking politically motivated measures when a bank wanted to merge. Under these circumstances it was vital that management and owners cooperated; otherwise it would be easier for the state to carry out its political intentions.

INTERNATIONALIZATION AND DIVERSIFICATION—MERGERS IN THE PERIOD 1985–2009

After a period of struggle between economists, bankers and the international wave of deregulation on the one hand and *Riksbanken* and politicians on the other, the deregulation of the Swedish financial sector gradually began in the early 1980s (Englund, 1999: 80–84; Marquardt 1994). In addition to abolishing regulation which had hampered competition, deregulation lifted the long-term 'moratorium' on bank mergers.[3]

In 1985 there were six regional commercial banks, but by January 1, 1986, there were only four. This situation marked the end of a long process of lobbying and later negotiation to merge two medium-sized regional banks, *Uplandsbanken* and *Sundsvallsbanken*, into the new *Nordbanken*. This was also the beginning of a general transformation of the Swedish banking market.[4]

Although the actual merger process started in 1984, there was a long prologue. The discussion on how to survive in the shadow of the dominant banks in Sweden—*Skandinaviska Banken, Svenska Handelsbanken* and to some extent also *Stockholms Enskilda Bank*—had promoted cooperation between regional banks as early as the 1950s and 1960s. At that time their main concern was to grow large enough to operate on foreign markets, engage in active marketing and develop new computer systems (Jungerhem 1992: 91). This cooperation also resulted in plans for establishing a jointly owned company that could offer the services needed, but the proposal to this effect was turned down by the government in 1982 on the alleged ground that a current governmental inquiry was already handling this question. Meanwhile, the management as well as the owners of the provincial banks became more and more convinced that within the foreseeable future it would no longer be possible to survive as independent regional banks.[5]

Arguably the views expressed by significant owners and management at the time affected senior state officials as well. When the proposed merger between *Uplandsbanken* and *Sundsvallsbanken* was discussed with the Bank Inspection Board and the finance minister, there were no hesitation—the merger was accepted. This new state of affairs, with all remaining regional banks involved in merger discussions and later merging, marked the end of independent regional banks in Sweden (Jungerhem 1992; Svenska Bankföreningen)[6]

Even though the regulatory regime was more liberal as from 1986, the state had to intervene in the market quite forcefully. The financial crisis in the early 1990s almost brought on the collapse of the banking industry, and some of the mergers in the earlier years of this regulatory regime can be seen as a direct result of the crisis. According to the Banking Crisis Committee established by the Swedish Ministry of Finance, lending losses between 1989 and 1993 rose from 0.3 percent of total lending (2.1 billion SEK) to 7 percent (56.7 billion SEK) (Wallander 1994: 73). The explanations given for this are somewhat complex, but the root cause was the deregulation of the lending market during the late 1980s (Englund 1999: 83–85; Lybeck 1992: 62–70, 191). This deregulation made it possible to expand lending very rapidly, contributing to a speculative bubble in real estate. The combination of bad banking practice and weak supervision led to a critical situation for the Swedish financial system (Ingves and Lind 1997; Ingves and Lind 2008; Jungerhem and Lundh 1996). This situation called for vigorous and immediate action by the state as well as the owners. The former guaranteed the functioning of the system, and the latter were in some cases forced to infuse more capital (Ingves and Lind 2008). Some banks had severe problems and were more or less compelled to merge with better capitalized and stronger banks. This applies to the *Gotabank,* which was a result of a merger 1990 between three regional banks: *Götabanken, Wermlandsbanken* and *Skaraborgsbanken.* After the state takeover of *Gotabank* in 1993, it was merged with *Nordbanken.*

Swedbank, the most recently established of the largest commercial banks, was founded 1992 when the commercial bank owned by Swedish savings banks merged with a group of regionally based savings banks.[7] As in the case of the regional banks mentioned earlier, this was possible only after a long period of debate and lobbying leading to a general realization that banks had to attain sufficient size in order to survive on the market of the future (Körberg 1999: 77–86). A change in the legislation governing the savings banks made it possible to list the bank on the stock market, a step that was necessary after the losses suffered in the crisis of the 1990s. Later on (1997) the bank merged with another bank with a similar background, namely *Föreningsbanken* (the Swedish Raiffeisen bank).[8] However, the new bank, too, had ideas stemming from the savings bank tradition. With strong management and limited owner control, it gradually became a powerful competitor of the 'old' commercial banks, not only on local markets but also nationally. Back in 1998 Swedbank had started to merge its way outside national borders when *Hansabank*, an Estonian bank with operations in the Baltic countries, was taken over, followed by a merger with a Ukrainian bank in 2007.

The early mergers in the period were carried out during and after forceful deregulation. Some mergers in early 1990s can be explained by the financial crisis, whereas mergers in the late 1990s expanded bank operations beyond national borders and their previous scope of business. A decade into the twenty-first century, the Swedish banking industry has more participants than ever before, but four commercial banks dominate the market. They differ somewhat in market orientation (scope/specialization and geography), but they all bear a long history of mergers, which helps to explain their size. As shown in Table 12.1, the four banks are also predominant in merger activities. Together they accounted for more than 72 percent of all bank mergers during 1985–2009, and these mergers, as can be seen, were not only within Sweden and between banks.

Table 12.1 Mergers 1986–2009 by Major Banks

Bank	*Total no. of mergers*	*With Swedish bank*	*With foreign bank*	*Scope expanding*
Nordea	6	4	2	0
Handelsbanken*	8	1	5	2
SEB	11	0	9	2
Swedbank	8	4	4	0
% of total mergers	72	64	80	50

* Previously Svenska Handelsbanken

Note: Scope expanding includes mergers with non-banks as, for instance, insurance companies, etc.

Source: Svenska Bankföreningen

Nordea (formerly *Nordbanken*) is the largest of the four banks and the biggest financial group in the Nordic countries. But during the financial crisis in the 1990s, *Nordbanken* ran into difficulty and had to be rescued by its principal owner, the Swedish state. The takeover of *Gotabank* 1993, as mentioned previously, was also part of a general crisis solution (Englund 1999: 91). After some difficult years recuperating from losses, *Nordbanken* underwent several mergers, mainly with other Nordic banks. In 1998, after merging with the Finnish *Merita bank*, the new entity adopted the name of *MeritaNordbanken*. Two years later *Nordea* was created through a merger between *MeritaNordbanken* and the two Danish banks, *Unidanmark* and *Christiania spar og kreditkasse*. With 20 percent of the shares, the Swedish state was in 2010 one of the largest owners.

Except for considerable financial problems in the early 1990s, *SEB* has quite a different history. It is the only one of the four large banks still connected with a single family. Through foundations and a family-controlled investment company (*Investor*), the Wallenberg family has a major influence on SEBs strategy. From Table 12.1 we can see that *SEB* is a bank with international ambitions. All but one merger have been with banks and related firms outside Sweden. Growth within Sweden's borders is not sufficient if one wants to keep up a rapid rate of growth. *SEB* and *Swedbank* attempted a merger in 2001, but the process was halted by the EU Commission, which had demanded that the new entity drastically reduce the network of branches and local presence in Sweden. Thereafter *SEB* reinforced its internationalisation strategy and bought or merged with several banks in the Baltic countries, Germany, and the Ukraine.

Since the early 1970s the management of *Handelsbanken* has strongly advocated caution and decentralization. Step by step, *Handelsbanken* has bought other banks and related companies nearby. But as in the case of the other three large banks, the home market is 'crowded', and the branch networks cover all of Sweden. Instead of going east to emerging markets, *Handelsbanken* has chosen to go west, mainly to Norway and Denmark. In recent decades *Handelsbanken*, perhaps more than the other three banks, has relied on organic growth.

We can see that the international influence grew stronger during this period. The international trend of deregulating banks was used by owners and managers as an argument for more liberal legislation which would allow banks to act more freely. At this time the structure of the Swedish banking industry was changing, yet although the number of banks rose considerably, the Swedish market was still dominated by four banks. We can conclude that after the crisis in the 1990s Swedish banks have used mergers gradually to expand their operations. It does not seem to matter whether bank ownership is strong or not. Growth, or maybe a belief that size is the way to profitability, seems to be the prevailing philosophy. Or is the explanation that competition encourages banks to follow the leader? In any event, the period has shown that the deregulated market allowed Swedish banks to merge with foreign companies as a means to develop their international operations.[9]

CONCLUDING REMARKS

This chapter deals with stakeholders in bank mergers from a hundred-year perspective. We have shown that the interplay between bank owners, management, and the state is important for understanding the fluctuations in the concentration process within the banking industry. Because state intervention sets the rules of the game for the merger process, we must also consider the difference in political priorities and regulations over time in order to comprehend fully the merger process.

For the purposes of our research, the Swedish banking industry under three different regulatory regimes can be compared, with each regime representing different political goals and regulations but also different activities on the part of the stakeholders in focus in this chapter. By so doing, we can see fluctuations in merger activities and also in the driving forces behind mergers.

During the first financial regulatory regime—1910–1944—the majority of mergers were both expanding and overlapping geographical markets, but without the possibility of extending business beyond the existing scope (see arrow I in Figure 12.2). The majority of banks had a limited number of branches in the early 1910s and could therefore not cover a large area. Mergers in order to expand the regional market were therefore given priority, especially among the largest banks. For banks involved in industrial financing, the expansion of deposits was also of great importance. This expansion was not limited to new geographical areas, but could also take place in areas where the bank already had a strong position. There are numerous examples of mergers within the traditional geographical areas served by banks during this regulatory regime. This step enabled banks to improve efficiency—hopefully without losing deposits—and also to prevent other banks from penetrating into their regions. During this financial regulatory regime, mergers were promoted by the state (the Bank Inspection Board).

The limited number of mergers during the second financial regulatory regime, 1945–1984, were of the same type as in the first period—geographically overlapping, market-expanding, and within the same business scope (see arrow II in Figure 12.2). For example, the merger between *Göteborgs bank* and *Smålands Enskilda Bank* resulted in a larger regional market for the new bank, whereas the merger that resulted in the establishment of *SEB* in 1972 definitely entailed considerable overlapping. In this merger, improving efficiency was just as important as size. A larger bank could more easily handle the diversified services demanded by industrial companies. During this financial regulatory regime, the state maintained a negative attitude towards bank mergers. The banks' business activities as well as the structure of the banking sector were subjected to detailed regulation, which brought merger developments to a halt for extended periods.

During the third financial regulatory regime—1985–2009—the driving forces behind bank mergers changed radically. For the first time it became possible for banks to enter new business areas and engage in activities other than banking, such as insurance. At the same time banks were free to move beyond national borders (see arrows III in Figure 12.2). As a result, foreign banks entered the Swedish market—sometimes through mergers—but primarily through expansion by Swedish banks via mergers into neighbouring countries. These changes in types of mergers were basically a result of a financial regulatory regime that was modified—under the pressure of technological development—to allow both internationalisation and changes in the business scope.

Whereas, of course, different types of mergers entail various advantages or results, all mergers need to be carefully integrated to be successful. Among the desired or expected benefits of mergers, owners, and managers often emphasize the role of 'synergy effects', referring to savings through cost cutting and economies of scale—that is, in IT and system development, as well as economies of scope such as broadened markets and/or a wider range of services (Hughes, Mueller, and Singh 1980; Lubatkin 1983). In contrast, state authorities expect that bigger banks and thus also mergers will lead to a more stable financial sector. Although rarely mentioned, the critical element in successful bank mergers is that a large bank has a better position on the market, that is, size itself has a significant value. In this regard, history has shown that stakeholders may have difficulties in picking the right target in view of their goals and that strategic considerations do not guarantee a successful merger (Jemison and Sitkin 1986; Jungerhem 1992).

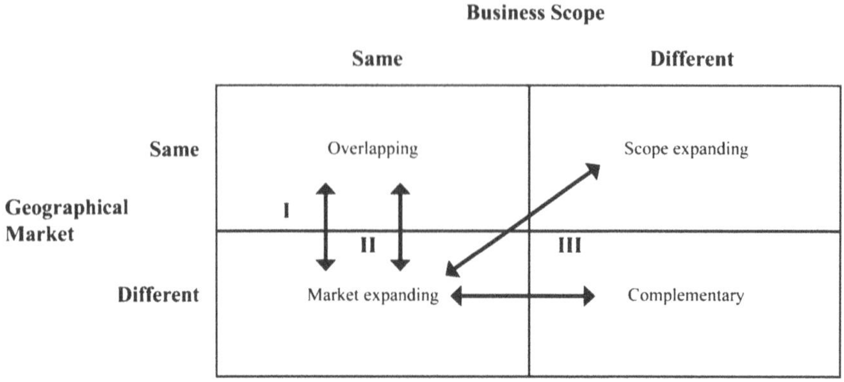

Figure 12.2 Model of mergers during three financial regulatory regimes.

Note: I = the financial regulatory regime 1910–1944. II = the financial regulatory regime 1945–1984. III = the financial regulatory regime 1985-2009

As already mentioned the state as a stakeholder also plays a vital part in the model. The state might act differently depending for example on the stability and competition on the market or as an effect of political priorities. If the state promotes market concentration, there will probably be an increase in the number of overlapping mergers. On the other hand, a desire to open the market for new financial instruments could result in a larger number of complementary or scope-expanding mergers.

A review of the past 100 years shows that the interplay between stakeholders—that is, the owners/managers and the state—has been altered. During the first and third financial regulatory regimes, the interest of the largest banks and the state coincided. This promoted the concentration of banking in larger units. With the growing concentration and larger banks, the role of the state was subject to potential change. In financial crises the state's responsibilities as lender of last resort could lead to increased support of individual banks rather than the financial system.

In a long-term perspective the changing position of the state in the financial system can be linked to certain special events. The positive state approach to bank mergers in the 1910s and 1920s was based on the belief that larger banks were more stable and easier to control than smaller banks, while at the same time they could more actively undertake large-scale financing. The banking crisis in the early 1920s undermined support for this standpoint to some extent, and with the collapse of the Kreuger business empire in the early 1930s—entailing heavy losses for the largest Swedish commercial bank—the state gradually changed its attitude toward bank mergers. From the late 1940s on—with the introduction of sweeping regulation for the financial sector—the state took a strong interest in promoting competition on the banking market, as expressed in administrative measures such as public banking and in a stand-off attitude towards bank mergers. The merger between *Stockholms Enskilda Bank* and *Skandinaviska Banken* in the early 1970s also played an important role in the cessation of bank mergers. Correspondingly, the acceptance of the merger between *Sundsvallsbanken* and *Uplandsbanken* in 1986 marks a new state attitude towards bank mergers.

During this century of banking mergers, the different roles of the state have been activated to a varying extent at different times. The role of *regulator* was the most commonly adopted. In the 1910s banking legislation was used to promote mergers and to create larger and financially stronger banks. But in the decades after World War II, informal and formal regulations hampered mergers. Since the early 1980s legislation has come to play a less important role in the process of bank mergers.

Basically state's role as *lender of last resort* is activated when the banking system is in a crisis. The main objective is then to save the financial system, and this often results in mergers which have been either organised or promoted by the state. One of the best examples was in the crises of the 1920s, when the state as lender of last resort promoted mergers between banks to enlarge their capital base. Another example can be found in the banking crisis of the 1990s, when the state took over *Gota Bank* in order to merge it later with state-owned *Nordbanken.* During both these crises the state also played a major role as a *controller* (Bank Inspection Board) in the preparation of both the banks and the financial system for the coming mergers. During the entire period the Bank Inspection Board was a pivotal intermediary between the commercial banks and other state authorities, transmitting for example information on new regulations.

The state's roles as *supplier* and *purchaser* of financial services have also been closely tied to bank mergers. Of special importance have been the measures taken to establish and promote the state-owned commercial bank, which has appeared under different names during different financial regulatory regimes. Especially after World War II, the state-owned commercial bank has been the centre of merger activities prompted by a desire to promote the state-owned bank but also as a part of rescue missions (as lender of last resort). These examples illustrate that the state has a variety of tools related to their different roles, that it is prepared to intervene in the bank merger process and that through the combination of these roles it can be a powerful stakeholder in mergers.

MANAGERIAL IMPLICATIONS

When viewing the development of the Swedish banking sector during the twentieth century, we can note some managerial implications. Banking, as a regulated business, is based on the interplay between bank owners and managers on the one hand and the state and its authorities on the other. Because the latter formally control the 'rules of the game', it has been of the utmost importance to develop strategies to handle this interplay, where the state is a stakeholder. On the firm level one may notice that a strong balance sheet can support arguments for more independent operations. From a managerial perspective the lesson taught by history is that in an industry of state interest it is vital to have working relationships with the principal parties. Because there is an inherent inertia in regulations, it is helpful to have a strategy for accomplishing one's objectives. From a state point of view this observation is somewhat contradictory. On the one hand, strong banks are desirable, but on the other, these banks have the potential to become strong counterparts.

NOTES

1. The concept of 'state' in this chapter includes the Government as well as other governmental and public organizations, such as the Ministry of Finance, the Bank Inspection Board, the central bank (*Riksbanken*), and the Bank Crisis Committee.
2. The name *Svenska Handelsbanken* was not adopted until 1926, when the bank merged with *Mälarbanken*. Before this merger the name was *Stockholms Handelsbank*, but the bank will be referred to as *Svenska Handelsbanken* throughout this chapter.
3. The Swedish banks had limited possibilities of doing business outside Swedish borders, and until 1986 foreign banks could not establish subsidiaries in Sweden. Before deregulation, establishing as well as closing branches required approval by the Bank Inspection Board.
4. *Nordbanken* later merged (1990) with the state-controlled and much larger *PK-banken*, and the new bank took the name *Nordbanken*.
5. In 1984 *Uplandsbanken*, *Wermlandsbanken*, and *Skaraborgsbanken* secretly initiated merger negotiations. However, the board of *Skaraborgsbanken* was not convinced of the merger's advantages and worried about losing their regional image, and it decided to terminate the negotiations. This encouraged *Sundsvallsbanken* to enter the scene and later merge with *Uplandsbanken* (Jungerhem 1992: 91–93).
6. However, this is only partly true as the Danish bank, *Danske Bank*, has registered many of the old regional banks' names and operates as a group of niche banks.
7. At the time the Swedish savings banks had changed their business scope into that of an increasingly commercial type of bank. The change of organizational structure from savings bank to commercial bank was therefore not very radical. However, even after the creation of Swedbank, there were still some independent local and regional savings banks.
8. *Föreningsbanken* was the only larger bank in Sweden organized as a co-operative credit institute according to the Raiffeisen principles. It originally specialised in lending to the agricultural sector but broadened the scope of its activities after 1970. However, the organizational structure made it difficult to expand the capital base, and after the crises in the 1990s, the bank was an easy target for a takeover.
9. The development of internationalization is consistent with earlier theories of internationalization (Engwall et al. 2001; Marquardt 1994; Wiedersheim-Paul and Hallén 1982). Although technological developments (Internet services and computer systems) diminish the geographical aspect of banking, a local presence still seems to be important. As for lending, it is often argued

that a local presence improves quality. However, the heavy losses of *Swedbank* and *SEB* in the Baltic countries during the recent financial crisis show that this is not always the case.

REFERENCES

Anell, B., Eliasson G., Henning, R., Hägg, I., and Larsson M. (1992) *Staten som ägare*, Stockholm: SNS förlag.

Annual Report of Nordea 2009.

Annual Report of SEB 2009.

Annual Report of Svenska Handelsbanken 2009.

Annual Report of Swedbank 2009.

Berglöf, E. and Sjögren, H. (1995) 'Husbanksrelationen i omvandling—förbindelserna mellan affärsbanker och storföretag i svenskt näringsliv 1885–1993', in *Bankerna under krisen. Fyra rapporter till bankkriskommittén*, Stockholm: Fritzes förlag.

Englund, P. (1999) 'The Swedish Banking Crisis: Roots and Consequences', *The Oxford Review of Economic Policy Limited*, 15(Autumn): 80–97.

Engwall, L., Marquardt, R., Pedersen, T., and Tschoegl, A.E. (2001) 'Foreign bank penetration of newly opened markets in the Nordic countries', *Journal of International Financial Markets, Institutions and Money*, 11: 53–63.

Forsyth, D.J. and Notermans, T. (eds.) (1997) *Regime Changes: Macroeconomic Policy and Financial Regulation in Europe from the 1930s to the 1990s*, Oxford: Berghahn.

Herring, R.J. and Santomero, A.M. (2000) 'What is Optimal Financial Regulation?'', bilaga 26, SOU 200:11, Stockholm: Fritzes offentliga publikationer.

Hildebrand, K.-G. (1971) *I omvandlingens tjänst. Svenska Handelsbanken 1871–1955*, Stockholm: Esselte.

Hughes, A., Mueller, D.C., and Singh, A. (1980) 'Mergers Concentration and Competition in Advanced Capitalist Economies: An International Perspective', in D.C. Mueller (ed.) *The Determinants and Effects of Mergers, An International Comparison*, Cambridge, Mass.: Oelgeschlager, Gunn & Hain, pp. 1–26.

Ingves, S. and Lind, G. (1997) 'Loan Losses Recoveries and Debt Resolution Agencies: The Swedish Experience', in C. Enoch and J.H. Green (eds.) *Banking Soundness and Monetary Policy. Issues and Experiences in the Global Economy*, Washington, DC: International Monetary Fund.

Ingves, S. and Lind, G. (2008) 'Stockholm solutions, A crucial lesson from the Nordic experience is the need for prominent state involvement in crisis resolution', *Finance & Development*, December.

Jemison, D.B. and Sitkin, S. (1986) 'Corporate acquisitions: A process perspective', *Academy of Management Review*, 11: 145–63.

Jungerhem, S. (1992) *Banker i fusion* [Banks in Merger], Doctoral Thesis, Department of Business Studies, Uppsala University.

Jungerhem, S. and Lundh, G. (1996) 'Krafter och motkrafter i kreditgivning—en studie av svenska bankers kreditorganisation' [Forces and Counter Forces in Loan Organisation—A study of Loan Organisation in Swedish Commercial Banks], Uppsala Papers in financial History, Ekonomisk Historiska institutionen, Uppsala University.

Körberg, L. (1999) *Ekluten: förändringsprocessen inom sparbanksrörelsen 1980–1995*, Stockholm: Ekerlid.

Larsson, M. (1998) *Staten och kapitalet. Det svenska finansiella systemet under 1900-talet*, Stockholm: SNS förlag.

Larsson, M. (2002) 'Storföretagande och industrikoncentration', in M. Isacson and M. Morell (ed.), *Industrialismens tid*, Stockholm: SNS Förlag.
Lindgren, H. (1988) *Bank, investmentbolag, bankirfirma. Stockholms Enskilda Bank 1924–1945*, Stockholm: Almqvist & Wiksell International.
Lindgren, H. (2007) *Jacob Wallenberg 1892–1980*, Stockholm: Atlantis förlag.
Llewellyn, T.D. (2001) *A Regulatory Regime for Financial Stability*. Vienna: Osterreichische Nationalbank.
Lubatkin, M. (1983) 'Merger and Performance of Acquiring Firm', *Academy of Management Review*, 8(2): 218–25.
Lundström, R. (1998) *Bank Industri Utlandsaffärer. Stockholms Enskilda Bank 1910–1924*, Stockholm: Almqvist & Wiksell International.
Lybeck (1992) *Finansiella kriser förr och nu*, Stockholm: SNS Förlag.
Marquardt, R. (1994) *Banketableringar i främmande länder*, Doctoral Thesis, Department of Business Studies, Uppsala University.
Nyberg, L., Viotti, S., and Wissén, P. (2006) *Penningmarknaden*, Stockholm: SNS Förlag.
Prop 1949:151 [Governmental proposition No 1949:151] angående inrättandet av en statlig affärsbank.
Revell, J. (1987) *Mergers and the Role of Large Banks*, Bangor: Institute of European Finance, University of North Wales Bangor.
Söderlund, E. (1978) *Skandinaviska Banken i det svenska bankväsendets historia*, Uppsala: Almqvist & Wiksell International.
SOS; Sveriges Officiella Statistik, Uppgifter om bankerna 1913–1991.
SOU 1949:13 *Förslag om inrättande av statlig affärsbank*, Stockholm: Fritzes.
Svenska Bankföreningen [Swedish Bankers´ Association], bankhistorik, http://www.swedishbankers.se/web/bf.nsf/pages/Bankhistorik.html?open. November 11, 2011.
Wallander, J. (1994) 'Bankkrisen—Omfattning, Orsaker, Lärdomar' [The Banking Crisis—Magnitude, Causes, Lessons], in *Bankkrisen*, Stockholm: Fritzes.
Wallerstedt, E. (1995) *Finansiärers fusioner: de svenska affärsbankernas rötter 1830–1993*, Uppsala.
Werin, L. (ed.) (1993) *Från räntereglering till inflationsnorm*, Stockholm: SNS Förlag.
Wiedersheim-Paul, F. and Hallén, L. (1982) 'Psychic distance in international marketing: an interaction approach', Working paper/CIF, Department of Business Studies, Uppsala University.

13 The Stake of High Failure Rates in Mergers and Acquisitions

Annette Risberg

INTRODUCTION

Scholars could be viewed as influential stakeholders in mergers and acquisitions because through their research focus they set the agenda for how mergers and acquisitions are viewed by other researchers as well as practitioners. So what stake do they have in mergers and acquisitions? I would argue their stake is to justify why they should study mergers and acquisitions, and their justification comes by their portraying mergers and acquisitions in a certain way. Let me explain what this portrayal might look like.

That mergers and acquisitions have high failure rates seems to be held as a well-known fact in the merger and acquisition academic community. Merger and acquisition researchers often claim that 50 percent or more of all mergers and acquisitions fail (Cartwright 1998; Hubbard 1999; Shrivastava 1986). To be more specific, Marks and Mirvis (2001: 80) state that '[t]hree out of four mergers and acquisitions fail to achieve their financial and strategic objectives' (2001: 80), whereas Cartwright and Cooper (1995) state that '[r]ecent estimates of merger failure rates vary from a pessimistic 77 percent reported by some US studies to a more optimistic 50 percent quoted by several UK sources' (1995: 33). So why are so many merger and acquisition scholars claiming high failure rates? Explaining variations in organizational performance or effectiveness is an enduring theme in the study of organizations in general (March and Sutton 1997) and mergers and acquisitions in particular. Following March and Sutton's reasoning for this focus on organizational performance, strategy and management scholars may have a professional goal to improve effectiveness of organizations through their research. Hence, many merger and acquisition scholars pursue the same objective: finding ways to improve the success of mergers and acquisitions.

One could consequently assert that merger and acquisition scholars have a stake in portraying mergers and acquisitions in a certain way in order to justify their research. This is not the only stake they may have. The analysis of citation behaviour in this study shows that certain citations recur in many texts. These citations could be interpreted as symbolic references, obligatory passage points considered by authors as necessary stops along the route to getting their work published (Macdonald and Kam 2010; Small 1978). Thus they cite these symbolic references in order to comply with the journal editors' and reviewers'—tacit or explicit—requirements. This reasoning will be elaborated upon later in the chapter.

METHOD FOR THE STUDY

The study is in the form of a review of books and articles claiming or referring to high failure rates in mergers and acquisitions. It began as a search for original sources for claims of high failure rates; therefore, the method chosen was to start with more recent publications and look up their citations,[1] moving backwards in time. When a citation was detected, it was examined to see whether there was a source for the claim in terms of an empirical study. If this was not the case, if instead there were other citations to support the claim of failure rates, then these citations were looked up. For example, NN cites XX; I look in XX and find that XX in turn cites YY, and in this manner I continue to look up the citations, step by step. I thus followed several chains of citations. I first searched for publications claiming failure or success rates and continued by looking up their citations in relation to these claims. The first search resulted in a list of 31 publications (a list of these publications and their citations can be obtained from the author upon request). However, when searching for articles and looking up the citations, I started to observe certain patterns in the citation behaviour of the texts I read. Consequently, I changed my research focus from searching for original sources to studying the citation behaviour I was observing. In order to analyse these patterns of behaviour in more depth, I decided to focus the analysis on a smaller number of publications (henceforth referred to as texts). The method will be described in detail here.

The texts were searched for in the Copenhagen Business School library catalogue and the two databases ABI/Proquest and EBSCO Business Source Premier using the search words *mergers* or *acquisitions* and *failures* or *success* together with the selection criterion 'peer-reviewed articles'. All articles found were scanned using the 'find' tool of the web browser to discover any claim of or reference to failure rates.

I found 31 texts that met my criteria. These texts were selected for further analysis. This number might seem small considering the number of articles in merger and acquisition research. The explanation is probably that the focus of the search was on failure or success rates and not on performance in general. If the search criteria had been post-merger and post-acquisition performance, the number would probably have been greater (see Meglio and Risberg 2011), but not all studies on performance address failure or success rates (see Risberg and Meglio 2012). The 31 selected texts were carefully read with the aim of finding a failure or success rate claim as well as citations to back up the claim. The claims and any citations were recorded in a table. Seventy different citations were found in connection to claims about failure or success rates in mergers and acquisitions. From these 70 citations, the sample was narrowed down to 32 references (not all citations had a full reference) in order to find the most *commonly used* citations regarding high failure rates. The selection criteria for this smaller sample of 32 texts were the following: (1) reference cited more than once in the first 31 texts, or (2) author(s) cited more than once. These 32 texts were analysed in regard to how they cite in connection with claims of failure or success rates. The citation behaviour found were categorised, for example as perfunctory, empty or recurring, but the citations were also analysed in relation to where they appeared, and for a smaller sample of 10 texts (see discussion here), to the type of study conducted in the citing text (see the analysis for more categories).

The results of the analysis will be discussed here. For this discussion a smaller number of texts (10) (see Table 13.1) will be used in order to illustrate the findings from the analysis of the 32 texts. These 10 texts are representative of many of the sample texts in the study in regard to their use of citations to support claims concerning failure rates. The 10 texts are also representative of the larger sample in the sense that the 32 texts are represented in the reference lists of the 10 texts. With this in mind, the citations of the 10 texts have been analysed in even more detail. Part of this analysis was to follow up the citation chains in detail for several chains. The purpose of this detailed discussion is to illustrate common citation behaviour in merger and acquisition texts. In the next section I will describe how the analysed texts cite failure rates. Later in the chapter I will discuss why these behaviours may be present in the literature on mergers and acquisitions.

Table 13.1 should be read in the following way: the first column simply numbers the texts from one to 10; the second provides name(s) of author(s) and publication year of the texts selected for detailed analysis. The third column briefly describes the research focus in the selected texts. In these excerpts from the selected texts, an effort has been made to stay as close as possible to the wording of the original text. The fourth column lists the claims of high failure rates as they are stated in the selected text. A claim could be expressed as a percentage (77 percent) or verbally, for example, termed unsuccessful. The fifth column lists the citations used in the selected texts to back up claims of failure rates. The sixth and last column provides the source for the citations in column five. If the citation refers to an empirical study, the results of this study are briefly mentioned in column six. If the citation cites another text (a second chain of citations), this source is also provided in column six. If there is no citation or no empirical study in column six, the citation in column five is listed as having no source. The full references for all citations can be found in the reference list of this chapter.

Table 13.1 Texts Selected for In-depth Analysis and Discussion

Selected texts	*Research focus—descriptions from the citing text*	*Claim made*	*Citations used in the selected text*	*Citations in the cited texts/comments about the cited text*
1. Cartwright & Cooper 1995	Examines the potential role played by people, the so-called soft issues in merger success	77% fr[1]	McKinsey in McManus & Hergert 1988	No source
			Marks 1988	No source
		50% fr	British Institute of Management 1986	No source
			Hunt 1988	Hunt et al. 1987
			Cartwright & Cooper 1992	British Institute of Management 1986 Hunt 1988 Ellis & Pekar 1987 Marks 1988 Cmnd. 7198. 1978
2. Bourantas & Nicandrou 1998	Post-acquisition employee behaviour	us[2]	Agrawal, Jaffe, & Mandelker 1992	Study of post-merger performance of companies listed on the NYSE
			Amihud, Lev, & Travlos 1990	Study of the market reaction to conglomerate merger announcements
			Businessweek 1988	
			Cartwright & Cooper 1990	Marks 1988
			Datta et al. 1992	Meta-analysis of post-acquisition performance
			Fowler & Schmidt 1988	Study on the performance of tender offers
			Marks 1988	No source
			Napier 1989	*Businessweek* 1985
			Ravenscraft & Scherer 1987	Study of merger success
			Travlos 1987	Study of the impact of payment for stock returns of bidding firms: losses for stock exchange gains for cash offers

[1] failure rate
[2] unsuccessful

3. Hubbard 1999	Explores the process of acquiring through an in-depth discussion of the various stages	50% fr	Baker, Miller, & Ramsberger 1981	Kitching 1967
			Lefkoe 1987	*Fortune* article referring to studies by McKinsey & Co. and the Hay Group (consultancy firms)
			Hunt et al. 1987	Study of success rates
			Porter 1987	Study of divesture rates in diversified companies
			Coopers and Lybrand 1992	I cannot locate the report
			KPMG Management Consulting 1997	Survey: 31% very successful, 50% quite successful, 11% not very successful, 8% don't know
		66% fr	Magnet 1984	*Fortune* article that refers to a study by McKinsey & Co.
			Lubatkin 1987	Study claiming 'mergers are a means to permanent gain in common stock value'
		75% fr	Kitching 1967	The study does not mention failure rates
4. & 5. Appelbaum, Gandell, Shapiro, Belisle, & Hoeven 2000; Appelbaum, Gandell, Yortis, Proper, & Jobin 2000	Part one of this article examined corporate culture and its effects on employees when two companies merge and considered the importance of lucid communication throughout the process.	us	Cartwright & Cooper 1993a	Hunt 1988
				Marks 1988
				British Institute of Management 1986
				Kitching 1967
				Farrant 1970[i]
				Hovers 1973
				Fairburn & Geroski 1989
				McKinsey et al. 1986[ii]
	Part two of the article addresses the critical issue of stress, which is an outcome within the new and uncertain environment.		Cartwright & Cooper 1993b	Kitching 1967
				British Institute of Management 1986
				Fairburn & Geroski 1989
			Marks 1999	No source
			British Institute of Management 1986	No source
			Hunt 1988	Hunt et al. 1987
			Marks 1988	No source
			Tetenbaum 1999	Tetenbaum (PhD) is the president of a consulting company. She does not cite but she does mention three references: Mark Sirower Businessweek in 1995 and Mercer Management Consulting plus an un-named reference referred to as 'one study'
			Weber 1996	Cartwright & Cooper 1993b

(continued)

Table 13.1 (continued)

Selected texts	*Research focus—descriptions from the citing text*	*Claim made*	*Citations used in the selected text*	*Citations in the cited texts/comments about the cited text*
6. Marks & Mirvis 2001	This article draws on the authors' experience with over 70 mergers and acquisitions to understand the managerial actions that distinguish successful from disappointing combinations.	75% fr	Elsass & Veiga 1994	Davidson 1991 Hitt et al. 1991 Lubatkin 1983 Ravenscraft & Scherer 1987
			Davidson 1991 (not an academic paper)	David Birch (statement made in a hearing) Mueller 1985
			Hitt et al. 1991	Jensen 1988 Amihud, Dodd, & Weinstein 1986 Fowler & Schmidt 1988 Lubatkin 1987 Lubatkin & O'Neill 1987 Porter 1987 Ravenscraft & Scherer 1987
			Lubatkin 1983	Literature review finding opposing opinions
			Wright, Hoskisson, & Busenitz 2001	Categorizes managerial buyouts
7. Panchal & Cartwright 2001	Investigates post-merger stress. Results revealed that group differences in both sources and effects of stress existed.	50% fr	Cartwright & Cooper 1996	Marks 1988 Hunt 1988 Ellis & Pekar 1987 Cmnd. 7198. 1978 Farrant 1970[iii] Ravenscraft & Scherer 1987

8. Very & Schweiger 2001	This study attempted to identify key problems faced and solutions employed by acquirers during the stages of the acquisition process for domestic and cross-border deals. Results showed that the acquisition process can be understood both as a learning process applied to the focal transaction, and as a learning process aimed at improving the acquisition process itself.	fail to create value	LaJoux 1998	Literature review of 15 references, which are a mixture of academic publications, consultancy reports, and newspaper articles
9. DiGeorgio 2002	This paper summarises what is known and not known about making M&As work, and identifies best practices where appropriate.	75% fr	Marks & Mirvis 1998	No source
		40–80% fr	LaJoux 1998	See above
		40–74% divest.	Porter 1987	Study of divesture rates in diversified companies

(continued)

Table 13.1 (continued)

Selected texts	*Research focus—descriptions from the citing text*	*Claim made*	*Citations used in the selected text*	*Citations in the cited texts/comments about the cited text*
10. Child et al. 2001	This is a book about acquisitions and their performance. It looks at the different ways in which companies from the major acquiring countries (UK, US, Japan, Germany, and France) set about integrating the acquisitions they make in the UK. The book illustrates different national styles at work, but also shows how common many management practices have become around the world.	50% fr	No reference	
		47% fr	Kitching 1967	Study of failure in European M&As
		45% fr	Hunt et al. 1987	Study of success rates
		54% fr	Coopers and Lybrand 1992	PPT presentation of 'A review of the acquisition experience of UK companies'
		65% fr	Skapinker 2000	*Financial Times* article. Interviews with 'experts'

Notes:
i. Cartwright and Cooper refer to Farrent; the correct reference, however, is Farrant.
ii. Cartwright and Cooper 1993a cite McKinsey with regard to success rates. The reference, however, is not listed in their reference list. For this reason, I have not been able to follow it up.
iii. See footnote i.

CITING FAILURE RATES IN MERGERS AND ACQUISITION STUDIES

The detailed analysis of the 10 selected texts demonstrated that only one (Child, Faulkner, and Pitkethly 2001) of them in some way measures merger or acquisition failure rates or performance. Child, Faulkner, and Pitkethly (2001) do not actually measure failure rates, but in one chapter they discuss management practices and other variables that may influence post-merger performance. The other texts studied many other aspects of merger and acquisition processes (see Table 13.1 for research focus). For example, Bourantas and Nicandrou (1998) propose a typology of employee behaviour in acquisitions. They claim that understanding employee reactions is important in assessing the dynamics of acquisitions and their possible success or failure, but they do not measure any failure or success rates. Even without measuring post-merger and post-acquisition performance, however, all these texts introduce the notion of mergers and acquisitions by means of citing high failure rates very early in their texts.

As only one of the chosen texts studies post-merger or post-acquisition performance, the failure rate citations in the analysed texts appear 'perfunctory'. Perfunctory citation means citing work that is not apparently relevant to the immediate concerns of the author (Gilbert 1977). At the same time, the assumption of high failure rates seems to be important to the authors. In a discussion of the logic and sequence of scientific texts, Woolgar (1980) describes the opening of a text. He claims that the opening of a text provides instructions to aid the reader in understanding later parts of the text. Consequently, if a claim of failure rates appears early in a text—and in the 10 texts it often came in the very first paragraph—one would assume that the rest of the text would address failure rates. Yet the texts analysed did not study failure rates. One could ask how a citation and a notion can be perfunctory and important at the same time? I will address this question later when I discuss possible reasons why merger and acquisition scholars cite high failure rates.

The analysis of the sample texts revealed another citation behaviour emphasizing that the belief in high failure rates has certain significance for merger and acquisition scholars. It appears that almost all citations of high failure rates were 'empty'. According to Harzing (2002: 130), empty references are 'references that do not contain any original evidence for the phenomenon under investigation, but strictly refer to other studies to substantiate their claim'. Among the 10 texts, the only one not using empty references was Child, Faulkner, and Pitkethly (2001). Although an empty reference ought to indicate that the citation is not of great importance, yet, it seems like failure rates are important for these studies. These seem to be contradictory findings, like the one mentioned earlier, which I will detail later in the chapter.

There are some examples of erroneous citations in the analysed texts where the results reported in a cited text have been incorrectly reproduced. For example, Lubatkin 1983 or Lubatkin 1987 are citations often used to support claims of high failure rates. Yet, the two articles do not conclude that failure rates in mergers and acquisitions are high. Lubatkin (1983) is a classic merger and acquisition article published in the Academy of Management Review. The article is a review of the literature on post-acquisition performance of acquiring firms. Lubatkin (1983) introduces the article as follows:

> 'The primary purpose of merging should be to improve overall performance. Conceptual works, mainly from the field of industrial organization theory and strategic management, suggest that merger may improve the performance of the acquiring firm. To date, empirical studies have not supported the conclusions of the conceptual works. Coming almost exclusively from the field of finance, these studies generally find that mergers do not benefit the acquiring firm with a return greater than it would receive from other investment-production activities with similar levels of risk'.
>
> (Lubatkin 1983: 218)

If one stops there, it appears as if Lubatkin claims that mergers are not profitable. However, his literature review shows that the post-acquisition performance record is inconsistent. In some studies that he reviews, the acquiring firm gains from the acquisition; in others it loses. He finds in the literature that there are *opposing* views as to whether acquisitions are profitable or not for the acquiring firm. Thus, Lubatkin does not make any definite claims about high or low failure rates.

In the 1987 article, Lubatkin reports a study where he tested the relationship between related mergers and stockholder value. The results of the study were somewhat of a surprise to Lubatkin. 'The results showed that mergers in general are a means to permanent *gains* in common stock value for both acquiring and acquired firms' stockholders' [italics added] (Lubatkin 1987: 50). Lubatkin observed that his results were contrary to most other studies on the subject. Neither article by Lubatkin (1983, 1987) supports claims of high failure rates in mergers and acquisitions. Yet many of the texts in the sample cite one of Lubatkin's studies (1983 or 1987) in order to support such claims (see Table 13.1).

Kitching (1967) is another classic, but often erroneously cited, text regularly used to support claims of high failure rates. In his study Kitching interviewed a number of managers to find out what they did to bring about either successful or unsuccessful acquisition outcomes. He discusses failure rates in certain types of acquisitions and finds that concentric acquisitions have the highest incidence of failure.[2] Kitching's numbers are quite easily misinterpreted as he talks about the share of the number of failures attributable to particular types of acquisition. Thus, when he states a 47 percent failure rate among concentric acquisitions, he means that these account for 47 percent of the total number of failures, not of the total number of acquisitions in the sample. Based on Exhibit 1 in his article, I have estimated the overall failure rate in his sample to be 27 percent.

The three citations discussed here (Kitching 1967; Lubatkin 1983, 1987) are classic in that they are commonly referred to in academic texts on mergers and acquisitions. They are also often misinterpreted and thereby cited incorrectly when used to support claims not made in the original texts.

The analysis of citation behaviour shows further that non-academic references are commonly used in the sample texts in order to back up the claim of high failure rates. Examples are consultant reports, newspaper articles, and practitioners' columns (see Table 13.1 for examples of these types of references). The newspaper articles often make vague references to different types of reports, academic or non-academic, and they refer to interviews with or statements by academics, CEOs, consultants, or others with experience in the field. The consultant reports are often based on a study by the consultant company, but the data, and the analysis thereof, are rarely available in the reports. These kinds of non-academic sources regularly claim that mergers and acquisitions have high failure rates, but their sources for these claims are vague if not non-existent. Citing such sources in an academic text increases the number of citations that emphasize the belief in high failure rates.

SO WHAT DOES THIS OBSERVED CITATION BEHAVIOUR MEAN?

This section cites texts from the sample of 10 texts as well as texts from the original sample of 31. The overall impression after analysing the merger and acquisition texts is that the citations repeatedly prove perfunctory, empty, or incorrect. There are so many articles on mergers and acquisitions starting with a statement of high failure rates that its veracity appears to be more or less mechanically taken for granted. Interestingly, though, the first sample of 31 texts included articles that actually study and discuss post-merger and post-acquisition performance without perfunctory citation (Brouthers, van Hastenburg, and van den Ven 1998; Capron, Mitchell, and Swaminathan 2001; Fluck and Lynch 1999, Haleblian and Finkelstein 1999; Hitt, Harrison, Ireland, and Best 1998; Kirshnan and Park 2002). These texts, though, are not frequently cited in relation to failure and success rates (for this reason they were not included in the list of 32 texts analysed in depth). In the sample texts, citations of merger failures and success seem to provide justification for the position taken in the article and to persuade readers that one's findings are new and contribute to the common knowledge in the field. However, as mentioned earlier most articles analysed here do not treat post-merger and post-acquisition performance or failure and success rates. The 10 texts selected for detailed discussion focus mostly on the integration process, discussing various ways to improve integration.

One could claim that the authors indirectly discuss performance in these cases as improved integration hopefully leads to better outcomes.

So why are there so many empty, perfunctory, or even secondary citations in the analysed merger and acquisition texts? One possible interpretation is that to mention failure or success rates has become an obligatory point of passage (cf., Macdonald and Kam 2010) or ritual in introducing and justifying a merger or acquisition study, especially if the study is not on performance but on processes of integration. The citations therefore appear perfunctory in relation to the actual research question, or empty, as they are not important for the study as such. Some citations are probably empty just because the claim is perfunctory. If the citation is not important to the actual study, most scholars would probably not find it meaningful to spend time trying to find a source for such a claim. Another reason for this behaviour could be to create a sort of drama around merger and acquisition research. If the scholars can show that mergers and acquisitions are problematic, using many citations pointing to problems, then studies on mergers and acquisitions may seem more urgent and important. Still another reason could be that one uses the same citations, a sort of given set of citations, in one's own publications.

The texts by Cartwright and Cooper are a case in point of such recurrent use of a given set of citations. Several of their publications mention high failure rates and refer to the same set of citations. For example: Kitching (1967) is cited in Cartwright and Cooper (1993a, 1993b); Farrent (1970—the correct spelling is Farrant 1970)—is found in two texts by Cartwright and Cooper (1993a, 1996); British Institute of Management (1986) is frequently cited in a number of texts Cartwright and Cooper (1992, 1993a, 1993b, 1995); as is Hunt (1988), cited in Cartwright and Cooper (1992, 1993a, 1995, 1996); finally Marks (1988) is cited in Cartwright and Cooper (1990, 1992, 1993a, 1995, 1996).

Cartwright and Cooper do not study merger and acquisition outcomes *per se*, though. Instead, their object of study is reasons for failures such as stress, cultures, or other human factors. They mention high failure rates *en passant*, on their way to justifying their own studies. They do not engage with their reference on high failure rates, nor do they account in detail for the degree of validity in these citations. Their referring to high failure rates is not something essential to their study at hand, but appears as an obligatory passage point through which they steer their publications on mergers and acquisitions.

In fact, justification for the study at hand seems to be the main purpose of citing high failure rates. However, if justification is a reason for citations, it is remarkable that citations used in the sample texts are rarely taken from studies on post-merger and post-acquisition performance. Only a few of the citations found in the analysis are studies on post-merger and post-acquisition performance in some aspect (see Table 13.1 for citations). For example, Datta, Pinches, and Narayanan (1992) conducted a meta-analysis of existing *ex-ante* event studies. Fowler and Schmidt (1988) studied tender offers and provided a comparison with ordinary acquiring firms, but their study does not mention mergers. Lubatkin (1987) found that mergers are in general a means to permanent *gain* in stock value for both the acquiring and acquired companies' shareholders. Ravenscraft and Scherer (1987) found that about one third of all acquisitions were divested. Porter (1987) discussed failures but only in diversified companies. Hitt, Hoskisson, Ireland, and Harrison (1991) did not study merger and acquisition outcomes in general, but how *R&D outputs* were affected by acquisitions. Kitching (1967, 1974) found varying results in his first study and in the second study that about 50 percent of mergers and acquisitions were failures. In his latter study, which was on international acquisitions, the results were based on managers' assessments of failure or success. Finally, Hunt, Lees, Grumbar, and Vivian (1987) did a study inspired by Kitching (1967) where they interpreted their results to mean that about 50 percent of all acquisitions succeed.

The previously mentioned citations are examples supporting the argument that there are somewhat high failure rates in mergers or acquisitions. It could, however, be worth pondering on what is regarded as a high failure rate. Is a 33 percent divesture rate high? Is 25 percent a high failure rate? And how should one interpret a so-so success (as in Hunt 1988; Hunt et al. 1987)? Hunt (1988) and Hubbard (1999) claim that Kitching (1967) found a 75 percent failure rate, which I would consider high. But Kitching never mentioned that number in his article. Moreover, failure is defined differently in these studies. Some measure the effect on shareholder value, others define failure in terms of divesture, still others refer to managers' perceptions and some measure the effects of an acquisition on R&D investment. To simply bundle all these studies under the heading of 'high failure rates in mergers and acquisitions' is like comparing apples to oranges, as different outcomes are measured (see Meglio and Risberg 2010).

If the purpose of citations is to persuade others, to position one's own study or even to appear scientific, then many of the citations in the texts studied do not seem useful. Citing articles not based on studies on merger or acquisition performance in order to argue for high failure rates is not very persuasive. Nor is citing an article that just refers to another article on the subject (empty reference, Harzing 2002).

Citations can sometimes function as a form of control; they may be imposed on scholars by their research environment in order to control the reputation of that environment. Whitley (2000) claims that when seeking to achieve good reputations, departments and universities force scholars to refer to the previous work of their colleagues. This convention, Whitley argues, is a way to exert social control, and by forcing scholars to relate only to references accepted by the local community, the institution can control novel ideas. Macdonald and Kam (2010) point to similar control by journals. If scholars want to improve their chances of being published in a journal, they cite articles from that journal. If the journal editors publish articles that cite articles from their own journal, they will improve their ISI impact factor. According to Macdonald and Kam, this means ultimately that the journal editors to some extent control what texts are cited in the articles published in the journal. In addition, many scholars are evaluated by their home institutions not only on number of publications but also on the journals in which they publish. The so-called A-journals require a certain standard and a certain form of writing to which scholars must conform if they want to be published in those journals—and if they want to have a career. Journals institutionalise through their requirements certain norms and procedures in the academic field (cf., Whitley 1980). These norms are difficult to break out of as they reflect the practices of the field as well as reproduce them. Such tacit social control could prevent novel approaches to merger and acquisition research as the careers of scholars might be at stake if they do not conform to the norms for publication and citation. As they do not want to put their careers at stake, this implicit control could be a reason why so many published texts start in the same manner.

IMPLICATIONS FOR THE M&A FIELD AND THE M&A SCHOLAR

What might be the implications of the citation behaviour found for the merger and acquisition community? First of all, such behaviour perpetuates a belief of merger and acquisition failures that is not supported by the citations used in the text (see Risberg and Meglio 2012 for an analysis of merger and acquisition outcomes). This seems to have become taken for granted as a truth that no one questions. If this is the case, it might also affect research agendas. If it is simply assumed that mergers and acquisitions have high failure rates, a large proportion of research might be directed towards improving post-merger and post-acquisition performance. This in turn could be a reason why so much merger and acquisition research is quantitative cross-sectional research aiming at finding explanatory variables and indicators for post-merger and post-acquisition performance (see Meglio and Risberg 2010, 2011 for further discussion). Most of the articles reviewed here are not of these kinds, yet the authors seem obliged to justify their research by referring to high failure rates. This could be a tacit norm that they feel required to follow in order not to stake their careers. It may be time for the merger and acquisition academic community to start a discussion on the purposes of research on mergers and acquisitions. Is it to improve post-merger and post-acquisition performance? Is it to better understand what takes place in an organization during merger and acquisition processes? Is it to improve the working lives of people employed by the merging organizations? Or is the purpose completely different? I am not making any claims here about what should be the correct purpose of research, but I would maintain that our research should have many different objectives. If most merger and acquisition research has the objective of solving problems of low performance, then the research, the methods used, and the outcomes will be rather limited. I hope instead that this analysis of citation behaviour will start a debate in the M&A research community on why we do merger and acquisition research, and what implications our research might have on companies, business life, and society at large.

Of the 10 texts discussed in more detail, few manage to convince the reader through their citation practices that there are high failure rates in mergers or acquisitions, because most of the citations used are empty (in Harzing's 2002 terms). The way in which citations are used, referring to secondary references and mixing citations of differing significance, gives rise to the assumption of high failure rates in mergers and acquisitions. There are studies supporting this fact (some of them mentioned earlier), but far fewer than the numbers of citations in the analysed texts would imply. If the purpose of the citations was to convince the reader of high failure rates in mergers and acquisitions, then the authors would have to cite other texts on post-merger and post-acquisition performance. My purpose here is not to verify or refute claims about failure rates in mergers and acquisitions, but merely to analyse citations in connection with such claims in order to learn about citation behaviour.

The findings of this study may say more about the academic world and its norms than about the author's citation behaviour. In the academic community there is a great pressure to publish. This pressure could lead to various behaviours such as sloppy, redundant, and perfunctory citation. To publish, one must be persuasive. To be persuasive, one should speak with authority, and using many references is a way to do achieve that objective. No scholar can manage to read everything that is published on her/his subject. A way to cope with the reading load is to read fragmentarily, quickly scanning articles for certain details. This practice could lead to misinterpretation of the article or at least missing important points. Another way to cope could be to use the literature reviews of others, that is, to use the citations of others.

The conclusion remains that much of the citation behaviour in the studied texts is casual and habitual, and that when scrutinized, the citations often fail to meet their purpose of convincing readers that there are high failure rates in mergers and acquisitions. A likely reason for these citation behaviours, I would claim, is that the merger and acquisition scholars have a stake in portraying mergers and acquisitions as failures in order to justify their research. I also would claim that sometimes the citations may be obligatory passages points used because the scholars have a stake in getting their research published.

Another implication is that recurrent resort to certain citations legitimises their use, no matter the quality of the references. Commenting upon a citation analysis by de Solla Price (1976), MacDonald and Kam note that '[i]t was becoming apparent that papers were often cited because they had been cited' (2010: 192). They concur with de Solla Price's finding: '[i]t was becoming *de rigeur* to cite certain papers to demonstrate knowledge of which papers were *de rigeur*, not because the papers were especially good or even relevant' (Macdonald and Kam 2010: 192). If citations that are perfunctory, empty or of low academic quality are repeatedly used, the credibility of our research might be put in doubt.

There might also be implications for practitioners. If practitioners cannot trust scholars to be careful and rigorous, or if they do not recognise their own reality in the research findings, they will probably not appreciate the results or any advice coming from research. According to Brouthers, van Hastenburg, and van den Ven (1998), for example, in previous research claiming that companies do not benefit from mergers and acquisitions, the wrong measure has been used. In their study they instead measured managers' fulfillment of their various motives for the merger or acquisition. Doing this, they found that most mergers are successful in achieving the goals set by managers.

Good citation behaviour is of extreme importance for academic rigour. Each and every citation in an academic paper reflects the quality of the research. Neglect of good citation practice calls into question the essence and value of academic research and its potential relevance to practitioners and the public at large.

NOTES

1. A citation is a reference to a published text made in running text (for example, Risberg 1999). A reference is an item providing all information regarding the citation. The reference is often included in a list of references at the end of the text. In this text I use the term citation when talking about the reference made in the running text and the term reference when I talk about the item in the list of references.
2. Kitching (1967: 85) defines concentric acquisitions as (i) 'concentric marketing—Same customer types as buying company but different technology'; (ii) 'concentric typology—Same technology as buying company but different customer types'.

REFERENCES

Agrawal, A., Jaffe, J.F., and Mandelker, G.N. (1992) 'The post-merger performance of acquiring firms: a re-examination of an anomaly', *Journal of Finance*, 47: 1605–21.

Amihud, Y., Dodd, P., and Weinstein, M. (1986) 'Conglomerate mergers, managerial motives and stockholder wealth', *Journal of Banking & Finance*, 10: 401–10.

Amihud, Y., Lev, B., and Travlos, N.G. (1990) 'Corporate control and the choice of investment financing: The case of corporate acquisitions', *Journal of Finance*, 45: 603–16.

Appelbaum, S.H., Gandell, J., Shapiro, B.T., Belisle, P., and Hoeven, E. (2000) 'Anatomy of a merger: behavior of organizational factors and processes throughout the pre- during- post- stages (part 2)', *Management Decision*, 38: 674–84.

Appelbaum, S.H., Gandell, J., Yortis, H., Proper, S., and Jobin, F. (2000) 'Anatomy of a merger: behavior of organizational factors and processes throughout the pre- during- post-stages (part 1)', *Management Decision*, 38: 649–62.

Baker, H.K., Miller, T., and Ramsberger, B.J. (1981) 'An Inside look at corporate mergers and acquisitions', *MSU Business Topics*, 29: 49–57.

Bourantas, D. and Nicandrou, I.I. (1998) 'Modelling post-acquisition employee behavior: typology and determining factors', *Employee Relations*, 20: 73–91.

British Institute of Management (BIM) (1986) 'The management of acquisitions and mergers', Discussion Paper No. 8, Economics Department.

Brouthers, K.D., van Hastenburg, P., and van den Ven, J. (1998) 'If most mergers fail why are they so popular?', *Long Range Planning*, 31: 347–53.

Businessweek (1985) 'Do mergers really work?', June 03: 88–100.

Businessweek (1988) 'A new strain of merger mania (Cover story)', March 21: 122–26.

Capron, L., Mitchell, W., and Swaminathan, A. (2001) 'Asset divestiture following horizontal acquisitions: a dynamic view', *Strategic Management Journal*, 22: 817–44.

Cartwright, S. (1998) 'International mergers and acquisitions: the issues and challenges', in M. Gertsen, A.-M. Søderberg, and J. Torp (eds.) *Cultural dimensions of international mergers and acquisitions*, New York, NY: Walter de Gruyter.

Cartwright, S. and Cooper, C.L. (1990) 'The Impact of Mergers and Acquisitions on People at Work: Existing Research and Issues', *British Journal of Management*, 1: 65–76.

Cartwright, S. and Cooper, C.L. (1992) *Merger and acquisition: The human factor.* Oxford: Butterworth-Heineman.

Cartwright, S. and Cooper, C.L. (1993a) 'The psychological impact of merger and acquisition on the individual: a study of building society managers', *Human Relations*, 46: 327–47.

Cartwright, S. and Cooper, C.L. (1993b) 'The role of culture compatibility in successful organizational marriage', *Academy of Management Executive*, 7: 57–70.

Cartwright, S. and Cooper, C.L. (1995) 'Organizational marriage: "hard" versus "soft" issues?', *Personnel Review*, 24(3): 32–42.

Cartwright, S. and Cooper, C.L. (1996) *Managing mergers, acquisitions and strategic alliances: Integrating people and cultures,* Oxford: Butterworth-Heineman.

Child, J., Faulkner, D., and Pitkethly, R. (2001) *The management of international acquisitions,* Oxford: Oxford University Press.

Cmnd. 7198. (1978) *A review of monopolies and mergers policy. A consultative document*, presented to Parliament by The Secretary of State for Prices and Consumer Protection by Command of Her Majesty, May 1978, London, UK: Her Majesty's Stationery Office 2.

Coopers and Lybrand (1992) *A review of acquisitions experience of major UK companies*, London, UK: Coopers and Lybrand.

Datta, D.K., Pinches, G.E., and Narayanan, V.K. (1992) 'Factors influencing wealth creation from mergers and acquisitions: A meta-analysis', *Strategic Management Journal*, 13: 67–84.

Davidson, K.M. (1991) 'Why acquisitions may not be the best route to innovation', *Journal of Business Strategy*, 12: 50–52.

de Solla Price, D. (1976) 'A general theory of bibliometric and other cumulative advantage processes', *Journal of the American Society for Information Science*, 27: 292–306.

DiGeorgio, R.M. (2002) 'Making mergers and acquisitions work: What we know and don't know—Part I', *Journal of Change Management*, 3: 134–48.
Ellis, D.J. and Pekar, P.P.J. (1987) 'Acquisitions: Is 50/50 good enough?', *Planning Review*, 6: 15–19.
Elsass, P.M. and Veiga, J.F. (1994) 'Acculturation in acquired organizations: A force-field perspective', *Human Relations*, 47: 431–53.
Fairburn, J. and Geroski, P. (1989) 'The empirical analysis of market structure and performance', in J. Fairburn and J. Kay (eds.) *Mergers and Merger Policy*, Oxford, UK: Oxford University Press.
Farrant, P. (1970) 'The truth about mergers', *Management Today*, May: 121–25, 164, 168.
Fluck, Z. and Lynch, A.W. (1999) 'Why do firms merge and then divest? A theory of financial synergy', *Journal of Business*, 72: 319–46.
Fowler, K.L. and Schmidt, D.R. (1988) 'Tender offers, acquisition, and subsequent performance in manufacturing firms', *Academy of Management Journal*, 31: 962–74.
Gilbert, N. (1977) 'Referencing as persuasion', *Social Studies of Science*, 7: 113–22.
Haleblian, J. and Finkelstein, S. (1999) 'The influence of organizational acquisition experience on acquisition performance: a behavioral learning perspective', *Administrative Science Quarterly*, 44: 29–56.
Harzing, A.-W. (2002) 'Are our referencing errors undermining our scholarship and credibility? The case of expatriate failure rates', *Journal of Organizational Behavior*, 23: 127–48.
Hitt, M.A., Harrison, J.S., Ireland, R.D., and Best, A. (1998) 'Attributes of successful and unsuccessful acquisitions of US firms', *British Journal of Management*, 9: 91–114.
Hitt, M.A., Hoskisson, Robert E., Ireland, R.D., and Harrison, J.S. (1991) 'Effects of acquisitions on R&D inputs and outputs', *Academy of Management Journal*, 34: 693–706.
Hovers, J. (1973) *Expansion through acquisitions*, London, UK: Business Books Limited.
Hubbard, N. (1999) *Acquisitions strategy and implementation*, Wiltshire, UK: Macmillan Business.
Hunt, J.W. (1988) 'Managing the successful acquisition: a people question', *London Business School Journal*, Summer: 2–15.
Hunt, J.W., Lees, S., Grumbar, J.J., and Vivian, P.D. (1987) *Acquisitions: The human factor*, Egon Zehnder International, London Business School.
Jensen, M.C. (1988) 'Takeovers: Their causes and consequences', *Journal of Economic Perspectives*, 2: 21–48.
Kirshnan, H.A. and Park, D. (2002) 'The impact of work force reduction on subsequent performance in major mergers and acquisitions. An exploratory study', *Journal of Business Research*, 55: 285–92.
Kitching, J. (1967) 'Why do mergers miscarry?', *Harvard Business Review*, 45: 84–101.
Kitching, J. (1974) 'Winning and losing with European acquisitions', *Harvard Business Review*, 52: 124–36.
KPMG Management Consulting (1997) *Colouring the map: Mergers and acquisitions in Europe*, Research Report, London: KPMG Management Consulting.
LaJoux, A.R. (1998) *The art of M&A integration*, New York, NY: McGraw-Hill.
Lefkoe, M. (1987) 'Why so many mergers fail', *Fortune*, 20 July: 113–14.
Lubatkin, M. (1983) 'Mergers and the performance of the acquiring firm', *Academy of Management Review*, 8: 218–25.
Lubatkin, M. (1987) 'Merger strategies and stockholder value', *Strategic Management Journal*, 8: 39–53.

Lubatkin, M. and O'Neill, H.M. (1987) 'Merger strategies and capital market risk', *Academy of Management Journal*, 30: 665–84.

Macdonald, S. and Kam, J. (2010) 'Counting footnotes: Citability in management studies', *Scandinavian Journal of Management*, 26: 189–203.

Magnet, M. (1984) 'Acquiring without smothering', *Fortune*, Nov 12: 22–28.

March, J.G. and Sutton, R.I. (1997) 'Organizational performance as a dependent variable', *Organization Science*, 8: 698–706.

Marks, M.L. (1988) 'The merger syndrome: the human side of corporate combinations', *Journal of Buyouts and Acquisitions*, January/February: 18–23.

Marks, M.L. (1999) 'Surviving a Merger', *Electric Perspectives*, 24: 26–35.

Marks, M.L. and Mirvis, P.H. (1998) *Joining forces*, San Francisco, CA: Jossey-Bass.

Marks, M.L. and Mirvis, P.H. (2001) 'Making mergers and acquisitions work: Strategic and psychological preparation', *Academy of Management Executive*, 15(2): 80–92.

McManus, M.L. and Hergert, M.L. (1988) *Surviving merger and acquisition*, Glenview, IL: Scott, Foresman and Co.

Meglio, O. and Risberg, A. (2010) 'Mergers and acquisitions—Time for a methodological rejuvenation of the field?', *Scandinavian Journal of Management*, 26: 87–95.

Meglio, O. and Risberg, A. (2011) 'The (mis)measurement of M&A performance—a systematic narrative literature review', *Scandinavian Journal of Management*, 27(4): 418–33.

Mueller, D.C. (1985) 'Mergers and market share', *Review of Economics & Statistics*, 67: 259–67.

Napier, N.K. (1989) 'Mergers and acquisitions, human resource issues and outcomes: a review and suggested typology', *Journal of Management Studies*, 26: 271–89.

Panchal, S. and Cartwright, S. (2001) 'Group differences in post-merger stress', *Journal of Managerial Psychology*, 16: 424–33.

Porter, M.E. (1987) 'From competitive advantage to corporate strategy', *Harvard Business Review*, 65: 43–59.

Ravenscraft, D.J. and Scherer, F.M. (1987) *Mergers, sell-offs and economic efficiency*, Washington, DC: Brookings Institution.

Risberg, A. and Meglio, O. (forthcoming) 'Merger and acquisition outcomes—Is it meaningful to talk about high failure rates?', in Y. Weber (ed.) *Handbook for Mergers and Acquisitions Research*, Edward Elgar Ltd, UK.

Shrivastava, P. (1986) 'Postmerger integration', *Journal of Business Strategy*, 7: 65.

Skapinker, M. (2000) 'Marrying in haste', *Financial Times*, April 12: 15.

Small, H.G. (1978) 'Cited documents as concept symbols', *Social Studies of Science*, 8: 327–40.

Tetenbaum, T.J. (1999) 'Beating the odds of merger & acquisition failure: seven key practices that improve the chance for expected integration and synergies', *Organizational Dynamics*, 28: 22–35.

Travlos, N.G. (1987) 'Corporate takeover bids, methods of payment, and bidding firms' stock returns', *Journal of Finance*, 42: 943–63.

Very, P. and Schweiger, D.M. (2001) 'The acquisition process as a learning process: evidence from a study of critical problems and solutions in domestic and cross-border deals', *Journal of World Business*, 36: 11–31.

Weber, Y. (1996) 'Corporate cultural fit and performance in mergers and acquisitions', *Human Relations*, 49: 1181–202.

Whitley, R. (1980) 'The context of scientific investigation', in W.R. Knorr, R. Krohn, and R. Whitley (eds.) *The Social Process of Scientific Investigation*.

Sociology of the Sciences, Volume IV, Dordrecht: D. Reidel Publishing Company, pp. 297–321.

Whitley, R. (2000) *The intellectual and social organization of the sciences*, 2nd ed., Oxford, UK: Oxford University Press.

Woolgar, S. (1980) 'Discovery: Logic and sequence in a scientific text (1)', in W.R. Knorr, R. Krohn, and R. Whitley (eds.) *The Social Process of Scientific Investigation. Sociology of the Sciences*, Volume IV, Dordrecht: D. Reidel Publishing Company, pp. 239–268.

Wright, M., Hoskisson, R.E., and Busenitz, L.W. (2001) 'Firm rebirth: Buyouts as facilitators of strategic growth and entrepreneurship', *The Academy of Management Executive*, 15: 111–25.

Epilogue

14 Reflection on the Critical Role of Stakeholders in Mergers and Acquisitions

Helén Anderson

In this final chapter, I consider the stakeholders in the context of a merger or acquisition process and discuss the nature of the stakes that are in focus. The literature in the mergers and acquisitions field is extensive and vast, as has been noted in Chapter 1. Regarding the merger or acquisition process, the literature has essentially suggested that it consists of two parts. The first is often described as pre-merger, ending with a decision to acquire or merge. The second part after the formal decision is made would be called post-merger. The initial part of the process typically includes very few core stakeholders formulating and articulating the motives that are later made public and official. Examples of typical motives in the literature are: to obtain economies of scale, to acquire new technology, or to increase market share. The different chapters of this book modify these findings. The contributions of the various authors have shown that there may be both explicit, official goals and more implicit ones that also change during the interaction among the stakeholders.

The application of a multi-stakeholder approach challenges the view of the merger and acquisition process as linear and rational. The book views stakeholders from both acquirers' and targets' perspectives, and their respective stakes that may conflict in some cases. The acknowledgement of stakeholders also sheds light on how their respective stakes are their basis for action and thus determine their role agenda in the process of implementation and integration following a merger or acquisition decision. I see the stakeholders as actors perceiving and making sense of their context, in which other stakeholders are included. Their roles are based on their respective understanding and interests—that is, their stakes. Similarly, the evaluation, viewed by some as a final part of the merger or acquisition process where performance would be measured, involves a number of stakeholders. The outcome of a merger or acquisition is the result of interaction among many stakeholders, where any one of them may play a critical role in the process.

A MODEL OF A MERGER OR AN ACQUISITION PROCESS

The literature discusses motives and goals for mergers and acquisitions as a basis for suggesting and deciding on such strategic activity. Based on the context and approach in this book, I would characterize that part of the process as one of estimation, in which stakeholders estimate what may be the pro's and con's of a merger or an acquisition. All decisions in such a process are based on estimates of what the future may hold even though the estimates may take the shape of refined and sophisticated calculations. The model in Figure 14.1 shows that the beginning of the process includes several estimation points and that these initial activities may overlap with the implementation and integration process that follows. The official and formal decision to acquire or merge is but a part of the process and serves as the official expression of strategic intent that justifies the formal decision. Therefore, several estimation points for several stakeholders precede the announcement of a merger or an acquisition.

Traditionally, implementation and integration start when the decision to merge or acquire is made official. The chapters in this book, however, show that the activities of various stakeholders undertaken to implement and integrate the two organizations may start at different times and places. In fact they overlap in time. There may be instructions on how to implement the strategy underlying the acquisition or merger decision, but surprisingly often there are not. The integration process becomes the principal strategic means for realizing the expected pro's and containing the con's. In that part of the process, other stakeholders like middle managers and employees are also involved. Thus, early in the process, the evaluation of performance in terms of benefits and sacrifices has already been initiated by the different

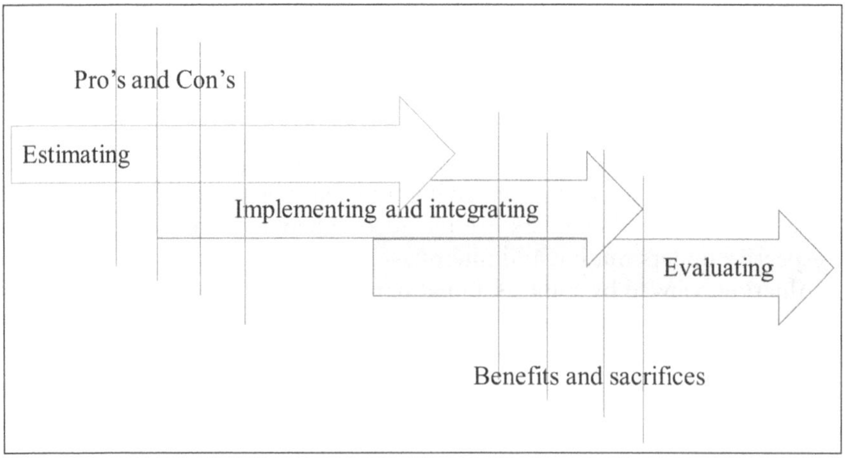

Figure 14.1 A model of an acquisition or a merger process.

stakeholders involved. For a company on the stock exchange, for example, the value of the shares would be measured the day after the announcement of a merger or an acquisition.

As claimed in Chapter 1, there are studies showing the complexities of preparing the business case, negotiating and closing the deal. Moreover, there is considerable research identifying the many challenges following a merger. The complexity of co-ordinating a merger (implementation and integration) is acknowledged in literature but still far from understood and recognized by practitioners. To realize the synergies can be a difficult task. Examples of especially challenging areas identified in this book relate to people (i.e., the perceptions and reactions of managers and employees) and structure (i.e., organization and information systems). The difficult measurement of synergies and performance (post-merger) is finally addressed in the model. The findings confirm the complexity, while also illustrating various forms of rationality present. In addition, as the integration process advances, more stakeholders may perceive and act in both expected and unexpected ways. Only after an activity can an evaluation be made; thus, what I called estimation *ex ante* will be called evaluation *ex post*. Moreover, because the book emphasizes the presence of many stakeholders in interaction, I have chosen to refer to the evaluation as the determination of benefits and sacrifices rather than performance, which relates to company performance only.

ESTIMATING PRO'S AND CON'S

In this part I will reflect on the left side of the model, emphasizing the estimation of what I call pro's and con's, by revisiting chapters in the book.

The shareholders represent a critical group in any kind of merger or acquisition. Their interest is primarily financial, according to Borglund (Chapter 2). The contributions in this book indicate that the shareholders make up a very heterogeneous group where some are more active than others.[1] Individual shareholders may be satisfied with different levels of return on investments than institutional ones, whereas other parties, like venture capitalists, would expect yet another level of return on investment. Also, the professional advisers to investors, like investment bankers, may have interests of a professional as well as a financial nature.

Synergy is a motive for many mergers and acquisitions and represents the activity that will in turn generate financial benefits. Most often synergy is related to internal issues such as production facilities, but synergy can also be expected in relation to customers of the merging companies (Chapter 10 by Öberg), to business partners (Chapter 8 by Schriber), or to suppliers (Chapter 9 by Holtström). The most striking aspect of synergy is its character of being expected. It is presented in the form of benefits that will be realized in the integration of the two companies.

In Chapter 12, by Jungerhem and Larsson, the government, or the state, is acting as an owner of banks. But the state is also the legislator defining the rules of the game, and in Chapter 12 I can observe the exercise of that role as the rules change over time. The state also has a stakeholder role as owner of public insurance, as is noted in Chapter 11, by Bringselius. As owner of public insurance the state wants to reorganise the business, but it may also have different goals for its ownership. Thus, the state can be an active owner, but also operate as a player on the market. I suggest that such a role would be an expression of some kind of power stake in addition to the financial one already presented.

In Chapter 12, the authors also point out that there are ownership interests linked to different industrial spheres consisting of groups of companies. Power stakes seem to provide the rationale for the hostile bid confronting the CEO in one of the paper and pulp companies, a situation described by Ericson in Chapter 3 as '. . .the most spectacular power struggle in Swedish business life at the time'. The Iggesund case illustrates the character of a hostile takeover. The bidder has gained power the very minute the bid is announced, putting the target in a position of having to react to what may come and be made public without any previous 'warning'.

The CEO in Chapter 3 does not immediately understand why a takeover bid has been made on the firm of which he is the top manager. The strategic objectives presented for and against a merger or an acquisition may be many and well-articulated, according to the literature, or obscure as in Chapter 3. The process by which the parties interpret and interact, based on their motives, is also very important. In order to make sense of the situation, the CEO of the target company had to take action to gather information from his current personal network and like pieces of a puzzle put them together into a frame shaped also by his past experience of the same industry and interaction with the same parties. Thus, he perceives that a hostile takeover has been initiated, where another company has as the primary objective of strengthening its position in the market. He views the companies as rivals on the market and therefore he also includes a future outlook for the market in his understanding of the situation. Furthermore, he acts according to his own interpretation of the situation, not according to what has been put forward to him or what is discussed in the media. Thus, whereas the chapter shows that a top manager may be acting as the agent of the owner (the principal), there are also other interests at stake. The case is, according to me, an example of how a top manager within a year changes his interpretation and moves from estimation to evaluation.

Borglund (Chapter 2) discusses a line of research claiming that strategic moves and activities are influenced by trends. The present trend of corporate social responsibility forces the key players in mergers and acquisitions to go beyond rhetoric and also to broaden their perspectives when preparing and evaluating their strategic initiative. In the case of Vin & Sprit, the different stakeholder influence is multifold. First there is the seller, the government, which is concerned about obtaining a high price, but in a way that would not jeopardize its political reputation. Secondly, the very business of the company, providing the Swedish market with wine and liquor, is in itself a societal concern. Thirdly, several of the stakeholders, like the union representing many of the employees at the Swedish facility, and the farmers supplying the same facility, took action when news of the acquisition came out. The case shows that the shareholders also need to relate to what is discussed in the media on the acquisition and on social responsibility.

Bringselius notes in Chapter 11 that the empirical phenomenon of mergers and acquisitions is frequent in the public sector as well. First the business sector seems to be held out as a role model for reducing costs. Because that issue is even more important to both politicians and authorities administering tax money, a merger between organisations is viewed as a means to improve efficiency. The second reason, according to Bringselius, is an ambition of elected politicians to distance themselves from what the authorities do. In that way the role of government as a stakeholder is not only changing but may also include stakes that are not easily combined, giving rise to ambiguity.

In summing up the reflection on stakes in the form of pro's and con's, firstly there are expectations of financial returns. There are also expectations of synergies, which are claimed to benefit stakeholders like clients and customers. Thirdly, the cases also revealed motives related to power in the sense of becoming 'big' on the market, but also in terms of influencing the rules of the game. Finally motives seem related to general trends inspired by value statements that include societal concerns. It is also quite obvious that concerns or arguments against a merger or an acquisition do not emanate from the driving stakeholders, but from stakeholders who perceive that they will be affected in a negative way.

IMPLEMENTING AND INTEGRATING

When a formal decision is made on an acquisition or a merger, the implementation and integration of the organizations involved are launched. Depending on the goals, there may of course be more or less integration. In this part I will reflect on the middle part of the model, emphasizing implementation and integration, in revisiting chapters of the book.

Usually not until top managers and shareholders, probably supported by different types of advisors, have initiated a merger or an acquisition process can other stakeholders learn about the news. I have already touched upon the public arena that media provides for such actions. The obvious internal stakeholders are employees and managers within the organizations involved in the merger or the acquisition. Four chapters (Chapters 4, 5, 6, and 7), described in more detail here, take as their point of departure different internal stakeholder groups in both the acquiring and the target company. These stakeholders are the ones expected to realize the synergy or multiple synergies that have been sought by the stakeholders taking the initiative in the merger or acquisition.

Chapter 4 by Schweizer concerns the merger between two Swiss-based companies, Sandoz and Ciba. They were already multinationals at the time of their merger, and Novartis, the new company formed in the merger nine months later, was even bigger. The complexity of the new MNC was also a concern for the managers of the Indian subsidiaries of Sandoz and Ciba that had to merge. As employees they were not part of the decision process, and as managers they did not fight the order given. Besides, both subsidiaries were part of the vertical in-house value chain, so that any protesting might interfere with operations; such protesting is not part of the task for an operations manager. After being initially shocked, they were confused and uncomfortable, feelings that were passed on to the local employees. Thus, the local managers were not as prepared to support the integration positively and constructively as they could have been had they been informed. Furthermore the case illustrates that the different hierarchical levels within an MNC—and what Schweizer calls 'global industry dynamics'—also create many arenas for interpretation. The pro's articulated and perceived at the top level of the MNC were not shared by the employees of the subsidiaries, where negative reactions and even counterarguments were expressed, leaving the managers of the subsidiaries caught in the middle. Another problem with not involving the subsidiary managers in the decision process was that of not exploiting their expertise on how the respective organizations function. Not involving the subsidiary managers is taking a high risk in that respect, according to Schweizer. Such involvement, on the other hand, must be balanced against the risk that top managers will lose control over a process where the stakes of many parties may conflict.

In Chapter 6, Nilsson, Olve, and Arwinge highlight the internal auditor, who is supporting primarily the board but also top management. To what extent, however, is their knowledge acknowledged and used by acquirers? And do they have stakes of their own? The authors particularly emphasize the increasing awareness of risk in strategic actions in general but for mergers and acquisitions in particular. Claiming that risk assessment is a continuous activity of ongoing strategic processes, the internal auditor could also be involved in evaluating a merger or an acquisition. Their findings show that the expertise of the internal auditor is little used, and in the execution rather than the design of the strategic transaction that constitutes a merger or an acquisition. They reason that the role of an independent yet internal auditor may prevent involvement by the auditors themselves. A third and interesting explanation for not using auditor expertise, according to the authors, relates to the very expertise the auditors possess. Perhaps, as Nilsson, Olve, and Arwinge argue, an auditor is focused on processes and procedures rather than on the content of strategic activities.

Despite earlier evidence from research on the complexities of integration, companies seem to run into the same or similar problems again and again. When companies are about to be integrated, much is at stake for internal groups and individuals. Not only culture and brand, routines and procedures of the organization, but also positions and employment contracts, may be altered or even abolished.

According to Frostenson, in Chapter 5, the employees of the acquiring or the target company are more or less at the core of the firm. But are they at the core of a merger or acquisition? They are most likely affected in some way, but do they exert any influence? A manager needs a mandate, an internal license to operate, Frostenson claims: 'The employees must be able to trust the new owners, to see a potential gain from them, and also to understand their activities and intentions'. Such legitimacy is important in any organisations, but becomes paramount in a merger or an acquisition. Employees are not a homogeneous group but are in fact very heterogeneous both as individuals and as groups. And because a high degree of legitimacy must be derived from many rather than few in an organisation, legitimacy has to be earned, again and again, after a merger or an acquisition. Not only are employees heterogeneous, but so are their perceptions of their respective organisation and the acquirer or target. Moreover, their stakes are not likely to be articulated or known in the organisation because most mergers and acquisitions are the concern of a limited group of core players, as discussed initially in this chapter.

Many mergers and acquisitions also lead to changes, as illustrated in the chapter by Beusch (Chapter 7), where the control system was reorganized. Therefore, the degree of insecurity may increase, not only about the individual's role and task in the organisation, but also on a more general level as to how things are going to be done. So legitimacy is likely to be reconstructed again and again in the integration process and needs considerate management attention and effort.

Chapter 7 by Beusch describes the critical operational task of the Part Numbering System when Ford acquired Volvo. He particularly addresses the important issue of effectiveness and efficiency that is also raised in Chapter 6 by Nilsson, Olve, and Arwinge. The ambition of Ford, the acquiring company, was to improve accounting and calculation methods. An additional acquisition motive for Ford was that the acquisition would also lead to optimization of product variety in the both Ford and Volvo brands. This task was to be performed primarily by the designers of management control systems at both companies, stakeholders by profession, having managed their respective control systems. At the same time, they were seen as stakeholders by the owners, who wanted them to redesign the systems into one common system. The challenges were identified early on because Ford was following a cost leadership strategy, whereas Volvo had a typical differentiation strategy. In the translation of strategic intent into operations, numerous critical issues had to be addressed by the managers of the control systems. In order to optimize at all in the target company, the two companies needed a similar way to identify the 30,000 components that make up a car. And the value chain included some 1,000 suppliers, 6–8 business units, 40–50 manufacturing facilities, and about 40 transporters—many stakeholders indeed.

The integration of control systems revealed different cognitive and cultural mindsets for the management controllers on what constituted a good Part Numbering System. The process was further complicated by high staff turnover in Volvo in connection with the acquisition. Thus, there was a confrontation of professional stakes with managerial stakes. The managers were responsible for realizing the synergies expected by the new owners, who were more convinced than the target-company employees about the benefits of a new system. The case illustrates that the acquirer has a form of first-mover advantage when exercising managerial power and taking strategic action. The power dimension can of course also give rise to competition between controllers and their respective stakes. If arguments are not understood, they will generate counterarguments. Winning a 'battle' on numbering parts gave control system designers at the target company a sense of pride and satisfaction. The process of negotiation to achieve the expected changes took more time and resources than expected, and by the end of the case description, it had still not led to the expected economies of scale and scope. The process is called the 'supposed' integration by Beusch.

In implementation and integration, synergy is going to be realized. However, synergy for the merging partners is not always perceived as synergy for other stakeholders, according to Schriber (Chapter 8). Schriber takes as his point of departure acquisition managers in the bakery industry and discusses how they handle stakeholders such as retailers during the integration process. By relating the discussion to the resource-dependence approach, he also touches upon power as one dimension of business relationships. But in contrast to what was discussed earlier in this chapter, power is not necessarily about ownership or setting the rules. Rather, control over resources and the exercise of power are not only ends, but also means, in an acquisition process.

In several chapters (Chapter 2 by Borglund, Chapter 3 by Ericson, and Chapter 11 by Bringselius) media are presented as an important channel when stakeholders are concerned about maintaining trustful relationships with other stakeholders. The merging or acquiring shareholders and key players, for example, assess the risk of receiving bad publicity. Such publicity may risk the whole venture; in less severe forms it may disturb the integration process between the companies.

In summing up, stakeholders within the acquiring and target company are part of the implementation and integration process following a merger or an acquisition. Thus, they are affected by it in one way or another. Their stakes in the process are formed on an individual, team, or group level and also through interaction with their respective managers. In some cases the employees are informed before the formal decision is made, but in most cases it seems they are not. Their stakes are not articulated in advance but develop during the integration process. And stakes can be different even when based on the same facts. For example, what seemed to be similar facts in Ford and Volvo turned out to have a different meaning for system engineers in the acquiring and target companies. Whether or not stakes are articulated by stakeholders in the acquiring and the target company, they need to take part of the management of the integration process.

Business partners of the companies involved in mergers and acquisitions perceive the strategic activity of a merger or acquisition from their own perspective. They may act as expected, but they may also change their interaction in unexpected ways. The interaction can support the development of synergy, but it can also give rise to unanticipated synergy. Actions by parties such as retailers, suppliers, or customers can also prevent synergy from being realized. Thus, the synergies that emerge from such integration processes are very difficult to evaluate and measure.

My conclusion of this discussion is that the pro's and con's—the stakes—in a merger or acquisition are not only differently perceived and interpreted depending on the stakeholder, but also on how and with whom the stakeholder interacts.

EVALUATING BENEFITS AND SACRIFICES

This discussion shows that no clear boundary separates implementation and integration from what can be regarded as post-merger activities. Thus, a post-merger process can be viewed as starting immediately after the merger or acquisition contract is signed. But it can also be seen as starting when integration is considered finalized. This is yet another manifestation of the non-linearity of the process. Evaluation seems to start as soon as the merger or the acquisition becomes known. An important observation is that evaluation of the earlier estimated pro's and con's, and what they mean, is part of implementation and integration. Similarly, the evaluation in terms of benefits and sacrifices becomes a part of the very operationalization of the merger or the acquisition. In this part I will reflect on the right side of the model, emphasizing the evaluation of what I call benefits and sacrifices, while revisiting chapters in the book.

In the bakery-industry acquisition studied by Schriber (Chapter 8), there is an expectation of synergies that explicitly concern suppliers. The first is reduction of logistic cost. The second expected synergy is increased margins through new products, and the third is strengthened brand loyalty among customers. However, the retailers selling the bakery products were very active in pursuing an agenda of their own, where they exercised power that forced acquisition managers to be more cautious in realizing synergies. That process included interaction with retailers both in the nature of negotiation and in the form of win-win discussions. Schriber suggests that there is not only synergy between the merging companies; the interconnectedness of the distribution chain leads to (re)action among other parties, creating unexpected synergy there as well.

Holtström (Chapter 9) claims that supplier relationships will likely be affected in mergers and acquisitions. He claims, further, that the stakes differ depending on type of supply, not just in terms of possible scale economies. And like Schriber, he emphasizes the interactive dimension of synergy where external stakeholders such as suppliers are concerned. Even with a quite obvious expected scale economy like increasing the volumes of purchased components, synergy realization may encounter difficulty because of co-ordination problems. Given that in Chapter 7 (by Beusch) the components in car assembly can number in the thousands, the complexity of synergy realization becomes obvious. In addition, suppliers of components and material for products are likely to realize the strategic character of their customers' integration, and in order to strengthen their own negotiating position they will also engage in restructuring. Equipment suppliers are likely to perceive the situation in the same way as product-related suppliers, whereas non-product related suppliers may be the ones perceived easiest to change from the merging firms' point of view. Holtström, however, notes that even in the latter case there is invariability in the process because so much of assembly and production nowadays is built into complex logistics and IT-integrated systems.

Öberg (Chapter 10) finds that customer relationships can dissolve if the product or products are replaced, or because of staff leaving, an (unfavourable) perception of the acquirer or simply because there are too many acquisitions. The perception of the situation and the context may also mean that the business relationships will continue as long as there is no change in product, in other customers and/or in key personnel. Also, the financial dimension can be a reason to maintain a supplier relationship. Her overall analysis shows the multi-dimensionality in a business relationship. And that multi-dimensionality also determines the content of the interaction between the target's customers and the target company and its new owner. The possible loss of a customer may thus seem to be a strategic risk worth taking into account in mergers and acquisitions. It becomes quite clear that the customers' perception of benefit and sacrifice is what becomes the basis for the post-merger evaluation.

The merger process in public insurance described in Chapter 11 (Bringselius) suffered from high employee turnover, but it also led to the replacement of the director general responsible. Bringselius' analysis reflects a media discussion and thus sheds light on external legitimacy in terms of who is to blame. She describes a very difficult integration process where both employees and clients (citizens) have difficulties seeing benefits, not just sacrifices. From her case presentation it becomes quite obvious that the parallel media discussion influences the stakeholders' interpretation.

Chapter 12, by Jungerhem and Larsson, provides an account of the merger history of Swedish banks up to 2009 and shows the development from many smaller banks into far fewer but much bigger ones. In their analysis the state (what Bringselius in Chapter 11 calls central government) is given several different stakeholder roles. In the first period the state was not very active, but when it was, it served as regulator of the financial system, in which it promoted mergers and acquisitions. That role changed dramatically in the second period, where the state was active as regulator and controller; here the Central bank (Riksbanken), too, assumed an active role. The state also reacted forcefully to the activity going on in the financial market. The third period began with a deregulation of the bank sector in Sweden, initiated by the state. Because of a financial crisis, the state served as a lender of last resort during this period, and it was also very active as a lender and a buyer. Another state-owned bank—Nordea—ran into severe financial difficulties from which it had to be rescued by its owner—the state. During all periods the state also acted as a supplier and purchaser of banking services. The analysis shows that the state not only has different stakeholder roles but also activates them differently over time, thus being an actor with multiple roles at the same time and in the same context.

A very common statement in research on mergers and acquisitions is the claim that many of them fail. This is the starting point for Risberg in Chapter 13. By going into depth in core articles in the area and systematically scrutinizing what the citations really say, she offers an answer. In addition, she elaborates on the stakes that can be ascribed to researchers. Of course they want to justify their field of research, but that may not be enough. In the competitive striving to get published, a researcher may yield to the temptation of citing what may seem to be the prevalent paradigm in the field, thereby repeating arguments again and again without the support of any empirical research. In fact, she found that only one of her analyzed texts actually measures failure rates. Risberg makes us aware that also stakes not directly related to a merger or an acquisition may have an influence on how we understand the phenomenon.

If I extend my reflection to questioning the benefits of trying to measure high failure rates, I can turn the argument around. In what way is there a benefit in showing success rates for mergers and acquisitions? Success or failure, or rather benefits and sacrifices, are evaluated from the perspective of each stakeholder. Through extending coverage to include many stakeholders, as has been the case in this book, the multi-dimensionality of what may constitute good progress in a merger or an acquisition process is emphasized. And because measurement procedures and tools seem still to be underdeveloped, at least among researchers, we must persist in claiming that we need to learn more about the what's and how's of performance in mergers and acquisitions.

In concluding, I want to stress that it seems to be researchers who use the terminology of success or failure regarding mergers and acquisitions. In the empirical cases the determination of whether the strategic activity was successful seems to be made with less definitive measures, by the stakeholders involved according to their criteria, using tools constructed underway, or not at all. At least the stakes identified are not evaluated in an explicit or formal way.

CRITICAL ROLES?

In the heterogeneous crowd of stakeholders in a merger or an acquisition, some articulate their stakes, while some do not. Stakes made explicit may be evaluated, as may implicit stakes. But first and foremost, it seems as if stakeholder stakes are made sense of, articulated, argued, and worked for in interaction with others in the complex process of integrating two or more companies. The critical role of a stakeholder seems to be a result of how the stakeholder perceives, acts, and interacts.

In preparing and proposing a merger or acquisition, the driving stakeholders interact in coming up with the pro's of taking this step. Early on, however, there may be other stakeholders interacting and arguing against a merger or an acquisition based on what they see as con's. In an implementation and integration process more stakeholders are involved. They may be more strongly dependent, like an employee, or less strongly dependent, like a customer. Irrespective of dependence, they will probably be influenced and exercise influence based on their stakes in the process. Finally what ends up being evaluated is the outcome of an interactive process involving many participants. Depending on how different stakes have influenced the process, the results in terms of benefits and sacrifices may be very different from what has been argued as pro's and con's before a merger or an acquisition.

NOTES

1. The many shareholders represented by institutions like pension funds and their employed professionals like financial analysts are not studied in this book. I believe that they would represent even more stakes.

Contributors

Helén Anderson has been professor of Business Administration, especially Marketing, at Jönköping International Business School since 2003. She obtained her PhD from the Stockholm School of Economics in 1994 and was appointed associate professor at Linköping University in 1998. Her current research interests are in business dynamics, innovation, strategic change, and mergers and acquisitions. She has previously published in journals such as *Frontiers of Entrepreneurship Research*, *Industrial Marketing Management*, *Journal of Brand Management*, *Management of Environmental Quality*, *Nordic Organization Studies*, *Scandinavian Journal of Management*, and *Supply Chain Management.*

Olof Arwinge obtained his licentiate in economics from Linköping University in conjunction with a research programme for auditors and consultants. Currently he is at Uppsala University finalizing his doctoral dissertation, which concerns internal control systems and risk management in the financial services industry. In addition to his research, he is a senior manager at the accounting firm of Grant Thornton, where he specializes in internal audit services, internal control, risk management and compliance. He has co-authored a paper in a Swedish professional journal for accountants, auditors, and consultants. In addition, he is co-author of a chapter on the link between internal control and management control in a comprehensive Swedish handbook on management control.

Peter Beusch is an assistant professor and senior lecturer with the department of Business Administration, School of Business, Economics, and Law at the University of Gothenburg. His research focuses on the role and function of management control, in particular the relationship between ideological and rhetorical elements and the more system-related features of control systems. Another area of interest is communication and management control, with a more actor-based view of management control, as evidenced, e.g., in P. Beusch (2011) 'Colliding and disintegrated topoi as the result of intended integration', in M. Jakobsen, I.L. Johansson, and H. Norreklit (eds.) *An Actor's Approach to Management: Conceptual Framework and Company Practice*, Copenhagen: DJØF Publishing.

Tommy Borglund is Head of Corporate Social Responsibility (CSR) Services at the consultancy of Hallvarsson & Halvarsson King Worldwide. He is a member of the CR group of the Swedish Society of Financial Analysts and the Commission on ESG at the European Federation of Financial Analysts Societies. In addition, he is an associate researcher with the Department of Business Studies at Uppsala University. His current research includes CSR communication, CSR strategies, and the role of CSR in mergers and acquisitions. He has co-authored 'Increasing responsibility through transparency?', a government report on sustainability reporting, as well as *Value creating CSR*, a book introducing CSR to Swedish readers. He holds a PhD from the Stockholm School of Economics, and his dissertation, published in 2006, was a study of changing stakeholder relations in connection with mergers and acquisitions. Tommy Borglund also has a background in business journalism and was editor of business news at Swedish Radio.

Louise Bringselius is a research fellow with the Lund Institute of Economic Research, Lund University. Her dissertation concerned mergers in central government and was presented in 2008. While currently continuing her research on public sector mergers, she is also focusing on auditing in central government (in particular at Supreme Audit Institutions). She is the author of a forthcoming article in the *International Journal of Public Administration* and has also published in Nordic Organization Studies (*Nordiske Organisasjonsstudier*). In 2012/2013 she will release a book on public-sector auditing. She is also involved in a research project on hospital mergers.

Mona Ericson is a professor at the Jönköping International Business School. She received her doctoral degree from the Stockholm School of Economics, where she also earned an associate professorship. Her dissertation focused on a complex merger and acquisition process, strategic actors, and their interactions and rationalities. Her principal research interest is in strategic change, with an emphasis on human interaction, temporal relationality, and emotions. Among her recent publications is the article 'Toward a sensed decision-making approach', published in *Management Decision*, and two books: *Business Growth—Activities, Themes and Voices*, and *A Narrative Approach to Business Growth*, both published by Edward Elgar. Mona Ericson has several years' experience in commercial banking, as well as managing her own consulting business and involvement in academic managerial duties.

Magnus Frostenson received his PhD from the Stockholm School of Economics in 2006. His dissertation focused on issues of ethics and culture in newly internationalized Swedish firms. He is currently a researcher with the Department of Business Studies at Uppsala University and is also a senior lecturer at the Örebro University School of Business. He is the author of several journal articles, books, and book chapters, primarily in business ethics and corporate social responsibility. He has published in *Journal of Business Ethics, Philosophy of Management* and *Business Ethics—a European Review*, among other academic periodicals. In 2011, he published a monograph on business ethics, to be followed in 2012 by a new book on sustainability reporting.

Virpi Havila has been Professor of Business Studies, especially Industrial Marketing, with the Department of Business Studies at Uppsala University since 2007. Her dissertation—defended in 1996—was a study on the role of intermediary in international business-to-business relationships. Her current research interests include mergers and acquisitions, management of project ending, and effects of ending business-to-business relationships on other companies. She has published in journals that include *Industrial Marketing Management*, *International Marketing Review*, *Journal of Management Studies*, *Journal of Strategic Marketing*, and *Scandinavian Journal of Management*. She is also co-author of the book *Managing Project Ending* (Routledge, together with Asta Salmi) and co-editor of *Critical Perspectives on Internationalisation* (Elsevier Science, together with Håkan Håkansson and Mats Forsgren).

Johan Holtström, PhD, is an assistant professor of industrial marketing at Linköping University. His dissertation studies synergy as a concept to enhance understanding of it, both within a company and in a business network of companies undergoing integration. The dissertation elaborates on implementation of synergy in mergers and acquisitions and in business relationships with customers and suppliers. His research is based on an interest in the dynamics of mergers and acquisitions and on the interrelationship of synergy, product development, and suppliers. He has previously published in *Journal of Business Research* on mergers and acquisitions as a driving force for further mergers and acquisitions. A recent publication in *Journal of Business-to-Business Marketing* concerns how competition authorities view business relationships. Johan Holtström has also had experience in managing and developing an executive MBA program in project management.

Sven Jungerhem is currently controller at Uppsala University and researcher at Uppsala Centre of Business History. Jungerhem presented his dissertation, *Banks in Merger*, in 1992 and has thereafter continued his research on financial organizations. In the early 2000s he worked for several years in the Swedish financial sector, where he was practically involved in two bank mergers. His current research interests cover financial history, entrepreneurship, and knowledge and competence in organizations, as set forth in 'Labour and competitiveness in the Swedish financial Sector', 2000, an expert report included in an official Swedish government report, and in 'Management-Speak in the Academic Field' (L. Engwall and S. Jungerhem 2010).

Mats Larsson is a professor of economic History at Uppsala University, and since 2008 he has also headed the new established Uppsala Centre for Business History. His PhD thesis was presented in 1986 and treated the development of wages in the Swedish iron industry during the nineteenth century. Since the late 1980s Larsson has focused primarily on financial and business history, particularly the relationship between financial companies and the state. His research has included commercial and savings banks as well as insurance companies. A part of this research is summarised in *Staten och kapitalet* (State and Capital 1998). Larsson has also published both articles and monographs in media history, including two volumes about Bonnier, the Swedish multinational media group.

Fredrik Nilsson has been Professor of Business Studies, especially Accounting, at Uppsala University since 2010. Before then he was a professor in Economic Information Systems at Linköping University. His dissertation—defended in 1997—was a study on the design and use of management control systems following takeover. His research is focused on understanding the role of control systems in formulating and implementing strategies. He has published in such journals as *Accounting & Finance*, *British Journal of Management*, *European Management Journal*, *Management Accounting Research*, and *Scandinavian Journal of Management*. Two books co-authored by Fredrik Nilsson are *Understanding Competitive Advantage* (Springer, together with Birger Rapp) and *Controlling for Competitiveness* (Liber and Copenhagen Business School Press, together with Nils-Göran Olve and Anders Parment).

Christina Öberg, associate professor, Lund University, received her PhD in marketing from Linköping University. Her doctoral thesis concerned how customers impact and are impacted by a merger or acquisition. Her current research interests are in mergers and acquisitions, customer relationships, and innovation management. Her recent publications deal with how the identity of innovative firms is changed following acquisitions (*European Journal of Marketing* 2011), what roles customers have in innovation processes (*International Journal of Innovation Management* 2010), and how managers' views on company networks may be transformed following acquisitions (*Industrial Marketing Management* 2007).

Nils-Göran Olve is an adjunct professor at Linköping University and a visiting professor at Uppsala University. He wrote his dissertation (1977) on interactive planning as a process for balancing multiple objectives, a topic which later led to an interest in the balanced scorecard, information systems, and controllership. He has pursued this interest as educator, consultant, and writer, both inside and outside academia. He has published numerous articles and books in Swedish and English, the most recent being *Making Scorecards Actionable* (Wiley 2003) and *Controlling for Competitiveness* (CBSP 2011). His three international books on the balanced scorecard have been translated into Japanese, Portuguese, Russian, and other languages. He is currently engaged in research on usable IT and internal control, with a continued focus on their role in bridging strategy and performance in all kinds of organisations.

Annette Risberg is an associate professor with the Department of Intercultural Communication and Management, Copenhagen Business School, Denmark. Her doctoral thesis, *Ambiguities Thereafter—an Interpretive Approach to Acquisitions*, is an interpretive analysis of employee experience with acquisitions, with special emphasis on multiple realities and ambiguity in acquisitions. More recently, she has critically reviewed the conventional methodology in research on merger and acquisitions. She is also researching diversity in organisations.

Svante Schriber, PhD, Stockholm University School of Business. Dr. Schriber's doctoral thesis contributes in two ways to research on acquisitions, by not only developing a generic framework for realizing synergies in acquisitions, but also tying synergies to the often dynamic competitive landscape that surrounds acquisitions. In his current research he continues to focus on acquisitions—both through an integration perspective and by viewing how frequent acquirers build and draw upon experience from previous acquisitions—as well as on strategic management in dynamically competitive environments. He has published internationally, has a background as a management consultant, and is frequently invited as a speaker on acquisitions.

Roger Schweizer, assistant professor with the Department of Business Administration, School of Business, Economics, and Law at the University of Gothenburg, received his PhD in 2005. Using an institutional approach to viewing organizations, his dissertation examines how the local subsidiaries of two merging MNCs deal with the dilemma of MNCs caught between their need to integrate activities globally in pursuing economies of scale and scope, and their equally compelling need to respond to local conditions in each host country. His current research interests are international strategy issues in general and, in particular, firms' internationalisation processes, international entrepreneurship, the relationship between headquarters and subsidiaries, and mergers and acquisitions.

Index

For Product Safety Concerns and Information please contact our EU representative GPSR@taylorandfrancis.com Taylor & Francis Verlag GmbH, Kaufingerstraße 24, 80331 München, Germany